AMERICA IN PERSON

96 first-person accounts of America's past

Edited by George D. Youstra

BOB JONES UNIVERSITY PRESS, INC.
GREENVILLE, SOUTH CAROLINA 29614

America in Person
Ninety-Six Eyewitness Accounts
edited by George D. Youstra

© Bob Jones University Press, Inc. 1975
Greenville, South Carolina 29614
ISBN 0-89084-026-1

Printed in the United States of America

To my mother,
sixth generation American and
great-great-great granddaughter
of Ephraim Root,
Corporal, Continental Army, 1777.

PREFACE

The aim of this volume is to present striking insights into great epochs in the history of the United States from the pre-Columbus era to the present. All of the events are described by men who participated in them or were personal eyewitnesses, something which enhances the interest and authenticity of the accounts.

Archaic spelling and syntax have been changed where necessary; the language of most articles, however, preserves its original flavor.

I have made here no attempt to give all historical periods equal weight and emphasis. A history so "balanced" can only be absurd, for not all periods have an equal impact on the future. For instance, the conflicts of the mid-nineteenth century have affected—and continue to affect—the social, racial, commercial, and political life of present-day America; accordingly those years are more amply represented here than are other periods.

Furthermore, unavoidably enmeshed as we are in our own century, we are less able to weigh properly the events of our day than will be, should the Lord tarry, our more dispassionate great-grandchildren. I have therefore chosen, in the most modern readings, to select only those articles most broadly representative of the first three quarters of the twentieth century.

When compared with the nations of the Old World, America is young, her history short. The American story is perhaps even more glorious for that. The United States has provided more individual liberty and more equality of opportunity for a wider range of people than has any other nation in the history of our globe. Is that not a goal more devoutly to be sought than the splendor of a monarch's court, than the conquests of a Trajan or a Napoleon?

Evidently other peoples thought so, for they came to America in millions. And still they come, to be welcomed by the Statue of Liberty and the nation whose philosophy it expresses:

"Keep, ancient lands, your storied pomp!" cries she,
With silent lips. "Give me your tired, your poor,
Your huddled masses yearning to breathe free,
The wretched refuse of your teeming shore,
Send these, the homeless, tempest-tost to me,
I lift my lamp beside the golden door!"

George D. Youstra
Greenville, South Carolina
September, 1975

TO THE READER:

History is *His* story. God's hand can be seen in the affairs of men. But history is also man's story. Parts of man's story—including his thoughts, deeds, and ways of life—are sometimes unacceptable to Christians. This part of man's story cannot be wholly denied without distorting the past and losing valuable lessons.

The fact that this volume of history has been published by the Bob Jones University Press does not mean, therefore, that the University endorses all deeds, beliefs, and ways of life which there appear. Bob Jones University's support of Biblical morality and orthodox Christianity are well known.

About the Author

A Chicago native, George D. Youstra received his B.S. and M.A. from Bob Jones University and an M.A. and Ph.D. from Michigan State University, East Lansing. He is a member of Phi Delta Kappa and the Association of Teacher Educators and is president of his local chapter of the Sons of the American Revolution. A longtime history teacher, Dr. Youstra currently serves as principal of Bob Jones Academy and teaches in the graduate school of Bob Jones University. He is married and has three children.

CONTENTS

IV. *GROWTH AND STRUGGLES*

V. *A GLOBAL POWER*

DISCOVERY

DISCOVERY

Probably the earliest journeys to America were made from Asia, but the hearty Northmen of the Viking Age were the first Europeans to set foot on the North American continent. They found it a rich, fertile land and named it Vinland.

Nevertheless, within a century their discovery had been virtually forgotten, not only because the Vikings understood so little of its importance, but also because Europe at that time (1000 A.D.) was eminently self-centered. She had troubles enough to absorb all her energies. Most European rulers were grimly struggling to hold what they had—to hold it from their ambitious nobles and from their land-hungry neighbors.

Columbus, then, was not the first to discover America, but he was the first to awaken in Europe an interest in the discovery leading to further explorations, disclosing a new continent, and ending in permanent settlements. The men who followed him, Vespucius and the Cabots, confirmed and extended his discovery. Cabot first found the mainland of North America, Vespucius the mainland of South America. Within a century after Columbus's voyage, Spanish explorers and adventurers were flocking to America in pursuit of silver and gold. Their countrymen had already found rich mineral deposits in Mexico and Peru; and after seeing Indians farther north wearing golden trinkets, the new explorers were persuaded that mineral wealth also existed in the lands now called the United States, and especially in the fabled "Seven Cities of Cibola" in the Southwest. Out of this belief sprang the bold enterprises of Ponce de Leon, Coronado, and De Soto.

French, Dutch, and English explorers of later years, such as Cartier, Champlain, Marquette and Joliet, Hudson, and Drake had different motives. They came to fish for cod, to explore the country, to plant the banners of the "Sun King" and "Good Queen Bess" over new territories, to convert the Indians, and to find a northwest passage to India. Henry Hudson, an Englishman sailing under the Dutch flag, hoped to discover such a passage in 1609 when he entered New York harbor. Later, when he attempted once more to seek it out, in what we now call Hudson's Bay, he perished miserably when set adrift in an open boat, abandoned by his mutinous sailors.

Columbus steadfastly believed that he had found unknown parts of Asia and had opened a shorter and safer route for trade with the East. He never knew that he had discovered a new continent. Columbus returned from America poorer than when he sailed from Spain. He claimed to have found Asia; but when he brought home none of the wealth of that distant continent after several voyages, his creditors saw him imprisoned. He later died a broken-hearted man in Valladolid.

COLUMBUS'S FIRST VOYAGE
(1492–93)
by Christopher Columbus

The first letter of Columbus, descriptive of his first voyage, was written in Febru-
ary, 1493, when he was off the Azores, on his return home. It was addressed to Louis
de Santangel, the treasurer of King Ferdinand of Spain. Although addressed to the
treasurer, it was intended for the eyes of the King himself, and for those of his queen,
Isabella.

As I know that it will afford you pleasure that I have brought my
undertaking to a successful result, I have determined to write to you this
letter to inform you of everything that has been done and discovered in this
voyage of mine.

On the thirty-third day after leaving Cadiz, I came into the Indian Sea,
where I discovered many islands inhabited by numerous people. I took
possession of all of them for our most fortunate King by making public
proclamation and unfurling his standard, no one making any resistance.
To the first of them I have given the name of our blest Saviour, trusting
in whose aid I had reached this and all the rest; but the Indians call it
Guanahani. To each of the others also I gave a new name, ordering one
to be called Sancta Maria de Concepcion, another Fernandina, another
Isabella, another Johana; and so with all the rest.

The island called Johana, as well as the others in its neighborhood, is
exceedingly fertile. It has numerous harbors on all sides, very safe and
wide, above comparison with any I have ever seen. Through it flow many
very broad and health-giving rivers, and there are in it numerous very lofty
mountains. All these islands are very beautiful and of quite different
shapes, easy to be traversed, and full of the greatest variety of trees reaching to the stars. I think these never lose their leaves, as I saw them looking
as green and lovely as they are wont to be in the month of May in Spain.
Some of them were in leaf and some in fruit, each flourishing in the condition its nature required. The nightingale and various other little birds were
singing when I was rambling among them in the month of November.

There are also in the island called Johana seven or eight kinds of palms, which as readily surpass ours in height and beauty as do all the other trees, herbs, and fruits. There are also wonderful pine-woods, fields, and extensive meadows, birds of various kinds, and honey, and all the different metals except iron.

In the island, which I have called Hispana, there are very lofty and beautiful mountains, great farms, groves and fields, most fertile both for cultivation and for pasturage, and well adapted for constructing buildings. The convenience of the harbors in this island and the excellence of the rivers in volume and salubrity surpass human belief, unless one should see them. In it the trees, pasture-lands, and fruits differ much from those of Johana. Besides these, Hispana abounds in various kinds of spices, gold, and metals.

The inhabitants of both sexes of this and of all the other islands I have seen, or of which I have any knowledge, always go as naked as they came into the world, except that some of the women cover parts of their bodies with leaves or branches, or a veil of cotton, which they prepare themselves for this purpose. They are all, as I said before, unprovided with any sort of iron, and they are destitute of arms, which are entirely unknown to them, and for which they are not adapted, not on account of any bodily deformity, for they are well made, but because they are timid and full of terror. They carry, however, canes dried in the sun in place of weapons, upon whose roots they fix a wooden shaft, dried and sharpened to a point. But they never dare to make use of these, for it has often happened, when I have sent two or three of my men to some of their villages to speak with the inhabitants, that a crowd of Indians has sallied forth; but when they saw our men approaching, they speedily took to flight, parents abandoning their children, and children their parents.

This happened not because any loss or injury had been inflicted upon any of them. On the contrary, I gave whatever I had, cloth and many other things, to whomsoever I approached or with whom I could get speech, without any return being made to me; but they are by nature fearful and timid. But, when they see that they are safe and all fear is banished, they are very guileless and honest and very liberal of all they have. No one refuses the asker anything that he possesses; on the contrary, they themselves invite us to ask for it. They manifest the greatest affection toward all of us, exchanging valuable things for trifles, content with the very least thing or nothing at all. But I forbade giving them a very trifling thing and of no value, such as bits of plates, dishes, or glass, also nails and straps, although it seemed to them if they could get such that they had acquired the most beautiful jewels in the world.

For it chanced that a sailor received for a single strap as much weight of gold as three gold *solidi;* and so others for other things of less price, especially for new *blancas,* and for some gold coins, for which they gave whatever the seller asked; for instance, an ounce and a half or two ounces of gold, or thirty or forty pounds of cotton, with which they were already familiar. So, too, for pieces of hoops, jugs, jars, and pots they bartered cotton and gold like beasts. This I forbade, because it was plainly unjust; and I gave them many beautiful and pleasing things, which I had brought with me, for no return whatever, in order to win their affection and that they might become Christians and inclined to love our king and queen and princes and all the people of Spain and that they might be eager to search for and gather and give to us what they abound in and we greatly need.

They do not practice idolatry; on the contrary, they believe that all strength, all power, in short, all blessings, are from Heaven and that I have come down from there with these ships and sailors; and in this spirit was I received everywhere, after they had got over their fear. They are neither lazy nor awkward but, on the contrary, are of an excellent and acute understanding.

Those who have sailed these seas give excellent accounts of everything; but they have never seen men wearing clothes or ships like ours.

As soon as I had come into this sea, I took by force some Indians from the first island, in order that they might learn from us and at the same time tell us what they knew about affairs in these regions. This succeeded admirably; for in a short time we understood them and they us, both by gesture and signs and words, and they were of great service to us. They are coming now with me and have always believed that I have come from Heaven, nothwithstanding the long time they have been, and still remain, with us. They were the first who told this wherever we went, one calling to another with a loud voice, "Come, come, you will see men from Heaven." Whereupon both women and men, children and adults, young and old, laying aside the fear they had felt before, flocked eagerly to see us, a great crowd thronging about our steps, some bringing food and others drink, with greatest love and incredible good will.

Although these matters are very wonderful and unheard of, they would have been much more so if the ships to a reasonable amount had been furnished me. But what has been accomplished is great and wonderful and not at all proportionate to my deserts, but to the sacred Christian faith and to the piety and religion of our sovereigns. For what the mind of man could not compass, the spirit of God has granted to mortals. For God is wont to listen to his servants who love his precepts, even in impossibilities, as has happened to me in the present instance, who have accomplished what human strength has hitherto never attained. For if any one has written or told anything about these islands, all have done so either obscurely or by guesswork, so that it has almost seemed to be fabulous.

Therefore let king and queen and princes and their most fortunate realms and all other Christian provinces, let us all return thanks to our Lord and Saviour Jesus Christ, who has bestowed so great a victory and reward upon us; let there be processions and solemn sacrifices prepared; let the churches be decked with festal boughs; let Christ rejoice upon earth as He rejoices in Heaven, as He forsees that so many souls of so many people heretofore lost are to be saved; and let us be glad not only for the exaltation of our faith, but also for the increase of temporal prosperity, in which not only Spain but all Christendom is about to share.

As these things have been accomplished, so have they been briefly narrated. Farewell.

VESPUCIUS IN SOUTH AMERICA
(1505–06)
by Amerigo Vespucius

Americus Vespucius was born in Florence in 1452 and died in Seville in 1512. He was the son of a notary in Florence, was educated by a Dominican friar and became connected with the commercial house which fitted out the second expedition of Columbus.

Vespucius claimed to have been four times in America. His letters describing his four voyages were published originally in Italian in Florence in 1505–06. The letter here given was addressed by Vespucius to Pier Soderini, the Gonfalonier of Florence.

Vespucius has been unjustly accused of appropriating to himself an honor which belonged to Columbus—that of giving a name to the new continent. This injustice, however, was not due to Vespucius, but to a German schoolmaster named Hylacomylus, or "Miller of the Wood-pond," who published a book in 1507.

Vespucius, in spite of several voyages, discovered very little in America. The continent ought not to have been named after him.

We left the port of Cadiz in four consort ships and began our voyage in direct course to the Fortunate Isles, which are called today *la gran Canaria,* which are situated in the ocean-sea at the extremity of the inhabited west and set in the third climate over which the North Pole has an elevation of twenty-seven and one-half degrees beyond their horizon. They are 280 leagues distant from this city of Lisbon, by the wind between *mezzo di* and *libeccio,* where we remained eight days, taking in provision of water and wood and other necessary things; and from here, having said our prayers, we weighed anchor and gave the sails to the wind, beginning our course to westward, taking one-quarter by southwest. And so we sailed on, till at the end of thirty-seven days we reached a land which we deemed to be a continent, which is distant westwardly from the isles of Canary about a thousand leagues beyond the inhabited region within the torrid zone, for we found the North Pole at an elevation of sixteen degrees above its horizon, and it was westward, according to the showing of our instruments, seventy-five degrees from the isles of Canary, whereat we anchored with our ships a league and a half from land, and we put out our boats freighted with men and arms.

We made toward the land and before we reached it had sight of a great number of people who were going along the shore.

This same day we put to land with the boats and sprang on shore full forty men in good trim, and still the land's people appeared shy of converse with us, and we were unable to encourage them so much as to make them come to speak with us. And this day we labored so greatly in giving them of our wares, such as rattles and mirrors, beads, spalline, and other trifles, that some of them took confidence and came to discourse with us. After having made good friends with them, the night coming on, we took our leave of them and returned to the ships. The next day when the dawn appeared, we saw that there were infinite numbers of people upon the beach, and they had their women and children with them. We went ashore and found that they were all laden with their worldly goods which are suchlike as in its proper place shall be related. Before we reached the land, many of them jumped into the sea and came swimming to receive us at a bowshot's length from the shore, for they are very great swimmers, with as much confidence as if they had for a long time been acquainted with us, and we were pleased with this their confidence.

For so much as we learned of their manner of life and customs, it was that they go entirely naked, as well the men as the women. They are of medium stature, very well proportioned, their flesh is of a color that verges into red like a lion's mane, and I believe that if they went clothed, they would be as white as we. They have not any hair upon the body, except the hair of the head, which is long and black, and especially in the women, whom it renders handsome. In aspect they are not very good-looking because they have broad faces so that they would seem Tartar-like. They let no hair grow on their eyebrows nor on their eyelids nor elsewhere, except the hair of the head, for they hold hairiness to be a filthy thing. They are very light-footed in walking and in running, as well the men as the women, so that a woman thinks nothing of running a league or two, as many times we saw them do, and herein they have a very great advantage over us Christians. They swim with an expertness beyond all belief, and the women better than the men, for we have many times found and seen them swimming two leagues out at sea without anything to rest upon. Their weapons are bows and arrows very well made, save that the arrows are not tipped with iron nor any other kind of hard metal, and instead of iron they put animals' or fishes' teeth or a spike of tough wood with the point hardened by fire. They are sure marksmen, for they hit whatever they aim at, and in some places the women use these bows. They have other weapons, such as fire-hardened spears, and also clubs with knobs, beautifully carved. Warfare is used amongst them, which they carry on against people not of their own language, very cruelly, without granting life to any one, except to reserve him for greater suffering.

We decided to leave that place and to go farther on, continuously coasting the shore upon which we made frequent descents and held converse with a great number of people, and at the end of some days we went into a harbor where we underwent very great danger. It pleased the Holy Ghost to save us, and it was in this wise.

We landed in a harbor, where we found a village built like Venice upon the water. There were about forty-four large dwellings in the form of huts erected upon very thick piles, and they had their doors or entrances in the style of drawbridges, and from each house one could pass through all by means of the drawbridges, which stretched from house to house. When the people thereof had seen us, they appeared to be afraid of us, and immediately drew up all the bridges. While we were looking at this strange action, we saw coming across the sea about twenty-two canoes, which are a kind of boat of theirs constructed from a single tree, which came toward our boats, as they had been surprised by our appearance and clothes and kept wide of us. Thus remaining, we made signals to them that they should approach us, encouraging them with every token of friendliness; and seeing that they did not come, we went to them, and they did not stay for us, but made to the land and by signs told us to wait and that they should soon return. And they went to a hill in the background and did not delay long. When they returned, they led with them sixteen of their girls and entered with these into their canoes and came to the boats, and in each boat they put four of the girls.

That we marveled at this behavior your Magnificence can imagine how much, and they placed themselves with their canoes among our boats, coming to speak with us, insomuch that we deemed it a mark of friendliness. While thus engaged, we beheld a great number of people advance swimming toward us across the sea, who came from the houses, and as they were drawing near to us without any apprehension, just then there appeared at the doors of the houses certain old women, uttering very loud cries and tearing their hair to exhibit grief, whereby they made us suspicious, and we each betook ourselves to arms. Instantly the girls whom we had in the boats threw themselves into the sea, and the men of the canoes drew away from us and began with their bows to shoot arrows at us. Those who were swimming each carried a lance held as covertly as they could beneath the water, so that recognizing the treachery, we engaged with them, not merely to defend ourselves but to attack them vigorously, and we overturned with our boats their canoes. We made a slaughter of them, and they all flung themselves into the water to swim, leaving their canoes abandoned. With considerable loss on their side, they went swimming away to the shore. There died of them about fifteen or twenty, and many were left wounded, and of ours five were wounded, and all, by the grace of God, escaped death. We captured two of the girls and two men, and we proceeded to their houses and entered therein, and in them all we found nothing else than two old women and a sick man. We took away from them many things but of small value, and we would not burn their houses, because it seemed to us as though that would be a burden upon our conscience. We returned to our boats with five prisoners and betook ourselves to the ships and put a pair of irons on the feet of each of the captives, except the little girls. When the night came on, the two girls and one of the men fled away in the most subtle manner possible, and the next day we decided to quit the harbor and go farther onwards.

We proceeded, continuously skirting the coast, until we had sight of another tribe distant perhaps some eighty leagues from the former tribe, and we found them very different in speech and customs. We resolved to cast anchor and went ashore with the boats, and we saw on the beach a great number of people amounting probably to four thousand souls. When we had reached the shore, they did not stay for us, but betook themselves to flight through the forests, abandoning their things. We jumped on land and took a pathway that led to the forest, and at the distance of a bow-shot we found their tents where they had made very large fires; and two of them were cooking their victuals and roasting several animals and fish of many kinds, where we saw that they were roasting a certain animal which seemed to be a serpent, save that it had wings, and was in its appearance so loathsome that we marveled much at its savageness.

This land is very populous and full of inhabitants and of numberless rivers and animals, few of which resemble ours—excepting lions, panthers, stags, pigs, goats, and deer—and even these have some dissimilarities of form. They have no horses nor mules nor, saving your reverence, asses nor dogs nor any kind of sheep or oxen; but so numerous are the other animals which they have, and all are savage, and of none do they make use for their service, that they could not be counted. What shall we say of others, such as birds, which are so numerous and of so many kinds and of such various-colored plumages that it is a marvel to behold them. The soil is very pleasant and fruitful, full of immense woods and forests, and it is always green, for the foliage never drops off. The fruits are so many that they are numberless and entirely different from ours. This land is within the torrid zone, close to or just under the parallel described by the Tropic of Cancer, where the pole of the horizon has an elevation of twenty-three degrees at the extremity of the second climate. Many tribes came to see us and wondered at our faces and our whiteness, and they asked us whence we came, and we gave them to understand that we had come from Heaven and that we were going to see the world, and they believed it. In this land we placed baptismal fonts, and an infinite number of people were baptized, and they called us in their language *carabi,* which means "men of great wisdom."

CARTIER'S CANADIAN EXPLORATIONS
(1535)
by Jacques Cartier

From a letter written by Cartier, a Frenchman who explored widely in Canada, claimed that territory for France, and is credited with discovering the St. Lawrence River.

Upon Thursday being the eighth of the month, because the wind was not good to go out with our ships, we set our boats in a readiness to go to discover the said bay, and that day we went twenty-five leagues within it. The next day the wind and weather being fair, we sailed until noon, in which time we had notice of a great part of the said bay, and how that over the low lands there were other lands with high mountains, but seeing that there was no passage at all, we began to turn back again. Taking our way along the coast and sailing, we saw certain wild men, and by and by in clusters they came with their boats to the shore where we were, bringing with them skins and other such things as they had, to have of our wares 'til they had nothing but their naked bodies; for they gave us all whatsoever they had, and that was but of small value. We perceived that this people might very easily be converted to our religion. They go from place to place. They live only with fishing. They have an ordinary time to fish for their provision. The country is hotter than the country of Spain and the fairest that can possibly be found, altogether smooth, and level. There is no place, be it never so little, but it hath some trees (yea, albeit it be sandy) or else is full of wheat, that hath an ear like unto rye; and small peas as thick as if they had been sown and plowed; white and red roses, with many other flowers of very sweet and pleasant smell. There be also many goodly meadows, full of grass, and lakes wherein great plenty of salmon be. They call a hatchet in their tongue *cochi,* and a knife *bacon:* we named it the Bay of Heat.

After we had sailed along the said coast for the space of two hours, behold, the tide began to turn against us with so swift and raging a course that it was not possible for us with thirteen oars to row or get one stone's cast farther, so that we were constrained to leave our boats with some of our men to guard them. Ten or twelve men went ashore to the said Cape, where we found that the land begins to bend southwest; which having seen, we came to our boats again and so to our ships, which were still ready under sail, hoping to go forward. But for all that, they were fallen more than four leagues to leeward from the place where we had left them, where so soon as we came, we assembled together all our captains, masters, and mariners to have their advice and opinion what was best to be done. After that every one had said, considering that the easterly winds began to bear away and blow, and that the flood was so great that we did but fall, and that there was nothing to be gotten, and that storms and tempests began to reign in Newfoundland, and that we were so far from home, not knowing the perils and dangers that were behind, for either we must agree to return home again or else to stay there all the year. Moreover, we did consider that if the northern winds did take us, it were not possible for us to depart thence. All which opinions being heard and considered, we altogether determined to address ourselves homeward. Now because upon Saint Peter's Day we entered into the said strait, we named it Saint Peter's Strait.

In the year of our Lord 1535 upon Whitsunday, being May 16, by the commandment of our Captain James Cartier and with a common accord in the Cathedral Church of St. Malo, we devoutly each one confessed ourselves and received the sacrament. And all entering into the choir of the said church, we presented ourselves before the Reverend Father in Christ, the Lord Bishop of St. Malo, who blessed us all, being in his bishop's robes. The Wednesday following, being May 19, there arose a good gale of wind, and therefore we hoisted sail with three ships. We stayed and rested ourselves in the said haven until the seventh of August, being Sunday, on which day we hoisted sail and came toward land on the south side toward Cape Robast, distant from the said haven about twenty leagues north-northeast, and south-southwest. But the next day there rose a stormy and contrary wind, and because we could find no haven there toward the south, thence we went coasting along toward the north, beyond the above said haven about ten leagues, where we found a goodly great gulf full of islands, passages, and entrances, toward what wind soever you please to bend. For the knowledge of this gulf there is a great island that is like to a cape of land, stretching somewhat farther forth than the others; and about two leagues within the land, there is an hill fashioned as it were an heap of corn. We named the said gulf Saint Lawrence Bay. The twelfth of the said month we went from the said Saint Lawrence Bay, or gulf, sailing westward and discovered a cape of land toward the south that runneth west and by south, distant from the said Saint Lawrence Bay about five and twenty leagues.

The seventh of the month being Our Lady's Even, after service we went to go up higher into the river and came to fourteen islands seven or eight leagues from the island of Filberds where the country of Canada begins, one of which islands is ten leagues in length, and five in breadth, greatly inhabited of such men as only live by fishing of such sorts of fishes as the river affords, according to the season of them. The next day following, the Lord of Canada (whose proper name was Donnacona, but by the name of Lord they call him Agouhanna) with twelve boats came to our ships, accompanied with many people, who causing ten of his boats to go back with the other two, approached unto us with sixteen men. Our captain then caused our boats to be set in order, that with the next tide he might go up higher into the river to find some safe harbor for our ships. We passed up the river against the stream about ten leagues, coasting the said island, at the end whereof we found a goodly and pleasant sound, where is a little river and haven, where by reason of the flood there is about three fathoms water. This place seemed to us very fit and commodious to harbor our ships therein, and so we did very safely: we named it the Holy Cross, for on that day we came thither. Near unto it, there is a village, whereof Donnacona is lord, and there he keeps his abode; it is called Stadacone [Quebec], as goodly a plot of ground as possibly may be seen.

The next day being September 19, we hoisted sail and with our pinnace and two boats departed to go up the river with the flood, where on both shores of it we began to see as goodly a country as possibly can with eye be seen, all replenished with very goodly trees and vines laden as full of grapes as could be all along the river, which rather seemed to have been planted by man's hand than otherwise. True it is, that because they are not dressed and wrought as they should be, their bunches of grapes are not so great nor sweet as ours.

The next day our captain seeing from that time it was not possible for our pinnace to go on any farther, he caused our boats to be made ready, and as much munition and victuals to be put in them as they could well bear. He departed with them, accompanied with many gentlemen, that is to say, Claudius of Ponte Briand, cupbearer to the Lord Dolphin of France; Charles of Pommeraye; John Gouion; John Powlet, with twenty and eight mariners; and Mace Jallobert and William Briton, who had the charge under the captain of the other two ships to go up as far as they could into that river. We sailed with good and prosperous weather until the second of October, on which day we came to the town of Hochalaga [Montreal], distant from the place where we had left our pinnace five and forty leagues.

CORONADO IN THE AMERICAN SOUTHWEST

(1540)

by Francisco Vasquez de Coronado

This is an excerpt from Coronado's letter to Mendoza, dated August 3, 1540, Mendoza being Viceroy of Mexico, by whom Coronado had been sent out. Coronado's expedition was a great disappointment to all concerned, inasmuch as it resulted in failure to find the fabled "seven cities of Cibola." He had three hundred Spaniards with him and eight hundred Indians. Instead of finding great towns, he discovered only a poor village of two hundred people, situated on a rocky eminence. The expedition, however, in spite of this failure, remains one of the most important exploring expeditions ever undertaken in America. Opinions differ as to how far north Coronado went, some maintaining that he reached a point north of the boundary line between Kansas and Nebraska.

The wanderer ventured as far as the Missouri and would have gone still farther eastward but for his inability to cross the swollen river. Cooperating parties explored the upper valleys of the Rio Grande and Gila, ascended the Colorado for two hundred and forty miles above its mouth, and visited the Grand Canyon of the same river. Coronado at last returned, satisfied that he had been victimized by the idle tales of travelers. He was rewarded with contempt and lost his place as governor of New Galicia, but his romantic march stands in history as one of the most remarkable expeditions of modern times.

Francisco Vasquez de Coronado was born at Salamanca, Spain, about 1500 and died in Mexico some time after 1542. He is believed to have gone to Mexico in 1535 with Mendoza, the viceroy, who in 1539 made him governor of a province.

At length I arrived at the valley of the people called Caracones, on May 26; and from Culiacan until I came thither, I could not help myself, save only with a great quantity of bread of maize. For seeing the maize in the fields were not yet ripe, I was constrained to leave them all behind me. In this valley of the Caracones we found more store of people and great store of tillage than in any other part of the country which we had passed. But I understood that there was store thereof in another valley called the Lord's Valley, which I would not disturb with force, but sent thither Melchior Diaz with wares of exchange to procure some and to give the said maize to the Indians, our friends which we brought with us, and to some others that had lost their cattle in the way and were not able to carry their victuals so far which they brought from Culiacan. It pleased God that we gave some small quantity of maize with this traffic, whereby certain Indians were relieved and some Spaniards.

And by that time that we were come to this valley of the Caracones, some ten or twelve of our horses were dead through weariness. For being overcharged with great burdens and having but little meat, they could not endure the travail. Likewise some of our Indians died here, which was no small want unto us for the performance of our enterprise. They told me that this valley of the Caracones is five days' journey from the Western Sea. I sent for the Indians of the sea coast to understand their estate, and while I stayed for them, the horses rested. I stayed there four days, in which space the Indians of the sea coast came unto me, which told me that two days' sailing from their coast of the sea there were seven or eight islands right over against them, well inhabited with people, but badly furnished with victuals, and were a rude people. And they told me that they had seen a ship pass by not far from the shore, which I knew not what to think whither it were one of those that went to discover the country or else a ship of the Portugals.

Fernando Alvarado returned to advise me that certain Indians were come unto them in peaceable manner and that two of them stayed for my coming with the master of the field. Whereupon I went unto them and gave them beads and certain short slokes, willing them to return unto their city and bid them to stay quiet in their houses and fear nothing. And this done, I sent the master of the field to search whether there were any bad passage which the Indians might keep against us and that he should take and defend it until the next day that I should come thither. So he went and found in the way a very bad passage where we might have sustained a very great harm. Wherefore there he seated himself with his company that were with him, and that very night the Indians came to take that passage to defend it; and finding it taken, they assaulted our men there and, as they tell me, they assaulted them like valiant men, although in the end they retired and fled away, for the master of the field was watchful and was in order with his company. The Indians in token of retreat sounded on a certain small trumpet and did no hurt among the Spaniards. The very same night the master of the field certified me hereof. Whereupon the next day in the best order that I could, I departed in so great want of victual that I thought that if we should stay one day longer without food we should all perish for hunger, especially the Indians, for among us all we had not two bushels of corn. Wherefore it behooved me to move forward without delay. The Indians here and there made fires and were answered again afar off as orderly as we for our lives could have done, to give their fellows understanding how we marched and where we arrived.

I arrived within sight of this city of Granada with all the rest of the horsemen and footmen, and found in the fields a great sort of the Indians which began to shoot at us with their arrows. And because I would obey your will and the command of the Marques, I would not let my people charge them, forbidding my company, which intreated me that they might set upon them in any wise to provoke them, saying that that which the enemies did was nothing and that it was not meet to set upon so few people. On the other side the Indians perceiving that we stirred not, took great stomach and courage unto them, insomuch that they came hard to our horses' heels to shoot at us with their arrows. Whereupon seeing that there was not time to stay longer and that the friars also were of the same opinion, I set upon them without any danger. For suddenly they fled part to the city which was near and well fortified, and other into the field, which way they could shift. Some of the Indians were slain, and more would have been if I had suffered them to have been pursued.

But since we had need of the food in the city, I assembled my people and divided them as I thought best to assault the city, and I compassed it about. And because the famine which we sustained suffered no delay, myself with certain of these gentlemen and soldiers put ourselves on foot and commanded that the crossbows and harquebusiers should give the assault and should beat the enemies from the walls, that they might not hurt us, and I assaulted the walls on one side, where they told me there was a scaling ladder set up and that there was one gate. But the crossbowmen suddenly broke the strings of their bows, and the harquebusiers did nothing at all, for they came thither so weak and feeble that scarcely could they stand on their feet.

It remains now to certify your Honor of the seven cities and of the kingdoms and provinces whereof the Father Provincial made report unto your Lordship. And to be brief, I can assure your Honor, he said the truth in nothing that he reported, but all was quite contrary, saving only the names of the cities and great houses of stone. For although they be not wrought with turquoises nor bricks, yet are they very excellent good houses of three or four or five lofts high, wherein are good lodgings and fair chambers with ladders instead of stairs and certain cellars under the ground very good and paved, which are made for winter; they are in manner like stoves. The ladders which they have for their houses are all in a manner moveable and portable, which are taken away and set down when they please, and they are made of two pieces of wood with their steps, as ours be. The seven cities are seven small towns, all made with these kinds of houses that I speak of. They stand all within four leagues together, and they are all called the kingdom of Cibola, and every one of them has its particular name. None of them is called Cibola, but altogether they are called Cibola.

And this town which I call a city I have named Granada, as well, because it is somewhat like unto it, as also in remembrance of your Lordship. In this town where I now remain, there may be some two hundred houses, all compassed with walls, and I think that with the rest of the houses which are not so walled, they may be together five hundred. There is another town near this, which is one of the seven, and it is somewhat bigger than this, and another of the same bigness that this is of, and the other four are somewhat less. I send them all painted unto your Lordship with the voyage. And the parchment, wherein the picture is, was found here with other parchments. The people of this town seem unto me of a reasonable stature and witty, yet they seem not to be such as they should be of that judgment and wit to build these houses in such sort as they are.

For the most part they go all naked, except their private parts which are covered; and they have painted mantles like those which I send unto your Lordship. They have no cotton wool growing because the country is cold, yet they wear mantles thereof as your Honor may see by the show thereof. True it is that there was found in their houses certain yarn made of cotton wool. They wear their hair on their heads like those of Mexico, and they are well nurtured and conditioned. They have turquoises, I think good quantity, which with the rest of the goods which they had, except their corn, they had conveyed away before I came thither. For I found no women there nor youth under fifteen years old nor no old folks above sixty, saving two or three old folks who stayed behind to govern all the rest of the youth and men of war. There were found in a certain paper two points of emeralds and certain small stones broken which are in color somewhat like garnets very bad and other stones of crystal, which I gave one of my servants to lay up to send them to your lordship, and he hath lost them as he tells me. We found here guinea cocks, but few. The Indians tell me in all these seven cities that they eat them not, but that they keep them only for their feathers. I believe them not, for they are excellent good and greater than those of Mexico. The season which is in this country and the temperature of the air is like that of Mexico, for sometime it is hot, and sometime it rains. Hitherto I never saw it rain, but once there fell a little shower with wind, as they are known to fall in Spain.

The snow and cold are known to be great, for so say the inhabitants of the country. And it is very likely so to be, both in respect to the manner of the country and by the fashion of their houses and their furs and other things which this people have to defend them from cold. There is no kind of fruit nor trees of fruit. The country is all plain and is on no side mountainous, albeit there are some hilly and bad passages. There are small store of fowls, the cause whereof is the cold and because the mountains are not near. Here is no great store of wood, because they have wood for their fuel sufficient four leagues off from a wood of small cedars. There is most excellent grass within a quarter of a league hence for our horses as well to feed them in pasture as to mow and make hay, whereof we stood in great need, because our horses came hither so weak and feeble. The victuals which the people of this country have is maize, whereof they have great store, and also small white peas and venison, which by all likelihood they feed upon (though they say no), for we found many skins of deer, of hares, and rabbits. They eat the best cakes that ever I saw, and everybody generally eats of them. They have the finest order and way to grind that we ever saw in any place. And one Indian woman of this country will grind as much as four women of Mexico. They have most excellent salt in kernel, which they fetch from a certain lake a day's journey from hence.

Three days after this city was taken, certain Indians of these people came to offer me peace and brought me certain turquoises and bad mantles, and I received them in his Majesty's name with all the good speeches that I could devise, certifying them of the purpose of my coming into this country, which is in the name of his Majesty and by the commandment of your Lordship, that they and all the rest of the people of this province should become Christians and should know the true God for their Lord and receive his Majesty for their King and earthly Sovereign. And herewithal they returned to their houses, and suddenly the next day they set in order all their goods and substance, their women and children, and fled to the hills, leaving their towns as it were abandoned, wherein remained very few of them. When I saw this, I went to the city, which I said to be greater than this where I am, and found there some few of them, to whom I said that they should not be afraid and that they should call their governor unto me. Howbeit forasmuch as I can learn or gather, none of them hath any governor, for I saw not there any chief house whereby any preeminence of one over another might be gathered.

I would have sent your Lordship with this dispatch many lists of things which are in this country, but the way is so long and rough that it is hard for me to do so; nevertheless I send your Honor one oxhide, certain turquoises, two earrings of the same, fifteen combs of the Indians, certain tablets set with these turquoises, and two small baskets made of wicker, whereof the Indians have great store. I sent your Lordship also two rolls which the women in these parts are known to wear on their heads when they fetch water from their wells, as we do in Spain. And one of these Indian women with one of these rolls on her head will carry a pitcher of water up a ladder without touching the same with her hand. I send you also a list of the weapons wherewith these people are known to fight; a buckler, a mace, a bow, and certain arrows, as these conquerors say, have never been seen.

THE DEATH OF DE SOTO

(1542)

by Alvaro Fernandez

From the Narrative of the Gentleman of Elvas. *The piece was written by one of De Soto's companions, Alvaro Fernandez, a Spaniard, and was first printed in 1557. Of noble birth and a lieutenant and close friend of Pizarro, De Soto was appointed governor of Cuba and Florida with the privilege of exploring and conquering at his pleasure. He led an unsuccessful treasure hunt from Florida northward through what is today Georgia, Tennessee, Oklahoma, Alabama, Mississippi, and Missouri. After fighting several desperate battles with Indians, where only Spanish weapons and discipline saved De Soto and his men from destruction, and after enduring starvation and sickness, the hearty cavalier who had dreamed of finding gold along the Mississippi died of a "malignant" fever and was buried secretly by his companions in the great Mississippi River in 1542.*

The Governor fell into great dumps to see how hard it was to get to the sea, and worse because his men and horses every day diminished, being without succor to sustain themselves in the country, and with that thought he fell sick. But before he took his bed, he sent an Indian to the Cacique of Quigalta to tell him that he was the child of the sun and that all the way that he came all men obeyed and served him, that he requested him to accept of his friendship and come unto him, for he would be very glad to see him, and in sign of love and obedience to bring something with him of that which in his country was most esteemed.

By the time the Indian returned with his arrogant answer, the Governor had betaken himself to bed, being evil handled with fevers, and was so enraged that he was ready to pass presently the river and to seek him, to see if he could abate that pride of his. The river went now very strongly in those parts, for it was near half a league broad and sixteen fathoms deep and very furious and ran with a great current; and on both sides there were many Indians, and his power was not now so great but that he had need to help himself rather by sleights than by force. The Indians of Guachoya came every day with fish in such numbers that the town was full of them.

The Governor felt in himself that the hour approached wherein he was to leave this present life and called for the king's officers, captains, and principal persons, to whom he made a speech. Baltasar de Gallegos answered in the name of all the rest. And first of all comforting him, he set before his eyes how short the life of this world was and with how many troubles and miseries it is accompanied and how God showed him a singular favor which soonest left it, telling him many other things fit for such a time. And touching the Governor which he commanded they should elect, he besought him that it would please his lordship to name him which he thought fit, and him they would obey. And presently he named Luys de Moscoso de Alvarado, his captain-general. And presently he was sworn by all that were present and elected for governor. The next day being May 21, 1542, departed out of this life the valorous, virtuous, and valiant captain, Don Fernando de Soto, Governor of Cuba and *Adelantado* of Florida, whom fortune advanced as it useth to do others, that he might have the higher fall. He departed in such a place and at such a time as in his sickness he had but little comfort, and the danger which appeared before their eyes wherein all his people in that country were perishing was cause sufficient why every one of them had need of comfort and why they did not visit nor accompany him as they ought to have done. Luys de Moscoso determined to conceal his death from the Indians, because Fernando de Soto had made them believe that the Christians were immortal and also because they took him to be hardy, wise, and valiant; and if they should know that he was dead, they would be bold to set upon the Christians, though they lived peaceably by them.

As soon as he was dead, Luys de Moscoso commanded to put him secretly in the house where he remained three days; and moving him from thence, commanded him to be buried in the night at one of the gates of the town within the wall. And as the Indians had seen him sick and missed him, so did they suspect what might be. And passing by the place where he was buried, seeing the earth moved, they looked and spoke one to another. Luys de Moscoso, understanding of it, commanded him to be taken up by night and to cast a great deal of sand into the mantles wherein he was wound up, wherein he was carried in a canoe and thrown into the midst of the river.

The Cacique of Guachoya inquired for him, demanding what was become of his brother and lord, the Governor. Luys de Moscoso told him that he was gone to Heaven, as many other times he did, and because he was to stay there certain days, he had left him in his place. The Cacique thought with himself that he was dead and commanded two young and well-proportioned Indians to be brought thither and said that the use of that country was, when any lord died, to kill Indians to wait upon him and serve him by the way, and for that purpose be his commandment were those come thither, and he prayed Luys de Moscoso to command them to be beheaded that they might attend and serve his lord and brother. Luys de Moscoso told him that the Governor was not dead, but gone to Heaven and that of his own Christian soldiers he had taken such as he needed to serve him and prayed him to command those Indians to be loosed and not to use any such bad custom from thenceforth. Straightway he commanded them to be loosed and to get them home to their houses.

HUDSON'S DISCOVERY OF THE HUDSON RIVER
(1609)
by Robert Juet

Juet, on a previous voyage with Hudson, had been Hudson's mate, but on the voyage to New York harbor he was his clerk and kept a journal, from which the account here given is taken. Hudson himself also kept a journal, but this has been lost. It is curious that Juet, on the last voyage which Hudson made—the one to Hudson Bay, in which he was set adrift in a small boat and left to perish—became the leader in the mutiny.

Before coming to America, Henry Hudson, an Englishman in Dutch service, had sailed to the east coast of Greenland, visited Spitzbergen, and attempted to find a northeast passage from the Atlantic to the Pacific. It was his attempt to find a northwest passage which led him, in September 1609, into the harbor of New York and up to the river named after him. In the following year he sailed again from Holland, seeking a northwest passage and thus entered Hudson Bay. Here he spent the winter. In the following June, when about to return home, the crew mutinied; Hudson and eight others were seized, bound, and set afloat in a small boat that was never heard from again.

The fourth of September 1609 in the morning as soon as the day was light, we saw that it was good riding farther up. So we sent out a boat to sound and found that it was a very good harbor of four and five fathoms, two cables' length from the shore. Then we weighed and went in with our ship. Then our boat went on land with our net to fish and caught ten great mullets of a foot and a half long apiece and a ray as great as four men could haul into the ship. So we trimmed our boat and stayed still all day. At night the wind blew hard at the northwest, our anchor came home, and we drove on shore, but took no hurt, thanks be to God, for the ground is soft sand and ooze. This day the people of the country came aboard of us, seeming very glad of our coming, and brought green tobacco and gave us of it for knives and beads. They go in loose deer skins, well-dressed. They have yellow copper. They desire clothes and are very civil. They have great store of maize, or Indian wheat, whereof they make good bread. The country is full of great and tall oaks.

The fifth in the morning as soon as the day was light, the wind ceased and the flood came. So we heaved off our ship again into five fathoms and sent our boat to sound the bay, and we found that there were three fathoms hard by the southern shore. Our men went on land there and saw great store of men, women, and children, who gave them tobacco at their coming on land. So they went up into the woods and saw great store of very goodly oaks and some currants. For one of them came aboard and brought some dried and gave me some which were sweet and good. This day many of the people came aboard, some in mantles of feathers and some in skins of divers sorts of good furs. Some women also came to us with hemp. They had red copper tobacco pipes, and other things of copper they did wear about their necks. At night they went on land again, so we stayed very quietly, but dared not trust them.

The sixth in the morning was fair weather, and our master sent John Colman with four other men in our boat over to the north side to sound the other river, being four leagues from us. They found by the day shoaled water, two fathoms; but at the north of the river eighteen and twenty fathoms, and very good riding for ships; and a narrow river to the westward between two islands. The lands, they told us, were as pleasant with grass and flowers and goodly trees as ever they had seen, and very sweet smells came from them.

The eleventh was fair and very hot weather. At one o'clock in the afternoon we weighed and went into the river, the wind at south-southwest, little wind. Our soundings were seven, six, five, six, seven, eight, nine, ten, twelve, thirteen, and fourteen fathoms. Then it shoaled again and came to five fathoms. Then we anchored and saw that it was a very good harbor for all winds and stayed all night. The people of the country came aboard of us, making show of love and gave us tobacco and Indian wheat and departed for that night, but we dared not trust them.

The twelfth was very fair and hot. In the afternoon at two o'clock we weighed, the wind being variable between the north and the northwest. So we turned into the river two leagues and anchored. This morning there came eight and twenty canoes full of men, women, and children to betray us; but we saw their intent and suffered none of them to come aboard of us. At twelve o'clock they departed. They brought with them oysters and beans, whereof we bought some. They have great tobacco pipes of yellow copper and pots of earth to dress their meat in.

The fourteenth in the morning being very fair weather, the wind southeast, we sailed up the river twelve leagues and had five fathoms and five fathoms and a quarter less; and we came to a strait between two points and had eight, nine, and ten fathoms. It attended northeast by north one league, and we had twelve, thirteen, and fourteen fathoms. The river is a mile broad; there is very high land on both sides. Then we went up northwest a league and a half deep water, then northeast by north five miles, then northwest by north two leagues, and anchored. The land grew very high and mountainous. The river is full of fish.

The seventeenth brought fair, sunshiny weather and was very hot. In the morning as soon as the sun was up, we set sail and ran up six leagues higher and found shoals in the middle of the channel, and small islands, but seven fathoms of water on both sides. Toward night we drifted so near the shore that we grounded; so we laid out our small anchor and heaved off again. Then we neared the bank of the channel and came aground again; while the flood ran, we heaved off again and anchored all night.

The eighteenth in the morning was fair weather, and we stayed still. In the afternoon our master's mate went on land with an old savage, a governor of the country, who carried him to his house and made him good cheer. The nineteenth was fair and hot weather. At the flood, being near eleven o'clock, we weighed and ran higher up two leagues above the shoals and had no less water than five fathoms. We anchored and rode in eight fathoms. The people of the country came flocking aboard and brought us beavers' skins and otters' skins, which we bought for beads, knives, and hatchets. So we stayed there all night.

The twentieth in the morning was fair weather. Our master's mate with four men more went up with our boat to sound the river and found two leagues above us but two fathoms and the channel very narrow, and above that place seven or eight fathoms. Toward night they returned, and we stayed still all night. The one and twentieth was fair weather, and the wind all southerly. We determined yet once more to go farther up into the river to try what depth and breadth it did bear, but much people resorted aboard, so we went not this day. Our carpenter went on land and made a foreyard. And our master and his mate determined to try some of the chief men of the country, whether they had any treachery in them. So they took them down into the cabin and gave them so much wine and aqua vita that they were all merry; and one of them had his wife with them, which sat so modestly as any of our country women would do in a strange place. In the end one of them was drunk which had been aboard our ship all the time that we had been there; and that was strange to them, for they could not tell how to take it. The canoes and folk went all on shore, but some of them came again and brought strings of beads—some had six, seven, eight, nine, ten and gave him. So he slept all night quietly.

The two and twentieth was fair weather. In the morning our master's mate and four more of the company went up with our boat to sound the river higher up. The people of the country came not aboard till noon; but when they came and saw the savages well, they were glad. So at three o'clock in the afternoon they came aboard and brought tobacco and more beads and gave them to our master and made an oration and showed him all the country round about. Then they sent one of their company on land, who presently returned and brought a great platter full of venison dressed by themselves, and they caused him to eat with them. Then they made him reverence and departed, all save the old man that lay aboard. This night at ten o'clock our boat returned in a shower of rain from sounding the river and found it to be at an end for shipping to go in. For they had been up eight or nine leagues and found but seven foot water and unconstant soundings.

The four and twentieth was fair weather. The wind at the northwest, we weighed and went down the river seven or eight leagues, and at half ebb we came on ground on a bank of ooze in the middle of the river and sat there till the flood. Then we went on land and gathered good store of chestnuts. At ten o'clock we came off into deep water and anchored.

The second was fair weather. At break of day we weighed, the wind being at northwest, and got down seven leagues; then the flood was come strong, so we anchored. Then came some of the savages that swam away from us at our going up the river, thinking to betray us. But we perceived their intent and suffered none of them to enter our ship. Whereupon two canoes full of men, with their bows and arrows, shot at us after our stern. In recompense whereof we discharged six muskets and killed two or three of them. Then above a hundred of them came to a point of land to shoot at us. There I shot a cannon at them and killed two of them; whereupon the rest fled into the woods. Yet they manned off another canoe with nine or ten men which came to meet us. So I shot at it also a cannon and shot it through and killed one of them. Then our men with their muskets killed three or four more of them. So they went their way. Within a mile after we got down two leagues beyond that place and anchored in a bay clear from all danger of them on the other side of the river, we saw a very good piece of ground, and hard by it there was a cliff that looked of the color of a white green, as though it were either a copper or silver mine; and I think it to be one of them by the trees that grow upon it, for they be all burned, and the other places are green as grass. It is on that side of the river that is called Mannahatta. There we saw no people to trouble us and rode quietly all night, but had much wind and rain.

We continued our course toward England without seeing any land by the way all the rest of the month of October, and on the seventh day of November, being Saturday, by the grace of God we safely arrived in the range of Dartmouth in Devonshire in the year 1609.

A BATTLE WITH THE IROQUOIS
(1609)
by Samuel de Champlain

Champlain, who has been called "The Father of New France," was born in Brouage, France, in 1567, and died in Quebec in 1635. In Champlain were embodied the religious zeal of New France and her romantic spirit of adventure. Champlain's first explorations in America were made in 1603-07. Quebec was founded by him in 1608, and Lake Champlain discovered in 1609.

We continued our course to the entrance of Lake St. Peter, where the country is exceedingly pleasant and level, and crossed the lake in two, three, and four fathoms of water, which is some eight leagues long and four wide. On the north side we saw a very pleasant river extending some twenty leagues into the interior, which I named St. Suzanne; on the south side, there are two—one called Riviere du Pont, the other Riviere de Gennes—which are very pretty and in a fine and fertile country. The water is almost still in the lake, which is full of fish. On the north bank there are seen some slight elevations at a distance of some twelve or fifteen leagues from the lake. After crossing the lake, we passed a large number of islands of various sizes, containing many nut trees and vines and fine meadows with quantities of game and wild animals, which go over from the mainland to these islands. Fish are here more abundant than in any other part of the river that we have seen. From these islands we went to the mouth of the River of the Iroquois where we stayed two days, refreshing ourselves with good venison, birds, and fish which the savages gave us. Here there sprang up among them some difference of opinion on the subject of the war, so that a portion only determined to go with me, while the others returned to their country with their wives and the merchandise which they had obtained by barter.

I set out accordingly from the fall of the Iroquois River on July 2. All the savages set to carrying their canoes, arms, and baggage overland some half a league in order to pass by the violence and strength of the fall, which was speedily accomplished.

The next day we entered the lake, which is of great extent, say eighty or a hundred leagues long, where I saw four fine islands, ten, twelve, and fifteen leagues long, which were formerly inhabited by the savages, like the River of the Iroquois; but they have been abandoned since the wars of the savages with one another prevail. There are also many rivers falling into the lake, bordered by many fine trees of the same kinds as those we have in France, with many vines finer than any I have seen in any other place; also many chestnut trees on the border of this lake, which I had not seen before.

Continuing our course over this lake on the western side, I noticed, while observing the country, some very high mountains on the eastern side, on the top of which there was snow. I made inquiry of the savages, whether these localities were inhabited, when they told me that the Iroquois dwelt there and that there were beautiful valleys in these places with plains productive in grain, such as I had eaten in this country, together with many kinds of fruit without limit. They said also that the lake extended near mountains some twenty-five leagues distant from us, as I judge. I saw on the south other mountains no less high than the first, but without any snow.

When it was evening, we embarked in our canoes to continue our course; and as we advanced very quietly and without making any noise, we met the Iroquois on May 29, about ten o'clock at evening at the extremity of a cape which extends into the lake on the western bank. They had come to fight. We both began to utter loud cries, all getting their arms in readiness. We withdrew out on the water, and the Iroquois went on shore where they drew up all their canoes close to each other and began to fell trees with poor axes, which they acquire in war sometimes, using also others of stone. Thus they barricaded themselves very well.

Our forces also passed the entire night, their canoes being drawn up close to each other and fastened to poles, so they they might not get separated and that they might be all in readiness to fight if occasion required. After arming ourselves with light armor, we each took an arquebuse and went on shore. I saw the enemy go out of their barricade, nearly two hundred in number, stout and rugged in appearance. They came at a slow pace toward us, with a dignity and assurance which greatly amused me, having three chiefs at their head. Our men also advanced in the same order, telling me that those who had three large plumes were the chiefs, that they had only three, that they could be distinguished by these plumes which were much larger than those of their companions, and that I should do what I could to kill them. I promised to do all in my power and said that I was very sorry they could not understand me so that I might give order and shape to their mode of attacking their enemies, and then we should without doubt defeat them all; but this could not now be obviated, and I was very glad to show them my courage and good-will when we began to engage in the fight.

As soon as we had landed, they began to run for some two hundred paces toward their enemies who stood firmly, not having as yet noticed my companions who went into the woods with some savages. Our men began to call me with loud cries; and in order to give me a passageway, they opened in two parts and put me at their head where I marched some twenty paces in advance of the rest until I was within about thirty paces of the enemy who at once noticed me, and, halting, gazed at me as I did also at them. When I saw them making a move to fire at us, I rested my musket against my cheek and aimed directly at one of the three chiefs. With the same shot two fell to the ground, and one of their men was so wounded that he died some time after. I had loaded my musket with four balls. When our side saw this shot so favorable for them, they began to raise such loud cries that one could not have heard it thunder. Meanwhile, the arrows flew on both sides. The Iroquois were greatly astonished that two men had been so quickly killed, although they were equipped with armor woven from cotton thread and with wood which was a proof against their arrows. This caused great alarm among them. As I was loading again, one of my companions fired a shot from the woods which astonished them anew to such a degree that, seeing their chiefs dead, they lost courage and took to flight, abandoning their camp and fort and fleeing into the woods whither I pursued them, killing still more of them. Our savages also killed several of them and took ten or twelve prisoners. The remainder escaped with the wounded. Fifteen or sixteen on our side were wounded with arrow shots, but they were soon healed.

After gaining the victory, our men amused themselves by taking a great quantity of Indian corn and some meal from their enemies and also their armor which they had left behind that they might run better. After feasting sumptuously, dancing and singing, we returned three hours after with the prisoners. The spot were this attack took place is in latitude forty-three degrees and some minutes, and the lake was called Lake Champlain.

After going some eight leagues, toward evening they took one of the prisoners to whom they had a harangue, enumerating the cruelties which he and his men had already practiced toward them without any mercy and that in like manner he ought to make up his mind to receive as much. They commanded him to sing if he had courage, which he did, but it was a very sad song.

DISCOVERY OF THE MISSISSIPPI
(1673)
by Father Marquette

Father Marquette was born at Laon, France, in 1637 and died on the eastern shore of Lake Michigan in 1675. Marquette had kept daily memoranda of his expedition, but during the return voyage up the Mississippi his papers were lost. He afterward composed from memory his narrative published under the title Travels and Discoveries in North America.

In this journey, occupying about four months, Marquette and Joliet paddled their canoes more than twenty-five hundred miles. Joliet and Marquette were as much the real discoverers of the Mississippi as Columbus was the discoverer of America. While Europeans had actually reached the Mississippi before them, just as Asiatics and Norwegians probably had reached America before Columbus, it was Joliet and Marquette who first wrote narratives of their expedition, prepared excellent maps, and were followed by others who opened the region to enterprise and settlement. Of De Soto's century-and-a-quarter earlier discovery, nothing came, while the contention put forth for La Salle that he made an earlier visit than Joliet and Marquette is based on surmise.

I embarked with Monsieur Joliet, who had been chosen to conduct this enterprise, on May 13, 1673, with five other Frenchmen in two bark canoes. We laid in some Indian corn and smoked beef for our voyage. We first took care, however, to draw from the Indians all the information we could concerning the countries through which we designed to travel and drew up a map on which we marked down the rivers, nations, and points of the compass to guide us in our journey. The first nation we came to was called the Folles-Avoines, or the nation of wild oats. The wild oats, from which they derive their name, grow spontaneously in their country. I entered the river to visit them, as I had preached among them some years before.

I acquainted them with my design of discovering other nations, to preach to them the mysteries of our holy religion, at which they were much surprised and said all they could to dissuade me from it. They told me I would meet Indians who spare no strangers and whom they kill without any provocation or mercy; that the war they have one with the other would expose me to be taken by their warriors, as they are constantly on the look-out to surprise their enemies; that the Great River was exceedingly dangerous and full of frightful monsters who devoured men and canoes together; and that the heat was so great that it would positively cause our death. I thanked them for their kind advice, but told them I would not follow it as the salvation of a great many souls was concerned in our undertaking, for whom I should be glad to lose my life. I added that I defied their monsters, and their information would oblige us to keep more upon our guard to avoid a surprise. And having prayed with them and given them some instructions, we set out for the Bay of Paun.

Before embarking, we all offered up prayers to the Holy Virgin, which we continued to do every morning, placing ourselves and the events of the journey under her protection, and after having encouraged each other, we got into our canoes. The river upon which we embarked is called Mesconsin [Wisconsin]; the river is very wide, but the sand bars make it very difficult to navigate, which is increased by numerous islands covered with grapevines. The country through which it flows is beautiful; the groves are so dispersed in the prairies that it makes a noble prospect, and the fruit of the trees shows a fertile soil. These groves are full of walnut, oak, and other trees unknown to us in Europe. We saw neither game nor fish, but roebuck and buffaloes in great numbers. After having navigated thirty leagues we discovered some iron mines, and one of our company who had seen such mines before said these were very rich in ore. They are covered with about three feet of soil and situated near a chain of rocks whose base is covered with fine timber. After having rowed ten leagues farther, making forty leagues from the place where we had embarked, we came into the Mississippi on June 17, [1673].

The mouth of the Mesconsin [Wisconsin] is in about forty-two and a half degrees north latitude. Behold us, then, upon this celebrated river, whose singularities I have attentively studied. The Mississippi takes its rise in several lakes in the north. Its channel is very narrow at the mouth of the Mesconsin and runs south until it is affected by very high hills. Its current is slow because of its depth. In sounding we found nineteen fathoms of water. A little farther on, it widens nearly three-quarters of a league, and the width continues to be more equal. We slowly followed its course to the south and southeast to forty-two degrees north latitude. Here we perceived the country change its appearance. There were scarcely any more woods or mountains. The islands were covered with fine trees, but we could not see any more roebucks, buffaloes, bustards, and swans. We met from time to time monstrous fish which struck so violently against our canoes that at first we took them to be large trees which threatened to upset us. We saw also a hideous monster; his head was like that of a tiger, his nose was sharp and somewhat resembled a wildcat, his beard was long, his ears stood upright, the color of his head was grey, and his neck black. He looked upon us for some time, but as we came near him our oars frightened him away. When we threw our nets into the water, we caught an abundance of sturgeons and another kind of fish like our trout, except that the eyes and nose are much smaller, and they have near the nose a bone three inches broad and a foot and a half long, the end of which is flat and broad, and when it leaps out of the water the weight of it throws it on its back.

Having descended the river as far as forty-one degrees and twenty-eight minutes, we found that turkeys took the place of game, and the pisikious that of other animals. We called the pisikious wild buffaloes, because that very much resemble our domestic oxen; they are not so long, but twice as large. We shot one of them, and it was as much as thirteen men could do to drag him from the place where he fell.

We took leave of our guides about the end of June and embarked in presence of all the village, who admired our birch canoes, as they had never before seen anything like them. We descended the river, looking for another called Pekitanoni [Missouri], which runs from the northwest into the Mississippi.

As we were descending the river, we saw high rocks with hideous monsters painted on them, and upon which the bravest Indians dare not look. Each is as large as a calf, with head and horns like a goat; its eyes red; beard like a tiger's; and a face like a man's. Their tails are so long that they can pass over their heads and between their fore-legs, under their belly, and ending like a fish's tail. They are painted red, green, and black. They are so well drawn that I cannot believe they were drawn by the Indians. And for what purpose they were made seems to me a great mystery. As we fell down the river and while we were discoursing upon these monsters, we heard a great rushing and bubbling of waters and small islands of floating trees coming from the mouth of the Pekitanoni [Missouri] with such rapidity that we could not trust ourselves to go near it. The water of this river is so muddy that we could not drink it. It so discolors the Mississippi as to make the navigation of it dangerous. This river comes from the northwest and empties into the Mississippi, and on its banks are situated a number of Indian villages. We judged by the compass that the Mississippi discharged itself into the Gulf of Mexico. It would, however, have been more agreeable if it had discharged itself into the South Sea or Gulf of California.

Having satisfied ourselves that the Gulf of Mexico was in latitude thirty-one degrees and forty minutes and that we could reach it in three or four days' journey from the Akansea [Arkansas River] and that the Mississippi discharged itself into it, not to the eastward of the Cape of Florida nor into the California Sea, we resolved to return home. We considered that the advantage of our travels would be altogether lost to our nation if we fell into the hands of the Spaniards, from whom we could expect no other treatment than death or slavery; besides, we saw that we were not prepared to resist the Indians, the allies of the Europeans, who continually infested the lower part of this river; we therefore came to the conclusion to return and make a report to those who had sent us. So that having rested another day, we left the village of the Akansea on the seventeenth of July, 1673, having followed the Mississippi from the latitude forty-two degrees to thirty-four degrees, and preached the Gospel to the utmost of my power to the nations we visited. We then ascended the Mississippi with great difficulty against the current and left it in the latitude of thirty-eight degrees north to enter another river [Illinois], which took us to the lake of the Illinois [Michigan], which is a much shorter way than through the River Mesconsin [Wisconsin], by which we entered the Mississippi.

COLONIZATION

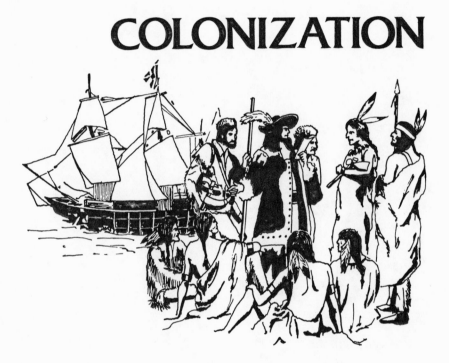

COLONIZATION

After the years of discovery and exploration came the first colonial settlements—Spaniards in Florida, Dutch in New York, Swedes in New Jersey and Delaware, French Huguenots in Florida and Carolina, French Catholics in Louisiana. The English founded several colonies: Protestants in New England, Catholics in Maryland, Quakers in Pennsylvania, and inmates of debtors' prisons in Georgia.

Some settlements were disastrous failures. The Huguenots in Florida and the English in Roanoke perished. Others who survived faced severe hardships at first. The English in Jamestown and Plymouth, the Dutch in New York, and the French in New Orleans were saved by good leaders such as John Smith, Bradford, Minuet, and Bienville.

No two settlements were alike. Each had been inspired by a different motive. Although some were similar in providing a haven from religious or political persecution, they were usually divided by years, if not by generations, in time; they were geographically isolated from one another; their settlers were different in nationality, government, and religion. Hence, the New World communities seldom had much contact with their neighbors.

The Spaniards who founded St. Augustine continued long to live there, but there was no real social and political growth in Spanish Florida. Spain was often absorbed in expensive and exhausting continental wars, especially in a furious contest with Holland, which dragged on for forty years and from which Spain retired ultimately in failure. England also smashed Spain's "Invincible Armada" in those years and gained control of the seas. The Spaniards began slowly to lose their hold on the New World.

Of the French settlements outside of Canada, the chief was New Orleans, French from the beginning, and so to remain in religion and government for a century and a half after Bienville founded it. Much of it remains the same to our day. But elsewhere the French gave to the United States almost no permanent settlements. Numbers of them came to Florida, only to perish by the sword; others settled in South Carolina, only to merge with other groups such as the English.

On Manhattan Island and in the valley of the Hudson River settled the Dutch (1626). They erected forts and partitioned vast tracts of fertile lands among favorite patroons; they built up a successful fur trade with the Indians and sent the profits home. They did not found permanent local settlements strong in population and industry. Holland soon surrendered its colony to England, and New Amsterdam became New York.

Sir Walter Raleigh sought to establish an English colony in Virginia, futilely spending much of his wealth and energy in the attempt. Out of his failure at Roanoke Island, however, English successes came in later years at Jamestown and in New England.

The first permanent English colony in America was Jamestown (1607). There, ten years after the arrival of the first settlers, a legislative assembly was organized. It was the first legislature in the New World, a miniature Parliament, modeled on the English House of Commons. In Jamestown, too, black slavery began in the United States.

English colonies at Plymouth (1620) and Massachusetts Bay (1630) followed the one at Jamestown. After several years the Plymouth group numbered only three hundred souls, but the Bay colony grew rapidly. By 1634 nearly four thousand of Winthrop's followers had arrived, many of them university graduates. Two years later Harvard College was established to train future ministers. From this parent colony went forth Roger Williams to Rhode Island, Hooker to Hartford, Davenport to Hew Haven, so that by the middle of the seventeenth century five English colonies had been planted in New England.

In the same century came the Maryland (1623) and Pennsylvania (1681) settlements, founded by Lord Baltimore and William Penn as Lords Proprietor. In the next century (1732) Oglethorpe arrived with his insolvent debtors to start a new settlement named for King George II.

The French and Dutch had come to North America to trade with the Indians, but the English had come to stay. And stay they did. Two hundred and fifty years after Columbus's first voyage to the New World, England controlled the eastern American seaboard from French Canada to Spanish Florida.

THE RETURN OF THE COLONISTS WITH SIR FRANCIS DRAKE

(1586)

by Ralph Lane

In 1585 Ralph Lane went to Virginia with one hundred other householders in ships dispatched by Raleigh and commanded by Sir Richard Grenville. After landing at Roanoke, Grenville returned to England for supplies and left Lane in charge of the colony. Lane has left an important account of the experiences and sufferings of the colonists during the absence of Grenville, whose return was delayed. In the meantime, Drake came up to Roanoke Island from St. Augustine in 1586, and the whole company returned to England with him. Grenville afterward arrived on Roanoke Island and found no one there. Leaving fifteen men on the island, he then returned to England. In the following year Raleigh sent John White out to Roanoke. When White arrived he found that these men had all been massacred by the Indians. Other expeditions were sent out later, but none was able to establish any colony at Roanoke Island.

This fell out of the first of June, 1586, and the eighth of June came advertisement to me from Captain Stafford, lying at my lord Admiral's island, that he had discovered a great fleet of three and twenty sails, but whether they were friends or foes, he could not yet discern. He advised me to stand upon as good guard as I could.

The ninth of June he himself came unto me, having that night before and that same day traveled by land twenty miles, and I must truly report of him from the first to the last. He was a gentleman who never spared labor or peril either by land or water, fair weather or foul, to perform any service committed unto him.

He brought me a letter from the General Sir Francis Drake, with a most bountiful and honorable offer for the supply of our necessities to the performance of the action we were entered into. And that not only of victuals, munition, and clothing, but also of barks, pinnaces, and boats; they also by him to be victualled, manned and furnished to my contention.

The tenth of June he arrived in the road of our bad harbor and anchored. The eleventh of June I came to him, whom I found indeed most honorably to perform that which in writing and message he had most courteously offered. He aforehand propounded the matter to all the captains of his fleet and got their liking and consent thereto.

I gave such thanks unto him and his captains for his care, both of us and of our action, as I could, though not as much as the matter deserved. I (being aforehand prepared what I would desire) craved at his hands if it would please him to take with him to England a number of weak men unfit for any good action, which I would deliver to him, and in place of them to supply me of his company with oarmen, artificers, and others.

Also, I asked if he would leave us enough shipping and victuals to last us until about August, when he would carry me and all my company into England. But we discovered that they had lack of needful provision and left us still without provisions.

I also asked that, if it would please him, to leave sufficient masters not only to carry us into England, when time should be, but also to search the coast for some better harbor, if there were any, and especially to help us to some small boats and oarmen. Also for a supply of hand weapons, match and lead, tools, apparel, and such like.

He having received my requests, the General came ashore and made a proffer unto me, which was a ship of 170 tons, called the *Bonner,* with a sufficient master and guide to tarry with me the time appointed, and victualled sufficiently to carry me and my company into England, with all provisions as before. But he told me that he would not for anything undertake to have her brought into our harbor, and therefore he was to leave her in the road, and to leave the care of the rest unto myself. He advised me to consider our case with my company and to deliver presently unto him in writing what I would require him to do for us; which being within his power, he did assure me as well for his captains as for himself, should be most willingly performed.

Hereupon I called such captains and gentlemen of my company as then were at hand, who were all as privy as myself to the General's offer. Their whole request to me was to consider the case that we stood in—the weakness of our company, the small number of the same, the carrying away of our first appointed bark (with those two special masters), with our principal provisions in the same. The very hand of God, it seemed, stretched out to take us from thence. Considering also, that his second offer, though most honorable on his part, yet could not be accepted by us since there was no possibility for the ship to be brought into the harbor in safety. Seeing furthermore our hope for supply with Sir Richard Grenville (so undoubtedly promised us before Easter, not yet come) neither then likely to come this year, considering the doings in England for Flanders, and also for America; therefore, I resolved myself with my company to go into England in that fleet and accordingly to make request to the General in all our names, that he would be pleased to give us present passage with him. Which request of ours I delivered unto him, and he most readily assented unto. And so he sent immediately his pinnaces unto our island for the fetching away of a few that there were left with out baggage. The weather was so boisterous, and the pinnesses so often on ground, that the most of all we had, with all our cards, books, and writings were by the sailors cast overboard, the greater number of the fleet being much aggrieved with their long and dangerous abode in that miserable road.

From whence the General in the name of the Almighty weighed his anchors, having bestowed us among his fleet. For the relief of us he had in that storm sustained more peril of wreck than in all his former most honorable actions against the Spaniards. With praises unto God for all, we set sail the nineteenth of June, 1596 and arrived in Portsmouth the twenty-seventh of July the same year.

THE BIRTH OF VIRGINIA DARE
(1587)
by John White

Virginia Dare was the first child of English parentage born in America. Her parents, Eleanor and Ananias Dare, named her after the colony that had already received the name in compliment to Queen Elizabeth.

July 22 we came safely to Cape Hatteras, where our ship and pinnace anchored. The Governor went aboard the pinnace accompanied by forty of his best men, intending to pass up to Roanoke. He hoped to find those fifteen Englishmen whom Sir Richard Grenville had left there the year before. With these he meant to have a conference concerning the state of the country and the savages, intending then to return to the fleet and pass along the coast to the Bay of Chesapeake. Here we intended to make our settlement and fort according to the charge given us among other directions in writing under the hand of Sir Walter Raleigh. We passed to Roanoke and the same night at sunset went ashore on the island, in the place where our fifteen men were left. But we found none of them nor any sign that they had been there, saving only that we found the bones of one of them, whom the savages had slain long before.

The Governor with several of his company walked the next day to the north end of the island, where Master Ralph Lane, with his men the year before, had built his fort with sundry dwelling houses. We hoped to find some signs here or some certain knowledge of our fifteen men.

When we came thither, we found the fort razed but all the houses standing unhurt, saving that the lower rooms of them, and of the fort also, were overgrown with melons of different sorts, and deer were in rooms feeding on those melons. So we returned to our company without the hope of ever seeing any of the fifteen men living.

The same day an order was given that every man should be employed in remodeling those houses which we found standing and in making more cottages.

On the eighteenth a daughter was born in Roanoke to Eleanor, the daughter of the Governor and the wife of Ananias Dare. This baby was christened on the Sunday following, and because this child was the first Christian born in Virginia she was named Virginia Dare.

By this time our shipmasters had unloaded the goods and victuals of the planters and taken wood and fresh water, and were newly calking and trimming their vessels for their return to England. The settlers also prepared their letters and news to send back to England.

THE FOUNDING OF JAMESTOWN
(1607)
by Captain John Smith

Edward Arber, a noted nineteenth century English scholar, has contended that had not John Smith "strove, fought and endured as he did the present United States of America might never had come into existence." Spaniards and French alike had failed in their attempts at colonization and so had the repeated expeditions sent out by Sir Walter Raleigh. Smith, "self-denying, energetic, so full of resources, and so trained in dealing with the savage race," carried the Jamestown settlement through its difficulties. Had Jamestown failed, the Pilgrim fathers "would not have gone to New England."

Captain Bartholomew Gosnoll, one of the first founders of this plantation, for many years solicited many of his friends but found few willing assistants. At last he prevailed with some gentlemen, as Captain John Smith, Master Edward-maria Wingfield, Master Robert Hunt, and diverse others, who depended a year upon his projects. But nothing could be effected, till by their great charge and industry it came to be noticed by certain of the nobility, gentry, and merchants, so that his Majesty by his letters gave commission for establishing councils to direct here and to govern and to execute there. To effect this, another year was spent, and by that, three ships were provided: one of one hundred tons, another of forty, and a pinnace of twenty. The transportation of the company was committed to Captain Christopher Newport, a mariner well practiced for the western parts of America. But their orders for government were put in a box, not to be opened, nor the governors known until they arrived in Virginia. On December 19, 1606, we set sail from Blackwell, but by unprosperous winds were kept six weeks in the sight of England; all which time, Master Hunt our preacher, was so weak and sick that few expected his recovery.

We watered at the Canaries; we traded with the savages at Dominica. Three weeks we spent in refreshing ourselves amongst these West India isles; in Guadalupa we found a bath so hot, that in it we boiled pork as well as it could be cooked over the fire. And a little isle called Monica, we took from the bushes with our hands nearly two hogsheads full of birds in three of four hours. In Mevis, Mona, and the Virgin Isles, we spent some time, where, on a loathsome beast like a crocodile, called a gwayn, tortoises, pelicans, parrots, and fishes, we daily feasted.

Gone from thence in search of Virginia, the company was not a little discomforted, seeing the mariners had three days passed their reckoning and found no land; so that Captain Ratliffe (captain of the pinnace) rather desired to bear up the helm to return for England, than to make further search. But God the Guider of all good actions, forcing them by an extreme storm to hull all night, did drive them by His providence to their desired port, beyond all their expectations, for not one of them had ever seen that coast.

The first land they made they called Cape Henry, where thirty of them recreating themselves on shore, were assaulted by five savages, who hurt two of the English very dangerously.

That night the box was opened and the orders read, in which Bartholomew Gosnoll, John Smith, Edward Wingfield, Christopher Newport, John Ratliffe, John Martin, and George Kendall were named to be the council and were to choose a president amongst them for a year, who with the council should govern. Matters of moment were to be examined by a jury but determined by the major part of the council, in which the president had two votes.

Until May 13 they sought a place to plant in. Then the council was sworn, Master Wingfield was chosen president, and an oration made why Captain Smith was not admitted to the council as the rest.

Now falleth every man to work; the council contrived the fort; the rest cut down trees to make a place to pitch their tents. Some provided clapboard to reload the ships, some made gardens, some nets, etc. The savages often visited us kindly. The president's overweening jealousy would admit no exercise at arms or fortification but the boughs of trees cast together in the form of a half moon by the extraordinary pains and diligence of Captain Kendall.

Newport, Smith, and twenty others were sent to discover the head of the river. By diverse small habitations they passed; in six days they arrived at a town called Powhatan, consisting of some twelve houses, pleasantly seated on a hill; before it were three fertile isles, about it many of their cornfields. The place is very pleasant and strong by nature. Of this place the prince is called Powhatan and his people Powhatans. To this place the river is navigable, but higher within a mile, by reason of the rocks and isles, there is not passage for a small boat; this they call the Falls. The people in all parts kindly entreated them; however, when they arrived at the fort the next day, they found seventeen men hurt and a boy slain by the savages. Had it not chanced a cross bar shot from the ships struck down a bough from a tree amongst them and caused them to retire, our men would have all been slain, being securely all at work, and their arm in dry fats.

Hereupon the president was contented the fort should be palisaded, the ordinance mounted, his men armed and exercised, for many were the assaults and ambushes of the savages, and our men by their disorderly straggling were often hurt, when the savages by the nimbleness of their heels well escaped.

What toil we had, with no small power to guard our workmen during the days, watch all night, resist our enemies, and effect our business, to reload the ships, cut down trees, and prepare the ground to plant our corn, etc. I refer to the reader's consideration. Six weeks being spent in this manner, reader's Captain Newport (who was hired only for our transportation) was to return with the ships.

Being thus left to our fortunes, it fortuned that within ten days scarcely ten among us could either go or well stand, such extreme weakness and sickness oppressed us. And thereat none need marvel, if they consider the cause and reason, which was this.

While the ships stayed, our allowance was somewhat bettered by a daily proportion of biscuit, which the sailors would pilfer to sell, give, or exchange with us, for money, sassafras, furs, or charity. But when they left there remained neither tavern, beer house, nor place of relief, but the common kettle. Had we been as free from all sins as gluttony and drunkenness, we might have been canonized for saints. But our president would never have been admitted, for he ingrossed for his private use oatmeal, white wine, oil, aqua vitae, beef, eggs, or what not. But the kettle, that aqua vitae indeed he allowed equally to be distributed, and that was half a pint of wheat and as much barley boiled with water for a man a day, and this having fried some six weeks in the ship's hold, contained as many worms as grains; so that we might truly call it rather so much bran than corn. Our drink was water, our lodgings castles in the air.

With this lodging and diet, our extreme toil in bearing and planting palisades so strained and bruised us, and our continual labor in the extremity of the heat had so weakened us, and were sufficient cause to have made us as miserable in our native country or any other place in the world.

From May to September those that escaped lived upon sturgeon and sea-crabs. Fifty in this time we buried; the rest seeing that the president (who all this time had neither felt want nor sickness) planned to escape these miseries in our pinnace deposed Wingfield and established Ratcliffe in his place, Godnoll being dead and Kendall deposed. Smith newly recovered, Martin and Ratcliff were by his care preserved and relieved, and the most of the soldiers recovered with the skillful diligence of Master Thomas Wotton, our surgeon general.

But now was all our provision spent, the sturgeon gone, all helps abandoned, each hour expecting the fury of the savages, when God the patron of all good endeavors, in that desperate extremity so changed the hearts of the savages that they brought so much of their fruits and provision that no man wanted for anything.

The new president and Martin, being little beloved, weak judgment in dangers, and less industrious in peace, committed the managing of all things abroad to Captain Smith who by his own example, good words, and fair promises, set some to mow, others to bind thatch, some to build houses, others to thatch them. He himself always bore the greatest task for his own share, so that in short time, he provided most of them with lodging, neglecting any for himself.

This done, seeing the savages' superfluity begin to decrease, he (with some of his workmen) shipped himself in the shallop to search the country for trade. The want of the language, knowledge to manage his boat without sails, the want of a sufficient power (knowing the multitude of the savages), apparel for his men, and other necessaries, were infinite impediments.

Being but six or seven in company he went down the river to Kecoughtan where at first they scorned him as a famished man and would in derision offer him a handful of corn, a piece of bread, for their swords and muskets, and such like proportions also for their apparel. But seeing by trade and courtesy there was nothing to be gained, he decided to try such conclusions as necessity enforced. Though contrary to his commission, he let fly his muskets, and ran his boat on shore, whereat they all fled into the woods.

So marching towards their houses, the men saw great heaps of corn. Much trouble he had to restrain his hungry soldiers from taking of it, expecting that the savages would assault them, as they did not long after with a most hideous noise. Sixty or seventy of them, some black, some red, some white, some party-colored, came in a square order, singing and dancing out of the woods, with their Okee (which was an idol made of skins, stuffed with moss, all painted and hung with chains and copper) carried before them. In this manner, being well armed with clubs, targets, bows and arrows, they charged the English, who so kindly received them with their muskets loaded with pistol shot, that down fell their god and lay sprawling on the ground. The rest fled again to the woods and ere long sent one of their Quiyoughkasoucks to offer peace and redeem their Okee.

Smith told them that if only six of them would come unarmed and load his boat, he would not only be their friend, but restore them their Okee and give them beads, copper, and hatchets besides. This was performed to the contentment of both sides. And then they brought venison, turkeys, wild fowl, bread, and what they had, singing and dancing in sign of friendship till they departed.

On his return he discovered the town and country of Warraskoyack.

> Thus God unboundless in his power,
> Made them thus kind, that would us devour.

Smith perceiving (notwithstanding their late misery) that no one was storing provisions but all were living from hand to mouth (the company being well recovered) had the pinnace provided with provisions for the year following. But in the iterim he made three or four journeys and discovered the people of Chickahamania. Yet what he carefully provided, the rest carelessly spent.

Wingfield and Kendall living in disgrace, seeing much confusion during the absence of Smith, the companies' dislike of their president's weakness and their small love of Martin's never-mending sickness, strengthened themselves with the sailors and other confederates in order to regain their former credit and authority, and sought to alter the course of the pinnace and to go for England.

Smith unexpectedly returning discovered the plot. Much trouble he had to prevent it, till with saker and musket shot he forced them stay or sink in the rivers. This action cost the life of Captain Kendall.

These brawls are so disgustful, as some will say they were better forgotten, yet all men of good judgment will conclude that it were better their baseness should be made manifest to the world, than the business bear the scorn and shame of their excused disorders.

The president and Captain Archer not long after also intended to abandon the country, which project also was curbed and suppressed by Smith. The Spaniard never more greedily desired gold than he victual; nor his soldiers more to abandon the country, than he to keep it. He eventually found plenty of corn in the river of Chickahamania, where hundreds of savages in diverse places stood with baskets expecting his coming.

And now the winter approaching, the rivers became so covered with swans, geese, ducks, and cranes, that we daily feasted with good bread. Virginia peas, pumpkins, and putchamins, fish, fowl, and diverse sorts of wild beasts as fat as we could eat them were also discovered so that none of our tuftaffaty humorists desired to go for England.

But our comedies never endured long without a tragedy. Some idle statements were being muttered against Captain Smith for not discovering the mouth of the Chickahamania River, and he was also taxed by the council for being slow in so worthy an attempt. The next voyage he proceeded so far that only with much labor of cutting of trees did he make his passage. But when his barge could pass no farther, he left her in a broad bay out of danger of shot, commanding none should go ashore till his return. With two English and two savages, he went up higher in a canoe. He was not long absent, when his men went ashore. Their lack of government gave both occasion and opportunity to the savages to surprise one George Cassen, whom they slew. They did not fail by too much to have captured the boat and slain all the rest of the men.

Smith, little dreaming of that accident, was at the marshes at the river's head, twenty miles in the desert, and had his two men slain (as is supposed) as they were sleeping by the canoe while he by fowling sought them victual. He found himself beset with two hundred savages; two of them he slew still defending himself with the aid of a savage his guide, whom he bound to his arm with his garters, and used him as a buckler. Yet he was shot in his thigh a little and had many arrows that stuck in his clothes, but he sustained no great hurt, till at last they took him prisoner.

When this news came to Jamestown, much was their sorrow for his loss, few expecting what ensued. Six or seven weeks those Barbarians kept him prisoner; many strange triumps and conjurations they made of him, yet he so demeaned himself among them that he not only diverted them from surprising the fort, but procured his own liberty and got himself and his company such estimation among them, that those savages admired him more than their own Quiyoughkasoucks.

At last they brought him to Meronocomoco, where was Powhatan their emperor. Here more than two hundred of those grim courtiers stood wondering at him, as though he were a monster, till Powhatan and his train had put themselves in their greatest braveries. Before a fire upon a seat like a bedstead, he sat covered with a great robe made of Rarowcun skins, and with all the tails hanging by. On either hand sat a young wench of fifteen or eighteen years, and along on each side the house, two rows of men and behind them as many women, with all their heads and shoulders painted red. Many of their heads were bedecked with the white down of birds, but every one had something, and a great chain of white beads about their necks.

At his entrance beofre the king, all the people gave a great shout. The Queen of Appamatuck was appointed to bring him water to wash his hands, and another brought him a bunch of feathers instead of a towel to dry them. Having feasted him after their best barbarous manner, a long consultation was held, but the conclusion was that two great stones were to be brought before Powhatan. Then as many as could laid hands on him, dragged him to them, and thereon laid his head, and were ready with their clubs, to beat out his brains. Pocohontas, the King's dearest daughter, when no entreaty could prevail, got his head in her arms and laid her own upon his to save him from death, whereat the emperor was contented he should live to make him hatchets and her bells, beads, and copper, for they thought him as capable of all occupations as themselves.

> They say he bore a pleasant show,
> But sure his heart was sad.
> For who can pleasant be, and rest,
> That lives in fear and dread:
> And having life suspected, doth
> It still suspected lead.

Two days after, Powhatan having disguised himself in the most fearful manner he could, caused Captain Smith to be brought forth to a great house in the woods, and there upon a mat by the fire to be left alone. Not long after from behind a mat that divided the house was made the most doleful noise he ever heard. Then Powhatan more like a devil than a man, with some two hundred more as black as himself, came unto him and told him now they were friends, and presently he should go to Jamestown, for which he would give him the country of Capahowosick and forever esteem him as his son Nantaquoud.

So to Jamestown with twelve guides Powhatan sent him. That night they quartered in the woods, he still expecting (as he had done all this long time of his imprisonment) every hour to be put to one death or other, for all their feasting. But almighty God (by His divine providence) had mollified the hearts of those stern barbarians with compassion. The next morning they came early to the fort, where Smith having used the savages with what kindness he could, showed Rawhunt, Powhatan's trusty servant, two muskets and a millstone to carry to Powhatan. They found them somewhat too heavy, but when they did see him discharge them, being loaded with stones, among the boughs of a great tree loaded with icicles, the ice and branches came so tumbling down, that the poor savages ran away half dead with fear. But at last we regained some confidence with them and gave them such toys and sent to Powhatan, his women, and children such presents as made them generally well content.

Now in Jamestown they were all in combustion; the strongest preparing once more to run away with the pinnace, which with the hazard of his life, with saker falcon and musket shot, Smith forced now the third time to stay or sink.

Some no better than they should be had plotted with the president the next day to have put Smith to death by the Levitical law for the lives of Robinson and Emry, pretending the fault was his that had led them to their ends. But he quickly took such order with such lawyers that he laid them by the heels till he sent some of them prisoners for England.

Now once in every four or five days, Pocahontas with her attendants brought him so much provision, that many of their lives were saved that else for all this would have starved with hunger.

Thus you may see what difficulties still crossed any good endeavors, and the good success of the business being thus oft brought to the very point of destruction; yet you see by what strange means God hath still delivered it.

Now whether it had been better for Captain Smith to have concluded with any of those several projects, to have abandoned the country with some ten or twelve of them, who were called the better sort, and have left Master Hunt, our preacher. Master Anthony Gosnoll, a most honest, worthy, and industrious gentleman. Master Thomas Wotton; and some twenty-seven others of his countrymen to the fury of the savages, famine, and all manner of mischiefs, and inconveniences (for they were but forty in all to keep possession of this large country) or starve himself with them for company for want of lodging or but adventuring abroad to make them provision or by his opposition to preserve the action and save all their lives, I leave to the censure of all honest men to consider.

THE FIRST AMERICAN LEGISLATIVE ASSEMBLY

(1619)
by John Twine

This account is taken from the official report of the assembly, of which Twine was clerk.

A report of the manner of proceedings in the General Assembly convened at Jamestown in Virginia, July 30, 1619, consisting of the Governor, the Council of Estate, and two burgesses elected out of each incorporation and plantation, and being dissolved August 4.

First. Sir George Yeardley, Knight Governor and Captain General of Virginia, sent his summons all over the country as well to invite those of the Council of Estate that were absent as also for the election of burgesses.

The most convenient place we could find to sit was the choir of the church where Sir George Yeardley, the Governor, sat in his accustomed place. Those of the Council of Estate sat next to him on both hands, except only the secretary then appointed speaker, who sat right before him; John Twine, clerk of the General Assembly, being placed next the speaker; and Thomas Pierse, the sergeant, standing at the bar to be ready for any service the Assembly should command him. But forasmuch as men's affairs do little prosper where God's service is neglected, all the burgesses took their places in the choir till a prayer was said by Mr. Bucke, the minister, that it would please God to guide and sanctify all our proceedings to His own glory and the good of this plantation. Prayer being ended, to the intent that as we had begun at God Almighty, so we might proceed with awful and due respect towards the lieutenant [i.e., the king], our most gracious and dread sovereign. All the burgesses were entreated to retire themselves into the body of the church, which being done, before they were fully admitted, they were called in order and by name, and so every man (none staggering at it) took the oath of supremacy and then entered the Assembly.

These obstacles removed, the speaker, who a long time had been extremely sickly and therefore not able to pass through long harangues, delivered in brief to the whole assembly the occasions of their meeting. Which done, he read unto them the commission for establishing the Council of Estate and the General Assembly, wherein their duties were described to the life.

Having thus prepared them, he read over unto them the great charter, or commission of privileges, orders and laws, sent by Sir George Yeardley out of England. For the more ease of the committees, he divided it into four books. He read the former two the same forenoon for expeditious sake a second time over, and so they were referred to the perusal of two committees, which did reciprocally consider both and accordingly brought in their opinions. But some men may here ask why we should presume to refer that to the examination of the committees which the council and company in England had already resolved to be perfect and did expect nothing but our assent thereunto? To this we answer that we did it not to the end to correct or control anything therein contained, but only in case we should find ought not perfectly squaring with the state of this colony or any law which did press or bind too hard, that we might by way of humble petition seek to have it redressed, especially because this great charter is to bind us and our heirs forever.

After dinner the Governor and those that were not of the committees sat a second time, while the said committees were employed in the perusals of those two books. And whereas the speaker had propounded four several objects for the Assembly to consider, namely, first, the great charter of orders, laws, and privileges; secondly, which of the instructions given by the Council in England to my lord was Captain Argall or Sir George Yeardley to make into laws; thirdly, what laws might issue out of the private concept of any of the burgesses or any other of the colony; and lastly, what petitions were fit to be sent home for England. It pleased the Governor for expedition sake to have the second object of the four to be examined and prepared by himself and the non-committees. Wherein after having spent some three hours conference, the two committees brought in their opinions concerning the two former books (the second of which begins at these words of the charter: "And forasmuch as our intent is to establish one equal and uniform kind of government over all Virginia," etc.), which the whole Assembly, because it was late, deferred to discuss the next morning.

There remaining no further scruple in the minds of the Assembly touching the said great charter of laws, orders, and privileges, the speaker put the same to the question, and so it had both the general assent and the applause of the whole Assembly, who, as they professed themselves in the first place most submissively thankful to Almighty God, therefore commanded the speaker to return (as now he doth) their due and humble thanks to the treasurer, Council, and company for so many privileges and favors as well in their own names as in the names of the whole colony whom they represented.

This being dispatched, we fell once more debating of such instructions given by the Council in England to several governors as might be converted into laws, the last whereof was the establishment of the price of tobacco, namely, of the best at three penny and the second at eighteen penny per pound.

Here begin the laws drawn out of the instructions given by his Majesty's Counsel of Virginia in England to my lord, Captain Argall, and Sir George Yeardley, knight. By this present General Assembly be it enacted that no injury or oppression be wrought by the English against the Indians whereby the present peace might be disturbed and ancient quarrels might be revived. And further be it ordained that the Chicohomini are not to be excepted out of this law until either that such order come out of England or that they do provoke us by some new injury.

Against idleness, gaming, drunkenness, and excess in apparel the Assembly hath enacted as followeth:

First, in detestation of idleness be it enacted that if any men be found to live as an idler or renegade, though a freedman, it shall be lawful for that incorporation or plantation to which he belongs to appoint him a master to serve for wages till he shows apparent signs of amendment.

Against gaming at dice and cards be it ordained by this present Assembly that the winner or winners shall lose all his or their winnings and both winners and losers shall forfeit ten shillings a man, one ten shillings whereof to go to the discoverer, and the rest to charitable and pious uses in the incorporation where the fault is committed.

Against drunkenness be it also decreed that if any private person be found culpable thereof, for the first time he is to be reproved privately by the minister, the second time publicly, the third time to lie in bolts twelve hours in the house of the provost marshal and to pay his fee; and if he still continue in that vice, to undergo such severe punishment as the Governor and Council of Estate shall think fit to be inflicted on him. But if any officer offend in this crime, the first time he shall receive a reproof from the

Governor, the second time he shall openly be reproved in the church by the minister, and the third time he shall first be committed and then degraded, provided it be understood that the Governor hath always power to restore him when he shall in his discretion think fit.

Against excess in apparel, let every man be taxed, if he be unmarried according to his own apparel, if he be married according to his own and his wife's, or either of their apparel.

Be it enacted by this present Assembly that for laying a surer foundation of the conversion of the Indians to Christian religion, each town, city, borrough, and particular plantation are to obtain unto themselves by just means a certain number of the natives' children to be educated by them in the true religion and civil course of life—of which children the most promising boys in wit and graces of nature are to be brought up by them that from thence they may be sent to that work of conversion.

As touching the business of planting corn, this present Assembly doth ordain that year by year all and every householder and householders have in store for every servant he or they shall keep and also for his or their own persons, whether they have any servants or no, one spare barrel of corn to be delivered out yearly, either upon sale or exchange as need shall require. For the neglect of which duty he shall be subject to the censure of the Governor and Council of Estate. Provided always that the first year of every new man this law shall not be of force.

All ministers shall duly read divine service and exercise their ministerial function according to the ecclesiastical laws and orders of the Church of England and every Sunday in the afternoon shall catechize such as are not yet ripe to come to the communion. And whosoever shall be found negligent or faulty in this kind shall be subject to the censure of the Governor and Council.

All persons whatsoever upon the Sabbath day shall frequent divine service and sermons both forenoon and afternoon, and all such as bear arms shall bring their pieces, swords, powder, and shot. And every one that shall transgress this law shall forfeit three shillings a time to the dues of the church, all lawful and necessary impediments excepted. But if a servant in this case shall willfully neglect his master's command, he shall suffer bodily punishment.

No maid or woman servant, either now resident in the colony or hereafter to come, shall contract herself in marriage without either the consent of her parents or of her master or mistress or of the magistrate and minister of the place both together. And whatsoever minister shall marry or con-, tract any such persons without some of the foresaid consents shall be subject to the severe censure of the Governor and Council of Estate.

In sum, Sir George Yeardley, the Governor suspended the said General Assembly till the first of March, 1619, and presently adjourned the Assembly.

THE VOYAGE OF THE MAYFLOWER
(1620)
by Governor William Bradford

William Bradford had already been a leading member of a little dissenting congregation in England when in 1608 it fled from England to Holland and in 1620 settled at Plymouth, Massachusetts. A year after the arrival at Plymouth, Bradford was elected Governor of the Colony and, with the exception of two short intervals, held this office until his death nearly forty years afterward.

September 6. These troubles being blown over, and now all being compact together in one ship, they put to sea again with a prosperous wind, which continued several days together, which was some encouragement unto them; yet according to the usual manner many were afflicted with seasickness.

After they had enjoyed fair winds and weather for a season, they were encountered many times with cross winds and met with many fierce storms, with which the ship was shrewdly shaken, and her upper works made very leaky. One of the main beams in the mid ships was bowed and cracked which put them in some fear that the ship could not be able to perform the voyage. So some of the chief of the company, perceiving by their mutterings that the mariners feared the sufficiency of the ship, they entered into serious consultation with the master and other officers of the ship, to consider in time of the danger and whether to return or to cast themselves into a desperate and inevitable peril. And truly there was great distraction and difference of opinion amongst the mariners themselves. Fain would they do what could be done for their wage sake, (being now half the seas over) and on the other hand they were loathe to hazard their lives too desperately. But in examining of all opinions, the master and others affirmed that they knew the ship to be strong and firm under water; and for the buckling of the main beam, there was a great iron screw that the passengers had brought out of Holland, which would raise the beam into his place. This being done, the carpenter and master affirmed that with a post put under it, set firm in the lower deck, and otherways bound, he would make it sufficient.

And as for the decks and upper works, they would calk them as well as they could, and though with the working of the ship they would not long keep staunch, yet there would otherwise be no great danger, if they did not overpress her with sails. So they committed themselves to the will of God and resolved to procede. In some of these storms the winds were so fierce and the seas so high that they could not bear a knot of sail, but were forced to hull for several days together. And in one of them, as they thus lay at hull in a mighty storm, a lusty young man (called John Howland) coming upon some occasion above the gratings, was, with a seal of the ship thrown into the sea. But it pleased God that he caught hold of the topsail halliards, which hung overboard and ran out at length. Yet he held his hold (though he was several fathoms under water) till he was hauled up by the same rope to the brim of the water, and then with a boat hook and other means got into the ship again, and his life saved. Though he was something ill with it, yet he lived many years after and became a profitable member both in church and commonwealth. In all this seige there died but one of the passengers, which was William Butten, a youth, servant to Samuel Fuller, when they drew near the coast.

But to omit other things (that I may be brief), after long beating at sea they fell with that land which is called Cape Cod, the which being made and certainly known to be it, they were not a little joyful. After some deliberation amongst themselves and with the master of the ship, they tacked about and resolved to stand for the southward (the wind and weather being fair) to find some place about Hudson's River for their habitation. But after they had sailed that course about half a day, they fell amongst dangerous shoals and roaring breakers, and they were so far entangled there that they conceived themselves in great danger; and the wind shrinking upon them withal, they resolved to bear up again for the Cape and thought themselves happy to get out of those dangers before night overtook them, as by God's providence they did. The next day they got into the Cape harbor where they rode in safety. A word or two by the way of this cape. It was thus first named by Captain Gosnoll and his company, A.D. 1602, and after by Captain Smith was called Cape James, but it retains the former name amongst seamen. Also that point which first showed those dangerous shoals unto them, they called Point Care and Tucker's Terror; but the French and Dutch to this day call it Malabarr, by reason of those perilous shoals and the losses they have suffered there.

Being thus arrived in a good harbor and brought safe to land, they fell upon their knees and blessed the God of heaven Who had brought them over the vast and furious ocean and delivered them from all the perils and miseries thereof, again to set their feet on the firm and stable earth, their proper element. And no marvel if they were thus joyful, seeing wise Seneca was so affected when he had sailed only a few miles on the coast of his own Italy; as he affirmed, that he had rather remain twenty years on his way by land, than pass by sea to any place in a short time, so tedious and dreadful was the same to him.

But here I cannot but stay and make a pause and stand half amazed at this poor people's present conditions; and so I think will the reader too when he well considers the same. Having thus passed the vast ocean and a sea of troubles before in their preparation (as may be remembered by that which went before), they had now no friends to welcome them, nor inns to entertain or refresh their weatherbeaten bodies, no houses or much less towns to repair to, to seek for aid. It is recorded in Scripture as a mercy to the apostle and his shipwrecked company, that the barbarians showed them no small kindness in refreshing them, but these savage barbarians, when they met with them (as after will appear) were readier to fill their sides full of arrows than otherwise. And it was winter, and they that know the winters of that country know them to be sharp and violent and subject to cruel and fierce storms, dangerous to travel to known places, much more to search an unknown coast. Besides, what could they see but a hideous and desolate wilderness, full of wild beasts and wild men? And what multitudes there might be of them they knew not. Neither could they, as it were, go up to the top of Pisgah, to view from this wilderness a more goodly country to feed their hopes; for which way soever they turned their eyes (save upward to the heavens) they could have little solace or content in respect of any outward objects.

For summer being done, all things around them have weatherbeaten faces; and the whole country full of woods and thickets, represented a wild and savage view. If they looked behind them, there was the mighty ocean which they had passed and was now as a main bar and gulf to separate them from all the civil parts of the world. If it be said they had a ship to succor them, it is true; but what heard they daily from the master and company? But that with speed they should look out a place with their shallop, where they would be at some near distance; for the season was such as he would not stir from thence till a safe harbor was discovered by them where they would be, and he might go without danger; and that victuals consumed apace, but he must and would keep sufficient for themselves and their return. Yea, it was muttered by some, that if they got not a place in time, they would turn them and their goods ashore and leave them.

Let it also be considered what weak hopes of supply and succor they left behind them that might bear up their minds in this sad condition and trials they were under, and they could not but be very small. It is true, indeed, the affections and love of their brethren at Leyden was cordial and entire towards them, but they had little power to help them, or themselves; and how the case stood between them and the merchants at their coming away, has already been declared. What could now sustain them but the spirit of God and His grace?

Being thus arrived at Cape Cod November 11, and necessity calling them to look out a place for habitation (as well as the master and mariners' importunity), they having brought a large shallop with them out of England, stowed in quarters in the ship, they now got her out and set their carpenters to work to trim her up. But being much bruised and shattered in the ship with foul weather, they saw she would be long in mending. Whereupon a few of them decided to go by land and discover those nearest places whilst the shallop was in mending; as they went into that harbor there seemed to be an opening some two or three leagues off, which the master judged to be a river. It was conceived there might be some danger in the attempt, yet seeing them resolute, they were permitted to go, being sixteen of them well armed, under the conduct of Captain Standish, having such instructions given them as was thought meet.

At length they found water and refreshed themselves, being the first New England water they had drunk of and was now in their great thirst as pleasant unto them as wine or beer had been in foretimes. Afterwards they directed their course to come to the other shore, for they knew it was a neck of land they were to cross over, and so at length got to the seaside and marched to this supposed river, and by the way found a pond of clear, fresh water, and shortly after, a good quantity of clear ground where the Indians had formerly set corn and some of their graves. And proceeding farther they saw new stubble where corn had been set the same year, also they found where lately a house had been, where some planks and a great kettle was remaining and heaps of sand newly paddled with their hands, which they, digging up, found in them several fair Indian baskets filled with corn, and some in ears, fair and good, of diverse colors, which seemed to them a very goodly sight (having never seen such before).

The month of November being spent in these affairs, and much foul weather falling in, December 6 they sent out their shallop again with ten of their principal men and some seamen, upon further discovery, intending to circulate that deep bay of Cape Cod. The weather was very cold, and it froze so hard that the spray of the sea lighting on their coats made them seem as if they had been glazed. Yet early that night they got down into the bottom of the bay, and as they drew near the shore they saw some ten or twelve Indians very busy about something. They landed about a league or two from them. Being landed, it grew late, and they made themselves a barricade with logs and bows as well as they could in the time and set out their sentinel and betook them to rest, and saw the smoke of fire the savages made that night.

When morning was come they divided their company, some to coast along the shore in the boat, and the rest to march through the woods to see the land, if any fit place might be for their dwelling. They came also to the place where they saw the Indians the night before and found they had been cutting up a great fish like a grampus, being some two inches thick of fat like a hog, some pieces whereof they had left by the way. The shallop found two more of these fishes dead on the sands, a usual thing after storms in that place, by reason of the great flats of sand that lie off.

So they ranged up and down all that day, but found no people, nor any place they liked. When the sun grew low, they hasted out of the woods to meet with their shallop, to whom they made signs to come to them into a creek nearby, which they did at high water. They were very glad, for they had not seen each other all day, since the previous morning.

So they made them a barricade (as usually they did every night) with logs, stakes, and thick pine boughs, the height of a man, leaving it open to leeward, partly to shelter them from the cold and wind (making their fire in the middle and lying round about it) and partly to defend them from any sudden assaults of the savages, if they should surround them. So being very weary, they betook them to rest. But about midnight they heard a hideous and great cry, and their sentinel called, "Arm, arm!" So they bestirred them and stood to their arms and shot off a couple of muskets, and then the noise ceased. They concluded it was a company of wolves or such like beasts, for one of the seamen told them he had often heard such a noise in Newfoundland. So they rested till about five o'clock in the morning. The tide and their purpose to go from thence made them be stirring early. So after prayer they prepared for breakfast, and it being day dawning, it was thought best to be carrying things down to the boat. But some said it was not best to carry the arms down; others said they would be the readier, for they had bundled them up in their coats from the dew.

But some three or four would not carry theirs till they went themselves, yet as it fell out, the water being not high enough, they laid them down on the bank side and came up to breakfast. But presently, all of the sudden, they heard a great and strange cry, which they knew to be the same voices they heard in the night, though they varied their notes, and one of their company being abroad came running in and cried, "Men, Indians, Indians!" Withal their arrows came flying amongst them. The men ran with all speed to recover their arms, as by the good providence of God they did. In the meantime, of those that were there ready, two muskets were discharged at them, and two more stood ready in the entrance of their rendezvous, but were commanded not to shoot till they could take full aim at them. The other two charged again with all speed, for there were only four that had arms there, and defended the barricade which was first assaulted. The cry of the Indians was dreadful, especially when they saw their men run out of the rendezvous towards the shallop to recover their arms, the Indians wheeling about upon them. But some came running out with cutlasses in their hands. They soon got their arms and let fly among them and quickly stopped their violence.

Yet there was a lusty man and no less valiant stood behind a tree within half a musket shot and let his arrows fly at them. He withstood three shots of a musket, till one taking full aim at him and made the bark or splinters of the tree fly about his ears, after which he gave an extraordinary shriek, and away they went all of them. They left some to keep the shallop and followed them about a quarter of a mile and shouted once or twice and shot off two or three pieces and so returned. This they did that they might show them that they were not afraid of them or in any way discouraged. Thus it pleased God to vanquish their enemies and give them deliverance, and by His special providence so to dispose that not any one of them were either hurt or hit, though their arrows came close by them and on every side them, and several of their coats which hung up in the barricade were shot through and through. Afterwards they gave God solemn thanks and praise for their deliverance and gathered up a bundle of their arrows and sent them into England afterward by the master of the ship and called that place The First Encounter.

From hence they departed and coasted all along but discerned no place likely for harbor, and therefore hasted to a place that their pilot (one Mr. Coppin who had been in the country before) did assure them was a good harbor, which he had been in, and they might reach it before night, of which they were glad, for it began to be foul weather. After some hours sailing, it began to snow and rain; and about the middle of the afternoon, the wind increased and the sea became very rough, and they broke their rudder. It was as much as two men could do to steer her with a couple of oars. But their pilot bade them be of good cheer, for he saw the harbor. The storm increasing and night drawing on, they bore what sail they could to get in while they could see. But here they broke their mast in three pieces, and their sail fell overboard into a very high sea, so as they had like to have been cast away. By God's mercy they recovered themselves, and having the flood with them, struck into the harbor. But when they came into the harbor, the pilot was deceived in the place and said the Lord be merciful unto them, for his eyes never saw that place before, and he and the master mate would have run her ashore in a cove full of breakers before the wind. But a lusty seaman which steered, bade those which rowed, if they were men, about with her, or else they were all cast away; the which they did with speed. So he bid them be of good cheer and row lustily, for there was a fair sound before them, and he doubted not but they should find one place or other where they might ride in safety.

And though it was very dark and rained sore, yet in the end they got under the lee of a small island and remained there all that night safely. But they knew not this to be an island till morning, but were divided in their minds; some stayed aboard the boat for fear they might be among the Indians; others were so weak and cold they could not endure, but got ashore, and with much ado got fire (all things being so wet); and the rest were glad to come to them, for after midnight the wind shifted to the northwest and it froze hard. But though this had been a day and night of much trouble and danger unto them, yet God gave them a morning of comfort and refreshing (as usually He doth to His children), for the next day was a fair, sunshining day, and they found themselves to be on an island secure from the Indians, where they might dry their stuff, fix their pieces, and rest themselves, and gave God thanks for His mercies, in their manifold deliverances. And this being the last day of the week, they prepared there to keep the Sabbath. On Monday they sounded the harbor and found it fit for shipping and marched into the land and found several cornfields and little running brooks, a place (as they supposed) fit for situation. At least it was the best they could find, and the season and their present necessity made them glad to accept it. So they returned to their ship again with this news to the rest of their people, which greatly comforted their hearts.

On December 15 they weighed anchor to go to the place they had discovered and came within two leagues of it but were fain to bear up again. The next day the wind came fair, and they arrived safe in this harbor. Afterwards they took better view of the place and resolved where to pitch their dwelling. December 25 they began to erect the first house for common use to receive them and their goods.

I shall go back a little and begin with an agreement made by them before they came ashore, being the first foundation of their government in this place, occasioned partly by the discontented and mutinous speeches that some of the strangers amongst them had let fall from them in the ship—that when they came ashore they would use their own liberties, for none had power to command them, the patent they had being for Virginia and not for New England, which belonged to another government, with which the Virginia Company had nothing to do. This was also partly done so that such an act done by them (this their condition considered) might be as firm as any patent and in some respects more sure. The form was as follows:

"In the name of God, Amen. We whose names are underwritten, the loyal subjects of our dread sovereign lord, King James, by the grace of God, of Great Britain, France, and Ireland king, defender of the faith, etc., having undertaken, for the glory of God and advancement of the Christian faith, and honor of our king and country, a voyage to plant the first colony in the northern parts of Virginia, do by these present solemnly and mutually in the presence of God, and one of another, covenant and combine ourselves together into a civil political body, for our better ordering and preservation and furtherance of the ends aforesaid; and by virtue hereof to enact, constitute, and frame such just and equal laws, ordinances, acts, constitutions, and offices, from time to time, as shall be thought most meet and convenient for the general good of the colony, unto which we promise all due submission and obedience. In witness whereof we have hereunder subscribed our names at Cape Cod November 11, in the year of England, France, and Ireland the eighteenth, and of Scotland the fifty-fourth. A.D. 1620."

THE BEGINNINGS OF THE MASSACHUSETTS BAY COLONY
(1627-1631)
by Governor Thomas Dudley

Dudley came over to America with Winthrop and was at one time made governor of the Massachusetts Bay Colony. The following is an excerpt from Dudley's letter to the Countess of London

Touching the plantation which we here have begun, it happened that about the year 1627 some friends being together in Lincolnshire, they began some discourse about New England and the planting of the Gospel there. After some deliberation, we imparted our reasons by letters and messages to some in London and the west country where it was likewise deliberately thought upon. At length, with often negotiation, we procured in 1628 a patent from his Majesty for our planting between the Massachusetts Bay and Charles River on the south, and the River of Merimack on the north and three miles on either side of those rivers' bays, as also for the government of those who did or should inhabit within that compass. The same year we sent Mr. John Endicott and some with him to begin a plantation and to strengthen such as he should find there.

The next year 1629, we sent diverse ships over with about three hundred people, and some cows, goats, and horses many of which arrived safely. These by their too large commendations of the country and the commodities thereof, invited us so strongly to go on that Mr. Winthrop of Soffolk (who was well-known in his own country and well approved here for his piety, liberality, wisdom, and gravity) coming in to us, we came to such resolution that in April 1630, we set sail from Old England with four good ships. And in May following, eight more followed, two having gone before in February and March, and two more following in June and August, besides another set out by a private merchant. These seventeen ships arrived all safe in New England, for the increase of the plantation here this year 1630.

Our four ships which set out in April arrived here in June and July, where we found the colony in a sad and unexpected condition, above eighty of them being dead the winter before and many of those alive were weak and sick. All the corn and bread among them was hardly sufficient to feed them a fortnight. When the remainder of one hundred and eighty servants we had sent over two years before came to us for victuals to sustain them, we found ourselves wholly unable to feed them by reason that the provisions shipped for them were taken out of the ship they were put in, and they who were trusted to ship them in another failed us and left them behind. Whereupon necessity forced us (to our extreme loss) to give them all liberty who had cost us about sixteen or twenty sterling pounds a person furnishing and sending over.

But bearing these things as we might, we began to look at the place of our settling, for Salem where we landed pleased us not. And for that purpose some were sent to the bay to search up the rivers for a convenient place. Upon their return they reported to have found a good place upon Mistick; but some other of us disliked their judgment, and we found a place that we liked better three leagues up Charles River. And thereupon we unshipped our goods into other vessels and with much cost and labor brought them in July to Charles Towne [Charleston]. But there receiving notice by some of the late arrived ships from London and Amsterdam of some French preparations against us (many of our people brought with us were sick of fevers and the scurvy, and we were thereby unable to carry up our ordinance and baggage so far), we were forced to change counsel and for our present shelter to plant dispersedly, some at Charles Towne which standeth on the north side of the mouth of Charles River; some on the south side thereof, which place we named Boston (as we intended to have done the place we first resloved on); some of us upon Mistick, which we named Meadford; some of us westward on Charles River, four miles from Charles Towne, which place we named Watertown; others of us two miles from Boston in a place we named Rocksbury; others upon the river of Sawgus between Salem and Charles Towne. And the western men settled four miles south from Boston at a place we named Dorchester.

This dispersion troubled some of us, but we could not help it, lacking ability to remove to any place fit to build a town upon and the time too short to deliberate any longer lest the winter should surprise us before we had builded our houses.

Of the people who came over with us from the time of their setting sail from England in April, 1630 until December following there died by estimation about two hundred at the least. So low hath the Lord brought us! Well, yet they who survived were not discouraged but bearing God's corrections with humility and trusting in His mercies and considering how after a greater ebb He had raised up our neighbors at Plymouth, we began again in December to consult about a fit place to build a town upon, leaving all thoughts of a fort, because upon any invasion we were necessarily to lose our horses when we should retire thereinto. So after diverse meetings at Boston, Rocksbury, and Watertown, on the twenty-eighth of December we grew to this resolution to bind all the assistants, Mr. Endicott and Mr.

Sharpe excepted (whose purpose it was to return by the next ships into England) to build houses at a place a mile east from Watertown near Charles River the next spring and to winter there the next year, that so by our examples and by removing the ordinance and munition thither, all who were able, might be drawn thither, and such as shall come to us hereafter to their advantage be compelled so to do. So if God would, a fortified town might there grow up, the place fitting reasonably well thereto.

But now having some leisure to discourse of the motives for other men coming to this place or their abstaining from it, after my brief manner I say this—that if any come hither to plant for worldy ends that can live well at home, he commits an error of which he will soon repent. But if for spiritual ends and that no particular obstacle hinder his removal, he may find here what may well content him: materials to build, fuel to burn, ground to plant, seas and rivers to fish in, a pure air to breathe, good water to drink till wine or beer can be made, which together with the cows, hogs and goats brought hither already may suffice for food. As for fowl and venison, they are dainties here as well as in England. For clothes and bedding they must bring them with them till time and industry produce them here. In a word, we yet enjoy little to be envied but endure much to be pitied in the sickness and mortality of our people.

KING PHILIP'S WAR
(1676)
by William Hubbard

William Hubbard was graduated from Harvard in 1642 in the first class sent out by the college. In 1666 he was settled as minister at Ipswich, Massachusetts, and died in 1704. His qualities as a minister, his learning, and his ability as a writer were praised by John Eliot, the apostle to the Indians. Some five hundred colonists and one thousand Indians died in this year-long war. The war was precipitated by the settlers' continued expansion of the frontier. King Philip was an Indian chieftain.

The occasion of Philip's so suddenly taking up arms the last year was this: There was one John Sausaman, a very cunning and plausible Indian, well skilled in the English language and bred up in the profession of Christian religion, employed as a schoolmaster at Natick, the Indian town, who upon some misdemeanor fled from his place to Philip, by whom he was entertained in the room and office of secretary and his chief counselor, whom he trusted with all his affairs and secret counsels. But afterwards, whether upon the sting of his own conscience or by the frequent solicitations of Mr. Eliot, who had known him from a child and instructed him in the principles of our religion and who was often laying before him the heinous sin of his apostasy and returning to his old vomit, he was at last prevailed with to forsake Philip and return to the Christian Indians at Natick where he was baptized, manifested public repentance for all his former offences, made a serious profession of the Christian religion, and did apply himself to preach to the Indians, wherein he was better gifted than any other of the Indian nation, since he was observed to conform more to the English manners than any other Indian.

Yet having occasion to go up with some others of his countrymen to Namasket, whether for the advantage of fishing or some such occasion, it matters not; being there not far from Philip's country, he had occasion to be much in the company of Philip's Indians and of Philip himself, by which means he discerned by several circumstances that the Indians were plotting anew against us; out of faithfulness to the English the said Sausaman informed the Governor of this, adding also that if it were known that he had revealed it, he knew they would presently kill him. There appearing so many concurrent testimonies from others, making it the more probable that there was certain truth in the information, some inquiry was made into the business by examining Philip himself and several of his Indians, who although they could do nothing, yet could not free themselves from just suspicion. Philip therefore soon after contrived the said Sausaman's death, which was strangely discovered. It was, however, cunningly effected, for they that murdered him met him upon the ice on a great pond, and presently after they had knocked him down, put him under the ice, yet leaving his gun and his hat upon the ice that it might be thought he fell in accidently through the ice and was drowned. But being missed by his friends, who finding his hat and his gun, they were thereby led to the place where his body was found under the ice. When they took it up to bury him, some of his friends, especially one David, observed some bruises about his head, which made them suspect he was first knocked down before he was put into the water. However, they buried him near about the place where he was found, without making any further inquiry at present. Nevertheless David, his friend, reported these things to some English at Taunton (a town not far from Namasket), occasioned the Governor to inquire further into the business, wisely considering that, as Sausaman had told him, if it were known that he had revealed any of their plots, they would murder him for his pains.

Wherefore by special warrant the body of Sausaman being digged again out of his grave, it was very apparent that he had been killed and not drowned. And by a strange providence an Indian was found that by accident was standing unseen upon a hill and had seen them murder the said Sausaman, but durst never reveal it for fear of losing his own life likewise, until he was called to court at Plymouth or before the Governor, where he plainly confessed immediately before his death, that his father (one of the counselors and special friends of Philip) was one of the two that murdered Sausaman, himself only looking on.

This was done at Plymouth Court, held in June, 1674. Philip, apprehending the danger his own head was in next, never used any further means to clear himself from what was like to be laid to his charge, either about his plotting against the English nor yet about Sausaman's death, but kept his men continually about him in arms and gathered what strangers he could to join with him, marched up and down constantly in arms, both all the while the courts sat as well as afterwards. The English of Plymouth hearing of all this, yet took no further notice than only to order a militia watch in all the adjacent towns, hoping that Philip, finding himself not likely to be arraigned by order of the said court, the present cloud might blow over, as some others of the like nature had done before; but in conclusion, the matter proved otherwise. For Philip, finding his strength daily increasing by the flocking of neighbor Indians unto him and sending over their wives children to the Narragansets for security (as they do when they intend war with any of their enemies), immediately they began to alarm the English at Swanzy (the next town to Philip's country), as it were daring the English to begin. At last their insolencies grew to such a height that they began not only to use threatening words to the English, but also to kill their cattle and rifle their houses; whereat an Englishman was so provoked that he let fly a gun at an Indian but did only wound, not kill him. Whereupon the Indians immediately began to kill all the English they could, so as on June 24, 1675, was the alarm of war first sounded in Plymouth Colony, when eight or nine of the English were slain in and about Swanzy.

About this time several parties of English within Plymouth jurisdiction were willing to have a hand in so good a matter as catching of Philip would be, who, perceiving that he was now going down the wind, were willing to hasten his fall. Amongst others, a small party, on July 31, 1676, went out of Bridgewater upon discovery and by providence were directed to fall upon a company of Indians where Philip was. They came up with them and killed some of his special friends; Philip himself was next to his uncle, that was shot down, and had the soldier had his choice which to shoot at, known which had been the right bird, he might as well have taken him as his uncle, but 'tis said that he had newly cut off his hair, that he might not be known. The party that did this exploit were few in number, and therefore not being able to keep altogether close in the rear, that cunning fox escaped away through the bushes undiscerned in the rear of the English.

Within two days after, Captain Church, the terror of the Indians in

Plymouth Colony, marching in pursuit of Philip, with but thirty English-men and twenty reconciled Indians, took twenty-three of the enemy, and the next day following them by their tracks, fell upon their headquarters and killed and took about a hundred and thirty of them but with the loss of one Englishman. In this engagement God did appear in a more than ordinary manner to fight for the English, for the Indians, by their number and other advantages of the place, were so conveniently provided that they might have made the first shot at the English and done them much dam-age; but one of their own countrymen in Captain Church's company spying them, called aloud unto them in their own language, telling them that if they shot a gun, they were all dead men. With which they were so amazed that they dared not once offer to fire at the English, which made the victory the more remarkable. Philip made a very narrow escape at that time, being forced to leave his treasures, his beloved wife, and only son to the mercy of the English; skin for skin, all that a man hath will he give for his life.

Philip, like a savage and wild beast, having been hunted by the English forces through the woods above a hundred miles backward and forward, at last was driven to his own den upon Mount Hope, where retiring himself with a few of his best friends into a swamp, which proved but a prison to keep him safe till the messengers of death came by divine permission to execute vengeance upon him, which was thus accomplished.

Such had been his inveterate malice and wickedness against the English that, despairing of mercy from them, he could not bear that anything should be suggested to him about a peace, insomuch as he caused one of his confederates to be killed for propounding an expedient of peace. This so provoked some of his company, not altogether so desperate as himself, that one of them (being near of kin that was killed) fled to Rhode Island (where that active champion Captain Church was newly retired, to recruit his men for a little time, being much tired with hard marches all that week), informing them that Philip was fled to a swamp in Mount Hope whither he would undertake to lead them that would pursue him. This was welcome news and the best cordial for such martial spirits. Whereupon he immediately with a small company of men, part English and part Indians, began another march, which proved fatal to Philip and brought an end to that controversy betwixt the English and him. For coming very early to the side of the swamp, his soldiers began presently to surround it, and whether the devil appeared to him in a dream that night, as he did unto Saul, forboding his tragic end, it matters not. As he intended to make his escape out of the swamp, he was shot through the heart by an Indian of his own nation, as is said, that had all this while kept himself in a neutrality until this time, but now had the casting vote in his power, by which he determined the quarrel that had held so long in suspense.

LORD BALTIMORE IN MARYLAND

(1633)

by Cecil Calvert

This account was compiled from letters written to friends in England by some of the original settlers of Maryland about a year after their arrival. George Calvert, first Lord Baltimore and founder of Maryland, had sent a group of colonists to Newfoundland in 1621, but the venture being unsuccessful, he secured a new grant north of the Potomac, to which at the request of Charles I he gave the name of Maryland, in honor of Queen Henrietta Maria. Calvert, after a visit to Virginia, returned to England and died there before his charter was actually issued. In consequence the grant was made out to Calvert's son Cecil. Cecil Calvert at once organized a company of more than two hundred men, who effected a permanent settlement at St. Mary's, which for sixty years was the capital of the colony of Maryland, Annapolis being afterward chosen. Baltimore was not founded until 1729.

The account given here was published in London in 1634 and is the first extant description of the province. Cecil Calvert prepared it from letters written by his brothers, Leonard and George.

On Friday, November 22, 1633, a small gale of wind coming gently from the northwest weighed from the Cowes in the Isle of Wight about ten in the morning; and having stayed by the way twenty days at the Barbados and fourteen days at St. Christopher's, upon some necessary occasions, we arrived at Point Comfort in Virginia on February 24, 1634; the Lord be praised for it. At this time one Captain Claybourne was come from parts where we intended to plant to Virginia, and from him we understood that all the natives of these parts were in preparation of defense by reason of a rumor somebody had raised amongst them of six ships that were come with a power of Spaniards whose meaning was to drive all the inhabitants out of the country.

On March 3 we came into Chesapeake Bay and made sail to the north of Potomac River, the bay running between two sweet lands in the channel of seven, eight, and nine fathoms deep, ten leagues broad, and full of fish at the time of the year. It is one of the most delightful waters I ever saw, except the Potomac, which we named St. Gregory's. And now being in our own country, we began to give names to places and called the southern point Cape Saint Gregory and the northern point Saint Michael's.

The river, of all I know, is the greatest and sweetest, much broader than the Thames, so pleasant that I for my part was never satisfied in beholding it. There are few marshes or swamps, but the greatest part solid good earth with great curiosity of woods which are not choked up with undershrubs, but set commonly one from the other in such distance as a coach and four horses may easily travel through them.

At our first trip upon the river, we found (as it was foretold us) all the country in arms. The king of the Paschattowayes had drawn together fifteen hundred bowmen, which we ourselves saw. Our vessel was the greatest that ever those Indians saw; the scouts reported we came in a canoe as big as an island and had as many men as there be trees in the woods.

We went to a place where a large tree was made into a cross; taking it on our shoulders, we carried it to the place appointed for it, the Governor and commissioners putting their hands first unto it, then the rest of the chiefest adventurers. At the place prepared we all kneeled down and said certain prayers, taking possession of the country for our Saviour and for our sovereign lord the King of England.

The Governor being returned, we came some nine leagues lower on the north side of that land to a river as big as the Thames which we called Saint Gregory's River. It runs up to the north about twenty miles before it comes to the fresh. This river makes two excellent bays for three hundred sail of ships of one thousand tons to harbor in with great safety. The one bay we named Saint George's, the other (and more inward) Saint Marie's. The king of Wicomico dwells on the left hand or side thereof, and we took up our seat on the right, one mile within the land. It is as brave a piece of ground to set down on as most is in the country, and I suppose as good as (if not much better than) the primest parcel of English ground.

Our town we call Saint Mary's and to avoid all just occasion of offense and color of wrong, we bought for the king—paying with hatchets, axes, and clothes—a quantity of some thirty miles of land, which we call Augusta Carolina. And what made them the more willing to sell it were the wares they had with the Susquehannas, a mighty bordering nation who came often into their country to waste and destroy and forced many of them to leave their country and pass over Potomac to free themselves from peril before we came. God no doubt disposing all this for them, who were to bring His law and light among the infidels. Yet, seeing we came so well prepared with arms, their fear was much less, and they could be content to dwell by us. Yet do they daily relinquish their houses, lands, and cornfields and leave them to us. Is not this a piece of wonder that a nation which a few days before was in arms with the rest against us should yield themselves now unto us like lambs and give us their houses and land, for a trifle? *Digitus Dei est hic,*[1] and surely some good is intended by God to His nation. Some few families of Indians are permitted to stay by us till next year, and then the land is free.

And now to return to the place itself chosen for our plantation. We have been upon it but one month and therefore can make no large relation

---

[1] "The finger of God is here."

of it. Yet thus much I can say of it already. For our own safety we have built a good strong fort or *palizado* and have mounted upon it one good piece of ordinance and four murderers and have seven more pieces of ordinance ready to mount forthwith. For our provision here is some store of peas and beans and wheat left on the ground by the Indians who had satisfaction for it.

We have planted since we came as much maize (or Indian wheat) as will suffice (if God prosper it) much more company than we have. It is up about knee high above ground already, and we expect return of one thousand for one, as we have reason for our hope from the experience of the yield in other parts of this country, as is very credibly related to us.

We have also English peas and French beans, cotton, oranges, lemons, apples, potatoes, and sugarcanes of our own planting, besides other garden crops coming up very well.

But such is the quantity of vines and grapes now already upon them (though young) that I dare say if we had vessels and skill we might make many a ton of wine, even from about our plantation, and such wine, as those of Virginia say (for yet we can say nothing) as is as good as the wine of Spain. I fear they exaggerate, but surely it is very good. For the climate of this country is near the same with Seville and Cordova, lying between thirty-eight and forty degrees north latitude.

Of hogs, we have already got from Achomack (a plantation in Virginia) to the number of one hundred and more and some thirty cows, and more we expect daily with goats and hens. Our horses and sheep we must get out of England or some other place by the way, for we can find none in Virginia.

THE FOUNDING OF PENNSYLVANIA
A. An Account of the Colony
(1684)
by William Penn

Penn had already been part proprietor of West Jersey when in 1681 he received the grant of Pennsylvania as compensation for a claim of his father's estate against the English government. He came out in person to America in 1682, made his famous treaty with the Indians, and founded Philadelphia. He returned to England in 1684 and again visited Pennsylvania in 1699–1701.

The first planters in these parts were the Dutch and soon after them the Swedes and Finns. The Dutch applied themselves to traffic, the Swedes and Finns to husbandry. There were some disputes between them for some years; the Dutch looking upon the Swedes as intruders upon their purchase and possession, which was finally ended in the surrender made by John Rizeing, the Swedish governor, to Peter Stuyvesant, governor for the States of Holland, A.D. 1655.

The Dutch inhabit mostly those parts of the province that lie upon or near the bay, and the Swedes the freshes of the river Delaware. There is no need of giving any description of them, who are better known there than here; but they are a plain, strong, industrious people, yet have made no great progress in culture or propagation of fruit-trees, as if they desired rather to have enough than plenty or traffic. But I presume the Indians made them the more careless by furnishing them with the means of profit, to wit, skins and furs for rum and such strong liquors. They kindly received me as well as the English, who were few before the people concerned with me came among them. I must needs commend their respect to authority and kind behavior to the English. They do not degenerate from the old friendship between both kingdoms. As they are people proper and strong of body, so they have fine children, and almost every house full. It is rare to find one of them without three or four boys and as many girls; some have six, seven, and eight sons. And I must do them that right; I see few young men more sober and laborious.

The Dutch have a meeting place for religious worship at Newcastle, and the Swedes three: one at Christina, one at Tenecum, and one at Wicoco, within half a mile of this town.

There rests that I speak of the condition we are in and what settlement we have made, in which I will be as short as I can. The country lies bounded on the east by the river and bay of Delaware and Eastern Sea. It has the advantage of many creeks, or rivers, that run into the main river or bay, some navigable for great ships, some for small craft. Those of most eminency are Christian, Brandywine, Skilpot, and Sculkil, any one of which has room to lay up the royal navy of England, there being from four to eight fathoms of water.

The lesser creeks or rivers, yet convenient for sloops and ketches of good burden, are Lewis, Mespillion, Cedar, Dover, Cranbrook, Feversham, and George's below; and Chichester, Chester, Toacawny, Pammapecka, Portquessin, Meshimenck, and Pennberry in the freshes. There are many lesser that admit boats and shallops. Our people are mostly settled upon the upper rivers, which are pleasant and sweet and generally bounded with good land.

The planted part of the province and territories is cast into six counties: Philadelphia, Buckingham, Chester, Newcastle, Kent, and Sussex, containing about four thousand souls. Two general assemblies have been held and with such concord and dispatch that they sat but three weeks, and at least seventy laws were passed without one dissent in any material thing. But of this more hereafter, being yet raw and new in our gear. However, I cannot forget their singular respect to me in this infancy of things, who, by their own private expenses, so early considered mine for the public as to present me with an impost upon certain goods imported and exported, which, after my acknowledgment of their affection, I did as freely remit to the province and the traders to it. And for the well-government of the said counties, courts of justice are established in every county with proper officers, as justices, sheriffs, clerks, constables, which courts are held every two months. But to prevent lawsuits there are three peacemakers chosen by every county court, in the nature of common arbitrators, to hear and end differences between man and man. And spring and fall there is an orphans' court in each county, to inspect and regulate the affairs of orphans and widows.

Philadelphia: the expectation of those who are concerned in this province is at last laid out to the great content of those here who are anyways interested therein. The situation is a neck of land and lies between two navigable rivers, Delaware and Sculkill, whereby it hath two fronts upon the water, each a mile, and two from river to river. Delaware is a glorious river; but the Sculkill, being an hundred miles boatable above the falls, and its course northeast toward the fountain of Susquehanah (that tends to the heart of the province and both sides our own), it is like to be a great part of the settlement of this age. I say little of the town itself because a platform will be shown you by my agent, in which those who are purchasers of me will find their names and interests. But this I will say, for the good providence of God, that of all the many places I have seen in the world, I remember not one better seated. So that it seems to me to have been appointed for a town whether we regard the rivers or the conveniency of the coves, ducks, and springs, the loftiness and soundness of the land, and the air, held by the people of those parts to be very good.

It is advanced within less than a year to about fourscore houses and cottages, such as they are, where merchants and handicrafts are following their vocations as fast as they can, while the countrymen are close at their farms. Some of them got a little winter corn. They reaped their barley this year in the month called May, the wheat in the month following. There is time in these parts for another crop of several things before the winter season. We are daily in hopes of shipping to add to our number; for, blessed be God! here is both room and accommodation for them. The stories of our necessity are either the fear of our friends or the scarecrows of our enemies, for the greatest hardship we have suffered hath been salt meat, which, by fowl in winter and fish in summer, together with some poultry, lamb, mutton, veal, and plenty of venison, the best part of the year, hath been made very passable. I bless God I am fully satisfied with the country and entertainment I got in it, for I find that particular content, which hath always attended me, where God in His providence hath made it my place and service to reside. You cannot imagine my station can be at present free of more than ordinary business, and, as such, I may say it is a troublesome work. But the method things are putting in will facilitate the charge and give an easier motion to the administration of affairs. However, as it is some men's duty to plow, some to sow, some to water, and some to reap, so it is the wisdom as well as the duty of a man to yield to the mind of providence and cheerfully as well as carefully embrace and follow the guidance of it.

THE FOUNDING OF PENNSYLVANIA
B. Penn's Treaty with the Indians
(1683)
by William Penn

This letter dated August 16, 1683, is from Penn to the Free Society of Traders.

Every king [i.e., Indian chief] had his council and that consists of all the old and wise men of his nation, which perhaps is two hundred people. Nothing of moment is undertaken, be it war, peace, selling of land, or traffic, without advising with them, and, which is more, with the young men, too. It is admirable to consider how powerful the kings are, and yet how they move by the breath of their people. I have had occasion to be in council with them upon treaties for land and to adjust the terms of trade.

Their order is thus: The king sits in the middle of an half-moon and has his council, the old and wise, on each hand. Behind them, or at a little distance, sit the younger fry in the same figure. Having consulted and resolved their business, the king ordered one of them to speak to me. He stood up, came to me, and in the name of the king saluted me, then took me by the hand and told me that he was ordered by his king to speak to me, and that now it was not he but the king who spoke, because what he should say was the king's mind. He first prayed me to excuse them, that they had not complied with me the last time. He feared there might be some fault in the interpreter, being neither Indian nor English. Besides, it was the Indian custom to deliberate and take up much time in council before they resolved, and that if the young people and owners of the land had been as ready as he, I had not met with so much delay.

Having thus introduced his matter, he fell to the bounds of the land they had agreed to dispose of and the price, which now is little and dear, that which would have bought twenty miles not buying now two. During the time that this person spoke, not a man of them was observed to whisper or smile—the old grave, the young reverent in their deportment. They speak little, but fervently and with elegance. I have never seen more natural sagacity, considering them without the help (I was going to say the spoil) of tradition, and he will deserve the name of wise who outwits them in any treaty about a thing they understand.

When the purchase was agreed, great promises passed between us of kindness and good neighborhood, and that the English and Indians must live in love as long as the sun gave light. That done, another made a speech to the Indians, in the name of all the sachamakers or kings; first, to tell them what was done; next, to charge and command them to love the Christians and particularly to live in peace with me and the people under my government. Many governors had been in the river, but no governor had come himself to live and stay here before; and having now such an one, who had treated them well, they should never do him or his any wrong; at every sentence of which they shouted and said Amen in their way.

We have agreed that in all differences between us six of each side shall end the matter. Do not abuse them, but let them have justice, and you win them.

BIRTH OF A NATION

BIRTH OF A NATION

The French were the first to grasp the territories watered by the Mississippi and many of its tributaries. The steps by which this area was wrested by the English from the French, and those by which English colonists wrested their new homeland from the mother country, constitute this third chapter of American history.

A long struggle between England and France for domination of North America began during Count Frontenac's first term as French governor of Canada (1762). For three quarters of a century, the conflict went on, now by the peaceful methods of increasing and spreading population, trade, and industry, now by open attacks on settlements, the burning of homes, and the massacre of settlers. Count Frontenac's purpose in coming to America for his second term was to secure the Hudson valley, which, added to the St. Lawrence, Ohio, Mississippi, and the Great Lakes, already in French hands, would have meant French control of the North American continent. But by making war on the Iroquois Indians, Frontenac gave the English the powerful aid of that tribe in the border and barrier state of New York. The English alliance with this strong Indian confederation turned the scale in English favor.

The periods of outright warfare are known as King William's War (1689–1697), Queen Anne's War (1702–1713), and King George's War (1740–1748). These were scarcely more than skirmishes and raids against forest clearings, but after them came a grim, final struggle, an all-out contest to decide whether the French or the British would control North America. This conflict was the French and Indian War.

Just as in Frontenac's time, more than seventy years before, the struggle was for control of the Hudson Valley. The ensuing land battles were mainly fought in New York territory—Fort Niagara, Fort Oswego, Lake George, and Ticonderoga.

Important battles took place elsewhere, too, notably the stunning defeat of British General Braddock at Pittsburgh (then Fort Duquesne) by the French and their Indian allies, and the decisive victory of Wolfe over the French at Quebec. This last victory forced France to seek peace.

The American Revolution was a direct outgrowth of the French and Indian War. In England, that war had led to special taxation for the colonies to reimburse the mother country for the expense of ridding the colonists of their troublesome French neighbors. But the war had awakened in the colonies a consciousness of their own strength and ability to stand alone. The Stamp Act of 1765 was part of the English policy, and the colonists' bitter opposition to it reflected their new sense of strength and independence.

The war which eventually ensued in 1775 began in New England with local conflicts between English regulars and Colonial militiamen, at Lexington, at Concord, at Bunker Hill. The struggle closed in the southern states, where Cornwallis surrendered to Washington. But the real war was fought in New York, Pennsylvania, and New Jersey. Here again was the vital ground: control of the Hudson Valley meant everything. In the long contest for this central area occurred the battles of Long Island, Princeton, Trenton, Brandywine, Germantown, Monmouth, and Stony Point. The British planned a three-fold advance designed to split the colonies along the Hudson. Saratoga, where they were defeated, was the first great American victory of the war, and probably the turning point of the Revolution.

The first years after the war, from 1783 until 1787, have been called "the critical period." The newborn United States was weak, chiefly because there was no central government with supreme authority to govern the whole country. Under the Articles of Confederation, Congress had no power to act on important measures affecting all the states, except by consent of nine of them. Obliged for several years to maintain an army of 10,000 men, it could not raise the money to pay them, and at one time was obliged ignominiously to leave Philadelphia in the face of soldiers in revolt for want of pay. No credit could be had in Europe; an attempt to raise $300,000 in Amsterdam in 1784 had utterly failed. Money was so scarce that cattle, sheep, and unimproved real estate were by law made legal tender.

Furthermore, the states failed to agree upon a common policy in commercial matters. They made tariff laws of their own, waging commercial war on one another. At one time four states—Massachusetts, Pennsylvania, North Carolina, and Georgia—in direct violation of the Articles of Confederation, began to raise troops for their own defense. In 1786 Rhode Island recalled her delegates to Congress and refused to appoint others. Shay's rebellion in western Massachusetts was a revolt against mortgage foreclosures, and a symptom of the discontent of the times. Europe, hearing of these disorders, believed the Union would not long keep itself together. George III thought the states would soon beg England to take them back. The whole country was on the verge of civil war.

The time had come for change. Wiser minds saw a constitution delegating authority to a Federal government as the only remedy. The resulting Constitution of 1787 was not so much a new creation as an outgrowth of the experience of eight years of war and four of subsequent disintegration. Much of it was drawn from systems of government that had already been tried and found adequate in some of the states.

Alexander Hamilton rendered his greatest services to his country as Secretary of the Treasury in the new Federal government. He found the national finances bordering on bankruptcy. There was a foreign debt of $10,000,000; a domestic debt of $29,000,000; and accrued interest amounting to $13,000,000. Our bonds had been selling for as little as 25 per cent of par; but five years later, after his fiscal reorganization, they sold at par. Hamilton also caused the Federal government to assume the debts of the several states. This act at once raised the credit of the whole country and cemented the states more firmly in a Union. He found a large source of revenue in sales of land from the Northwest Territory, which Virginia had given up for the common good.

Washington's first administration closed in 1793. The Union then seemed complete. Two new states had been added—Vermont and Kentucky. Taxes were uncomplainingly borne.

Under John Adams' administration, however, trouble arose with England over her aggressions on our commerce, such as the impressment of seamen seized on board our ships. Intense indignation arose throughout the country. Congress sent John Jay to London to try diplomatic persuasion, but the resulting treaty was so disliked in America that Jay was burned in effigy. Nevertheless, the treaty prevailed, and war with Britain was averted, if only temporarily.

THE DEFEAT OF BRADDOCK

(1754)

by George Washington

Letter from Washington to his mother, written at Fort Cumberland, after the battle, and dated July 18, 1755. Washington had accompanied Braddock as a volunteer aide-de-camp.

HONORED MADAM: As I doubt not but you have heard of our defeat, and, perhaps, had it represented in a worse light, if possible, than it deserves, I have taken this earliest opportunity to give you some account of the engagement as it happened, within ten miles of the French fort, on Wednesday the 9th instant.

We marched to that place, without any considerable loss having only now and then a straggler picked up by the French and scouting Indians. When we came there, we were attacked by a party of French and Indians, whose number, I am persuaded, did not exceed three hundred men; while ours consisted of about one thousand three hundred well-armed troops, chiefly regular soldiers, who were struck with such a panic that they behaved with more cowardice than it is possible to conceive. The officers behaved gallantly, in order to encourage their men, for which they suffered greatly, there being near sixty killed and wounded; a large proportion of the number we had.

The Virginia troops showed a good deal of bravery, and were nearly all killed; for I believe, out of three companies that were there, scarcely thirty men are left alive. Captain Peyrouny, and all his officers down to a corporal, were killed. Captain Polson had nearly as hard a fate, for only one of his was left. In short, the dastardly behavior of those they call regulars exposed all others, that were inclined to do their duty, to almost certain death: and, at last, in despite of all the efforts of the officers to the contrary, they ran, as sheep pursued by dogs, and it was impossible to rally them.

The General was wounded, of which he died three days after. Sir Peter

Halket was killed in the field, where died many other brave officers. I luckily escaped without a wound, though I had four bullets through my coat, and two horses shot under me. Captains Orme and Morris, two of the aids-de-camp, were wounded early in the engagement, which rendered the duty harder upon me, as I was the only person then left to distribute the General's orders, which I was scarcely able to do, as I was not half recovered from a violent illness, that had confined me to my bed and a wagon for above ten days. I am still in a weak and feeble condition, which indures me to halt here two or three days in the hope of recovering a little strength, to enable me to proceed homewards; from whence, I fear, I shall not be able to stir till toward September; so that I shall not have the pleasure of seeing you till then, unless it be in Fairfax. I am, honored Madam, your most dutiful son.

WOLFE'S VICTORY AT QUEBEC
(1759)
by Captain John Knox

From Knox's Historical Journal of the Campaign in North America. *Knox accompanied the expedition and wrote his "journal" from day to day. It was published in London, in two volumes, a few years after the battle. The victory of Wolfe has been recognized by many writers to be of utmost importance in modern history. John Fiske wrote that "the triumph of Wolfe marks the greatest turning point as yet discovered in modern history." The battle decided for North America that her civilization should be English rather than French.*

Before daybreak this morning [September 13, 1759] we made a descent upon the north shore, about half a quarter of a mile to the eastward of Sillery; and the light troops were fortunately by the rapidity of the current carried lower down between us and Cape Diamond. We had in this debarkation thirty flat-bottomed boats, containing about sixteen hundred men. This was a great surprize on the enemy, who from the natural strength of the place did not suspect, and consequently were not prepared against so bold an attempt. The chain of sentries which they had posted along the summit of the heights galled us a little, and picked off several men and some officers before our light infantry got up to dislodge them. This grand enterprise was conducted and executed with great good order and discretion.

As fast as we landed the boats put off for reenforcements, and the troops formed with much regularity. The general, with Brigadiers Monckton and Murray, was ashore with the first division. We lost no time here, but clambered up one of the steepest precipices that can be conceived, being almost a perpendicular, and of an incredible height. As soon as we gained the summit all was quiet, and not a shot was heard, owing to the excellent conduct of the light infantry under Colonel Howe. It was by this time clear daylight. Here we formed again, the river and the south country in our rear, our right extending to the town, our left to Sillery, and halted a few minutes. The general then detached the light troops to our left to route the enemy from their battery, and to disable their guns, except they could be rendered serviceable to the party who were to remain there; and this service was soon performed. We then faced to the right, and marched toward the town by files till we came to the Plains of Abraham, an even piece of ground which Mr. Wolfe had made choice of, while we stood forming upon the hill. Weather showery. About six o'clock the enemy first made their appearance upon the heights between us and the town, whereupon we halted and wheeled to the right, thereby forming the line of battle.

The enemy had now likewise formed the line of battle, and got some cannon to play on us, with round and canister shot; but what galled us most was a body of Indians and other marksmen they had concealed in the corn opposite to the front of our right wing, and a coppice that stood opposite to our center inclining toward our left. But Colonel Hale, by Brigadier Monckton's orders, advanced some platoons alternately from the forty-seventh regiment, which after a few rounds obliged these skulkers to retire. We were now ordered to lie down, and remained some time in this position. About eight o'clock we had two pieces of short brass six-pounders playing on the enemy, which threw them into some confusion, and obliged them to alter their disposition; and Montcalm formed them into three large columns. About nine the two armies, moved a little nearer each other. The light calvary made a faint attempt upon our parties at the battery of Sillery, but were soon beat off; and Monsieur de Bougainville, with his troops from Cape Rouge, came down to attack the flank of our second line, hoping to penetrate there. But, by a masterly disposition of Brigadier Townshend, they were forced to desist; and the third battalion of Royal Americans was then detached to the first ground we had formed on after we gained the heights, to preserve the communication with the beach and our boats.

About ten o'clock the enemy began to advance briskly in three columns, with loud shots and recovered arms, two of them inclining to the left of our army, and the third toward our right, firing obliquely at the two extremities of our line, from the distance of one hundred and thirty, until they came within forty yards, which our troops withstood with the greatest intrepidity and firmness, still reserving their fire and paying the strictest obedience to their officers. This uncommon steadiness, together with the havoc which the grape-shot from our field-pieces made among them, threw them into some disorder and was most critically maintained by a well-timed, regular, and heavy discharge of our small arms, such as they could no longer oppose. Hereupon they gave way, and fled with precipitation, so that by the time the cloud of smoke was vanished our men were again over them, pursued them almost to the gates of town and the bridge over the little river, redoubling our fire with great eagerness, making many officers and men prisoners.

The weather cleared up, with a comfortably warm sunshine. The Highlanders chased them vigorously toward Charles River, and the fifty-eighth to the suburb close to John's gate, until they were checked by the cannon from the two hulks. At the same time a gun which the town had brought to bear upon us with grape-shot galled the progress of the regiments to the right, who were likewise pursuing with equal ador, while Colonel Hunt Walsh, by a very judicious movement, wheeled the battalions of Bragg and Kennedy to the left, and flanked the coppice where a body of the enemy made a stand as if willing to renew the action; but a few platoons from these corps completed our victory. Then it was that Brigadier Townshed came up, called off the pursuers, ordered the whole line to dress and recover their former ground.

Our joy at this success is inexpressibly damped by the loss we sustained of one of the greatest heroes which this or any other age can boast of,— General James Wolfe,—who received his mortal wound as he was exerting himself at the head of the grenadiers of Louisbourg; and Brigadier Monckton was unfortunately wounded upon the left of the forty-third and right of the forty-seventh regiment at much the same time, whereby the command devolved on Brigadier Townshend, who, with Brigadier Murray, went to the head of every regiment and returned thanks for their extraordinary good behavior, congratulating the officers on our success. There is one incident very remarkable, and which I can affirm from my own personal knowledge,—that the enemy were extremely apprehensive of being rigorously treated; for, conscious of their inhuman behavior to our troops upon a former occasion, the officers who fell into our hands most piteously (with hats off) sued for quarter, repeatedly declaring they were not at Fort William Henry (called by them Fort George) in the year 1757. A soldier of the Royal Americans who deserted from us this campaign, and fought against us to-day, was found wounded on the field of battle. He was immediately tried by a general court-martial, and was shot to death pursuant to his sentence.

While the two armies were engaged this morning there was an incessant firing between the town and our south batteries. By the time that our troops had taken a little refreshment, a quantity of intrenching tools were brought ashore, and the regiments were employed in redoubting our ground and landing some cannon and ammunition. The officers who are prisoners say that Quebec will surrender in a few days. Some deserters who came out to us in the evening agree in that opinion, and inform us that the Sieur de Montcalm is dying, in great agony, of a wound he received today in their retreat.

Thus has our late renowned commander by his superior eminence in the art of war, and a most judicious *coup d'ètat,* made a conquest of this fertile, healthy, and hitherto formidable country, with a handful of troops only, in spite of the political schemes and most vigorous efforts of the famous Montcalm, and many other officers of rank and experience at the head of an army considerably more numerous. My pen is too feeble to draw the character of this British Achilles; but the same may, with justice, be said of him as was said of Henry IV of France: he was possessed of courage, humanity, clemency, generosity, affability, and politeness.

Deserters who are come over to us since the action inform us that it was very difficult to persuade Monsieur de Montcalm and the other commanders that the flower of our army were behind the town; and, after the marquis had marched his troops over the river Charles, and taken a view of us, he said: "They have at last got to the weak side of this miserable garrison. Therefore, we must endeavor to crush them with our numbers, and scalp them all before twelve o'clock." Every coppice, bush, or other cover that stood on our ground this morning were cut down before night, and applied to the use of our new works. The houses were all fortified and several redoubts thrown up round our camp, which is about one thousand yards from the garrison, before ten o'clock.

The Sieur de Montcalm died late last night. When his wound was dressed and he settled in bed, the surgeons who attended him were desired to acquaint him ingenuously with their sentiments of him; and, being answered that his wound was mortal, he calmly replied, "he was glad of it." His Excellency then demanded "whether he could survive it long, and how long." He was told, "About a dozen hours, perhaps more, peradventure less." "So much the better," rejoined this eminent warrior. "I am happy I shall not live to see the surrender of Quebec." He then ordered his secretary into the room to adjust his private affairs, which, as soon as they were dispatched, he was visited by Monsieur de Ramsey, the French king's lieutenant, and by other principal officers who desired to receive his Excellency's commands, with the farther measures to be pursued for the defense of Quebec, the capital of Canada. To this the marquis made the following answer: "I'll neither give orders nor interfere any farther. I have much business that must be attended to, of greater moment than your ruined garrison and this wretched country. My time is very short, therefore pray leave me. I wish you all comfort, and to be happily extricated from your present perplexities." He then called for his chaplain, who, with the bishop of the colony, remained with him till he expired. Some time before this great man departed, we are assured he paid us this compliment: "Since it was my misfortune to be discomfited, and mortally wounded, it is a great consolation to me to be vanquished by so brave and generous an enemy. If I could survive this wound, I would engage to beat three times the number of such forces as I commanded this morning with a third of their number of British troops."

After our late worthy general of renowned memory was carried off wounded to the rear of the front line, he desired those who were about him to lay him down. Being asked if he would have a surgeon, he replied, "It is needless: it is all over with me." One of them then cried out, "They run, see how they run!" "Who runs?" demanded our hero with great earnestness, like a person roused from sleep. The officer answered: "The enemy, sir. Egad, they give way everywhere." Thereupon the general rejoined: "Go, one of you, my lads, to Colonel Burton—; tell him to march Webb's regiment with all speed down to Charles River, to cut off the retreat of the fugitives from the bridge." Then, turning on his side, he added, "Now, God be praised, I will die in peace!" and thus expired.

BOONE'S MIGRATION TO KENTUCKY

(1773)
by Daniel Boone

Boone wrote this account many years after his migration. As his education was extremely limited, the article was put into literary form by a friend. Boone, in 1773, made the first white settlement west of the Alleghenies.

It was on the first of May, in the year 1769, that I resigned my domestic happiness for a time, and left my family and peaceable habitation on the Yadkin River, in North Carolina, to wander through the wilderness of America, in quest of the country of Kentucky, in company with John Finley, John Stewart, Joseph Holden, James Monay, and William Cool.

We proceeded successfully, and after a long and tiresome journey through a mountainous wilderness, in a westward direction, on the seventh day of June following, we found ourselves on Red River, where John Finley had formerly gone trading with the Indians; and, from the top of an eminence, saw with pleasure the beautiful level of Kentucky.

We found everywhere abundance of wild beasts of all sorts, through this vast forest. The buffalo were more frequent than I have seen cattle in the settlements, browzing on the leaves of the cane, or cropping the herbage on those extensive plains, fearless, because ignorant of the violence of man. Sometimes we saw hundreds in a drove, and the numbers about the salt springs were amazing.

As we ascended the brow of a small hill, near Kentucky River, a number of Indians rushed out of a thick cane-brake upon us, and made us prisoners. The time of our sorrow was now arrived, and the scene fully opened. They plundered us of what we had, and kept us in confinement seven days, treating us with common savage usage. During this time we showed no uneasiness or desire to escape, which made them less suspicious of us. But in the dead of night, as we lay in a thick cane-brake by a large fire, when sleep had locked up their senses, my situation not disposing me for rest, I touched my companion and gently woke him.

We improved this favorable opportunity, and departed, leaving them to take their rest, and speedily directed our course toward our old camp, but found it plundered, and the company dispersed and gone home.

Soon after this my companion in captivity, John Stewart, was killed by the savages, and the man that came with my brother returned home by himself. We were then in a dangerous, helpless situation, exposed daily to perils and death among savages and wild beasts, not a white man in the country but ourselves.

One day I undertook a tour through the country, and the diversity and beauties of nature I met with in this charming season expelled every gloomy and vexatious thought. I laid me down to sleep, and I awoke not until the sun had chased away the night. I continued this tour, and in a few days explored a considerable part of the country, each day equally pleased as the first.

I returned again to my old camp, which was not disturbed in my absence. I did not confine my lodging to it, but often reposed in thick cane-brakes to avoid the savages, who, I believe, often visited my camp, but fortunately for me, in my absence. In this situation I was constantly exposed to danger and death. How unhappy such a situation for a man! Tormented with fear, which is vain if no danger comes. The prowling wolves diverted my nocturnal hours with perpetual howlings.

In 1772 I returned safe to my old home, and found my family in happy circumstances. I sold my farm on the Yadkin, and what goods we could not carry with us; and on the twenty-fifth day of September, 1773, bade a farewell to our friends and proceeded on our journey to Kentucky, in company with five families more, and forty men that joined us in Powel's Valley,which is one hundred and fifty miles from the now settled parts of Kentucky.

This promising beginning was soon overcast with a cloud of adversity; for upon the tenth day of October the rear of our company was attacked by a number of Indians, who killed six and wounded one man. Of these my eldest son was one that fell in the action.

Tho we defended ourselves, and repulsed the enemy, yet this unhappy affair scattered our cattle, brought us into extreme difficulty, and so discouraged the whole company that we retreated forty miles to the settlement on Clench River.

Within fifteen miles of where Boonsborough now stands we were fired upon by a party of Indians that killed two and wounded two of our number; yet altho surprized and taken at a disadvantage, we stood our ground. This was on the twentieth of March, 1775.

Three days after we were fired upon again, and had two men killed and three wounded. Afterward we proceeded on to Kentucky River without opposition; and on the first day of April began to erect the fort of Boonsborough at a salt lick, about sixty yards from the river, on the south side. On the fourth day the Indians killed one man.

In a short time I proceeded to remove my family from Clench to this garrison, where we arrived safe without any other difficulties than such as are common to this passage, my wife and daughter being the first white women that ever stood on the banks of Kentucky River. On the twenty-fourth day of December following we had one man killed and one wounded by the Indians, who seemed determined to persecute us for erecting this fortification.

On the fourteenth day of July, 1776, two of Colonel Calaway's daughters and one of mine were taken prisoners near the fort. I immediately pursued the Indians, with only eight men, and on the sixteenth overtook them, killed two of the party and recovered the girls. The same day on which this attempt was made the Indians divided themselves into different parties and attacked several forts, which were shortly before this time erected, doing a great deal of mischief. This was extremely distressing to the new settlers. The innocent husbandman was shot down while busy in cultivating the soil for his family's supply. Most of the cattle around the stations were destroyed. They continued their hostilities in this manner until the fifteenth of April, 1777, when they attacked Boonsborough with a party of above one hundred in number, killed one man and wounded four. Their loss in this attack was not certainly known to us.

On the fourth day of July following a party of about two hundred Indians attacked Boonsborough, killed one man and wounded two. They besieged us forty-eight hours; during which time seven of them were killed, and finding themselves not likely to prevail, they raised the siege and departed.

The Indians had disposed their warriors in different parties at this time and attacked the different garrisons to prevent their assisting each other, and did much injury to the inhabitants.

On the nineteenth day of this month Colonel Logan.s fort was besieged by a party of about two hundred Indians. During this dreadful siege they did a great deal of mischief, distrest the garrison, in which were only fifteen men, killed two and wounded one.

This campaign in some measure damped the spirits of the Indians, and made them sensible of our superiority. Their connections were dissolved, their armies scattered, and a future invasion put entirely out of their power; yet they continued to practise mischief secretly upon the inhabitants, in the exposed parts of the country.

In October following a party made an excursion into that district called the Crab Orchard, and one of them, who was advanced some distance before the others, boldly entered the house of a poor defenseless family, in which was only a negro man, a woman and her children, terrified with the apprehensions of immediate death. The savage, perceiving their defenseless situation, without offering violence to the family, attempted to captivate the negro, who happily proved an overmatch for him, threw him on the ground, and, in the struggle, the mother of the children drew an ax from a corner of the cottage and cut his head off, while her little daughter shut the door. The savages instantly appeared, and applied their tomahawks to the door. An old rusty gun-barrel, without a lock, lay in a corner, which the mother put through a small crevice, and the savages, perceiving it, fled. In the mean time the alarm spread through the neighborhood; the armed men collected immediately, and pursued the ravagers into the wilderness. Thus Providence, by the means of this negro, saved the whole of the poor family from destruction. From that time until the happy return of peace between the United States and Great Britain the Indians did us no mischief.

To conclude, I can now say that I have verified the saying of an old Indian who signed Colonel Henderson's deed. Taking me by the hand, at the delivery thereof, Brother, says he, we have given you a fine land, but I believe you will have much trouble in settling it. My footsteps have often been marked with blood, and therefore I can truly subscribe to its original name. Two darling sons, and a brother, have I lost by savage hands, which have also taken from me forty valuable horses and abundance of cattle. Many dark and sleepless nights have I been a companion for owls, separated from the cheerful society of men, scorched by the summer's sun and pinched by the winter's cold, an instrument ordained to settle the wilderness. But now the scene is changed: peace crowns the sylvan shade.

THE BOSTON TEA PARTY
(1773)
by Governor Hutchinson

From Hutchinson's History of Massachusetts Bay. *Hutchinson's position has awakened much sympathy. Although Governor of the province, and thus obligated to enforce the unpopular English tax on tea, he was a native of Boston and a graduate of Harvard. His* History *has been much admired for its fair and temperate spirit. Especially valuable are the portraits he gives of his contemporaries, "the men who bore him down after the fiercest possible struggle." For an interesting account of this royal governor's problems at the time of the revolution, consult* The Ordeal of Thomas Hutchinson *by Bernard Bailyn.*

The Governor was unable to judge what would be the next step. The secretary had informed him in the hearing of the deputy secretary, that, if the Governor should refuse a pass [permitting the ship to return to England], he would demand it himself, at the head of one hundred and fifty men, etc.; and he was not without apprehensions of a further application. But he was relieved from his suspense, the same evening, by intelligence from town of the total destruction of the tea.

It was not expected that the Governor would comply with the demand; and, before it was possible for the owner of the ship to return from the country with an answer, about fifty men had prepared themselves, and passed by the house where the people were assembled to the wharf where the vessels lay, being covered with blankets, and making the appearance of Indians. The body of the people remained until they had received the Governor's answer; and then, after it had been observed to them that, everything else in their power having been done, it now remained to proceed in the only way left, and that, the owner of the ship having behaved like a man of honor, no injury ought to be offered to his person or property, the meeting was declared to be dissolved, and the body of the people repaired to the wharf, and surrounded the immediate actors, as a guard and security, until they had finished their work. In two or three hours they hoisted out of the holes of the ships three hundred and forty-two chests of tea, and emptied them into the sea.

The Governor was unjustly censured by many people in the province, and much abused by the pamphlet and newspaper writers in England for refusing his pass, which, it was said, would have saved the property thus destroyed; but he would have been justly censured if he had granted it. He was bound, as all the king's governors were, by oath, faithfully to observe the acts of trade, and to do his endeavor that the statute of King William, which establishes a custom-house, and is particularly mentioned in the oath, be carried into execution. His granting a pass to a vessel which had not cleared at the custom-house would have been a direct violation of his oath, by making himself an accessory in the breach of those laws which he had sworn to observe. It was out of his power to have prevented this mischief without the most imminent hazard of much greater mischief. The tea could have been secured in the town in no other way than by landing marines from the men of war, or bringing to town the regiment which was at the castle, to remove the guards from the ships, and to take their places. This would have brought on a greater convulsion than there was any danger of in 1770, and it would not have been possible, when two regiments were forced out of town, for so small a body of troops to have kept possession of the place. Such a measure the Governor had no reason to suppose would have been approved of in England.

Notwithstanding the forlorn state he was in, he thought it necessary to keep up some show of authority, and caused a council to be summoned to meet at Boston the day after the destruction of the tea, and went to town himself to be present at it; but a quorum did not attend. The people had not fully recovered from the state of mind which they were in the preceding night. Great pains had been taken to persuade them that the obstruction they had met with, which finally brought on the loss of the tea, were owing to his influence; and, being urged to it by his friends, he left the town, and lodged that night at the castle, under pretense of a visit to his sons, who were confined there with the other consignees of the tea. Failing in an attempt for a council the next day at Milton, he met them, three days after, at Cambridge, where they were much divided in their opinion. One of them declared against any step whatever. The people, he said, had taken the powers of government into their hands,—any attempt to restrain them would only enrage them, and render them more desperate; while another observed that, having done everything else in their power to prevent the tea from being landed, and all to no purpose, they had been driven to the necessity of destroying it, as a less evil than submission to the duty. So many of the actors and abetters were universally known that a proclamation, with a reward for discovery, would have been ridiculed. The attorney-general, therefore, was ordered to lay the matter before the grand jury, who, there was no room to expect, would ever find a bill for what they did not consider as an offense. This was the boldest stroke which had yet been struck in America.

THE CONCORD FIGHT
April 19, 1775
By Rev. William Emerson

William Emerson, a clergyman of Concord, was the grandfather of Ralph Waldo Emerson. He became a chaplain in the Continental Army and lost his life in the Ticonderoga expedition.

This morning between one and two o'clock we were alarmed by the ring of the bell and upon examination found that the troops to the north of eight hundred had stolen their march from Boston in boats and barges from the bottom of the Common over to a point in Cambridge, near to Inman's farm, and were at the Lexington Meeting House half an hour before sunrise, where they had fired upon a body of our men and (as we afterward heard) had killed several. This intelligence was brought us at first by Dr. Samuell Prescott, who narrowly escaped the guard that was sent before on horses, purposely to prevent all posts and messengers from giving us timely information. He, by the help of a very fleet horse crossing several walls and fences, arrived at Concord at the time above mentioned.

When several posts were immediately dispatched, that returning confirmed the account of the regulars' arrival at Lexington, and that they were on their way to Concord. Upon this a number of our minutemen belonging to this town, and Acton and Lyncoln, with several others that were in readiness, marched out to meet them, while the alarm company were preparing to receive them in the town. Captain Minot who commanded them, thought it proper to take possession of the hill above the Meeting House as the most advantageous situation. No sooner had he gained it, than we were met by the companies that were sent out to meet the troops, who informed us that they were just upon us and that we must retreat as their number was more than triple ours. We then retreated from the hill near the Liberty Pole and took a new post back of the town, upon a rising eminence, where we formed into two battalions and waited the arrival of the enemy.

Scarcely had we formed before we saw the British troops at the distance of one-quarter of a mile, glittering in arms, advancing towards us with the greatest speed. Some were for making a stand, notwithstanding the superiority of their number, but others more prudent thought best to retreat till our strength should be equal the enemy's by recruits from neighboring towns that were continually coming in to our assistance. Accordingly we retreated over the bridge. When the troops came into the town, they set fire to several carriages for the artillery, destroyed sixty barrels of flour, rifled several houses, took possession of the Townhouse, destroyed five hundred pounds of balls, set a guard of one hundred men at the north bridge, and south sent up a party to the house of Colonel Barrett, where they were in expectation of finding a quantity of warlike stores. But these were happily secured just before their arrival by transportation into the wood and other by-places.

In the meantime, the guards set by the enemy to secure the pass at the north bridge were alarmed by the approach of our people who had retreated as mentioned before and were now advancing with special orders not to fire upon the troops unless fired upon. These orders were so punctually observed that we received the fire of the enemy in three several and separate discharges of their pieces before it was returned by our commanding officer. The firing then soon became general for several minutes, in which skirmish two were killed on each side and several of the enemy wounded. It may here be observed by the way, that we were the more cautious to prevent beginning a rupture with the King's troops as we were then uncertain what had happened at Lexington and knew not that they had begun the quarrel there by first firing upon our people and killing eight men on the spot.

The three companies of troops soon quitted their post at the bridge and retreated in greatest discord and confusion to the main body, who were soon upon the march to meet them. For half an hour the enemy by their marches and countermarches discovered great fickleness and inconstancy of mind, sometimes advancing, sometimes returning to their former posts, till at length they quitted the town and retreated by the way they came. In the meantime, a party of our men (150) took the back way through the great fields into the east quarter and had placed themselves to advantage, laying in ambush behind walls, fences, and buildings, ready to fire upon the enemy on their retreat.

DRAFTING THE DECLARATION OF INDEPENDENCE

(1776)

by John Adams

Adams wrote this account long after the event—in 1822. This distinguished American family produced John Adams, second President of the United States and John Quincy Adams, sixth President of the United States.

You inquire why so young a man as Mr. Jefferson was placed at the head of the Committee for preparing a Declaration of Independence? I answer: It was the Frankfort advice, to place Virginia at the head of everything. Mr. Richard Henry Lee might be gone to Virginia, to his sick family, for aught I know, but that was not the reason of Mr. Jefferson's appointment. There were three committees appointed at the same time. One for the Declaration of Independence, another for preparing articles of Confederation, and another for preparing a treaty to be proposed to France. Mr. Lee was chosen for the Committee of Confederation, and it was not thought convenient that the same person should be upon both.

Mr. Jefferson came into Congress in June, 1775, and brought with him a reputation for literature, science, and a happy talent of composition. Writings of his were handed about, remarkable for the peculiar felicity of expression. Tho a silent member in Congress, he was so prompt, frank, explicit, and decisive upon committees and in conversation, not even Samuel Adams was more so, that he soon seized upon my heart; and upon this occasion I gave him my vote, and did all in my power to procure the votes of others. I think he had one more vote than any other, and that placed him at the head of the committee. I had the next highest number, and that placed me the second. The committee met, discust the subject, and then appointed Mr. Jefferson and me to make the draft, I suppose because we were the two first on the list.

The sub-committee met. Jefferson proposed to me to make the draft. I said, "I will not." "You should do it." "Oh, no!" "Why will you not? You ought to do it." "I will not." "Why?" "Reasons enough." "What can be your reasons?" "Reason first—You are a Virginian, and a Virginian ought to appear at the head of this business. Reason second—I am obnoxious, suspected, and unpopular. You are very much otherwise. Reason third

—You can write ten times better than I can." "Well," said Jefferson, "if you are decided, I will do as well as I can." "Very well. When you have drawn it up, we will have a meeting."

A meeting we accordingly had, and conned the paper over. I was delighted with its high tone and the flights of oratory with which it abounded, especially that concerning negro slavery, which, tho I knew his Southern brethren would never suffer to pass in Congress, I certainly never would oppose. There were other expressions which I would not have inserted, if I had drawn it up, particularly that which called the King tyrant. I thought this too personal; for I never believed George to be a tyrant in disposition and in nature; I always believed him to be deceived by his courtiers on both sides of the Atlantic, and in his official capacity only, cruel. I thought the expression too passionate, and too much like scolding, for so grave and solemn a document; but as Franklin and Sherman were to inspect it afterward, I thought it would not become me to strike it out. I consented to report it, and do not now remember that I made or suggested a single alteration.

We reported it to the committee of five. It was read, and I do not remember that Franklin or Sherman criticized anything. We were all in haste. Congress was impatient, and the instrument was reported, as I believe, in Jefferson's handwriting, as he first drew it. Congress cut off about a quarter of it, as I expected they would; but they obliterated some of the best of it, and left all that was exceptionable, if anything in it was. I have long wondered that the original draft has not been published. I suppose the reason is, the vehement Philippic against negro slavery.

As you justly observe, there is not an idea in it but what had been hackneyed in Congress for two years before. The substance of it is contained in the declaration of rights and the violation of those rights, in the Journals of Congress, in 1774. Indeed, the essence of it is contained in a pamphlet, voted and printed by the town of Boston, before the first Congress met, composed by James Otis, as I suppose, in one of his lucid intervals, and pruned and polished by Samuel Adams.

JOHN PAUL JONES'S SEA FIGHT
(1779)
by John Paul Jones

Jones wrote this account as his official report to Congress, sending it through Franklin, who then represented the Colonies in France. He wrote it on board the captured British ship Serapis, while she lay at anchor off Holland in October, 1779. The fight between the Bonhomme Richard and the Serapis had occurred in the North Sea late in September of this year, the Serapis being vastly the superior of Paul Jones's own ship. Jones gave the name Bonhomme Richard to his own ship out of compliment to Franklin. The expense of his expedition had been borne by the King of France and after achieving his victory, Jones was received in France with much enthusiasm. The battle is especially memorable for Jones's defiant response to a British demand for his surrender: "I have not yet begun to fight!"

On the morning of that day, the 23d, the brig from Holland not being in sight, we chased a brigantine that appeared laying to the windward. About noon we saw and chased a large ship that appeared coming round Flamborough Head from the northward, and at the same time I manned and armed one of the pilot boats to sail in pursuit of the brigantine, which now appeared to be the vessel that I had forced ashore. Soon after this a fleet of 41 sail appeared off Flamborough Head, bearing N.N.E. This induced me to abandon the single ship, which had then anchored in Burlington Bay. I also called back the pilot boat, and hoisted a signal for a general chase. When the fleet discovered us bearing down, all the merchant ships crowded sail toward the shore. The two ships of war that protected the fleet at the same time steered from the land, and made the disposition for the battle. In approaching the enemy, I crowded every possible sail, and made the signal for the line of battle, to which the *Alliance* showed no attention. Earnest as I was for the action, I could not reach the commodore's ship until seven in the evening. Being then within pistol shot, when he hailed the *Bonhomme Richard,* we answered him by firing a whole broadside.

The battle, being thus begun, was continued with unremitting fury. Every method was practised on both sides to gain an advantage, and rake each other; and I must confess that the enemy's ship, being much more manageable than the *Bonhomme Richard,* gained thereby several times an advantageous situation, in spite of my best endeavors to prevent it. As I had to deal with an enemy of *greatly superior force,* I was under the necessity of closing with him, to prevent the advantage which he had over me in point of maneuver. It was my intention to lay the *Bonhomme Richard* athwart the enemy's bow, but, as that operation required great dexterity in the management of both sails and helm, and some of our braces being shot away, it did not exactly succeed to my wishes. The enemy's bowsprit, however, came over the *Bonhomme Richard's* poop by the mizzen mast, and I made both ships fast together in that situation, which by the action of the wind on the enemy's sails forced her stern close to the *Bonhomme Richard's* bow, so that the ships lay square alongside of each other, the yards being all entangled, and the cannon of each ship touching the opponent's side.

When this position took place, it was 8 o'clock, previous to which the *Bonhomme Richard* had received sundry eighteen-pounds shot below the water, and leaked very much. My battery of 12-pounders, on which I had placed my chief dependence, being commanded by Lieut. Dale and Col. Weibert, and manned principally with American seamen and French volunteers, were entirely silenced and abandoned. As to the six old eighteen-pounders that formed the battery of the lower gun-deck, they did no service whatever. Two out of three of them burst at the first fire, and killed almost all the men who were stationed to manage them. Before this time, too, Col. de Chamillard, who commanded a party of 20 soldiers on the poop, had abandoned that station after having lost some of his men. These men deserted their quarters.

I had now only two pieces of cannon, nine-pounders, on the quarter-deck, that were not silenced; and not one of the heavier cannon was fired during the rest of the action. The purser, Mr. Mease, who commanded the guns on the quarter deck, being dangerously wounded in the head, I was obliged to fill his place, and with great difficulty rallied a few men, and shifted over one of the lee quarter-deck guns, so that we afterward played three pieces of 9-pounders upon the enemy. The tops alone seconded the fire of this little battery, and held out bravely during the whole of the action, especially the main top, where Lieut. Stack commanded. I directed the fire of one of the three cannon against the main-mast, with double-headed shot, while the other two were exceedingly well served with grape and canister shot to silence the enemy's musketry, and clear her decks, which was at last effected.

The enemy were, as I have since understood, on the instant of calling for quarters when the cowardice or treachery of three of my under officers induced them to call to the enemy. The English commodore asked me if I demanded quarters, and, I having answered him in the most determined negative, they renewed the battle with double fury. They were unable to stand the deck; but the fire of their cannon, especially the lower battery, which was entirely formed of 18-pounders, was incessant. Both ships were set on fire in various places, and the scene was dreadful beyond the reach of language. To account for the timidity of my three under officers,—I mean the gunner, the carpenter, and the master-at-arms,—I must observe that the two first were slightly wounded; and, as the ship had received various shots under water, and one of the pumps being shot away, the carpenter expressed his fear that she would sink, and the other two concluded that she was sinking, which occasioned the gunner to run aft on the poop without my knowledge to strike the colors. Fortunately for me, a cannon ball had done that before by carrying away the ensign staff. He was therefore reduced to the necessity of sinking, as he supposed, or of calling for quarter; and he preferred the latter.

All this time the *Bonhomme Richard* had sustained the action alone, and the enemy, though much superior in force, would have been very glad to have got clear, as appears by their own acknowledgments, and by their having let go an anchor the instant that I laid them on board, by which means they would have escaped, had I not made them well fast to the *Bonhomme Richard*.

At last, at half-past 9 o'clock, the Alliance appeared, and I now thought the battle at an end; but, to my utter astonishment, he discharged a broadside full into the stern of the *Bonhomme Richard*. We called to him for God's sake to forbear firing into the *Bonhomme Richard;* yet he passed along the off side of the ship, and continued firing. There was no possibility of his mistaking the enemy's ship for the *Bonhomme Richard,* there being the most essential difference in their appearance and construction; besides, it was then full moonlight, and the sides of the *Bonhomme Richard* were all black, while the sides of the prizes were yellow; yet, for the greater security, I shewed the signal of our reconnoissance by putting out three lanthorns, one at the head (bow), another at the stern, (quarter), and the third in the middle in a horizontal line.

Every tongue cried that he was firing into the wrong ship, but nothing availed. He passed round, firing into the *Bonhomme Richard's* head, stern, and broadside; and by one of his volleys killed several of my best men, and mortally wounded a good officer on the forecastle. My situation was really deplorable. The *Bonhomme Richard* received various shot under water from the *Alliance,* the leak gained on the pumps, and the fire increased much on board both ships. Some officers persuaded me to strike, of whose courage and good sense I entertain a high opinion. My treacherous master-at-arms let loose all my prisoners without my knowledge, and my prospect became gloomy indeed. I would not, however, give up the point. The enemy's main-mast began to shake, their firing decreased, ours increased, and the British colors were struck at half past 10 o'clock.

The prize proved to be the British ship of war the *Serapis,* a new ship of 44 guns, built on their most approved construction, with two complete batteries, one of them of 18-pounders, and commanded by the brave Commodore Richard Pearson. I had yet two enemies to encounter far more formidable than the Britons,—I mean fire and water. The *Serapis* was attacked only by the first, but the *Bonhomme Richard* was assailed by both. There were five feet of water in the hold, and, though it was moderate from the explosion of so much gunpowder, yet the three pumps that remained could with difficulty only keep the water from gaining. The fire broke out in various parts of the ship, in spite of all the water that could be thrown to quench it, and at length broke out as low as the powder magazine, and within a few inches of the powder.

In that dilemma I took out the powder upon deck, ready to be thrown overboard at the last extremity; and it was ten o'clock the next day, the 24th, before the fire was entirely extinguished. With respect to the situation of the *Bonhomme Richard,* the rudder was cut entirely off the stern frame, and the transoms were almost entirely cut away; the timbers, by the lower deck especially, from the mainmast to the stern, being greatly decayed with age, were mangled beyond my power of description; and a person must have been an eye-witness to form a just idea of the tremendous scene of carnage, wreck, and ruin that everywhere appeared. Humanity can not but recoil from the prospect of such finished horror, and lament that war should produce such fatal consequences.

After the carpenters, as well as Capt. de Cottineau, and other men of sense, had well examined and surveyed the ship (which was not finished before five in the evening), I found every person to be convinced that it was impossible to keep the *Bonhomme Richard* afloat so as to reach a port if the wind should increase, it being then only a very moderate breeze. I had but little time to remove my wounded, which now became unavoidable, and which was effected in the course of the night and next morning. I was determined to keep the *Bonhomme Richard* afloat, and, if possible, to bring her into port. For that purpose the first lieutenant of the Pallas continued on board with a party of men to attend the pumps, with boats in waiting ready to take them on board in case the water should gain on them too fast. The wind augmented in the night and the next day, on the 25th, so that it was impossible to prevent the good old ship from sinking. They did not abandon her till after 9 o'clock. The water was then up to the lower deck, and a little after 10 I saw with inexpressible grief the last glimpse of the *Bonhomme Richard.* No lives were lost with the ship, but it was impossible to save the stores of any sort whatever. I lost even the best part of my clothes, books, and papers; and several of my officers lost all their clothes and effects.

THE EXECUTION OF ANDRÉ

(1780)

by General William Heath

General Heath, a witness of the hanging of André, had been assigned to the command of the Hudson River posts in 1779, and except for a short interval, remained there until the close of the war.

The hanging of Major André, the British spy who collaborated with American traitor Benedict Arnold, took place at Tappan, a hamlet in Rockland County, New York, south of Nyack. A monument was later erected there. Another monument to André stands in Westminster Abbey, London.

October 2d—Major André is no more among the living. I have just witnessed his exit. It was a tragical scene of the deepest interest. During his confinement and trial, he exhibited those proud and elevated sensibilities which designate greatness and dignity of mind. Not a murmur or a sigh ever escaped him, and the civilities and attentions bestowed on him were politely acknowledged.

Having left a mother and two sisters in England, he was heard to mention them in terms of the tenderest affection, and in his letter to Sir Henry Clinton, he recommends them to his particular attention.

The principal guard officer who was constantly in the room with the prisoner, relates that when the hour of his execution was announced to him in the morning, he received it without emotion, and while all present were affected with silent gloom, he retained a firm countenance, with calmness and composure of mind. Observing his servant enter the room in tears, he exclaimed, "Leave me till you can show yourself more manly."

His breakfast being sent to him from the table of General Washington, which had been done every day of his confinement, he partook of it as usual, and having shaved and dressed himself, he placed his hat on the table, and cheerfully said to the guard officers, "I am ready at any moment, gentlemen, to wait on you."

The fatal hour having arrived, a large detachment of troops was paraded, and an immense concourse of people assembled; almost all our general and field officers, excepting his Excellency and his staff, were present on horseback; melancholy and gloom pervaded all ranks, and the scene was affectingly awful. I was so near during the solemn march to the fatal spot, as to observe every movement, and share in every emotion which the sad scene was calculated to produce.

Major André walked from the stone house, in which he had been confined, between two of our subaltern officers, arm in arm; the eyes of the immense multitude were fixed on him, who, rising superior to the fears of death, appeared as if conscious of the dignity which he displayed.

He betrayed no want of fortitude, but retained a complacent smile on his countenance, and politely bowed to several gentlemen whom he knew, which was respectfully returned. It was his earnest desire to be shot, as being the mode of death most fitting to the feelings of a military man, and he had indulged the hope that his request would be granted.

At the moment, therefore, when suddenly he came in view of the gallows, he involuntarily started backward, and made a pause. "Why this emotion, sir," said an officer by his side? Instantly recovering his composure, he said, "I am reconciled to my death, but I detest the mode." While waiting and standing near the gallows, I observed some degree of trepidation; placing his foot on a stone, and rolling it over and choking in his throat, as if attempting to swallow.

So soon, however, as he perceived that things were in readiness, he stepped quickly into the wagon, and at this moment he appeared to shrink, but instantly elevating his head with firmness, he said, "It will be but a momentary pang," and he took from his pocket two white handkerchiefs; the provost marshal with one loosely pinioned his arms, and with the other, the victim, after taking off his hat and stock, bandaged his own eyes with perfect firmness, which melted the hearts, and moistened the cheeks, not only of his servant, but of the throng of spectators.

When the rope was appended to the gallows, he slipped the noose over his head and adjusted it to his neck, without the assistance of the awkward executioner. Colonel Scammel now informed him that he had an opportunity to speak, if he desired it; he raised the handkerchief from his eyes and said, "I pray you to bear me witness that I meet my fate like a brave man."

The wagon being now removed from under him, he was suspended and instantly expired; it proved indeed "but a momentary pang." He was dressed in his royal regimentals and boots, and his remains, in the same dress, were placed in an ordinary coffin, and interred at the foot of the gallows; and the spot was consecrated by the tears of thousands. Thus died in the bloom of life, the accomplished Major André, the pride of the royal army.

THE CAPTURE OF VINCENNES
(1779)
by George Rogers Clark

From Clark's Memoirs. Historians are in agreement as to the importance of Clark's expedition. It was not only an act of heroism scarcely surpassed by any act of the Revolution, but secured for the future Republic all that country north and west of the Ohio River, of which Clark became master by conquest. At the close of the war, territory as far west as the Mississippi was thus held by the colonies, so that they were able to retain it under the treaty of Paris. Otherwise, the Ohio instead of the Mississippi would have been made our western boundary. The account here given was written by Clark at the special request of Jefferson and Madison.

Everything being ready, on the 5th of February, we crossed the Kaskaskia River with one hundred and seventy men, marched about three miles and encamped, where we lay until the 7th, and set out. The weather wet (but fortunately not cold for the season), and a great part of the plains under water several inches deep. It was difficult and very fatiguing marching.

Crossing a narrow deep lake in the canoes, and marching some distance, we came to a copse of timber called the Warrior's Island. We were now in full view of the fort and town, not a shrub between us, at about two miles' distance. Every man now feasted his eyes, and forgot that he had suffered anything, saying that all that had passed was owing to good policy and nothing but what a man could bear; and that a soldier had no right to think, etc.,—passing from one extreme to another, which is common in such cases. It was now we had to display our abilities. The plain between us and the town was not a perfect level. The sunken grounds were covered with water full of ducks.

Our situation was now truly critical—no possibility of retreating in case of defeat, and in full view of a town that had, at this time, upward of six hundred men in it—troops, inhabitants, and Indians. We were now in the situation that I had labored to get ourselves in. The idea of being made prisoner was foreign to almost every man, as they expected nothing but torture from the savages, if they fell into their hands. Our fate was now to be determined, probably in a few hours. We knew that nothing but the most daring conduct would insure success. I knew that a number of the inhabitants wished us well, that many were lukewarm to the interest of either, and I also learned that the grand chief, the Tobacco's son, had but a few days before openly declared, in council with the British, that he was a brother and friend to the Big Knives. These were favorable circumstances; and, as there was but little probability of our remaining until dark undiscovered, I determined to begin the career immediately, and wrote the following placard to the inhabitants:

"To the Inhabitants of Post Vincennes.

"Gentlemen: Being now within two miles of your village, with my army, determined to take your fort this night, and not being willing to surprize you, I take this method to request such of you as are true citizens and willing to enjoy the liberty I bring you to remain still in your houses; and those, if any there be, that are friends to the king will instantly repair to the fort, and join the hair-buyer general, and fight like men. And, if any such as do not go to the fort shall be discovered afterward, they may depend on severe punishment. On the contrary, those who are true friends to liberty may depend on being well treated; and I once more request them to keep out of the streets. For every one I find in arms on my arrival I shall treat him as an enemy.

"(Signed)   G. R. Clark."

We anxiously viewed this messenger until he entered the town, and in a few minutes could discover by our glasses some stir in every street that we could penetrate into, and great numbers running or riding out into the commons, we supposed, to view us, which was the case. But what surprized us was that nothing had yet happened that had the appearance of the garrison being alarmed—no drum nor gun. We began to suppose that the information we got from our prisoners was false, and that the enemy knew of us, and were prepared. A little before sunset we moved, and displayed ourselves in full view of the town, crowds gazing at us. We were plunging ourselves into certain destruction or success. There was no midway thought of.

The firing now commenced on the fort, but they did not believe it was an enemy until one of their men was shot down through a port, as drunken Indians frequently saluted the fort after night. The drums now sounded, and the business fairly commenced on both sides. Reenforcements were sent to the attack of the garrison, while other arrangements were making in town. We now found that the garrison had known nothing of us; that, having finished the fort that evening, they had amused themselves at different games, and had just retired before my letter arrived, as it was near roll-call. The placard being made public, many of the inhabitants were afraid to show themselves out of the houses for fear of giving offense, and not one dare give information. Our friends flew to the commons and other convenient places to view the pleasing sight.

The garrison was soon completely surrounded.

The firing immediately commenced on both sides with double vigor; and I believe that more noise could not have been made by the same number of men. Their shouts could not be heard for the firearms; but a continual blaze was kept around the garrison, without much being done, until about daybreak, when our troops were drawn off to posts prepared for them, about sixty or seventy yards from the fort. A loophole then could scarcely be darkened but a rifle-ball would pass through it. To have stood to their cannon would have destroyed their men, without a probability of doing much service. Our situation was nearly similar. It would have been imprudent in either party to have wasted their men, without some decisive stroke required it.

Thus the attack continued until about 9 o'clock on the morning of the 24th I sent a flag (with a letter) demanding the garrison.

We met at the church, about eighty yards from the fort, Lieutenant Governor Hamilton, Major Hay, superintendent of Indian affairs, Captain Helm, their prisoner, Major Bowman, and myself. The conference began. Hamilton produced terms of capitulation, signed, that contained various articles, one of which was that the garrison should be surrendered on their being permitted to go to Pensacola on parole. After deliberating on every article, I rejected the whole. He then wished that I would make some proposition. I told him that I had no other to make than what I had already made—that of his surrendering as prisoners at discretion.

We took our leave, and parted but a few steps, when Hamilton stopt, and politely asked me if I would be so kind as to give him my reasons for refusing the garrison any other terms than those I had offered. I told him him I had no objections in giving him my real reasons, which were simply these: that I knew the greater part of the principal Indian partisans of Detroit were with him; that I wanted an excuse to put them to death or otherwise treat them as I thought proper; that the cries of the widows and the fatherless on the frontiers, which they had occasioned, now required their blood from my hand, and that I did not choose to be so timorous as to disobey the absolute commands of their authority, which I looked upon to be next to divine; that I would rather lose fifty men than not to empower myself to execute this piece of business with propriety; that, if he chose to risk the massacre of his garrison for their sakes, it was his own pleasure; and that I might, perhaps, take it into my head to send for some of those widows to see it executed.

From that moment my resolutions changed respecting Hamilton's situation. I told him that we would return to our respective posts; that I would reconsider the matter, and let him know the result. No offensive measures should be taken in the meantime. Agreed to; and we parted. What had passed being made known to our officers, it was agreed that we should moderate our resolutions.

The business being now nearly at an end, troops were posted in several strong houses around the garrison and patroled during the night to prevent any deception that might be attempted. The remainder on duty lay on their arms, and for the first time for many days past got some rest. During the siege, I got only one man wounded. Not being able to lose many, I made them secure themselves well. Seven were badly wounded in the fort through ports.

THE SURRENDER OF CORNWALLIS
(1781)
by General Charles Cornwallis

From the General's official report, dated Yorktown, Virginia, October 20, 1781. Surrounded on land by the American Continental Army, at sea by the French fleet, Cornwallis finally surrendered to Washington.

I have the mortification to inform your Excellency that I have been forced to give up the posts of York and Gloucester, and to surrender the troops under my command, by capitulation, on the 19th instant, as prisoners of war to the combined forces of America and France.

I never saw this post in a very favorable light, but when I found I was to be attacked in it in so unprepared a state, by so powerful an army and artillery, nothing but the hopes of relief would have induced me to attempt its defense, for I would either have endeavored to escape to New York by rapid marches from the Gloucester side, immediately on the arrival of General Washington's troops at Williamsburg, or I would, notwithstanding the disparity of numbers, have attacked them in the open field, where it might have been just possible that fortune would have favored the gallantry of the handful of troops under my command; but being assured by your Excellency's letters that every possible means would be tried by the navy and army to relieve us, I could not think myself at liberty to venture upon either of these desperate attempts; therefore, after remaining for two days in a strong position in front of this place in hopes of being attacked, upon observing that the enemy were taking measures which could not fail of turning my left flank in a short time, and receiving on the second evening your letter of September 24th, informing me that the relief would sail about October 5th, I withdrew within the works on the night of September 29th, hoping by the labor and firmness of the soldiers to protract the defense until you could arrive. Everything was to be expected from the spirit of the troops, but every disadvantage attended their labor, as the works were to be continued under the enemy's fire, and our stock of entrenching tools, which did not much exceed four hundred when we began to work in the latter end of August, was now much diminished.

The enemy broke ground on the night of the 30th, and constructed on that night, and the two following days and nights, two redoubts, which, with some works that had belonged to our outward position, occupied a gorge between two creeks or ravines which come from the river on each side of the town. On the night of October 6th they made their first parallel, extending from its right on the river to a deep ravine on the left, nearly opposite to the center of this place, and embracing our whole left at a distance of six hundred yards. Having perfected this parallel, their batteries opened on the evening of the 9th against our left, and other batteries fired at the same time against a redoubt advanced over the creek upon our right, and defended by about a hundred and twenty men of the Twenty-third regiment and marines, who maintained that post with uncommon gallantry. The fire continued incessant from heavy cannon, and from mortars and howitzers throwing shells from 8 to 16 inches, until all our guns on the left were silenced, our work much damaged, and our loss of men considerable. On the night of the 11th they began their second parallel, about three hundred yards nearer to us. The troops being much weakened by sickness, as well as by the fire of the besiegers, and observing that the enemy had not only secured their flanks, but proceeded in every respect with the utmost regularity and caution, I could not venture so large sorties as to hope from them any considerable effect, but otherwise I did everything in my power to interrupt this work by opening new embrasures for guns and keeping up a constant fire from all the howitzers and small mortars that we could man.

This action, tho extremely honorable to the officers and soldiers who executed it, proved of little public advantage, for the cannon, having been spiked in a hurry, were soon rendered fit for service again, and before dark the whole parallel and batteries appeared to be nearly complete. At this time we knew that there was no part of the whole front attacked on which we could show a single gun, and our shells were nearly expended. I therefore had only to choose between preparing to surrender next day or endeavoring to get off with the greatest part of the troops, and I determined to attempt the latter.

In this situation, with my little force divided, the enemy's batteries opened at daybreak. The passage between this place and Gloucester was much exposed, but the boats, having now returned, they were ordered to bring back the troops that had passed during the night, and they joined us in the forenoon without much loss. Our works, in the mean time, were going to ruin, and not having been able to strengthen them by an abatis, nor in any other manner but by a slight fraising, which the enemy's artillery were demolishing whenever they fired, my opinion entirely coincided with that of the engineer and principal officers of the army, that they were in many places assailable in the forenoon, and that by the continuance of the same fire for a few hours longer they would be in such a state as to render it desperate, with our numbers, to attempt to maintain them. We at that time could not fire a single gun; only one 8-inch and little more than one hundred Cohorn shells remained. A diversion by the French ships-of-war that lay at the mouth of York River was to be expected.

Our numbers had been diminished by the enemy's fire, but particularly by sickness, and the strength and spirits of those in the works were much exhausted by the fatigue of constant watching and unremitting duty. Under all these circumstances I thought it would have been wanton and inhuman to the last degree to sacrifice the lives of this small body of gallant soldiers, who had ever behaved with so much fidelity and courage, by exposing them to an assault which, from the numbers and precautions of the enemy, could not fail to succeed. I therefore proposed to capitulate; and I have the honor to enclose to your excellency the copy of the correspondence between General Washington and me.

THE FIRST AMERICAN MINISTER MEETS GEORGE III
(1785)
by John Adams

The American Revolution had ended. George III, Britain's defeated king, was now to receive officially the triumphant Americans' first ambassador. What would happen? everyone wondered.

Adams wrote this account at his hotel in Westminster, London, on June 2, 1785, addressing it to John Jay, then secretary for foreign affairs in Washington's cabinet.

During my interview with the Marquis of Carmarthen, he told me that it was customary for every foreign minister, at his first presentation to the King, to make his Majesty some compliments conformable to the spirit of his letter of credence; and when Sir Clement Cottrell Dormer, the master of the ceremonies, came to inform me that he should accompany me to the secretary of state and to Court, he said that every foreign minister whom he had attended to the Queen had always made a harangue to her Majesty, and he understood, tho he had not been present, that they always harangued the King.

On Tuesday evening the Baron de Lynden called upon me, and said he came from the Baron de Nolken, and they had been conversing upon the singular situation I was in, and they agreed in opinion that it was indispensable that I should make a speech, and that that speech should be as complimentary as possible. All this was conformable to the advice lately given by the Count de Vergennes to Mr. Jefferson; so that, finding it was a custom established at both these great Courts, and that this Court and the foreign ministers expected it, I thought I could not avoid it, altho my first thought and inclination had been to deliver my credentials silently and retire.

At one, on Wednesday, the master of ceremonies called at my house, and went with me to the secretary of state's office, in Cleveland Row, where the Marquis of Carmarthen received me, and introduced me to his under secretary, Mr. Fraser, who has been, as his Lordship told me, uninterruptedly in that office, through all the changes in administration for thirty years, having first been appointed by the Earl of Holderness. After a short conversation upon the subject of importing my effects from Holland and France free of duty, which Mr. Fraser himself introduced, Lord Carmarthen invited me to go with him in his coach to Court. When we arrived in the antechamber, the master of the ceremonies met me and attended me, while the secretary of state went to take the commands of the King. While I stood in this place, where it seems all ministers stand upon such occasions, always attended by the master of ceremonies, the room very full of ministers of state, lords, and bishops, and all sorts of courtiers, as well as the next room, which is the King's bedchamber, you may well suppose I was the focus of all eyes.

I was relieved, however, from the embarrassment of it by the Swedish and Dutch ministers, who came to me, and entertained me in a very agreeable conversation during the whole time. Some other gentlemen, whom I had seen before, came to make their compliments too, until the Marquis of Carmarthen returned and desired me to go with him to his Majesty. I went with his Lordship through the levee room into the King's closet. The door was shut, and I was left with his Majesty and the secretary of state alone. I made the three reverences—one at the door, another about half way, and a third before the presence—according to the usage established at this and all the northern Courts of Europe, and then addressed myself to his Majesty in the following words:

"Sir:—The United States of America have appointed me their minister plenipotentiary to your Majesty, and have directed me to deliver to your Majesty this letter, which contains the evidence of it. It is in obedience to their express commands, that I have the honor to assure your Majesty of their unanimous disposition and desire to cultivate the most friendly and liberal intercourse between your Majesty's subjects and their citizens, and of their best wishes for your Majesty's health and happiness, and for that of your royal family. The appointment of a minister from the United States to your Majesty's Court will form an epoch in the history of England and of America. I think myself more fortunate than all my fellow citizens, in having the distinguished honor to be the first to stand in your Majesty's royal presence in a diplomatic character; and I shall esteem myself the happiest of men, if I can be instrumental in recommending my country more and more to your Majesty's royal benevolence, and of restoring an entire esteem, confidence, and affection, or, in better words, the old good nature and the old good humor between people, who, tho separated by an ocean, and under different governments, have the same language, a similar religion, and kindred blood.

"I beg your Majesty's permission to add, that, altho I have some time before been entrusted by my country, it was never in my whole life in a manner so agreeable to myself."

The King listened to every word I said, with dignity, but with an apparent emotion. Whether it was the nature of the interview, or whether it was my visible agitation, for I felt more than I did or could express, that touched him, I can not say. But he was much affected, and answered me with more tremor than I had spoken with, and said:

"Sir:—The circumstances of this audience are so extraordinary, the language you have now held is so extremely proper, and the feelings you have discovered so justly adapted to the occasion, that I must say that I not only receive with pleasure the assurance of the friendly dispositions of the United States, but that I am very glad the choice has fallen upon you to be their minister. I wish you, sir, to believe, and that it may be understood in America, that I have done nothing in the late contest but what I thought myself indispensably bound to do, by the duty which I owed to my people. I will be very frank with you. I was the last to consent to the separation; but the separation having been made, and having become inevitable, I have always said, as I say now, that I would be the first to meet the friendship of the United States as an independent power. The moment I see such sentiments and language as yours prevail, and a disposition to give to this country the preference, that moment I shall say, let the circumstances of language, religion, and blood have their natural and full effect."

I dare not say that these were the King's precise words, and, it is even possible, that I may have in some particular mistaken his meaning; for, altho his pronunciation is as distinct as I ever heard, he hesitated some time between his periods, and between the members of the same period. He was indeed much affected, and I confess I was not less so, and, therefore, I can not be certain that I was so cool and attentive, heard so clearly, and understood so perfectly, as to be confident of all his words or sense; and, I think, that all which he said to me should at present be kept secret in America, unless his Majesty, or his secretary of state, who alone was present, should judge proper to report it. This I do say, that the foregoing is his Majesty's meaning as I then understood it, and his own words as nearly as I can recollect them.

The King then asked me whether I came last from France, and upon my answering in the affirmative, he put on an air of familiarity, and, smiling, or rather laughing, said, "there is an opinion among some people that you are not the most attached of all your countrymen to the manners of France." I was surprized at this, because I thought it an indiscretion and a departure from my dignity. I was a little embarrassed, but determined not to deny the truth on one hand, nor leave him to infer from it any attachment to England on the other. I threw off as much gravity as I could, and assumed an air of gaiety and a tone of decision as far as was decent, and said, "that opinion, sir, is not mistaken; I must avow to your Majesty, I have no attachment but to my own country." The King replied, as quick as lightening, "an honest man will never have any other."

The King then said a word or two to the secretary of state, which, being between them, I did not hear, and then turned round and bowed to me, as is customary with all kings and princes when they give the signal to retire. I retreated, stepping backward, as is the etiquette, and, making my last reverence at the door of the chamber, I went my way. The master of the ceremonies joined me the moment of my coming out of the King's closet, and accompanied me through the apartments down to my carriage, several stages of servants, gentlemen-porters, and under-porters, roaring out like thunder, as I went along, "Mr. Adams' servants, Mr. Adams' carriage, etc." I have been thus minute, as it may be useful to others hereafter to know.

The conversation with the King, Congress will form their own judgment of. I may expect from it a residence less painful than I once expected, as so marked an attention from the King will silence many grumblers; but we can infer nothing from all this concerning the success of my mission.

ADVICE ON COMING TO AMERICA
(1784)
by Benjamin Franklin

Written by Benjamin Franklin while living in France, just after the conclusion of the treaty of peace with Great Britian, which he had helped to negotiate, and published in London as "Information to Those Who Would Remove to America."

Many persons in Europe having directly or by letters, expressed to the writer of this, who is well acquainted with North America, their desire of transporting and establishing themselves in that country; but who appear to him to have formed through ignorance, mistaken ideas and expectations of what is to be obtained there; he thinks it may be useful, and prevent inconvenient, expensive and fruitless removals and voyages of improper persons, if he gives some clearer and truer notions of that part of the world than appear to have hitherto prevailed.

The truth is, that tho there are in that country few people so miserable as the poor of Europe, there are also very few that in Europe would be called rich. It is rather a general happy mediocrity that prevails. There are few great proprietors of the soil, and few tenants; most people cultivate their own lands, or follow some handicraft or merchandise; very few [are] rich enough to live idly upon their rents or incomes; or to pay the high prices given in Europe, for painting, statues, architecture, and the other works of art that are more curious than useful.

Hence the natural geniuses that have arisen in America, with such talents, have uniformly quitted that country for Europe, where they can be more suitably rewarded. It is true that letters and mathematical knowledge are in esteem there, but they are at the same time more common than is apprehended; there being already existing nine colleges, or universities, viz.: four in New England, and one in each of the provinces of New York, New Jersey, Pennsylvania, Maryland, and Virginia, all furnished with learned professors; besides a number of smaller academies. These educate many of their youth in the languages, and those sciences that qualify men for the professions of Divinity, Law, or Physic. Strangers indeed are by no means excluded from exercising those professions; and the quick increase of inhabitants everywhere gives them a chance of employ, which they have in common with the natives. Of civil offices or employments, there are few; no superfluous ones as in Europe; and it is a rule established in some of the States, that no office should be so profitable as to make it desirable. These ideas prevailing more or less in all the United States, it can not be worth any man's while, who has a means of living at home, to expatriate himself in hopes of obtaining a profitable civil office in America; and as to military offices, they are at an end with the war, the armies being disbanded. Much less is it advisable for a person to go thither who has no other quality to recommend him but his birth. In Europe it has indeed its value; but it is a commodity that can not be carried to a worse market than to that of America, where people do not not inquire concerning a stranger, *What is he?* but *What can he do?* If he has any useful art, he is welcome; and if he exercises it, and behaves well, he will be respected by all that know him; but a mere man of quality, who on that account wants to live upon the public, by some office or salary, will be despised and disregarded.

With regard to encouragements for strangers from government, they are really only what are derived from good laws and liberty. Strangers are welcome because there is room enough for them all, and therefore the old inhabitants are not jealous of them; the laws protect them sufficiently, so that they have no need of the patronage of great men; and every one will enjoy securely the profits of his industry. But if he does not bring a fortune with him, he must work and be industrious to live. One or two years' residence give him all the rights of a citizen; but the Government does not at present, whatever it may have done in former times, hire people to become settlers, by paying their passages, giving land, negroes, utensils, stock, or any other kind of emolument whatsoever. In short, America is the land of labor, and by no means what the English call *Lubberland,* and the French *Pays de Cocagne,* where the streets are said to be paved with half-peck loaves, the houses tiled with pancakes, and where the fowls fly about ready roasted, crying, *Come eat me!*

Land being cheap in that country, from the vast forests still void of inhabitants, and not likely to be occupied in an age to come, insomuch that the propriety of an hundred acres of fertile soil full of wood may be obtained near the frontiers in many places, for eight or ten guineas, hearty young laboring men, who understand the husbandry of corn and cattle, which is nearly the same in that country as in Europe, may easily establish themselves there. A little money saved of the good wages they receive there while they work for others enables them to buy the land and begin their plantation, in which they are assisted by the good will of their neighbors, and some credit. Multitudes of poor people fron England, Scotland, and Germany, have by this means in a few years become wealthy farmers, who in their own countries, where all the lands are fully occupied, and the wages of labor low, could never have emerged from the mean condition wherein they were born.

From the salubrity of the air, the healthiness of the climate, the plenty of good provisions, and the encouragement to early marriages, by the certainty of subsistence in cultivating the earth, the increase of inhabitants by natural generation is very rapid in America, and becomes still more so by the accession of strangers; hence there is a continual demand for more artisans of all the necessary and useful kinds, to supply those cultivators of the earth with houses, and with furniture and utensils of the grosser sorts, which can not so well be brought from Europe. Tolerably good workmen in any of those mechanic arts are sure to find employ, and to be well paid for their work, there being no restraints preventing strangers from exercising any art they understand, nor any permission necessary. If they are poor, they begin first as servants or journeymen; and if they are sober, industrious, and frugal, they soon become masters, establish themselves in business, marry, raise families, and become respectable citizens.

Also, persons of moderate fortunes and capitals, who having a number of children to provide for, are desirous of bringing them up to industry, and to secure estates for their posterity, have opportunities of doing it in America, which Europe does not afford. There they may be taught and practise profitable mechanic arts, without incurring disgrace on that account; but on the contrary acquiring respect by such abilities. There small capitals laid out in lands, which daily become more valuable by the increase of people, afford a solid prospect of ample fortunes thereafter for those children. The writer of this has known several instances of large tracts of land, bought on what was then the frontier of Pennsylvania, for ten pounds per hundred acres, which, after twenty years, when the settlements had been extended far beyond them, sold readily, without any improvement made upon them, for three pounds per acre. The acre in America is the same with the English acre, or the acre of Normandy.

Several of the Princes of Europe having of late, from [formed?] an opinion of advantage to arise by producing all commodities and manufactures within their own dominions, so as to diminish or render useless their importations, have endeavored to entice workmen from other countries, by high salaries, privileges, etc. This, however, has rarely been done in America; and when it has been done it has rarely succeeded, so as to establish a manufacture, which the country was not yet so ripe for as to encourage private persons to set it up; labor being generally too dear there, and hands difficult to be kept together, every one desiring to be a master, and the cheapness of land inclining many to leave trades for agriculture. Some indeed have met with success, and are carried on to advantage; but they are generally such as require only a few hands, or wherein great part of the work is performed by machines. Great establishments of manufacture require great numbers of poor to do the work for small wages; these poor are to be found in Europe, but will not be found in America, till in lands are all taken up and cultivated, and the excess of people who can not get land, want employment.

Therefore the governments in America do nothing to encourage such projects. The people, by this means, are not imposed on, either by the merchant or mechanic; if the merchant demands too much profit on imported shoes they buy of the shoemaker; and if he asks too high a price they take them of the merchant: Thus the two professions are checks on each other. The shoemaker, however, has on the whole, a considerable profit upon his labor in America, beyond what he had in Europe, as he can add to his price a sum nearly equal to all the expenses of freight and commission, risk or insurance, etc., necessarily charged by the merchant. And the case is the same with the workmen in every other mechanic art. Hence it is, that artizans generally live better and more easily in America than in Europe; and such as are good economists make a comfortable provision for age, and for their children. Such may, therefore, remove with advantage to America.

In the old long-settled countries of Europe artisans who fear creating future rivals in business, refuse to take apprentices, but upon conditions of money, maintenance, or the like, which the parents are unable to comply with. In America the rapid increase of inhabitants takes away that fear of rivalship, and artisan willingly receive apprentices from the hope of profit by their labor, during the remainder of the time stipulated, after they shall be instructed. Hence it is easy for poor families to get their children instructed; for the artisans are so desirous of apprentices, that many of them will even give money to the parents, to have boys from ten to fifteen years of age bound apprentices to them, till the age of twenty-one; and many poor parents have, by that means, on their arrival in the country, raised money enough to buy land sufficient to establish themselves, and to subsist the rest of their family by agriculture.

These contracts for apprentices are made before a magistrate, who regulates the agreement according to reason and justice; and having in view the formation of a future useful citizen, obliges the master to engage by a written indenture, not only that during the time of service stipulated, the apprentice shall be duly provided with meat, drink, apparel, washing, and lodging, and at its expiration with a complete new suit of clothes, but also that he shall be taught to read, write, and cast accounts; and that he shall be well instructed in the art or profession of his master, or some other, by which he may afterward gain a livelihood, and be able in his turn to raise a family. This desire among the masters to have more hands employed in working for them, induces them to pay the passages of young persons, of both sexes, who on their arrival agree to serve them one, two, three, or four years; those who have already learned a trade, agreeing for a shorter term, in proportion to their skill, and the consequent immediate value of their service; and those who have none, agreeing for a longer term, in consideration of being taught an art their poverty would not permit them to acquire in their own country.

The almost general mediocrity of fortune that prevails in America, obliging its people to follow some business for subsistence, those vices that arise usually from idleness are in a great measure prevented. Industry and constant employment are great preservatives of the morals and virtue of a nation. Hence bad examples to youth are more rare in America, which must be a comfortable consideration to parents. To this may be truly added, that serious religion, under its various denominations, is not only tolerated, but respected and practised. Atheism is unknown there; Infidelity rare and secret; so that persons may live to a great age in that country without having their piety shocked by meeting with either an Atheist or an Infidel. And the Divine Being seems to have manifested his approbation of the mutual forbearance and kindness with which the different sects treat each other, by the remarkable prosperity with which he has been pleased to favor the whole country.

HOW SETTLEMENTS WERE PROMOTED

(1790)

by William Cooper

William Cooper was the father of the novelist, James Fenimore Cooper. His home originally was in Burlington, New Jersey, where he became interested in mortgages that had been foreclosed on large tracts of land around Lake Otsego in central New York. To investigate these lands, he went out to Otsego in 1785 and finally decided to move there with his family in 1790. His "Guide in the Wilderness" was a pamphlet issued in Dublin for the purpose of promoting immigration to Otsego. Cooper's son Fenimore, as a child about four years old, went to Otsego with him and grew up there in the wilderness, thus acquiring that familiarity with the Indians and with frontier life of which he has left such famous pictures in his Leatherstocking Tales.

I began with the disadvantage of a small capital, and the incumbrance of a large family, and yet I have already settled more acres than any man in America. There are forty thousand souls now holding directly or indirectly under me, and I trust, that no one among so many can justly impute to me any act resembling oppression. I am now descending into the vale of life, and I must acknowledge that I look back with self-complacency upon what I have done, and am proud of having been an instrument in reclaiming such large and fruitful tracts from the waste of the creation.

And I question whether that sensation is not now a recompense more grateful to me than all the other profits I have reaped. Your good sense and knowledge of the world will excuse this seeming boast; if it be vain, we all must have our vanities, let it at least serve to show that industry has its reward, and age its pleasures, and be an encouragement to others to persevere and prosper.

In 1785 I visited the rough and hilly country of Otsego, where there existed not an inhabitant, nor any trace of a road; I was alone three hundred miles from home, without bread, meat, or food of any kind; fire and fishing tackle were my only means of subsistence. I caught trout in the brook, and roasted them on the ashes. My horse fed on the grass that grew by the edge of the waters. I laid me down to sleep in my watch-coat, nothing but the melancholy wilderness around me. In this way I explored the country, formed my plans of future settlement, and meditated upon the spot where a place of trade or a village should afterward be established.

In May, 1786, I opened the sales of 40,000 acres, which, in sixteen days, were all taken up by the poorest order of men. I soon after established a store, and went to live among them, and continued so to do till 1790, when I brought on my family. For the ensuing four years the scarcity of provisions was a serious calamity; the country was mountainous, there were neither roads nor bridges.

But the greatest discouragement was in the extreme poverty of the people, none of whom had the means of clearing more than a small spot in the midst of the thick and lofty woods, so that their grain grew chiefly in the shade; their maize did not ripen; their wheat was blasted, and the little they did gather they had no mill to grind within twenty miles distance: not one in twenty had a horse, and the way lay through rapid streams, across swamps, or over bogs. They had neither provisions to take with them, nor money to purchase them; nor if they had, were any to be found on their way. If the father of a family went abroad to labor for bread, it cost him three times its value before he could bring it home, and all the business on his farm stood still till his return.

I resided among them, and saw too clearly how bad their condition was. I erected a storehouse, and during each winter filled it with large quantities of grain, purchased in distant places. I procured from my friend Henry Drinker a credit for a large quantity of sugar kettles; he also lent me some potash kettles, which we conveyed as we best could; sometimes by partial roads on sleighs, and sometimes over the ice. By this means I established potash works among the settlers, and made them debtor for their bread and laboring utensils. I also gave them credit for their maple sugar and potash, at a price that would bear transportation, and the first year after the adoption of this plan I collected in one mass forty-three hogsheads of sugar, and three hundred barrels of pot and pearl ash, worth about nine thousand dollars. This kept the people together and at home, and the country soon assumed a new face.

I had not funds of my own sufficient for the opening of new roads, but I collected the people at convenient seasons, and by joint efforts we were able to throw bridges over the deep streams, and to make, in the cheapest manner, such roads as suited our then humble purposes.

In the winter preceding the summer of 1789, grain rose in Albany to a price before unknown. The demand swept the whole granaries of the Mohawk country. The number of beginners who depended upon it for their bread greatly aggravated the evil, and a famine ensued, which will never be forgotten by those who, tho now in the enjoyment of ease and comfort, were then afflicted with the cruelest of wants.

A singular event seemed sent by a good Providence to our relief; it was reported to me that unusual shoals of fish were seen moving in the clear waters of the Susquehanna. I went and was surprized to find that they were herrings. We made something like a small net, by the interweaving of twigs, and by this rude and simple contrivance we were able to take them in thousands. In less than ten days each family had an ample supply with plenty of salt. I also obtained from the Legislature, then in session, seventeen hundred bushels of corn. This we packed on horses' backs, and on our arrival made a distribution among the families, in proportion to the number of individuals of which each was composed.

This was the first settlement I made, and the first attempted after the revolution; it was, of course, attended with the greatest difficulties; nevertheless, to its success many others have owed their origin. It was besides the roughest land in all the State, and the most difficult of cultivation of all that has been settled;-but for many years past it has produced everything necessary to the support and comfort of man. It maintains at present eight thousand souls, with schools, academies, churches, meeting-houses, turnpike roads, and a market town. It annually yields to commerce large droves of fine oxen, great quantities of wheat and other grain, abundance of pork, potash in barrels, and other provisions; merchants with large capitals, and all kinds of useful mechanics reside upon it; the waters are stocked with fish, the air is salubrious, and the country thriving and happy. When I contemplate all this, and above all, when I see these good old settlers meet together, and hear them talk of past hardships, of which I bore my share, and compare the misery they then endured with the comforts they now enjoy, my emotions border upon weakness, which manhood can scarcely avow. One observation more on the duty of landlords shall close my answer to your first inquiry.

If the poor man who comes to purchase land has a cow and a yoke of cattle to bring with him, he is of the most fortunate class, but as he will probably have no money to hire a laborer, he must do all his clearing with his own hands. Having no pasture for his cow and oxen, they must range the woods for subsistence; he must find his cow before he can have his breakfast, and his oxen before he can begin his work. Much of the day is sometimes wasted, and his strength uselessly exhausted. Under all these disadvantages, if in three years he attains a comfortable livelihood, he is pretty well off: he will then require a barn, as great losses accrue from the want of shelter for his cattle and his grain; his children, yet too young to afford him any aid, require a school, and are a burden upon him; his wife bearing children, and living poorly in an open house, is liable to sickness and doctors' bills will be to pay.

THE YELLOW FEVER EPIDEMIC IN PHILADELPHIA
(1793)
by Matthew Carey

Carey was born in Dublin in 1760, and died in Philadelphia in 1839. He was a noted publicist and founded in Philadelphia a large publishing business. He also founded a newspaper, receiving financial aid from Lafayette. Among his friends was Franklin.

Philadelphia, in the latter part of the eighteenth century, suffered from two epidemics of yellow fever—one in 1793, which caused the death of 4,000 persons, and one in 1798, when 5,000 died.

Philadelphia was our nation's first capital city.

The consternation of the people of Philadelphia, at this period, was carried beyond all bounds. Dismay and affright were visible in almost every person's countenance. Most of those who could, by any means, make it convenient, fled from the city. Of those who remained, many shut themselves up in their houses, being afraid to walk the streets. The smoke of tobacco being regarded as a preventive, many persons, even women and small boys, had cigars almost constantly in their mouths. Others, placing full confidence in garlic, chewed it almost the whole day; some kept it in their pockets and shoes. Many were afraid to allow the barbers or hairdressers to come near them, as instances had occurred of some of them having shaved the dead, and many having engaged as bleeders. Some, who carried their caution pretty far, bought lancets for themselves, not daring to allow themselves to be bled with the lancets of the bleeders. Many houses were scarcely a moment in the day free from the smell of gunpowder, burned tobacco, niter, sprinkled vinegar, etc.

Some of the churches were almost deserted, and others wholly closed.

The coffee-house was shut up, as was the city library, and most of the public offices—three, out of the four, daily papers were discontinued, as were some of the others. Many devoted no small portion of their time to purifying, scouring, and whitewashing their rooms. Those who ventured abroad had handkerchiefs or sponges, impregnated with vinegar or camphor, at their noses, or smelling-bottles full of thieves' vinegar. Others carried pieces of tarred rope in their hands or pockets, or camphor bags tied round their necks. The corpses of the most respectable citizens, even of those who had not died of the epidemic, were carried to the grave on the shafts of a chair, the horse driven by a negro, unattended by a friend or relation, and without any sort of ceremony. People uniformly and hastily shifted their course at the sight of a hearse coming toward them. Many never walked on the foot-path, but went into the middle of the streets, to avoid being infected in passing houses wherein people had died. Acquaintances and friends avoided each other in the streets, and only signified their regard by a cold nod.

The old custom of shaking hands fell into such general disuse, that many shrunk back with affright at even the offer of the hand. A person with a crape, or any appearance of mourning, was shunned like a viper. And many valued themselves highly on the skill and address with which they got to windward of every person whom they met. Indeed, it is not probable that London, at the last stage of the plague exhibited stronger marks of terror than were to be seen in Philadelphia from the 25th or 26th of August till late in September. When the citizens summoned resolution to walk abroad, and take the air, the sick cart conveying patients to the hospital, or the hearse carrying the dead to the grave, which were travelling almost the whole day, soon damped their spirits and plunged them again into despondency.

While affairs were in this deplorable state, and people at the lowest ebb of despair, we can not be astonished at the frightful scenes that were acted, which seemed to indicate a total dissolution of the bonds of society in the nearest and dearest connections. Who, without horror, can reflect on a husband, married perhaps for twenty years, deserting his wife in the last agony—a wife, unfeelingly, abandoning her husband on his death-bed—parents forsaking their children—children ungratefully flying from their parents, and resigning them to chance, often without an inquiry after their health or safety—masters hurrying off their faithful servants to Bushhill, even on suspicion of the fever, and that at a time, when, almost like Tartarus, it was open to every visitant, but rarely returned any—servants abandoning tender and humane masters, who only wanted a little care to restore them to health and usefulness—who, I say, can think of these things without horror? Yet they were often exhibited throughout our city; and such was the force of habit, that the parties who were guilty of this cruelty, felt no remorse themselves—nor met with the censure from their fellow citizens which such conduct would have excited at any other period. Indeed, at this awful crisis, so much did *self* appear to engross the whole attention of many, that in some cases not more concern was felt for the loss of a parent, a husband, a wife, or an only child, than, on other occasions, would have been caused by the death of a faithful servant.

A pregnant woman, whose husband and two children lay dead in the room with her, was in the same situation as the former, without a midwife, or any other person to aid her. Her cries at the window brought up one of the carters employed by the committee for the relief of the sick. With his assistance she was delivered of a child, which died in a few minutes, as did the mother, who was utterly exhausted by her labor, by the disorder, and by the dreadful spectacle before her. And thus lay, in one room, no less than five dead bodies, an entire family, carried off within a few hours. Instances have occurred, of respectable women, who, in their lying-in, have been obliged to depend on their maid-servants for assistance—and some have had none but from their husbands. Some of the midwives were dead— and others had left the city.

A servant-girl, belonging to a family in this city, in which the fever had prevailed, was apprehensive of danger, and resolved to remove to a relation's house, in the country. She was, however, taken sick on the road, and returned to town, where she could find no person to receive her. One of the guardians of the poor provided a cart, and took her to the almshouse, into which she was refused admittance. She was brought back, but the guardian could not procure her a single night's lodging. And in fine, after every effort made to provide her shelter, she absolutely expired in the cart. This occurrence took place before Bushhill hospital was opened.

A drunken sailor lay in the street, in the Northern Liberties, for a few hours asleep, and was supposed by the neighbors to be dead with the disorder; but they were too much afraid to make personal examination. They sent to the committee at the city hall for a cart and coffin. The carter took the man by the heels, and was going to put him into the coffin. Handling him roughly he awoke, and cursing his eyes, asked him what he was about? The carter let him drop in a fright, and ran off as if a ghost was at his heels.

A lunatic, who had the malignant fever, was advised by his neighbors to go to Bushhill. He consented, and got into the cart; but soon changing his mind, he slipped out at the end, unknown to the carter, who, after a while, missing him, and seeing him at a distance running away, turned his horse about, and trotted hard after him. The other doubled his pace; and the carter whipped his horse to a gallop; but the man turned a corner and hid himself in a house, leaving the mortified carter to return, and deliver an account of his ludicrous adventure. Several instances have occurred of the carters on their arrival at Bushhill, and proceeded to deliver up their charge, finding, to their amazement, the carts empty.

A woman, whose husband died, refused to have him buried in a coffin provided for her by one of her friends, as too paltry and mean. She bought an elegant and costly one—and had the other laid by in the yard. In a week she was herself a corpse—and was buried in the very coffin she had so much despised.

The wife of a man who lived in Walnut Street was seized with the malignant fever, and given over by the doctors. The husband abandoned her, and next night lay out of the house for fear of catching the infection. In the morning, taking it for granted, from the very low state she had been in, that she was dead, he purchased a coffin for her; but, on entering the house, was surprized to see her much recovered. He fell sick shortly after, died, and was buried in the very coffin which he had so precipitately bought for his wife, who is still living.

FAREWELL ADDRESS
(1796)
by George Washington

At the end of his second term as President, Washington gave this message of farewell to his countrymen, warning them to beware of sectionalism, political factions, and entangling foreign alliances. The speech as given here has been abridged.

The unity of government which constitutes you one people is also now dear to you. It is justly so, for it is a main pillar in the edifice of your real independence, the support of your tranquillity at home, your peace abroad, of your safety, of your prosperity, of that very liberty which you so highly prize. But as it is easy to foresee that from different causes and from different quarters much pains will be taken, many artifices employed, to weaken in your minds the conviction of this truth, it is of infinite moment that you should properly estimate the immense value of your national union to your collective and individual happiness.

For this you have every inducement of sympathy and interest. Citizens by birth or choice of a common country, that country has a right to con-centrate your affections. The name of American, which belongs to you in your national capacity, must always exalt the just pride of patriotism more than any appellation derived from local discriminations. With slight shades of difference, you have the same religion, manners, habits, and political principles. You have in a common cause fought and triumphed together. The independence and liberty you possess are the work of joint councils and joint efforts, of common dangers, sufferings, and successes.

While every part of our country feels an immediate and particular interest in union, all the parts combined cannot fail to find in the united mass of means and efforts greater strength, greater resource, proportionably greater security from external danger, a less frequent interruption of their peace by foreign nations, and what is of inestimable value, they must derive from union an exemption from those broils and wars between themselves which so frequently afflict neighboring countries not tied together by the same governments, which their own rivalships alone would be sufficient to produce, but which opposite foreign alliances, attachments, and intrigues would stimulate and embitter. Hence, likewise, they will avoid the necessity of those overgrown military establishments which, under any form of government, are inauspicious to liberty, and which are to be regarded as particularly hostile to republican liberty. In this sense it is that your union ought to be considered as a main prop of your liberty, and that the love of the one ought to endear to you the preservation of the other.

These considerations speak a persuasive language to every reflecting and virtuous mind, and exhibit the continuance of the union as a primary object of patriotic desire. Is there a doubt whether a common government can embrace so large a sphere? Let experience solve it. To listen to mere speculation in such a case were criminal. It is well worth a fair and full experiment. With such powerful and obvious motives to union affecting all parts of our country, while experience shall not have demonstrated its impracticability, there will always be reason to distrust the patriotism of those who in any quarter may endeavor to weaken its bands.

To the efficacy and permanency of your union a government for the whole is indispensable. No alliances, however strict, between the parts can be an adequate substitute. They must inevitably experience the infractions and interruptions which all alliances in all times have experienced. Sensible of this momentous truth, you have improved upon your first essay by the adoption of a constitution of government better calculated than your former for an intimate union and for the efficacious management of your common concerns. This government has a just claim to your confidence and your support. Respect for its authority, compliance with its laws, acquiescence in its measures, are duties enjoined by the fundamental maxims of true liberty. The basis of our political systems is the right of the people to make and to alter their constitutions of government. But the constitution which at any time exists till changed by an explicit and authentic act of the whole people is sacredly obligatory upon all. The very idea of the power and the right of the people to establish government presupposes the duty of every individual to obey the established government.

All obstructions to the execution of the laws, all combinations and associations, under whatever plausible character, with the real design to direct, control, counteract, or awe the regular deliberation and action of the constituted authorities, are destructive of this fundamental principle and of fatal tendency. They serve to organize faction; to give it an artificial and extraordinary force; to put in the place of the delegated will of the nation the will of a party, often a small but artful and enterprising minority of the community, and, according to the alternate triumphs of different parties, to make the public administration the mirror of the ill-concerted and incongruous projects of faction rather than the organ of consistent and wholesome plans, digested by common counsels and modified by mutual interests.

However combinations or associations of the above description may now and then answer popular ends, they are likely in the course of time and things to become potent engines by which cunning, ambitious, and unprincipled men will be enabled to subvert the power of the people, and to usurp for themselves the reins of government, destroying afterwards the very engines which have lifted them to unjust dominion.

Observe good faith and justice toward all nations. Cultivate peace and harmony with all. Religion and morality enjoin this conduct. And can it be that good policy does not equally enjoin it? The nation which indulges toward another an habitual hatred or an habitual fondness is in some degree a slave. It is a slave to its animosity or to its affection, either of which is sufficient to lead it astray from its duty and its interest.

Antipathy in one nation against another disposes each more readily to offer insult and injury, to lay hold of slight causes of umbrage, and to be haughty and intractable when accidental or trifling occasions of dispute occur.

So, likewise, a passionate attachment of one nation for another produces a variety of evils. Sympathy for the favorite nation, facilitating the illusion of an imaginary common interest in cases where no real common interest exists, and infusing into one the enmities of the other, betrays the former into a participation in the quarrels and wars of the latter without adequate inducement or justification. It leads also to concessions to the favorite nation of privileges denied to others, which is apt doubly to injure the nation making the concessions by unnecessarily parting with what ought to have been retained, and by exciting jealousy, ill will, and a disposition to retaliate in the parties from whom equal privileges are withheld.

As avenues to foreign influence in innumerable ways, such attachments are particularly alarming to the truly enlightened and independent patriot. How many opportunities do they afford to tamper with domestic factions, to practice the arts of seduction, to mislead public opinion, to influence or awe the public councils! Such an attachment of a small or weak toward a great and powerful nation dooms the former to be the satellite of the latter. Against the insidious wiles of foreign influence (I conjure you to believe me, fellow citizens) the jealousy of a free people ought to be *constantly* awake, since history and experience prove that foreign influence is one of the most baneful foes of republican government. But that jealousy, to be useful, must be impartial, else it becomes the instrument of the very influence to be avoided, instead of a defense against it. Excessive partiality for one foreign nation and excessive dislike of another cause those whom they actuate to see danger only on one side, and serve to veil and even second the arts of influence on the other. Real patriots who may resist the intrigues of the favorite are liable to become suspected and odious, while its tools and dupes usurp the applause and confidence of the people to surrender their interests.

The great rule of conduct for us in regard to foreign nations is, in extending our commercial relations to have with them as little *political* connection as possible. So far as we have already formed engagements let them be fulfilled with perfect good faith. Here let us stop.

Europe has a set of primary interests which to us have none or a very remote relation. Hence she must be engaged in frequent controversies, the causes of which are essentially foreign to our concerns. Hence, therefore, it must be unwise in us to implicate ourselves by artifical ties in the ordinary vicissitudes of her politics or the ordinary combinations and collisions of her friendships or enmities.

Our detached and distant situation invites and enables us to pursue a different course. If we remain one people, under an efficient government, the period is not far off when we may defy material injury from external annoyance; when we may take such an attitude as will cause the neutrality we may at any time resolve upon to be scrupulously respected; when belligerent nations, under the impossibility of making acquisitions upon us, will not lightly hazard the giving us provocation; when we may choose peace or war, as our interest, guided by justice, shall counsel.

Why forego the advantages of so peculiar a situation? Why quit our own to stand upon foreign ground? Why, by interweaving our destiny with that of any part of Europe, entangle our peace and prosperity in the toils of European ambition, rivalship, interest, humor, or caprice?

THE BEGINNINGS OF THE CITY OF WASHINGTON

(1800)

by Abigail Adams

Abigail Adams was the wife of President John Adams. It was near the end of Adams' administration that Washington was first occupied by the Federal government. At that time the place was entirely open country, scarcely more than a wilderness, in which appeared several buildings in process of construction. This letter, written in Washington on November 21, 1800, was addressed by Mrs. Adams to her daughter, Mrs. Smith.

I arrived here on Sunday last, and without meeting with any accident worth noticing, except losing ourselves when we left Baltimore, and going eight or nine miles on the Frederick road, by which means we were obliged to go the other eight through woods, where we wandered two hours without finding a guide or the path. Fortunately, a straggling black came up with us, and we engaged him as a guide, to extricate us out of our difficulty; but woods are all you see, from Baltimore until you reach the city, which is only so in name. Here and there is a small cot, without a glass window, interspersed among the forests, through which you travel miles without seeing any human being. In the city there are buildings enough, if they were compact and finished, to accommodate Congress and those attached to it; but as they are, and scattered as they are, I see not great comfort for them.

The river, which runs up to Alexandria, is in full view of my window, and I see the vessels as they pass and repass. The house is upon a grand and superb scale, requiring about thirty servants to attend and keep the apartments in proper order, and perform the ordinary business of the house and stables; an establishment very well proportioned to the President's salary. The lighting of apartments, from the kitchen to parlors and chambers, is a tax indeed; and the fires we are obliged to keep to secure us from daily agues is another very cheering comfort. To assist us in this great castle, and render less attendance necessary, bells are wholly wanting, not one single one being hung through the whole house, and promises are all you can obtain. This is so great an inconvenience that I know not what to do, or how to do. The ladies from Georgetown and in the city have many of them visited me. Yesterday I returned fifteen visits—but such a place as Georgetown appears—why, our Milton is beautiful. But no comparisons —if they will put me up some bells, and let me have wood enough to keep fires, I design to be pleased.

I could content myself almost anywhere three months; but, surrounded with forests, can you believe that wood is not to be had, because people can not be found to cut and cart it! Briesler entered into a contract with a man to supply him with wood. A small part, a few cords only, has he been able to get. Most of that was expended to dry the walls of the house before we came in, and yesterday the man told him it was impossible for him to procure it to be cut and carted. He has had recourse to coals; but we can not get grates made and set. We have, indeed, come into a new country.

You must keep all this to yourself, and when asked how I like it, say that I write you the situation is beautiful, which is true. The house is made habitable, but there is not a single apartment finished, and all withinside, except the plastering, has been done since Briesler came. We have not the least fence, yard, or other convenience, without, and the great unfinished audienceroom I make a drying-room of, to hang up the clothes in. The principal stairs are not up, and will not be this winter. Six chambers are made comfortable; two are occupied by the President and Mr. Shaw; two lower rooms, one for a common parlor, and one for a levee-room. Upstairs there is the oval room, which is designed for the drawing-room, and has the crimson furniture in it. It is a very handsome room now; but, when completed it will be beautiful.

If the twelve years in which this place has been considered as the future seat of government had been improved, as they would have been if in New England, very many of the present inconveniences would have been removed. It is a beautiful spot, capable of every improvement, and, the more I view it the more I am delighted with it.

Since I sat down to write I have been called down to a servant from Mount Vernon, with a billet from Major Custis, and a haunch of venison, and a kind, congratulatory letter from Mrs. Lewis, upon my arrival in the city, with Mrs. Washington's love, inviting me to Mount Vernon, where, health permitting, I will go, before I leave this place.

The Senate is much behindhand. No Congress has yet been made. 'Tis said—— ——is on his way, but travels with so many delicacies in his rear that he can not get on fast, lest some of them should suffer.

Thomas comes in and says a House is made; so to-morrow, tho Saturday, the President will meet them. Adieu, my dear. Give my love to your brother, and tell him he is ever present upon my mind.

GROWTH AND STRUGGLES

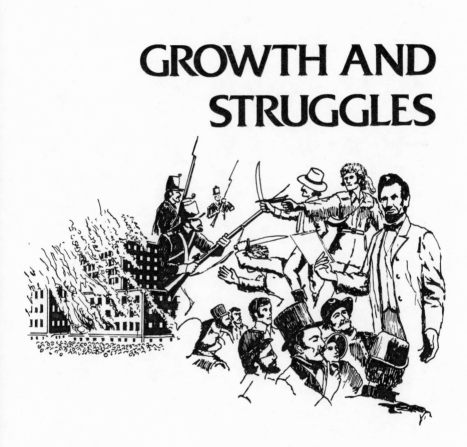

GROWTH AND STRUGGLES

Under Jefferson's administration, the United States made advances, population pushed westward, and, except during the embargo period, commerce increased. The purchase of Louisiana from Napoleon more than doubled the area of the country. The Lewis and Clark expedition opened that vast Northwestern region to the people and spurred emigration into it.

As Jefferson's administration drew to a close, however, the foreign relations of the United States were troubled. Jefferson declined a third election and was succeeded by James Madison of Virginia. The new President had been a member of the Continental Congress, a delegate to the Constitutional Convention of 1787, and Secretary of State under Jefferson. He owed his election to the Democratic party, whose sympathy with France and hostility to Great Britain were well-known.

The commercial troubles with England multiplied, until President Jefferson was forced by public sentiment to recommend an embargo; no vessel, American or foreign, could leave an American port unless the President suspended the act. The effects of the embargo a year later were disappointing to the United States. English and French trade had not been seriously injured, but the American export trade had been almost destroyed. Farmers faced ruin, New England ports closed down, and Virginia, unable to sell tobacco, found herself almost bankrupt. The embargo had been popular enough when imposed, but its effects turned the public against it. The embargo did, however, delay for a few years a second war with England.

A second war with England had long been foreshadowed by her aggressions on our commerce. Diplomacy had been tried in vain. Retaliation by non-intercourse acts and an embargo had resulted in greater harm to ourselves than to the offenders. Finally, Congress voted for war.

At the beginning, the war was popular throughout the country, except with New England shipmasters and merchants. Operations began on our northern frontier. Two expeditions were dispatched to Canada, one by way of Niagara, one by Detroit. The first failed to gain possession of the country beyond a few frontier forts, the second ended in a disastrous retreat and the loss of Detroit, Fort Dearborn (Chicago), and Mackinac Island, in what is today northern Michigan. These disasters were relieved by the splendid victory of Perry on Lake Erie and the work of our land forces at Chippewa.

More memorable still were the victories won by our Navy. On August 19, 1812, England's chief offender in making illegal searches of American ships, the H.M.S. *Guerriere,* was captured by the U.S.S. *Constitution* ("Old Ironsides"); the H.M.S. *Macedonian* by the U.S.S. *United States.* The *Constitution* went on to capture the H.M.S. *Java* and other ships. Later came MacDonough's victory on Lake Champlain. Six months of naval warfare led to American successes that astonished Europeans who remembered Nelson's victories at Copenhagen, Aboukir Bay, and Trafalgar. One notable defeat came to us—that of Lawrence, with the U.S.S. *Chesapeake* lost to the H.M.S. *Shannon.* American privateers took up the war in 1813, capturing more than four hundred prizes. In spite of all these successes our merchant ships suffered badly; by the end of the war the American flag had almost ceased to float on merchant ships.

The Treaty of Ghent, however, left matters between us and England very much where they were in 1812; not one of the distinctive issues of the war was settled or even mentioned. The advantages to us lay in a great and new prestige won for us in Europe by "Old Hickory" and "Old Ironsides."

The greatest American victory came after the articles of peace were signed. The battle of New Orleans, in which Andrew Jackson ("Old Hickory"), with his frontier riflemen, swept away the Peninsular Veterans of Sir Edward Pakenham, occurred fifteen days after peace had been made, but before the news had crossed the Atlantic to America.

After the war our population increased rapidly. Industries revived everywhere, and an era of prosperity set in. Meanwhile, in Florida the Seminoles had become troublesome to American settlers, and the Spanish authorities had completely failed to preserve order. General Jackson, in consequence, virtually took possession of Florida, and soon afterwards it was annexed to the United States. On every frontier, American soldiers and settlers were forcing back the Indians, opening new territories to settlements. Pioneers in great volume now poured into the Middle West.

These movements were helped forward immensely by new mechanical inventions such as the steamboat of Robert Fulton, which by 1820 had promoted much steam navigation on inland waters—the Hudson, the Mississippi, and the Great Lakes. Plans were made for an extensive system of roads and canals, first of which was the Erie Canal. Within a few years a vast network of railroads also covered the nation.

Andrew Jackson's accession to the Presidency in 1828 was in some measure a revolution, not only in the political but in the social tone of his administration. Hitherto all the presidents had been gentlemen, educated, and experienced in public affairs. Jackson made no pretensions to culture or refinement, and many of the coarse elements of his former life were evident during his term of office. The Jackson administration marked the victory of the boisterous, democratic West over the respectable, aristocratic East. When President Jackson vetoed the National Bank charter, he did so largely as a Westerner trying to keep the East from growing too powerful.

A new era had dawned upon the whole country. The era of canals, farm machinery, steamboats, railroads, and ocean steamships cemented the states together in an industrial union. The Jacksonian era, in the transformation it effected, was the most notable in the history of the country between the Revolution and the Civil War. That economic transformation was really the basis of the political transformation. Both had been made possible largely by the mechanical inventions of the age.

The Missouri Compromise of 1820 had preserved a numerical balance between slave states and free states, but it had also forbidden the expansion of slavery north of the 36° 30′ line. The Mexican-American War (1846–48), however, enabled the South to extend slavery below that parallel. The war with Mexico that followed American annexation of Texas was long foreseen, and by the frontiersman, if not by the Federal administration, was desired. Its conclusion secured to the Union a vast country in the southwest and far west, out of which five states and parts of two others have since been created. Except for California, which did not come directly from the defeat of Mexico, that war added an enormous area that soon became open to slavery.

Almost coincident with these events came the final settlement of the Oregon boundary, with new emigration to Oregon, and in 1848 the organization of that country into a territory. This addition of non-slaveholding territory counterbalanced the acquisitions made by Southern interests in the southwest. Within two years from the conclusion of peace with Mexico, the Fugitive Slave Law passed Congress. This law provided for the arrest and return of escaped slaves, who were to be considered as any other lost or stolen property. Two notable outcomes ensued from its enforcement. One was the "underground railway," by which Northern abolitionists assisted escaping slaves to reach Canada. The other was a book, which more than all the speeches of agitators and all the preaching from pulpits, made antislavery sentiment in the North a political rather than a social force—Mrs. Stowe's *Uncle Tom's Cabin.*

At this period the Abolition Movement, after eleven years of activity, had measurably overcome the strong opposition it had formerly encountered in the North and had drawn within its folds many eminent men. It found a powerful ally, one which eventually was to absorb it, in the Republican party. Then came the Supreme Court's Dred Scott Decision (1857), which in effect opened a vast territory beyond the Mississippi to slavery.

Republicans were furious; three years later, they nominated an enemy of slavery, Abraham Lincoln, for President. Meanwhile the Democrats split up between two candidates, Douglas and Breckenridge. Southerners talked openly of leaving the Union if Lincoln won.

The election of Lincoln was a triumph for many political elements that, before his ascendency, had been groping blindly toward similar ends. Some of these were old-time Whigs, others new-time Abolitionists, some Free Soil Men, others Union Democrats. But all were eager for the salvation of the Union, as they saw it, and all were now marching under a common banner as Republicans.

To the Southern states Lincoln's election came with a force of an appalling calamity. No longer did their leaders see any peaceable legislative way out of the country's wearisome intestinal strife. All the forces with which they had ever contended were now united against them, and victorious in their unity. They honestly believed Lincoln's election meant the overthrow of slavery, without which they could no longer prosper or perhaps exist. Lincoln insisted in vain that he had no intention to destroy slavery, that his prime purpose was to save the Union, and that so far as slavery was concerned, his only wish was to prevent its extension. A month before he was inaugurated six states had seceded and set up a government of their own. The Civil War opened on April 12, 1861, when Southern forces fired on Fort Sumter, off the coast of Charleston, South Carolina.

Once the war began, industrial conditions operated powerfully to the advantage of the North. The South had no large enterprises to supply an army with guns, powder, clothing, surgical instruments, and medicine. All these indispensable things it had to import from Europe. Early in the war the North blockaded Southern ports from the Chesapeake to the mouth of the Mississippi, and supplies had to be brought in by running the blockade or entering the country by way of Texas, which was a slow and costly process, and made supplies scarce.

The South also lacked money. Her great planters were rich in land, cotton, tobacco, and slaves, but until their crops had been sold, they were often in debt, and now with the ports blockaded, their market for sales of crops was cut off. Before the war their exports of cotton had amounted to $202,000,000 annually; in 1862 they fell to $4,000,000. The resources of the South constantly diminished, not only in arms, ammunition, and clothing, but in the supply of soldiers. In 1860 the population of the seceding states did not number much more than one-third as many men as the North, and of these much more than a quarter were slaves.

The ability of the South to prolong the war for four consecutive years was due to her intense spirit of devotion. Her soldiers were also better marksmen and better horsemen, the conditions of their domestic life having taught them skill in these matters. One other great advantage lay in being on the defensive against an invader. This not only awakened a livelier sense of wrong and a keener sense of duty, but also gave them the advantage of being in a country that was better known to them than to the enemy.

In four years of war, the two armies fought more than 10,000 military actions including over 70 full-scale battles. The deaths due to military operations are believed to have exceeded 500,000, of whom three-fifths were Northern and two-fifths Southern men. At Gettysburg 43,000 were killed and wounded; at Chickamauga and Chattanooga the losses were equally appalling.

What the war cost in money and property can never be known, but the North emerged from the war with a national debt of almost $3,000,000,-000. (The wars of Napoleon, extending over four and a half times as long a period, are estimated to have added to the national debt of France only $487,000,000.)

General Robert E. Lee and his exhausted Army of Virginia finally surrendered to Ulysses S. Grant of the North at Appomattox Court House on April 9, 1865. Soon the remaining Southern forces too gave up the struggle. During the summer of 1865 the great armies were disbanded, and the victors and vanquished returned to their homes to resume the work of peace.

On the evening of the fourteenth of April the President attended Ford's theater with his wife and a party of friends. As the play drew near its close, a disreputable actor, named John Wilkes Booth, stole unnoticed into the Presidential box, leveled a pistol at his head, and shot him through the brain. Lincoln fell forward in his seat, was borne from the building, lingered in an unconscious state until the following morning, and died. The assassin and his fellow conspirators were all soon caught and punished.

On March 2, 1867, an act was passed by Congress by which the ten seceded states were divided into five military districts, each district under the control of a governor appointed by the President. Of the desolation, the political and social misery inflicted on the South by the Reconstruction Act, no adequate story has been written. A horde of unscrupulous adventurers from the North were permitted to take control of the state governments, aided by mostly illiterate black men having majorities in the legislatures. These Negro legislatures and plundering "carpet-baggers," with federal troops helping them to maintain supremacy, debauched and made miserable the whole social, industrial, and political life of the South. After the final withdrawal of troops in 1877, more normal conditions returned to the South.

In addition reconstruction caused the nation further difficulties when friendly relations between Congress and the chief executive broke down completely. Lincoln's successor, Andrew Johnson, held views toward the

South very similar to those of Lincoln; what he lacked in woeful degree was Lincoln's tact and vision, and his experience of public life. On March 3 of 1868 articles of impeachment were agreed to by the House of Representatives, and the cause against the President of the United States was immediately remanded to the Senate for trial. Proceedings were instituted in that body on March 23, and continued until March 26, when the question was submitted to a vote of senators, acting as judges. Mr. Johnson was acquitted by a single vote. Thus the country was spared from further reconstruction disgrace.

Immediately after the war the Atlantic cable was laid successfully, by which the old world and the new, now at last, though divided by 3,000 miles of water, had almost instantaneous communication one with the other. The same period saw the purchase of Alaska for $7,200,000. A territory of 590,000 square miles, or more than the area of the original thirteen states, had now been added to the Republic.

In 1868 Ulysses S. Grant was elected the eighteenth President of the United States. The first event by which the new administration was signalized was the completion of the transcontinental railroad in May of 1869. In addition two new amendments to the Constitution were adopted. The first of these, the Fourteenth Amendment, extended the rights of citizenship to all persons born or naturalized in the United States. The Fifteenth Amendment provided that the rights of citizens of the United States to vote should not be denied or abridged on account of race, color, or previous condition of servitude. This article was intended to confer the right of suffrage on the emancipated blacks of the South.

In 1870 the ninth census of the United States showed that, notwithstanding the ravages of the Civil War, the American population had increased from 31,433,000 to 38,587,000. The national debt, though still enormous, had been considerably reduced, and now American manufacturers were competing with those of England in the markets of the world. The Union embraced 37 states and 11 territories. From the narrow limits of the 13 original colonies, with their 420,000 square miles of territory, the national domain had spread to 3,640,000 square miles.

In 1872, Grant overwhelmingly defeated Horace Greeley, the distinguished editor of the New York *Tribune,* and returned to the White House for a second term. Grant's second four years as President were contaminated with one scandal after another, the most famous being the Credit Mobilier investigation in Congress. In 1872 a law suit in Pennsylvania revealed the startling fact that much of the stock of the Credit Mobilier was owned by members of Congress. This led to a congressional investigation, in the course of which many scandalous transactions were brought to light; the faith of the people in the integrity of their public servants was greatly shaken. This precipitated in the autumn of 1873 one of the most disastrous financial panics in the history of the United States.

Meanwhile, gold was discovered among the Black Hills in the Dakotas, a region belonging by treaty to the Sioux nation. But no treaty could keep the hungry horde of white gold diggers and adventurers from overrunning the interdicted district. Congressional policy now became one of weakening the power of the chiefs and their tribal organizations. Pressured by a reform movement spearheaded by Helen Hunt Jackson's *A Century of Dishonor,* Congress passed the Dawes Act, giving plots of land and American citizenship to Indians. Although the act was not a panacea, it at least did not crush the Indian culture nor wipe their traditions from memory.

Rutherford Burchard Hayes, nineteenth President of the United States, was born in Ohio, completed his legal studies at Harvard, and later became the city solicitor in Cincinnati where he won a distinguished reputation as a lawyer. In his inaugural address he assured the South of right purposes on the part of the new chief executive; some have referred to this as the beginning of a second "Era of Good Feeling." The summer of 1877 was notable in American history for the great labor disturbance known as The Railroad Strike resulting in rioting in Pittsburgh, Chicago, St. Louis, Cincinnati, Columbus, Indianapolis, Louisville, and Fort Wayne. James A. Garfield was inaugurated the twentieth President of the United States in 1881 and on the morning of July 2, at the Baltimore Railway Station in Washington, was assassinated by a political radical named Charles Jules Guiteau. On the eightieth day after the shot was fired, Garfield died, making vice-president Chester A. Arthur the new chief executive. It was during this new administration that such inventions as the Bell telephone, the phonograph, and the electric light were consummated.

For six successive administrations the Republican party had been in control. But Grover Cleveland and the Democrats came to power in 1884. A lawyer and former governor of New York, the twenty-second President was inaugurated in 1885 for his first of two terms. During his second administration the panic of 1893 struck, causing considerable economic hardship to the nation. Benjamin Harrison interrupted Cleveland's two terms and is considered the twenty-third President of the United States. A Republican who served in the Civil War and was later elected a United States senator from Indiana, he stood for high tariffs and supported the first Pan-American conference in 1889.

A gold standard party platform and the economic conditions blamed on the Democrats assured Republican William McKinley's election as the twenty-fourth President of the United States. McKinley led the United States into war with Spain in 1898, although there is strong evidence that Spain was willing to make concessions to avoid bloodshed. After the American victory and the acquisition of the Philippine Islands, McKinley supported an Open Door Policy in China. He was reelected in 1900 only to be assassinated the following year in Buffalo, New York, by an anarchist named Leon Czolgosz.

FULTON'S STEAMBOAT
(1807)
by Robert Fulton

Two letters by Fulton, the first being addressed to a newspaper, The American
Citizen; *the second to Joel Barlow, the poet. Although his* Clermont, *launched in
1807, was not the first steamboat in America, it was the first commercial success on
this continent. In his day he was as well-known for his painting and engineering as
his inventions. Born in 1765, he died in 1815.*

FIRST LETTER

I arrived this afternoon at four o'clock in the steamboat from Albany.
As the success of my experiment gives me great hopes that such boats may
be rendered of great importance to my country, to prevent erroneous opinions and give some satisfaction to my friends of useful improvements, you
will have the goodness to publish the following statement of facts:

I left New York on Monday at one o'clock and arrived at Clermont,
the seat of Chancellor Livingston, at one o'clock on Tuesday: time, twenty-
four hours; distance, one hundred and ten miles. On Wednesday I departed
from the Chancellor's at nine in the morning, and arrived at Albany at five
in the afternoon: distance, forty miles; time, eight hours. The sum is one
hundred and fifty miles in thirty-two hours, equal to near five miles an
hour.

On Thursday, at nine o'clock in the morning, I left Albany, and arrived
at the Chancellor's at six in the evening. I started from thence at seven,
and arrived at New York at four in the afternoon: time, thirty hours; space
run through, one hundred and fifty miles, equal to five miles an hour.
Throughout my whole way, both going and returning, the wind was ahead.
No advantage could be derived from my sails. The whole has therefore
been performed by the power of the steam-engine.

SECOND LETTER

My steamboat voyage to Albany and back has turned out rather more
favorably than I had calculated. The distance from New York to Albany

is one hundred and fifty miles. I ran it up in thirty-two hours, and down in thirty. I had a light breeze against me the whole way, both going and coming; and the voyage has been performed wholly by the power of the steam-engine. I overtook many sloops and schooners beating to windward, and parted with them.

The power of propelling boats by steam is now fully proved. The morning I left New York there were not perhaps thirty persons in the city who believed that the boat would ever move one mile an hour or be of the least utility; and, while we were putting off from the wharf, which was crowded with spectators, I heard a number of sarcastic remarks. This is the way in which ignorant men compliment what they call philosophers and projectors.

Having employed much time, money, and zeal in accomplishing this work, it gives me, as it will you, great pleasure to see it answer my expectations. It will give a cheap and quick conveyance to the merchandize on the Mississippi, Missouri, and other great rivers, which are now laying open their treasures to the enterprise of our countrymen; and, altho the prospect of personal emolument has been some inducement to me, yet I feel infinitely more pleasure in reflecting on the immense advantage my country will derive.

"OLD IRONSIDES" DEFEATS THE GUERRIÈRE

(1812)

by Captain William Orme

Captain Orme was an American naval officer who had been captured by the Guerrière off Newfoundland only a few days before the battle with the Constitution. Here is his report to his superiors.

I commanded the American brig *Betsey,* in the year 1812, and was returning home from Naples, Italy, to Boston. When near the western edge of the Grand Bank of Newfoundland, on the 10th of August, 1812, I fell in with the British frigate *Guerrière,* Captain Dacres, and was captured by him. Myself and a boy were taken on board of the frigate; the remainder of my officers and men were left in the *Betsey,* and sent into Halifax, N.S., as a prize to the *Guerrière.*

On the 19th of the same month, the wind being fresh from the northward, the *Guerrière* was under double-reefed topsails during all the forenoon of this day. At 2 P.M. we discovered a large sail to windward, bearing about North from us. We soon made her out to be a frigate. She was steering off from the wind, with her head to the southwest, evidently with the intention of cutting us off as soon as possible.

Signals were soon made by the *Guerrière,* but as they were not answered, the conclusion of course was, that she was either a French or an American frigate. Captain Dacres appeared anxious to ascertain her character, and after looking at her for that purpose, handed me his spy-glass, requesting me to give him my opinion of the stranger. I soon saw from the peculiarity of her sails, and from her general appearance, that she was, without doubt, an American frigate, and communicated the same to Captain Dacres. He immediately replied, that he thought she came down too boldly for an American, but soon after added, "The better he behaves, the more honor we shall gain by taking him."

The two ships were rapidly approaching each other, when the *Guerrière* backed her maintopsail, and waited for her opponent to come down, and commence the action. He then set an English flag at each masthead, beat to quarters, and made ready for the fight. When the strange frigate came down to within two or three miles distance, he hauled upon the wind, took in all his light sails, reefed his topsails, and deliberately prepared for action. It was now about five o'clock in the afternoon, when he filled away and ran down for the *Guerrière.* At this moment, Captain Dacres politely said to me: "Captain Orme, as I suppose you do not wish to fight against your own countrymen, you are at liberty to go below the water-line." It was not long after this before I retired from the quarter-deck to the cockpit.

Of course I saw no more of the action until the firing ceased, but I heard and felt much of its effects; for soon after I left the deck, the firing commenced on board the *Guerrière,* and was kept up almost constantly until about six o'clock, when I heard a tremendous explosion from the opposing frigate. The effect of her shot seemed to make the *Guerrière* reel and tremble as tho she had received the shock of an earthquake. Immediately after this, I heard a tremendous crash on deck, and was told the mizzenmast was shot away. In a few moments afterward the cockpit was filled with wounded men.

At about half-past six o'clock in the evening, after the firing had ceased, I went on deck, and there beheld a scene which it would be difficult to describe: all the *Guerrière's* masts were shot away, and as she had no sails to steady her, she lay rolling like a log in the trough of the sea. The decks were covered with blood, the gun tackles were not made fast, and several of the guns got loose, and were surging to and fro from one side to the other.

Some of the petty officers and seamen, after the action, got liquor, and were intoxicated; and what with the groans of the wounded, the noise and confusion of the enraged survivors on board of the ill-fated ship, rendered the whole scene fearful beyond description.

THE BURNING OF WASHINGTON BY THE BRITISH
(1814)
by Rev. G. R. Gleig

By Rev. George Robert Gleig, who served in the British army during the war and was present at the capture and burning of Washington. He published, after the war, "A Narrative of the Campaign of the British Army at Washington and New Orleans."

Toward morning a violent storm of rain, accompanied with thunder and lightning, came on, which disturbed the rest of all those who were exposed to it. Yet, in spite of the disagreeableness of getting wet, I can not say that I felt disposed to grumble at the interruption, for it appeared that what I had before considered as superlatively sublime, still wanted this to render it complete. The flashes of lightning seemed to vie in brilliancy with the flames which burst from the roofs of burning houses, while the thunder drowned the noise of crumbling walls, and was only interrupted by the occasional roar of cannon, and of large depots of gunpowder, as they one by one exploded.

The consternation of the inhabitants was complete, and to them this was a night of terror. So confident had they been of the success of their troops, that few of them had dreamed of quitting their houses, or abandoning the city; nor was it till the fugitives from the battle began to rush in, filling every place as they came with dismay, that the President himself thought of providing for his safety. That gentleman, as I was credibly informed, had gone forth in the morning with the army, and had continued among his troops till the British forces began to make their appearance. Whether the sight of his enemies cooled his courage or not I can not say, but, according to my informer, no sooner was the glittering of our arms discernible than he began to discover that his presence was more wanted in the Senate than with the army; and having ridden through the ranks, and exhorted every man to do his duty, he hurried back to his own house, that he might prepare a feast for the entertainment of his officers, when they should return victorious. For the truth of these details I will not be answerable; but this much I know, that the feast was actually prepared, tho, instead of being devoured by American officers, it went to satisfy the less delicate appetites of a party of English soldiers. When the detachment, sent out to destroy Mr. Madison's house, entered his dining parlor, they found a dinner table spread, and covers laid for forty guests.

They sat down to it, therefore, not indeed in the most orderly manner, but with countenances which would not have disgraced a party of aldermen at a civic feast; and having satisfied their appetites with fewer complaints than would have probably escaped their rival *gourmands,* and partaken pretty freely of the wines, they finished by setting fire to the house which had so liberally entertained them.

But, as I have just observed, this was a night of dismay to the inhabitants of Washington. They were taken completely by surprize; nor could the arrival of the flood be more unexpected to the natives of the antediluvian world, than the arrival of the British army to them. The first impulse of course tempted them to fly, and the streets were in consequence crowded with soldiers and senators, men, women, and children, horses, carriages, and carts loaded with household furniture, all hastening toward a wooden bridge which crosses the Potomac. The confusion thus occasioned was terrible, and the crowd upon the bridge was such as to endanger its giving way. But Mr. Madison, having escaped among the first, was no sooner safe on the opposite bank of the river than he gave orders that the bridge should be broken down; which being obeyed, the rest were obliged to return, and to trust to the clemency of the victors.

In this manner was the night passed by both parties; and at daybreak next morning the light brigade moved into the city, while the reserve fell back to a height about half a mile in the rear. Little, however, now remained to be done, because everything marked out for destruction was already consumed. Of the senate-house, the President's palace, the barracks, the dockyard, etc., nothing could be seen, except heaps of smoking ruins; and even the bridge, a noble structure upward of a mile in length, was almost wholly demolished. There was, therefore, no farther occasion to scatter the troops, and they were accordingly kept together as much as possible on the Capitol hill.

"WHO READS AN AMERICAN BOOK?"
(1820)
by Sidney Smith

This article, immediately after its publication, and for many years, led to intense indignation in the United States; indeed, one frequently finds the title cited now. The article appeared originally in the Edinburgh Review *for January, 1820, Smith having been one of the founders of that periodical.*

Thus far we are the friends and admirers of Jonathan. But he must not grow vain and ambitious; nor allow himself to be dazzled by that galaxy of epithets by which his orators and newspaper scribblers endeavor to persuade their supporters that they are the greatest, the most refined, the most enlightened, and the most moral people upon earth. The effect of this is unspeakably ludicrous on this side of the Atlantic—and, even on the other, we should imagine, must be rather humiliating to the reasonable part of the population.

The Americans are a brave, industrious, and acute people; but they have hitherto given no indications of genius, and made no approaches to the heroic, either in their morality or character. They are but a recent offset indeed from England; and should make it their chief boast, for many generations to come, that they are sprung from the same race with Bacon and Shakespeare and Newton. Considering their numbers, indeed, and the favorable circumstances in which they have been placed, they have yet done marvelously little to assert the honor of such a descent, or to show that their English blood has been exalted or refined by their republican training and institutions. Their Franklins and Washingtons, and all the other sages and heroes of their revolution, were born and bred subjects of the King of England—and not among the freest or most valued of his subjects: And, since the period of their separation, a far greater proportion of their statesmen and artists and political writers have been foreigners, than ever occurred before in the history of any civilized and educated people.

During the thirty or forty years of their independence, they have done absolutely nothing for the Sciences, for the Arts, for Literature, or even for the statesman-like studies of Politics or Political Economy. Confining ourselves to our own country, and to the period that has elapsed since *they* had an independent existence, we would ask, Where are their Foxes, their Burkes, their Sheridans, their Windhams, their Horners, their Wilberforces?—where their Arkwrights, their Watts, their Davys?—their Robertsons, Blairs, Smiths, Stewarts, Paleys and Malthuses?—their Porsons, Parrs, Burneys, or Blomfields?—their Scotts, Campbells, Byrons, Moores, or Crabbes?—their Siddonses, Kembles, Keans, or O'Neils—their Wilkies, Laurences, Chantrys?—or their parallels to the hundred other names that have spread themselves over the world from our little island in the course of the last thirty years, and blest or delighted mankind by their works, inventions, or examples?

In so far as we know, there is no such parallel to be produced from the whole annals of this self-adulating race. In the four quarters of the globe, who reads an American book? or goes to an American play? or looks at an American picture or statue? What does the world yet owe to American physicians or surgeons? What new substances have their chemists discovered? or what old ones have they analyzed? What new constellations have been discovered by the telescopes of Americans?—what have they done in the mathematics? Who drinks out of American glasses? or eats from American plates? or wears American coats or gowns? or sleeps in American blankets?—Finally, under which of the old tyrannical governments of Europe is every sixth man a slave, whom his fellow creatures may buy and sell and torture?

When these questions are fairly and favorably answered, their laudatory epithets may be allowed: But, till that can be done, we would seriously advise them to keep clear of superlatives.

HOW A LOG CABIN WAS BUILT
(1822)
by A Pioneer Woman

In building our cabin it was set north and south; my brother used my father's pocket-compass on the occasion, for we had no idea of living in a house that did not stand square with the earth itself. This showed our ignorance of the comforts and conveniences of a pioneer life. The position of the house, end to the hill, necessarily elevated the lower end, and the determination to have both a north and south door, added much to the airiness of the house, particularly after the green ash puncheons had shrunk so as to leave cracks in the floor and doors from one to two inches wide. At both the doors we had high, unsteady, and sometimes icy steps, made by piling up the logs cut out of the wall. We had a window, if it could be called a window, when, perhaps, it was the largest spot in the top, bottom, or sides of the cabin at which the wind could not enter. It was made by sawing out a log, and placing sticks across; and then, by pasting an old newspaper over the hole, and applying some hog's lard, we had a kind of glazing which shed a most beautiful and mellow light across the cabin when the sun shone on it. All other light entered at the doors, cracks, and chimney.

Our cabin was twenty-four feet by eighteen. The west end was occupied by two beds, the center of each side by a door, and here our symmetry had to stop, for on the side opposite the window were our shelves, made of clapboards, supported on pins driven into the logs. Upon these shelves my sister displayed, in ample order, a host of pewter plates, basins, dishes, and spoons, scoured and bright. It was none of your new-fangled pewter made of lead, but the best of London pewter, which our father himself bought of the manufacturer. These were the plates upon which you could hold your meat so as to cut it without slipping and without dulling your knife. But, alas! the days of pewter plates and sharp dinner knives have passed away.

To return to our internal arrangements. A ladder of five rounds occupied the corner near the window. By this, when we got a floor above, we could ascend. Our chimney occupied most of the east end; there were pots and kettles opposite the window under the shelves, a gun on hooks over the north door, four split-bottom chairs, three three-legged stools, and a small eight by ten looking glass sloped from the wall over a large towel and combcase. Our list of furniture was increased by a clumsy shovel and a pair of tongs, made with one shank straight, which was a certain source of pinches and blood blisters. We had also a spinning-wheel and such things as were necessary to work it. It was absolutely necessary to have three legged stools, as four legs of anything could not all touch the floor at the same time.

The completion of our cabin went on slowly. The season was inclement, we were weak-handed and weak-pocketed—in fact laborers were not to be had. We got our chimney up breast high as soon as we could, and got our cabin daubed as high as the joists outside. It never was daubed on the inside, for my sister, who was very nice, could not consent to "live right next to mud." My impression now is, that the window was not constructed till spring, for until the sticks and clay were put on the chimney we could have no need of a window; for the flood of light which always poured into the cabin from the fireplace would have extinguished our paper window, and rendered it as useless as the moon at noonday.

We got a floor laid overhead as soon as possible, perhaps in a month; but when finished, the reader will readily conceive of its imperviousness to wind or weather, when we mention that it was laid of loose clapboards split from red oak, the stump of which may be seen beyond the cabin. That tree must have grown in the night, for it was so twisting that each board lay on two diagonally opposite corners; and a cat might have shaken every board on our ceiling.

It may be well to inform the unlearned reader that "clapboards" are such lumber as pioneers split throughout; they resemble barrel-staves before they are shaved, but are split longer, wider, and thinner; of such our roof and ceiling were composed. "Puncheons" are planks made by splitting logs to about two and a half or three inches in thickness, and hewing them on one or both sides with the broadax; of such our floor, doors, tables, and stools were manufactured. The "eave-bearers" are those end logs which project over to receive the butting poles, against which the lower tier of clapboards rest to form the roof. The "trapping" is the roof timbers, composing the gable end and the ribs. The "trap logs" are those of unequal length above the eave-bearers, which form the gable ends, and upon which the ribs rest. The "weight poles" are small logs laid on the roof, which weigh down the course of clapboards on which they lie, and against which the course above is placed. The "knees" are pieces of heart timber placed above the butting poles, successively, to prevent the weight poles from rolling off.

THE BUILDING OF THE ERIE CANAL
(1818–25)
by William H. Seward

Seward, at the time of the building of the Erie Canal, was a lawyer in Auburn, New York. In 1838 he was elected governor of New York, and reelected in 1840. He served under Lincoln as Secretary of State, continuing in that office during the administration of Andrew Johnson. On the night of Lincoln's assassination, an attempt on his life was made in his house by one of John Wilkes Booth's associates in the conspiracy, and he was severely wounded.

History will assign to Gouverneur Morris the merit of first suggesting a direct and continuous communication from Lake Erie to the Hudson. In 1800 he announced this idea from the shore of the Niagara River to a friend in Europe, in the following enthusiastic language:

"Hundreds of large ships will, in no distant period, bound on the billows of these inland seas. Shall I lead your astonishment to the verge of incredulity? I will! Know then that one-tenth part of the expense borne by Britain in the last campaign would enable ships to sail from London through the Hudson into Lake Erie. As yet we only crawl along the outer shell of our country. The interior excels the part we inhabit in soil, in climate, in everything. The proudest empire of Europe is but a bauble compared with what America may be, must be."

In 1808 Joshua Forman, a representative in the New York Assembly from Onondaga County, submitted his memorable resolution:

"*Resolved,* if the honorable the Senate concur herein, That a joint committee be appointed to take into consideration the propriety of exploring and causing an accurate survey to be made of the most eligible and direct route for a canal, to open a communication between the tide-waters of the Hudson River and Lake Erie, to the end that Congress may be enabled to appropriate such sums as may be necessary to the accomplishment of that great national object."

In pursuance of a recommendation by the committee, a resolution unanimously passed both houses, directing the surveyor-general, Simeon De Witt, to cause an accurate survey to be made of the various routes proposed for the contemplated communication.

The commissioners in March, 1811, submitted their report written by Gouverneur Morris, in which they showed the practicability and advantages of a continuous canal from Lake Erie to the Hudson, and stated their estimate of the cost at five million dollars, a sum which they ventured to predict would not exceed five per cent of the value of the commodities which, within a century, would be annually transported on the proposed canal. We may pause here to remark that the annual value of the commodities carried on the canals, instead of requiring a century to attain the sum of one hundred millions, reached that limit in twenty-five years.

The ground was broken for the construction of the Erie Canal on July 4, 1817, at Rome, with ceremonies marking the public estimation of that great event. De Witt Clinton, having just before been elected to the chief magistracy of the State, and being president of the Board of Canal Commissioners, enjoyed the high satisfaction of attending, with his associates, on the auspicious occasion.

In 1819 Governor Clinton announced to the Legislature that the progress of the public works equaled the most sanguine expectations and that the canal fund was flourishing. He recommended the prosecution of the entire Erie Canal. Enlarging upon the benefits of internal navigation, he remarked that he looked to a time, not far distant, when the State would be able to improve the navigation of the Susquehanna, the Allegheny, the Genesee, and the St. Lawrence; to assist in connecting the waters of the Great Lakes and the Mississippi; to form a junction between the Erie Canal and Lake Ontario through the Oswego River; and to promote the laudable intention of Pennsylvania to unite Seneca Lake with the Susquehanna, deducing arguments in favor of such enterprises, from the immediate commercial advantages of extended navigation, as well as from its tendency to improve the condition of society and strengthen the bonds of the Union.

The canal commissioners reported in 1824 that the Champlain Canal was finished; that both canals had produced revenues during the previous year of one hundred fifty-three thousand dollars; and that the commissioners had decided that the Erie Canal ought to be united with the Niagara River at Black Rock and terminate at Buffalo.

On the reassembling of the Legislature in January, 1825, De Witt Clinton, who, in November of the preceding year, had been again called to the office of governor, congratulated the Legislature upon the prospect of the immediate completion of the Erie Canal, and the reasonable certainty that the canal debt might soon be satisfied, without a resort to taxation, without a discontinuance of efforts for similar improvements, and without staying the dispensing hand of Government in favor of education, literature, science, and productive industry. Earnestly renewing his recommendation that a board of internal improvement should be instituted, he remarked that the field of operations was immense, and the harvest of honor and profit unbounded, and that, if the resources of the State should be wisely applied and forcibly directed, all proper demands for important avenues of communication might be satisfied.

The primary design of our system of artificial navigation, which was to open a communication between the Atlantic and the Great Lakes, was already, he observed, nearly accomplished, but would not be fully realized until Lake Ontario should be connected with the Erie Canal and with Lake Champlain, and the importance of these improvements would be appreciated when it was understood that the lake coast, not only of this State, but of the United States, was more extensive than their seacoast. The next leading object, he remarked, should be to unite the minor lakes and secondary rivers with the canals and to effect such a connection between the bays on the seacoast as would insure the safety of boat navigation against the tempests of the ocean in time of peace, and against the depredations of an enemy in time of war.

He stated also that ten thousand boats had passed the junction of the canals near tide-water during the previous season. Remarking that the creative power of internal improvement was manifested in the flourishing villages which had sprung up or been extended; in the increase of towns; and above all, in the prosperity of the city of New York. And noticing the fact that three thousand buildings had been erected in that city during the preceding year, Clinton predicted that in fifteen years its population would be doubled, and that in thirty years that metropolis would be the third city in the civilized world, and the second, if not the first, in commerce.

LAFAYETTE'S RETURN
(1824)
by Thurlow Weed

Thurlow Weed was editor of newspapers in Rochester and elsewhere, and was influential in New York politics. In 1830 he was made editor of the Albany Journal, a position he held for thirty-two years, during which he was one of the chief leaders in the Whig party, state and national.

General le Marquise de Lafayette, after an absence of thirty-nine years, revisited our country, on the invitation of Congress, as the nation's guest in 1824. He reached New York on the 15th of August, in the packet-ship *Cadmus*, Captain Allyn, with his son and secretary. The Government had tendered him a United States frigate, but always simple and unostentatious, he preferred to come as an ordinary passenger in a packet-ship.

There were no wires fifty years ago over which intelligence could pass with lightning speed, but the visit of Lafayette was expected, and the pulses and hearts of the people were quickened and warmed simultaneously through some mysterious medium throughout the whole Union. Citizens rushed from neighboring cities and villages to welcome the French nobleman, who, before he was twenty-one years old, had devoted himself and his fortune to the American colonies in their wonderful conflict with the mother country for independence; and who, after fighting gallantly by the side of Washington through the Revolutionary War, returned to France with the only reward he desired or valued—the gratitude of a free people. General Lafayette was now sixty-seven years of age, with some physical infirmities, but intellectually strong, and in manners and feeling cheerful, elastic, and accomplished.

The General's landing on the Battery, his reception by the military under General Martin, his triumphant progress through Broadway, his first visit to the City Hall, awakened emotions which can not be described. I have witnessed the celebration of the completion of the Erie Canal and the mingling of the waters of Lake Erie with the Atlantic Ocean, the completion of the Croton Water Works celebration, the reception of the Prince of Wales, and other brilliant and beautiful pageants, but they all lacked the heart and soul which marked and signalized the welcome of Lafayette. The joy of our citizens was exprest more by tears than in any other way. It is impossible to imagine scenes of deeper, higher or purer emotion than the first meeting between General Lafayette and Colonel Marinus Willett, Colonel Ebenezer Stevens, Colonel Varick, Major Platt, General Anthony, Major Popham, Major Fairlee, and other officers of the Revolution, whom he had not seen for nearly forty years, and whom without a moment's hesitation he recognized and named.

On a trip up the Hudson to Albany, General Lafayette in the most enthusiastic language and manner pointed out Stony Point, and described the manner in which the British garrison was surprized and captured by "mad Anthony Wayne." As you approached the West Point wharf, cheers of citizens lining the banks echoed and reechoed from hill to hill, well-burnished muskets dazzled the eye, tall plumes nodded their greetings, the ear-piercing fife, the spirit-stirring drum, and the loud bugle sent forth their loftiest notes, while the reverberating cheers filled the air with welcomes. The General was received by Colonel Thayer, and ascended the hill in a landau, escorted by the officers of the post, followed by the Revolutionary officers and a long procession of citizens. He was received by the cadets from their parade ground, and escorted to his marquee, where they paid him the marching salute. From the marquee he proceeded to the quarters of Generals Brown and Scott, where he was presented to the ladies and partook of refreshments. From thence he was conducted to the library and introduced to the cadets. Dinner was served in the mess-room of the cadets, which had been splendidly decorated for the occasion.

General Lafayette's happiness took every conceivable form of expression. He made an early visit to the ruins of old Fort Putnam, where he had been stationed. Almost every scene and object served to recall incidents of the Revolution, of which he spoke with the greatest enthusiasm. He pointed out the Robinson House, where General Washington, himself, and General Knox were breakfasting with Mrs. Arnold when the commander-in-chief received the first news of Arnold's treason. Early in the day a committee of citizens arrived from Newburg, where General Lafayette was expected to dine, and where the citizens of Orange County *en masse* anxiously awaited his arrival. But he was too much delighted with West Point to be hurried away. An early dinner had been ordered, so that the impatient thousands at Newburgh might be gratified with a sight of the General before evening. The dinner, however, with the associations and remembrances it suggested, proved irresistible. Hour after hour passed, but the interest increased rather than diminished, and it was not until seven o'clock that the General could be prevailed to rise from the table. It was dark, therefore, when we reached Newburgh.

Upon landing, a scene of indescribable confusion ensued; troops were in line, but powerless to preserve order. The desire to see the nation's guest was uncontrollable. The huzzas of men mingled with the shrieks of women and the cries of children. All were eager to see, but everywhere good humor and kindness prevailed. The village was illuminated, and the occasion was honored by a ball and supper. The festivities of the evening, however, were saddened by the sudden death of Hector Seward (a cousin of the late Governor Seward), who received a fatal kick from an excited horse. Notwithstanding the excitement and fatigues of the day and of the preceding night, General Lafayette was as cheerful and buoyant at the ballroom and at the supper-table as the youngest and gayest of the revelers.

The General reembarked at one o'clock A.M. At half past two our approach was announced by a discharge of cannon from the bluff, just below the landing at Poughkeepsie. Large piles of seasoned wood, saturated with tar and turpentine, were kindled on that bluff, fed by hundreds of boys who had been entrusted with the duty, and were kept blazing high, filling the atmosphere with lurid flame and smoke until daylight. Soon after sunrise, a large concourse of the citizens of Poughkeepsie, with a military escort, arrived at the wharf. The General, on disembarking, was shown to a splendid barouche, and the procession moved to and through the village of Poughkeepsie, where congratulatory speeches were made and reciprocated. A large party sat down to a bountiful breakfast.

The party reembarked at ten o'clock, when the steamer proceeded up the river to the then beautiful residence of Governor Morgan Lewis, where the party landed, proceeded to his fine old mansion, and partook of a sumptuous collation. About two o'clock the steamer glided through the placid waters until between four and five o'clock, when she reached Clermont, the manor-house of Chancellor Livingston, of Revolutionary memory. On landing the General was received by a large body of men, and was escorted by a military company from Hudson to the beautiful lawn in front of the manor-house, where the General was warmly welcomed by the master of the lodge with an appropriate speech. The afternoon was uncommonly beautiful; the scene and its associations were exceedingly impressive. Dinner was served in a greenhouse or orangery, which formed a sort of balcony to the southern exposure of the manor house. When the cloth was removed, and the evening came on, variegated lamps suspended from the orange-trees were lighted, producing a wonderfully brilliant and beautiful effect.

But the grand event of the occasion was the ball, which was opened by General Lafayette, who gracefully led out the venerable and blind widow of General Montgomery—who fell in the assault of Quebec in 1775—amid the wildest enthusiasm of all present. While the festivities were progressing within, the assembled tenantry, who were "to the manor born," were feasted upon the lawn, where there was music and dancing. The party broke up and returned to the boat about 3 A.M. The steamer hauled out into the river, but did not get under way until sunrise.

We reached Catskill at seven o'clock. A large procession, civic and military, awaited the General's arrival at the landing. General Lafayette and the Revolutionary officers were seated in open barouches, and the procession moved through the main street for more than a mile, affording the dense mass of men, women, and children the great happiness of seeing the compatriot and friend of Washington. Several beautiful arches, profusely drest with flags, flowers, and evergreens, each one bearing the inscription, "Welcome, Lafayette," were thrown across the street. In the center of the village a brief address was made, to which the General responded. After this he was escorted in the same order to the boat, and at eleven o'clock he reached Hudson, where a hearty welcome awaited the General. Not only the citizens of Columbia, but many of the inhabitants of Berkshire County, Mass., were present, whose acclamations, as General Lafayette was seen upon the main deck of the steamer, made the welkin ring. The ceremonies and festivities at Hudson consumed between three and four hours. A committee, consisting of the most distinguished citizens of Albany, awaited the General's arrival at Hudson, anxious that the steamer should reach Albany before dark, preparations having been made for a magnificent reception. But in this the Albanians were disappointed, for, on account of the low water above Coeyman's, the steamer's progress was so slow that it was quite dark when she reached Albany. What was lost, however, in one respect was gained in another, for between the illuminations and torches the procession, from Lydius Street landing to the Capitol, was alike brilliant and impressive.

The excursion from New York to Albany occupied three days, and afforded to all who enjoyed it an interest and a happiness more complete and more touching than tongue or pen can describe.

THE CLAY-RANDOLPH DUEL

(1826)

by Thomas H. Benton

Born in 1782, Thomas Hart Benton was elected both a United States Senator from Missouri between 1821 and 1851, and a United States representative from 1853 to 1855. A strong supporter of Andrew Jackson, he was responsible for the famous Specie Circular (1836) and was known for legislation supporting frontiersmen. He was also a strong opponent of slavery. His nephew, Thomas Hart Benton, was a famous American painter who was best known for his murals dramatizing Americans.

The Clay-Randolph duel was not historically important, as was the Burr-Hamilton conflict, but it well illustrates the atmosphere of the times. Henry Clay and John Randolph were prominent American senators of the early nineteenth century. Clay, from Kentucky, represented the new West, its settlers and frontiersmen. John Randolph of Virginia supported the interests of long-established Southern planters.

It was Saturday, the first day of April, toward noon, the Senate not being that day in session, that Mr. Randolph came to my room at Brown's Hotel, and (without explaining the reason of the question) asked me if I was a blood-relation of Mrs. Clay? I answered that I was, and he immediately replied that that put an end to a request which he had wished to make of me; and then went on to tell me that he had just received a challenge from Mr. Clay, had accepted it, was ready to go out, and would apply to Col. Tatnall to be his second. Before leaving, he told me he would make my bosom the depository of a secret which he should commit to no other person: it was, that he did not intend to fire at Mr. Clay. He told it to me because he wanted a witness of his intention, and did not mean to tell it to his second or anybody else; and enjoined inviolable secrecy until the duel was over. This was the first notice I had of the affair. The circumstances of the delivery of the challenge I had from General Jesup, Mr. Clay's second, and they were so perfectly characteristic of Mr. Randolph that I give them in detail, and in the General's own words: "I informed Mr. Randolph that I was the bearer of a message from Mr. Clay in consequence of an attack which he had made upon his private as well as public character in the Senate; that I was aware no one had the right to question him out of the Senate for anything said in debate, unless he chose voluntarily to waive his privileges as a member of that body. Mr. Randolph replied, that the Constitution did protect him, but he would never shield himself under such a subterfuge as the pleading of his privileges as a Senator from Virigina; that he did not hold himself accountable to Mr. Clay.

These were the circumstances of the delivery of the challenge, and the only thing necessary to give them their character is to recollect that, with this prompt acceptance and positive refusal to explain, there was a perfect determination not to fire at Mr. Clay. That determination rested on two grounds; first, an entire unwillingness to hurt Mr. Clay; and, next, a conviction that to return the fire would be to answer, and would be an implied acknowledgment of Mr. Clay's right to make him answer. This he would not do, neither by implication nor in words. He denied the right of any person to question him out of the Senate for words spoken within it. He took a distinction between man and senator. As senator he had a constitutional immunity, given for a wise purpose, and which he would neither surrender nor compromise; as individual he was ready to give satisfaction for what was deemed an injury. He would receive, but not return a fire. It was as much as to say: Mr. Clay may fire at me for what has offended him; I will not, by returning the fire, admit his right to do so. This was a subtle distinction, and that in case of life and death, and not very clear to the common intellect; but to Mr. Randolph both clear and convincing.

The acceptance, the refusal to explain, the determination not to fire, and the resolve to fall, if he fell, on the soil of Virginia—was all, to his mind, a single emanation, the flash of an instant. He needed no consultations, no deliberations to arrive at all these important conclusions. I dwell upon these small circumstances because they are characteristic, and show the man—a man who belongs to history, and had his own history, and should be known as he was. That character can only be shown in his own conduct, his own words and acts: and this duel with Mr. Clay illustrates it at many points.

The afternoon of Saturday, the 8th of April, was fixt upon for the time; the right bank of the Potomac within the State of Virginia, above the Little Falls bridge, was the place—pistols the weapons—distance ten paces; each party to be attended by two seconds and a surgeon, and myself at liberty to attend as a mutual friend. There was to be no practising with pistols, and there was none; and the words "one", "two," "three," "stop," after the word "fire," were, by agreement between the seconds, and for the humane purpose of reducing the result as near as possible to chance, to be given out in quick succession.

Saturday, the 8th of April—the day for the duel—had come, and almost the hour. It was noon, and the meeting was to take place at 4:30 o'clock. I had gone to see Mr. Randolph before the hour; He was making codicils to his will, all in the way of remembrance to friends; the bequests slight in value, but invaluable in tenderness of feeling and beauty of expression, and always appropriate to the receiver. To Mr. Macon he gave some English shillings, to keep the game when he played whist. His namesake, John Randolph Bryan, then at school in Baltimore, and since married to his niece, had been sent for to see him, but sent off before the hour for going out, to save the boy from a possible shock at seeing him brought back.

He wanted some gold—that coin not being then in circulation, and only to be obtained by favor or purchase—and sent his faithful man, Johnny, to the United States Branch Bank to get a few pieces, American being the kind asked for.

He delivered me a sealed paper, which I was to open if he was killed—give back to him if he was not; also an open slip, which I was to read before I got to the ground. This slip was a request to feel in his left breeches pocket, if he was killed, and find so many pieces of gold—I believe nine—take three for myself, and give the same number to Tatnall and Hamilton each, to make seals to wear in remembrance of him. We were all three at Mr. Randolph's lodgings then, and soon sat out, Mr. Randolph and his seconds in a carriage, I following him on horseback.

The preparations for the duel were finished; the parties went to their places; and I went forward to a piece of rising ground, from which I could see what passed and hear what was said. The faithful Johnny followed me close, speaking not a word, but evincing the deepest anxiety for his beloved master. The place was a thick forest, and the immediate spot a little depression, or basin, in which the parties stood. The principals saluted each other courteously as they took their stands. Col. Tatnall had won the choice of position, which give to Gen. Jesup the delivery of the word. They stood on a line east and west—a small stump just behind Mr. Clay; a low gravelly band rose just behind Mr. Randolph. This latter asked Gen. Jesup to repeat the word as he would give it; and while in the act of doing so, and Mr. Randolph adjusting the butt of his pistol to his hand, the muzzle pointing downward, and almost to the ground, it fired. Instantly Mr. Randolph turned to Col. Tatnall and said: "I protested against that hair trigger." Col. Tatnall took blame to himself for having sprung the hair. Mr. Clay had not then received his pistol. Senator Johnson, of Louisiana (Josiah), one of his seconds, was carrying it to him, and still several steps from him.

This untimely fire, tho clearly an accident, necessarily gave rise to some remarks, and a species of inquiry, which was conducted with the utmost delicacy, but which, in itself, was of a nature to be inexpressibly painful to a gentleman's feelings. Mr. Clay stopped it with the generous remark that the fire was clearly an accident; and it was so unanimously declared. Another pistol was immediately furnished; and exchange of shots took place, and, happily, without effect upon the persons. Mr. Randolph's bullet struck the stump behind Mr. Clay, and Mr. Clay's knocked up the earth and gravel behind Mr. Randolph, and in a line with the level of his hips, both bullets having gone so true close that it was a marvel how they missed.

The moment had come for me to interpose. I went in among the parties and offered my mediation; but nothing could be done. Mr. Clay said, with that wave of the hand with which he was accustomed to put away a trifle, "This is child's play!" and required another fire. Mr. Randolph also demanded another fire. The seconds were directed to reload. While this was doing I prevailed on Mr. Randolph to walk away from his post, and renewed to him, more pressingly than ever, my importunities to yield to some accommodation; but I found him more determined than I had ever seen him, and for the first time impatient, and seemingly annoyed and dissatisfied at what I was doing. He was indeed annoyed and dissatisfied. The accidental fire of his pistol preyed upon his feelings. He was doubly chagrined at it, both as a circumstance susceptible in itself of an unfair interpretation, and as having been the immediate and controlling cause of his firing at Mr. Clay. He regretted this fire the instant it was over. He felt that it had subjected him to imputations from which he knew himself to be free—a desire to kill Mr. Clay, and a contempt for the laws of his beloved State; and the annoyances which he felt at these vexatious circumstances revived his original determination, and decided him irrevocably to carry it out.

He declared to me that he had not aimed at the life of Mr. Clay; that he did not level as high as the knees—not higher than the knee-band; "for it was no mercy to shoot a man in the knee"; that his only object was to disable him and spoil his aim. And then added, with a beauty of expression and depth of feeling which no studied oratory can ever attain, and which

I shall never forget, these impressive words: "I would not have seen him fall mortally, or even doubtfully wounded, for all the land that is watered by the King of Floods and all his tributary streams."

He left me to resume his post, utterly refusing to explain out of the Senate any thing that he had said in it, and with the positive declaration that he would not return the next fire. I withdrew a little way into the woods, and kept my eyes fixt on Mr. Randolph, who I then knew to be the only one in danger. I saw him receive the fire of Mr. Clay, saw the gravel knocked up in the same place, saw Mr. Randolph raise his pistol—discharge it in the air; heard him say, "I do not fire at you, Mr. Clay"; and immediately advancing and offering his hand. He was met in the same spirit. They met half way, shook hands, Mr. Randolph saying, jocosely, "You owe me a coat, Mr. Clay"—(the bullet had passed through the skirt of the coat, very near the hip)—to which Mr. Clay promptly and happily replied, "I am glad the debt is no greater." I had come up, and was prompt to proclaim what I had been obliged to keep secret for eight days. The joy of all was extreme at this happy termination of a most critical affair; and we immediately left, with lighter hearts than we brought.

I stopt to sup with Mr. Randolph and his friends—none of us wanted dinner that day—and had a characteristic time of it. A runner came in from the bank to say that they had overpaid him, by mistake, $130 that day. He answered, "I believe it is your rule not to correct mistakes, except at the time, and at your counter." And with that answer the runner had to return. When gone, Mr. Randolph said, "I will pay it on Monday; people must be honest, if banks are not." He asked for the sealed paper he had given me, opened it, took out a check for $1,000, drawn in my favor, and with which I was requested to have him carried, if killed, to Virginia, and buried under his patrimonial oaks—not let him be buried at Washington, with an hundred hacks after him.

He took the gold from his left breeches pocket, and said to us (Hamilton, Tatnall, and I), "Gentlemen, Clay's bad shooting sha'n't rob you of your seals. I am going to London, and will have them made for you"; which he did, and most characteristically, so far as mine was concerned. He went to the herald's office in London and inquired for the Benton family, of which I had often told him there was none, as we only dated on that side from my grandfather in North Carolina. But the name was found, and with it a coat of arms—among the quarterings a lion rampant. That is the family, said he; and had the arms engraved on the seal, the same which I have habitually worn; and added the motto, *Factis non verbis;* of which he was afterward accustomed to say the *non* should be changed into *et.*

But, enough. I run into these details, not merely to relate an event, but to show character; and if I have not done it, it is not for want of material, but of ability to use it.

On Monday the parties exchanged cards, and social relations were formally and courteously restored. It was about the last high-toned duel that I have witnessed, and among the highest-toned that I have ever witnessed, and so happily conducted to a fortunate issue—a result due to the noble character of the seconds as well as to the generous and heroic spirit of the principals.

PETER COOPER'S
TOM THUMB *LOCOMOTIVE*
(1830)
by John H. B. Latrobe

The first American-built locomotive that made a successful trip on rails was the one described by Mr. Latrobe, and built by Peter Cooper. Peter Cooper's locomotive was merely a working model. In actual railway service, the first American-built locomotive put into use was one operated by the South Carolina Canal and Rail Road, which ran from Charleston to Hamburg, and was called the Best Friend of Charleston.

When steam made its appearance on the Liverpool and Manchester Railroad it attracted great attention here. But there was this difficulty about introducing an English engine on an American road. An English road was virtually a straight road. An American road had curves sometimes of as small radius as two hundred feet. For a brief season it was believed that this feature of the early American roads would prevent the use of locomotive engines. The contrary was demonstrated by a gentleman still living in an active and ripe old age, honored and beloved, distinguished for his private worth and for his public benefactions; one of those to whom wealth seems to have been granted by Providence that men might know how wealth could be used to benefit one's fellow creatures.

The speaker refers to Mr. Peter Cooper of New York. Mr. Cooper was satisfied that steam might be adapted to the curved roads which he saw would be built in the United States; and he came to Baltimore, which then possest the only one on which he could experiment, to vindicate his belief. He had another idea, which was, that the crank could be dispensed with in the change from a reciprocating to a rotary motion: and he built an engine to demonstrate both articles of his faith. The machine was not larger than the hand-cars used by workmen to transfer themselves from place to place; and as the writer now recalls its appearance, the only wonder is that so apparently insignificant a contrivance should ever have been regarded as competent to the smallest results. But Mr. Cooper was wiser than many of the wisest around him. His engine could not have weighed a ton; but he saw in it a principle which the forty-ton engines of to-day have but served to develop and demonstrate.

The boiler of Mr. Cooper's engine was not as large as the kitchen boiler attached to many a range in modern mansions. It was of about the same diameter, but not much more than half as high. It stood upright in the car, and was filled, above the furnace, which occupied the lower section, with vertical tubes. The cylinder was but three and a half inches in diameter, and speed was gotten up by gearing. No natural draft could have been sufficient to keep up steam in so small a boiler; and Mr. Cooper used therefore a blowing apparatus, driven by a drum attached to one of the car wheels, over which passed a cord that in its turn worked a pulley on the shaft of the blower.

Mr. Cooper's success was such as to induce him to try a trip to Ellicott's Mills; and an open car, the first used upon the road, already mentioned, having been attached to his engine, and filled with the directors and some friends, the Speaker among the rest, the first journey by steam in America was commenced. The trip was most interesting. The curves were passed without difficulty at a speed of fifteen miles an hour; the grades were ascended with comparative ease; the day was fine, the company in the highest spirits, and some excited gentlemen of the party pulled out memorandum books, and when at the highest speed, which was eighteen miles an hour, wrote their names and some connected sentences, to prove that even at that great velocity it was possible to do so. The return trip from the Mills—a distance of thirteen miles—was made in fifty-seven minutes. This was in the summer of 1830.

But the triumph of this Tom Thumb engine was not altogether without a drawback. The great stage proprietors of the day were Stockton & Stockes; and on this occasion a gallant gray of great beauty and power was driven by them from town, attached to another car on the second track— for the company had begun by making two tracks to the Mills—and met the engine at the Relay House on its way back. From this point it was determined to have a race home; and, the start being even, away went horse and engine, the snort of the one and the puff of the other keeping time and time. At first the gray had the best of it, for *his* steam would be applied to the greatest advantage on the instant, while the engine had to wait until the rotation of the wheels set the blower to work. The horse was perhaps a quarter of a mile ahead when the safety-valve of the engine lifted and the thin blue vapor issuing from it showed an excess of steam. The blower whistled, the steam blew off in vapory clouds, the pace increased, the passengers shouted, the engine gained on the horse, soon it lapped him—the silk was plied—the race was neck and neck, nose and nose—then the engine passed the horse, and a great hurrah hailed the victory. But it was not repeated, for just at this time, when the gray's master was almost giving up, the band which drove the pulley, which moved the blower, slipped from the drum, the safety-valve ceased to scream, and the engine, for want of breath, began to wheeze and pant. In vain Mr. Cooper, who was his own engineer and fireman, lacerated his hands in attempting to replace the band upon the wheel; in vain he tried to urge the fire with light wood; the horse gained on the machine and passed it, and, although the bank was presently replaced, and steam again did its best, the horse was too far ahead to be overtaken, and came in the winner of the race.

THE FIRST ANTISLAVERY CONVENTION
(1833)
by John G. Whittier

From the Prose Works *of John Greenleaf Whittier, a noted American Quaker poet of the Romantic period. An influential abolitionist, he is known for his* Legends of New England *(1831), and such poems as "Moll Pitcher," "Barbara Frietchie," and "The Barefoot Boy."*

In the gray twilight of a chill day of late November, forty years ago, a dear friend of mine, residing in Boston, made his appearance at the old farmhouse in East Harverhill. He had been deputed by the Abolitionists of the city, William L. Garrison, Samuel E. Sewall, and others, to inform me of my appointment as a delegate to the convention about to be held in Philadelphia for the formation of an American Anti-slavery Society, and to urge upon me the necessity of my attendance.

Few words of persuasion, however, were needed. I was unused to traveling, my life had been spent on a secluded farm; and the journey, mostly by stage-coach, at that time was really a formidable one. Moreover, the few Abolitionists were everywhere spoken against, their persons threatened, and in some instances a price set on their heads by Southern legislators. Pennsylvania was on the borders of slavery, and it needed small effort of imagination to picture to one's self the breaking up of the convention and maltreatment of its members. This latter consideration I do not think weighed much with me, altho I was better prepared for serious danger than for anything like personal indignity. I had read Governor Trumbull's description of the tarring and feathering of his hero MacFingal, when, after the application of the melted tar, the feather bed was ripped open and shaken over him, and, I confess, I was quite unwilling to undergo a martyrdom which my best friends could scarcely refrain from laughing at. But a summons like that of Garrison's bugle-blast could scarcely be unheeded by one who, from birth and education, held fast the traditions of that earlier abolitionism which, under the lead of Benezet and Woolman,[1] had effaced from the Society of Friends every vestige of slaveholding. I had thrown myself, with a young man's fervid enthusiasm, into a movement which commended itself to my reason and conscience, to my love of country and my sense of duty to God and my fellow-men. Under such circumstances I could not hesitate.

So the next morning I took the stage for Boston, stopping at the ancient hostelry known as the Eastern Stage Tavern; and on the day following, in company with William Lloyd-Garrison, I left for New York. At that city we were joined by other delegates, among them David Thurston, a Congregational minister from Maine. On our way to Philadelphia we took, as a matter of necessary economy, a second-class conveyance, and found ourselves, in consequence, among rough and hilarious companions, whose language was more noteworthy for strength than refinement.

On reaching Philadelphia, we at once betook ourselves to the humble dwelling of Fifth Street occupied by Evan Lewis, a plain, earnest man and lifelong Abolitionist, who had been largely interested in preparing the way for the convention. We found about forty members assembled in the parlors of our friend Lewis. Beriah Green, of the Oneida (New York) Institute, was chosen president, a fresh-faced, sandy-haired, rather common-looking man, but who had the reputation of an able and eloquent speaker. He had already made himself known to us as a resolute and self-sacrificing Abolitionist. Lewis Tappan and myself took our places at his side as secretaries, on the elevation at the west end of the hall.

Looking over the assembly, I noticed that it was mainly composed of comparatively young men, some in middle age, and a few beyond that period. They were nearly all plainly drest, with a view to comfort rather than elegance. Many of the faces turned toward me wore a look of expectancy and supprest enthusiasm. All had the earnestness which might be expected of men engaged in an enterprise beset with difficulty and perhaps with peril. The fine, intellectual head of Garrison, prematurely bald, was conspicuous. The sunny-faced young man at his side, in whom all the beatitudes seemed to find expression, was Samuel J. May, mingling in his

[1] Benezet and Woolman were both Quakers, the former a Frenchman who came to America, wrote pamphlets against the slave trade, and died in Philadelphia in 1784; the latter an American who also wrote against slavery, but is best known for his *Journal,* published after his death as edited by Whittier.

veins the best blood of the Sewalls and Quincys—a man so exceptionally pure and large-hearted, so genial, tender, and loving, that he could be faithful to truth and duty without making an enemy.

The committee on the declaration of principles, of which I was a member, held a long session discussing the proper scope and tenor of the document. But little progress being made, it was finally decided to entrust the matter to a subcommittee, consisting of William L. Garrison, S. J. May, and myself; and, after a brief consultation and comparison of each other's views, the drafting of the important paper was assigned to the former gentleman. We agreed to meet him at his lodgings in the house of a colored friend early the next morning. It was still dark when we climbed up to his room, and the lamp was still burning by the light of which he was writing the last sentence of the declaration. We read it carefully, made a few verbal changes, and submitted it to the large committee, who unanimously agreed to report it to the convention.

The paper was read to the convention by Dr. Atlee, chairman of the committee, and listened to with the profoundest interest. Commencing with a reference to the time, fifty-seven years before, when, in the same city of Philadelphia, our fathers announced to the world their Declaration of Independence—based on the self-evident truths of human equality and rights—and appealed to arms for its defense, it spoke of the new enterprise as one "without which that of our fathers is incomplete," and as transcending theirs in magnitude, solemnity, and probable results as much "as moral truth does physical force." It spoke of the difference of the two in the means and ends proposed, and of the trifling grievances of our fathers compared with the wrongs and sufferings of the slaves, which it forcibly characterized as unequaled by any others on the face of the earth. It claimed that the nation was bound to repent at once, to let the opprest go free, and to admit them to all the rights and privileges of others; because, it asserted, no man has a right to enslave or imbrute his brother; because liberty is inalienable; because there is no difference in principle between slave-holding and man-stealing, which the law brands as piracy; and because no length of bondage can invalidate man's claim to himself, or render slave laws anything but "an audacious usurpation."

After clearly and emphatically avowing the principles underlying the enterprise, and guarding with scrupulous care the rights of persons and states under the Constitution, in prosecuting it, the declaration closed with these eloquent words:

"These are our views and principles—these our designs and measures. With entire confidence in the overruling justice of God, we plant ourselves upon the Declaration of Independence and the truths of divine revelation as upon the everlasting rock.

"We shall organize anti-slavery societies, if possible, in every city, town, and village in our land.

"We shall send forth agents to lift up the voice of remonstrance, of warning, of entreaty and rebuke.

"We shall circulate unsparingly and extensively anti-slavery tracts and periodicals.

"We shall enlist the pulpit and the press in the cause of the suffering and the dumb.

"We shall aim at a purification of the churches from all participation in the guilt of slavery.

"We shall encourage the labor of freemen over that of the slaves, by giving a preference to their productions; and

"We shall spare no exertions nor means to bring the whole nation to speedy repentance."

On the morning of the last day of our session the declaration, with its few verbal amendments, carefully engrossed on parchment, was brought before the convention. Samuel J. May rose to read it for the last time. His sweet, persuasive voice faltered with the intensity of his emotions as he repeated the solemn pledges of the concluding paragraphs. After a season of silence, David Thurston, of Maine, rose as his name was called by one of the secretaries, and affixt his name to the document. One after another passed up to the platform, signed, and retired in silence. All felt the deep responsibility of the occasion: the shadow and forecast of a lifelong struggle rested upon every countenance.

Our work as a convention was now done.

CHICAGO: VILLAGE AND FORT
(1833)
by Patrick Shirreff

From Shirreff's Tour Through North America, *published in Edinburgh, 1835. The author was a Scotsman who came to this country for the purpose of studying agricultural conditions with a view to emigration by his countrymen.*

Chicago is situated on Lake Michigan, at the confluence of Chicago River, a small stream, affording the advantages of a canal to the inhabitants for a limited distance. At the mouth of the river is Fort Dearborn, garrisoned by a few soldiers, and one of the places which has been long held to keep the Indian tribes in awe. The entrance from the lake to the river is much obstructed by sand banks, and an attempt is making to improve the navigation.

Chicago consists of about 150 wood houses, placed irregularly on both sides of the river, over which there is a bridge. This is already a place of considerable trade, supplying salt, tea, coffee, sugar, and clothing to a large tract of country to the south and west; and when connected with the navigable point of the river Illinois, by a canal or railway, can not fail of rising to importance.

Almost every person I met regarded Chicago as the germ of an immense city, and speculators have already bought up, at high prices, all the building ground in the neighborhood. Chicago will, in all probability, attain considerable size, but its situation is not so favorable to growth as many other places in the Union. The country south and west of Chicago has a channel of trade to the south by New Orleans; and the navigation from Buffalo by Lake Huron is of such length, that perhaps the produce of the country to the south of Chicago will find an outlet to Lake Erie by the waters of the rivers Wabash and Mamee. A canal has been in progress for three years, connecting the Wabash and Mamee, which flows into the west end of Lake Erie; and there can be little difficulty in connecting the Wabash with the Illinois, which, if effected, will materially check the rise of Chicago.

At the time of visiting Chicago, there was a treaty in progress with the Pottawattamie Indians, and it was supposed nearly 8,000 Indians, of all ages, belonging to different tribes, were assembled on the occasion, a treaty being considered a kind of general merry-making, which lasts several weeks; and animal food, on the present occasion, was served out by the States government. The forests and prairies in the neighborhood were stubbed with the tents of the Indians, and numerous herds of horses were browsing in all directions. Some of the tribes could be distinguished by their peculiarities. The Sacs and Foxes have their heads shaven, with exception of a small tuft of hair on the crown. Their garments seemed to vary according to their circumstances, and not to their tribes. The dress of the squaws was generally blue cloth, and sometimes printed cotton, with ornaments in the ears, and occasionally also in the nose.

The men generally wore white blankets, with a piece of blue cloth round their loins; and the poorest of them had no other covering, their arms, legs, and feet being exposed in nakedness. A few of them had cotton trousers, and jackets of rich patterns, loosely flowing, secured with a sash; boots, and handkerchiefs or bands of cotton, with feathers in the head-dress, their appearance reminding me of the costume of some Asiatic nations. The men are generally without beards, but in one or two instances I saw tufts of hair on the chin, which seemed to be kept with care, and this was conspicuously so among the well-drest portion. The countenances of both sexes were frequently bedaubed with paint of different kinds, including red, blue, and white.

In the forenoon of my arrival, a council had been held, without transacting business, and a race took place in the afternoon. The spectators were Indians, with exception of a few travelers, and their small number showed the affair excited little interest. The riders had a piece of blue cloth round their loins, and in other respects were perfectly naked, having the whole of their bodies painted of different hues. The race-horses had not undergone a course of training. They were of ordinary breed, and, according to British taste at least, small, coarse, and ill-formed.

Besides the assemblage of Indians, there seemed to be a general fair at Chicago. Large wagons drawn by six or eight oxen, and heavily laden with merchandise, were arriving from, and departing to, distant parts of the country. There was also a kind of horse-market, and I had much conversation with a dealer from the State of New York, having serious intentions of purchasing a horse to carry me to the banks of the Mississippi, if one could have been got suitable for the journey. The dealers attempted to palm colts on me for aged horses, and seemed versed in all the trickery which is practised by their profession in Britain.

A person showed me a model of a threshing machine and a churn, for which he was taking orders, and said he furnished the former at $30, or £6, 10s. sterling. There were a number of French descendants, who are engaged in the fur-trade, met in Chicago, for the purpose of settling accounts with the Indians. They were drest in broadcloths and boots, and boarded in the hotels. They are a swarthy scowling race, evidently tinged with Indian blood, speaking the French and English languages fluently, and much addicted to swearing and whisky.

The hotel at which our party was set down, was so disagreeably crowded that the landlord could not positively promise beds, altho he would do every thing in his power to accommodate us. The house was dirty in the extreme, and confusion reigned throughout, which the extraordinary circumstances of the village went far to extenuate. I contrived, however, to get on pretty well, having by this time learned to serve myself in many things, carrying water for washing, drying my shirt, wetted by the rain of the preceding evening, and brushing my shoes. The table was amply stored with substantial provisions, to which justice was done by the guests, altho indifferently cooked, and still more so served up.

When bedtime arrived, the landlord showed me to an apartment about ten feet square, in which there were two small beds already occupied, assigning me in a corner a dirty pallet, which had evidently been recently used, and was lying in a state of confusion. Undressing for the night had become a simple proceeding, and consisted in throwing off shoes, neckcloth, coat, and vest, the two latter being invariably used to aid the pillow, and I had long dispensed with a nightcap. I was awoke from a sound sleep toward morning by an angry voice uttering horrid imprecations, accompanied by a demand for the bed I occupied. A lighted candle, which the individual held in his hand, showed him to be a French trader, accompanied by a friend, and as I looked on them for some time in silence, their audacity and brutality of speech increased.

At length I lifted my head from the pillow, leaned on my elbow, and with a steady gaze, and the calmest tone of voice, said: "Who are you that address me in such language?" The countenance of the angry individual fell, and he subduedly asked to share my bed. Wishing to put him to a further trial, I again replied: "If you will ask the favor in a proper manner, I shall give you an answer." He was now either ashamed of himself, or felt his pride hurt, and both left the room without uttering a word. Next morning, the individuals who slept in the apartment with me, discovered that the intruders had acted most improperly toward them, and the most noisy of the two entered familiarly into conversation with me during breakfast, without alluding to the occurrence of the preceding evening.

"REMEMBER THE ALAMO!"
A. A Call to Arms
(1836)
by William Barrett Travis

In a dispute of several years duration, American settlers in the Mexican state of Coahuila-Texas expressed dissatisfaction with inequities in the Mexican administration of the region. During one of the periodic Mexican revolutions, Santa Anna won the support of the Texans by promising to separate Texas from Coahuila, making it a Mexican state with self-rule. Upon coming to power in 1835, Santa Anna reneged on these promises and instituted an authoritarian government. The Texans revolted, founding the Republic of Texas in the 1836 Texan War of Independence. The war spanned only a few months and saw only one defeat—the Alamo—and one victory (San Jacinto), where Santa Anna himself was captured.

The defense of the Alamo may have been strategically questionable, but here a small group of men chose to make their final stand. The actual fortification was large (much larger than most depictions) and would have required a thousand soldiers for an adequate defense. Colonel Travis had only 182 men, including the famed Jim Bowie and Davy Crockett. With no thought of retreat, the commander of the Alamo called for more men to hold against the onslaught.

"COMMANDANCY OF THE ALAMO, Bexar, Feby. 24th, 1836. "*To the People of Texas and All Americans in the World—*
"FELLOW CITIZENS AND COMPATRIOTS: I am besieged by a thousand or more of the Mexicans under Santa Anna. I have sustained a continual Bombardment and cannonade for 24 hours and have not lost a man. The enemy has demanded a surrender at discretion, otherwise, the garrison are to be put to the sword, if the fort is taken. I have answered the demand with a cannon shot, and our flag still waves proudly from the walls. *I shall never surrender or retreat.* Then, I call on you in the name of Liberty, of patriotism and everything dear to the American character, to come to our aid with all dispatch. The enemy is receiving reinforcements daily and will no doubt increase to three or four thousand in four or five days. If this call is neglected, I am determined to sustain myself as long as possible and die like a soldier who never forgets what is due to his own honor and that of his country. VICTORY OR DEATH.

"WILLIAM BARRETT TRAVIS,
"*Lt. Col. comdt.*

"P.S. The Lord is on our side. When the enemy appeared in sight we had not three bushels of corn. We have since found in deserted houses 80 to 90 bushels and got into the walls 20 or 30 head of Beeves."

"TRAVIS."

"REMEMBER THE ALAMO!"
B. Orders of the Day: March 6
(1836)
by General Juan Amador

On the afternoon of March 5, Santa Anna had General Amador, his Chief of Staff, issue the following secret orders for storming the Alamo. Santa Anna is "His Excellency, the General-in-Chief" in the orders and remained at a safe distance during the fighting. The Mexican commander would show no mercy—no one would escape alive—and probably both sides knew this as they waited for the climactic battle of the siege.

"To the Generals, Chiefs of Sections and Commanding Officers.
    "The time has come to strike a decisive blow upon the enemy occupying the Fortress of the Alamo. Consequently, His Excellency, the General-in-Chief, has decided that, to-morrow at 4 o'clock a.m., the columns of

attack shall be stationed at musket-shot distance from the first entrench-
ments, ready for the charge, which shall commence, at a signal to be given
with the bugle, from the Northern Battery.

"The first column will carry ten ladders, two crowbars and two axes;
the second, ten ladders; the third, six ladders; and the fourth, two ladders.

"The men carrying the ladders will sling their guns on their shoulders,
to be enabled to place the ladders wherever they may be required.

"The companies of Grenadiers will be supplied with six packages of
cartridges to every man, and the centre companies with two packages and
two spare flints. The men will wear neither overcoats nor blankets, or
anything that may impede the rapidity of their motions. The Commanding
Officers will see that the men have the chin straps of their caps down, and
that they wear either shoes or sandals.

"The troops composing the columns of attack will turn in to sleep at
dark; to be in readiness to move at 12 o'clock at night.

"Recruits deficient in instruction will remain in their quarters. The
arms, principally the bayonets, should be in perfect order.

"As soon as the moon rises, the centre companies of the Active Battalion of San Luis will abandon the points they are now occupying on the line,
in order to have time to prepare.

"The cavalry, under Colonel Joaquin Ramirez y Sesma, will be stationed at the Alameda, saddling up at 3 o'clock a.m. It shall be its duty
to scout the country, to prevent the possibility of an escape.

"The honor of the nation being interested in this engagement against
the bold and lawless foreigners who are opposing us, His Excellency ex-
pects that every man will do his duty, and exert himself to give a day of
glory to the country, and of gratification to the Supreme Government, who
will know how to reward the distinguished deeds of the brave soldiers of
the Army of Operations."

"REMEMBER THE ALAMO!"
C. The Battle and the Burial
(1836)
by Francis Antonio Ruiz

*Francisco Ruiz was the alcade (administrator, or mayor) of San Antonio. His brief
narrative gives a good description of the battle, although later historians revised his
battle statistics. The Mexican army has been estimated at about 3,000 men, with
between 500 and 600 soldiers killed or wounded. Since there were only 182 defenders,*

each man inflicted a remarkable toll considering the primitive weaponry of the day.
We can only speculate on the emotions and actions of the defenders inside the
Alamo. They left no written record. Each of the 182 Texans died that morning.

"On the 6th March (1836) at 3 A.M., General Santa Anna at the head
of 4,000 men advanced against the Alamo. The infantry, artillery and cavalry had formed about 1,000 varas from the walls of the same fortress. The
Mexican army charged and were twice repulsed by the deadly fire of
Travis's artillery, which resembled a constant thunder. At the third charge
the Toluca battalion commenced to scale the walls and suffered severely.
Out of 830 men only 130 were left live.

"When the Mexican army entered the walls, I with the political chief,
Don Ramon Musquiz and other members of the corporation, accompanied
by the curate, Don Refugio de la Garza, who by Santa Anna's orders had
assembled during the night at a temporary fortification on Protero Street,
with the object of attending the wounded, etc. As soon as the storming
commenced we crossed the bridge on Commerce street, with this object
in view and about 100 yards from the same, a party of Mexican dragoons
fired upon us and compelled us to fall back on the river and the place we
occupied before. Half an hour had elapsed when Santa Anna sent one of
his aides-de-camp with an order for us to come before him. He directed
me to call on some of the neighbors to come with carts to carry the (Mexican) dead to the cemetery and to accompany him, as he was desirous to
have Col. Travis, Bowie, and Crockett shown to him.

"On the north battery of the fortress convent, lay the lifeless body of
Col. Travis on the gun carriage, shot only through the forehead. Towards
the west, and in a small fort opposite the city, we found the body of Col.
Crockett. Col. Bowie was found dead in his bed in one of the rooms on
the south side.

"Santa Anna, after all the Mexican bodies had been taken out, ordered
wood to be brought to burn the bodies of the Texans. He sent a company
of dragoons with me to bring wood and dry branches from the neighboring forests. About three o'clock in the afternoon of March 6, we laid the
wood and dry branches upon which a pile of dead bodies were placed, more
wood was piled on them and another pile of bodies was brought and
in this manner they were all arranged in layers. Kindling wood was
distributed through the pile and about 5 o'clock in the evening it was
lighted.

"The dead Mexicans of Santa Anna were taken to the grave-yard, but
not having sufficient room for them, I ordered some to be thrown into the
river, which was done on the same day.

"The gallantry of the few Texans who defended the Alamo was really
wondered at by the Mexican army. Even the generals were astonished at
their vigorous resistance and how dearly victory was bought.

"The generals, who under Santa Anna participated in the storming of the Alamo, were Juan Amador, Castrillon, Ramirez y Sesma and Andrade."

"The men [Texans] burnt were one hundred and eighty-two. I was an eye-witness, for as Alcalde of San Antonio, I was, with some of the neighbors, collecting the dead bodies and placing them on the funeral pyre."

THE BATTLE OF SAN JACINTO
(1836)
by General Sam Houston

Houston made this report in the third person. He was a native of Virginia, moved to Tennessee where he was elected to the United States Congress from 1823 to 1827 and served as that state's governor for the next two years. Houston was commander-in-chief of the Army of Texas and led those forces at San Jacinto. Three times he was elected President of the Texas republic, and then served in the United States Senate after Texas was annexed.

The Mexican army was literally caught napping at San Jacinto. It was a stunning victory for the Texans. Houston put his losses at 8 killed, 23 wounded; the Mexicans, at 630 killed, 208 wounded, and 730 prisoners.

The General[2] proceeded on his way and met many fugitives. The day on which he left Washington, the 6th of March, the Alamo had fallen. He anticipated it; and marching to Gonzales as soon as practicable, tho his health was infirm, he arrived there on the 11th of March. He found at Gonzales three hundred and seventy-four men, half fed, half clad, and half armed, and without organization. That was the nucleus on which he had to form an army and defend the country. No sooner did he arrive than he sent a dispatch to Colonel Fannin, fifty-eight miles, which would reach him in thirty hours, to fall back. He was satisfied that the Alamo had fallen. Colonel Fannin was ordered to fall back from Goliad, twenty-five miles to Victoria, on the Guadalupe, thus placing him within striking distance of Gonzales, for he had only to march twenty-five miles to Victoria to be on the east side of the Colorado, with the only succor hoped for by the General. He received an answer from Colonel Fannin, stating *that he had received his order; had held a council of war; and that he had determined to defend the place, and called it Fort Defiance, and had taken the responsibility to disobey the order.*

[2] That is, Houston himself.

Fannin, after disobeying orders, attempted, on the 19th, to retreat; and had only twenty-five miles to reach Victoria. His opinions of chivalry and honor were such that he would not avail himself of the night to do it in, altho he had been admonished by the smoke of the enemies' encampment for eight days previous to attempting a retreat. He then attempted to retreat in open day. The Mexican cavalry surrounded him. He halted in a prairie, without water; commenced a fortification, and there was surrounded by the enemy, who, from the hill tops, shot down upon him. Tho the most gallant spirits were there with him, he remained in that situation all that night, and the next day, when a flag of truce was presented; he entered into a capitulation, and was taken to Goliad, on a promise to be returned to the United States with all associated with him. In less than eight days, the attempt was made to massacre him and every man with him. I believe some few did escape, most of whom came afterward and joined the army.

The remarkable march brought the army in a little time to Harrisburg, opposite which it halted. Orders were given by the General immediately to prepare rations for three days, and to be at an early hour in readiness to cross the bayou.

The line of march was taken up for San Jacinto, for the purpose of cutting off Santa Anna below the junction of the San Jacinto and Buffalo bayou. In the morning the sun had risen brightly, and he determined with this omen, "today the battle shall take place." After the council was dismissed, the General sent for Deaf Smith and his comrade, Reeves, who came mounted, when he gave them the axes so as not to attract the attention of the troops. They placed them in their saddles, as Mexicans carry swords and weapons, and started briskly for the scene of action. The General announced to them: "You will be speedy if you return in time for the scenes that are to be enacted here."

They executed the order, and when the troops with the General were within sixty yards of the enemy's front, when charging, Deaf Smith returned and announced that the bridge was cut down. It had been preconcerted to announce that the enemy had received no reenforcement. It was announced to the army for the first time; for the idea that the bridge would be cut down was never thought of by any one but the General himself, until he ordered it to be done, and then only known to Smith and his comrade. It would have made the army polemics if it had been known that Vince's bridge was to be destroyed, for it cut off all means of escape for either Army. There was no alternative but victory or death.

With the exception of the Commander-in-Chief, no gentleman in the army had ever been in a general action, or even witnessed one; no one had been drilled in a regular army, or had been accustomed to the evolutions necessary to the maneuvering of troops. So soon as the disposition of the troops was made, according to his judgment, he announced to the Secretary of War the plan of battle. It was concurred in instantly. The Commander-in-Chief requested the Secretary of War to take command of the left wing, so as to possess him of the timber, and enable him to turn the right wing of the enemy. The General's plan of battle was carried out.

DICKENS' FIRST VISIT TO AMERICA
(1842)
by Charles Dickens

One of the most famous English fictional novelists of all times, Dickens was born into a poverty-stricken home in 1812. Some of his most famous novels include Oliver Twist *(1837);* David Copperfield *(1850);* A Tale of Two Cities *(1859);* Great Expectations *(1860); and* A Christmas Carol *(1843). These novels were published by newspapers in weekly installments, thus creating intense public interest.*

"As the Cunard boats [in Boston] have a wharf of their own at the customhouse, and that a narrow one, we [wrote Dickens] were a long time (an hour at least) working in. I was standing in full fig on the paddle-box beside the captain, staring about me, when suddenly, long before we were moored to the wharf, a dozen men came leaping on board at the peril of their lives, with great bundles of newspapers under their arms; worsted comforters (very much the worse for wear) round their necks; and so forth. 'Aha!' says I, 'this is like our London Bridge'; believing, of course, that these visitors were newsboys. But what do you think of their being editors? And what do you think of their tearing violently up to me and beginning to shake hands like madmen? Oh! if you could have seen how I wrung their wrists! And if you could but know how I hated one man in very dirty gaiters, and with very protruding upper teeth, who said to all comers after him, 'So you've been introduced to our friend Dickens—eh?' There was one among them, tho, who really was of use; a Doctor S., editor of the ————. He ran off here (two miles at least), and ordered rooms and dinner. And in course of time Kate, and I, and Lord Mulgrave (who was going back to his regiment at Montreal on Monday, and had agreed to live with us in the meanwhile) sat down in a spacious and handsome room to a very handsome dinner, bating peculiarities of putting on table, and had forgotten the ship entirely."

What further he had to say of that week's experience finds its first public utterance here. "How can I tell you," he continues, "what has happened since that first day? How can I give you the faintest notion of my reception here; of the crowds that pour in and out the whole day; of the people that line the streets when I go out; of the cheering when I went to the theater; of the copies of verses, letter of congratulation, welcomes of all kinds, balls, dinners, assemblies without end?

"I have had deputations from the Far West, who have come from more than two thousand miles' distance: from the lakes, the rivers, the backwoods, the log houses, the cities, factories, villages, and towns. Authorities from nearly all the States have written to me. I have heard from the universities, Congress, Senate, and bodies, public and private, of every sort and kind. 'It is no nonsense, and no common feeling,' wrote Dr. Channing to me yesterday. 'It is all heart. There never was, and never will be, such a triumph.' And it is a good thing, is it not, to find those fancies it has given me and you the greatest satisfaction to think of, at the core of it all? And if I know my heart, not twenty times this praise would move me to an act of folly."

Three days later he began another letter; and, as this will be entirely new to the reader, I shall print it as it reached me, with only such omission of matter concerning myself as I think it my duty, however reluctantly, to make throughout these extracts: "We left Boston on the fifth, and went away with the governor of the city to stay till Monday at his house at Worcester. He married a sister of Bancroft's, and another sister of Bancroft's went down with us. The village of Worcester is one of the prettiest in New England. On Monday morning at nine o'clock we started again by railroad and went on to Springfield.

"There, there was quite an English inn; except in respect of the bedrooms, which are always uncomfortable; and the best committee of management that has yet presented itself. They kept us more quiet, and were more considerate and thoughtful, even to their own exclusion, than any I have yet had to deal with. Kate's face being horribly bad, I determined to give her a rest here; and accordingly wrote to get rid of my engagement at New Haven, on that plea. We remained in this town until the eleventh: holding a formal levee every day for two hours, and receiving on each from two hundred to three hundred people. At five o'clock on the afternoon of the eleventh, we set off (still by railroad) for New Haven, which we reached about eight o'clock. The moment we had had tea, we were forced to open another levee for the students and professors of the college (the largest in the States), and the townspeople. I suppose we shook hands, before going to bed, with considerably more than five hundred people; and I stood, as a matter of course, the whole time.

"I was delighted to find on board a Mr. Felton whom I had known at Boston. He is the Greek professor at Cambridge, and was going on to the ball and dinner. Like most men of his class whom I have seen, he is a most delightful fellow—unaffected, hearty, genial, jolly; quite an Englishman of the best sort. We drank all the porter on board, ate all the cold pork and cheese, and were very merry indeed.

"About half-past 2 we arrived here (New York). In half an hour more, we reached this hotel, where a very splendid suite of rooms was prepared for us; and where everything is very comfortable, and no doubt (as at Boston) *enormously* dear. Just as we sat down to dinner, David Colden made his appearance; and when he had gone, and we were taking our wine, Washington Irving came in alone, with open arms. And here he stopt, until ten o'clock at night."

"Having got so far, I shall divide my discourse into four points. First, the ball. Secondly, some slight specimens of a certain phase of character in the Americans. Thirdly, international copyright. Fourthly, my life here, and projects to be carried out while I remain.

"Firstly, the ball. It came off last Monday (vide pamphlet.) 'At a quarter-past 9, exactly' (I quote the printed order of proceeding), we were waited upon by 'David Colden, Esquire, and General George Morris'; habited, the former in full ball costume, the latter in the full-dress uniform of Heaven knows what regiment of militia. The General took Kate, Colden gave his arm to me, and we proceeded down stairs to a carriage at the door, which took us to the stage-door of the theater, greatly to the disappointment of an enormous crowd who were besetting the main door and making a most tremendous hullaballoo.

"The newspapers were, if possible, unusually loquacious; and in their accounts of me, and my seeings, sayings, and doings on the Saturday night and Sunday before, they describe my manner, mode of speaking, dressing, and so forth. In doing this, they report that I am a very charming fellow (of course), and have a very free and easy way with me; 'which,' say they, 'at first amused a few fashionables'; but soon pleased them exceedingly. Another paper, coming after the ball, dwells upon its splendor and brilliancy; hugs itself and its readers upon all that Dickens saw, and winds up by gravely expressing its conviction that Dickens was never in such society in England as he has seen in New York, and that its high and striking tone can not fail to make an indelible impression on his mind! For the same reason I am always represented, whenever I appear in public, as being 'very pale': 'apparently thunderstruck'; and utterly confounded by all I see. You recognize the queer vanity which is at the root of all this? I have plenty of stories in connection with it to amuse you with when I return."

"I have the privilege of appearing on the floor of both Houses here [in Washington], and go to them every day. They are very handsome and commodious. There is a great deal of bad speaking, but there are a great many very remarkable men, in the legislature: such as John Quincy Adams, Clay, Preston, Calhoun, and others: with whom I need scarcely add I have been placed in the friendliest relations. Adams is a fine old fellow—seventy-six years old, but with most surprizing vigor, memory, readiness, and pluck. Clay is perfectly enchanting; an irresistible man. There are some very notable specimens, too, out of the West. Splendid men to look at, hard to receive, prompt to act, lions in energy, Crichtons in varied accomplishments, Indians in quickness of eye and gesture, Americans in affectionate and generous impulse. It would be difficult to exaggerate the nobility of some of these glorious fellows."

"Irving was with me at Washington yesterday, and *wept heartily* at parting. He is a fine fellow, when you know him well; and you would relish him, my dear friend, of all things. We have laughed together at some absurdities we have encountered in company, quite in my vociferous Devonshire Terrace style. The 'Merrikin' Government has treated him, he says, most liberally and handsomely in every respect. He thinks of sailing for Liverpool on the 7th of April, passing a short time in London, and then going to Paris. Perhaps you may meet him. If you do, he will know that you are my dearest friend, and will open his whole heart to you at once. His secretary of legation, Mr. Coggleswell, is a man of very remarkable information, a great traveler, a good talker, and a scholar."

The next letter described his experiences in the Far West, his stay in St. Louis, his visit to a prairie, the return to Cincinnati, and, after a stagecoach ride from that city to Columbus, the travel thence to Sandusky, and so, by Lake Erie, to the Falls of Niagara.

"A St. Louis lady complimented Kate upon her voice and manner of speaking, assuring her that she should never have suspected her of being Scotch, or even English. She was so obliging as to add that she would have taken her for an American, anywhere: which she (Kate) was no doubt aware was a very great compliment, as the Americans were admitted on all hands to have greatly refined upon the English language! I need not tell you that out of Boston and New York a nasal drawl is universal, but I may as well hint that the prevailing grammar is also more than doubtful; that the oddest vulgarisms are received idioms; that all the women who have been bred in slave states speak more or less like negroes, from having been constantly in their childhood with black nurses; and that the most fashionable and aristocratic (these are two words in great use), instead of asking you in what place you were born, inquire where you 'hail from'!

"I never in my life was in such a state of excitement as coming from Buffalo here [to Niagara Falls] this morning. You come by railroad, and are nigh two hours upon the way. I looked out for the spray, and listened for the roar, as far beyond the bounds of possibility as tho, landing in Liverpool, I were to listen for the music of your pleasant voice in Lincoln's Inn Fields. At last, when the train stopt, I saw two great white clouds rising up from the depths of the earth—nothing more. They rose up slowly, gently, majestically, into the air. I dragged Kate down a deep and slippery path leading to the ferry-boat; bullied Anne for not coming fast enough;

perspired at every pore; and felt, it is impossible to say how, as the sound grew louder and louder in my ears, and yet nothing could be seen for the mist. I went down alone, into the very basin. It would be hard for a man to stand nearer God than he does there. There was a bright rainbow at my feet; and from that I looked up to—great Heaven! to *what* a fall of bright green water! The broad, deep, mighty stream seems to die in the act of falling; and from its unfathomable grave arises that tremendous ghost of spray and mist which is never laid, and has been haunting this place with the same dread solemnity—perhaps from the creation of the world."

THE FIRST TELEGRAPH LINE
(1844)
by Samuel Morse

This account is contained in a letter that Morse wrote from Paris in 1866. Morse was an artist as well as an inventor. Having graduated from Yale in 1810, he studied art in London under Benjamin West, and opened a studio in New York in 1823, becoming the first president of the National Academy of Design (1826–42). Morse first designed the electric telegraph in 1832, and three years later exhibited a working model of it. In 1837 he applied for a patent, and in 1843 Congress granted an appropriation for the construction of a line as here described between Baltimore and Washington, the same being completed in 1844.

I had spent at Washington two entire sessions of Congress, one in 1837–38, the other in 1842–43, in the endeavor so far to interest the Government in the novel telegraph as to furnish me with the means to construct a line of sufficient length to test its practicability and utility.

The last days of the last session of that Congress were about to close. A bill appropriating thirty thousand dollars for my purpose had passed the House, and was before the Senate for concurrence, waiting its turn on the calendar. On the last day of the session (3d of March, 1843), I had spent the whole day and part of the evening in the Senate chamber, anxiously watching the progress of the passing of the various bills, of which there were, in the morning of that day, over one hundred and forty to be acted upon, before the one in which I was interested would be reached; and a resolution had a few days before been passed, to proceed with the bills on the calendar in their regular order, forbidding any bill to be taken up out of its regular place.

As evening approached, there seemed to be but little chance that the Telegraph Bill would be reached before the adjournment, and consequently I had the prospect of the delay of another year, with the loss of time, and all my means already expended. In my anxiety, I consulted with two of my senatorial friends—Senator Huntington, of Connecticut, and Senator Wright, of New York—asking their opinion of the probability of reaching the bill before the close of the session. Their answers were discouraging, and their adivce was to prepare myself for disappointment. In this state of mind I retired to my chamber, and made all my arrangements for leaving Washington the next day. Painful as was this prospect of renewed disappointment, you, my dear sir, will understand me when I say that, knowing from experience whence my help must come in any difficulty I soon disposed of my cares, and slept as quietly as a child.

In the morning, as I had just gone into the breakfast-room, the servant called me out, announcing that a young lady was in the parlor, wishing to speak with me. I was at once greeted with the smiling face of my young friend, the daughter of my old and valued friend and classmate, the Hon. H. L. Ellsworth, the Commissioner of Patents. On expressing my surprize at so early a call, she said, "I have come to congratulate you." "Indeed, for what?" "On the passage of your bill." "Oh, no, my young friend, you are mistaken; I was in the Senate chamber till after the lamps were lighted, and my senatorial friends assured me there was no chance for me." "But," she replied, "it is you that are mistaken. Father was there at the adjournment, at midnight, and saw the President put his name to your bill; and I asked father if I might come and tell you, and he gave me leave. Am I the first to tell you?" The news was so unexpected that for some moments I could not speak. At length I replied: "Yes, Annie, you are the first to inform me; and now I am going to make you a promise: the first dispatch on the completed line from Washington to Baltimore shall be yours." "Well," said she, "I shall hold you to your promise."

In about a year from that time the line from Washington to Baltimore was completed. I was in Baltimore when the wires were brought into the office and attached to the instrument. I proceeded to Washington, leaving word that no dispatch should be sent through the line until I had sent one from Washington. On my arrival there, I sent a note to Miss Ellsworth, announcing to her that everything was ready, and I was prepared to fulfil my promise of sending the first dispatch over the wires, which she was to indite. The answer was immediately returned. The dispatch was, *"What hath God wrought!"* It was sent to Baltimore, and repeated to Washington, and the strip of paper upon which the telegraphic characters are printed was claimed by Governor Seymour, of Hartford, Connecticut, then a member of the House, on the ground that Miss Ellsworth was a native of Hartford. It was delivered to him by Miss Ellsworth, and is now preserved in the archives of the Hartford Museum, or Atheneum.

I need only add that no words could have been selected more expressive of the disposition of my own mind at that time, to ascribe all the honor to Him to whom it truly belongs.

PAINLESS SURGERY INTRODUCED
(1846)
by Dr. William James Morton

From Dr. Morton's Memoranda Relating to the Discovery of Surgical Anesthesia.

In November, 1844, Dr. Morton entered the Harvard Medical School in Boston in a regular course as a matriculate and attended lectures for two years, expecting soon to receive his full degree. While pursuing his studies and practising dentistry at the same time as a means of earning the money necessary to continue them, his attention was drawn vividly to the pain attending certain severe dental operations. The suffering involved made a deep impression upon his mind and he set about to discover some means to alleviate it.

He read in his text-books extensively upon the subject, and finally began a series of experiments upon insects, fish, dogs, and lastly upon himself. Satisfied that his favorite spaniel, "Nig," had not been harmed by the inhalation of sulfuric ether vapor, even subsequent to a state of complete unconsciousness, he determined to inhale the ether himself. In his memoir to the Academy of Arts and Sciences, at Paris, presented by M. Arago, in the autumn of 1847, he thus describes the experiment, and his next almost immediate experiment upon a patient:

"Taking the tube and flask, I shut myself up in my room, seated myself in the operating chair, and commenced inhaling. I found the ether so strong that it partially suffocated me, but produced no decided effect. I then saturated my handkerchief and inhaled it from that. I looked at my watch and soon lost consciousness. As I recovered, I felt a numbness in my limbs, with a sensation like nightmare, and would have given the world for some one to come and arouse me. I thought for a moment I should die in that state, and the world would only pity or ridicule my folly. At length I felt a slight tingling of the blood in the end of my third finger, and made an effort to touch it with my thumb, but without success. At a second effort, I touched it, but there seemed to be no sensation. I gradually raised my arm and pinched my thigh but I could see that sensation was imperfect. I attempted to rise from my chair, but fell back. Gradually I regained power over my limbs and found that I had been insensible between seven and eight minutes.

"Delighted with the success of this experiment, I immediately announced the result to the persons employed in my establishment, and waited impatiently for some one upon whom I could make a fuller trial. Toward evening, a man residing in Boston came in, suffering great pain, and wishing to have a tooth extracted. He was afraid of the operation, and asked if he could be mesmerized. I told him I had something better, and saturating my handkerchief, gave it to him to inhale. He became unconscious almost immediately. It was dark, and Dr. Hayden held the lamp while I extracted a firmly-rooted bicuspid tooth. There was not much alteration in the pulse and no relaxing of the muscles. He recovered in a minute and knew nothing of what had been done for him. He remained for some time talking about the experiment. This was on the 30th of September, 1846."

The first public notice of this event appeared in the Boston *Daily Journal* of October 1, 1846, in the following terms:

"Last evening, as we were informed by a gentleman who witnessed the operation, an ulcerated tooth was extracted from the mouth of an individual without giving him the slightest pain. He was put into a kind of sleep, by inhaling a preparation, the effects of which lasted for about three-quarters of a minute, just long enough to extract the tooth."

This publication induced the eminent surgeon, Dr. Henry J. Bigelow, to visit Dr. Morton's office, and he was present at a large number of successful inhalations of ether vapor by the new method in which teeth were extracted without pain. So imprest was he with the magnitude of the event and the perfection of the method of anesthetic inhalation in Morton's hands, that he at once warmly espoused Morton's desire to make public demonstration of his method. Largely through his instrumentality, permission was secured from Dr. John C. Warren, senior surgeon of the Massachusetts General Hospital, to make trial of the new method, and on October 16, 1846, at this hospital, occurred the first public demonstration of surgical anesthesia, in the presence of the surgical and medical staffs in an amphitheater crowded to overflowing with students and physicians.

The trustees of the Massachusetts General Hospital, quickly following the public demonstration of October, 1846, made a report according the honor and credit of the discovery to Dr. Morton, and presented him with a silver box containing $1,000, "In honor of the ether discovery of September 30, 1846," adding the further inscription, "He has become poor in a cause which has made the world his debtor."

THE STORMING OF CHAPULTEPEC

(1847)

by General Winfield Scott

From Scott's official report, written at the National Palace in Mexico, September 18, 1847. Scott, a native of Virginia, entered the army as a captain in 1808, served in the War of 1812, became a brevet major-general in 1814 and commanded in South Carolina during the Nullification troubles of 1832. He served afterward against the Seminoles and Creeks, became commander in chief in 1841, and commanded in Mexico during the war with that country.

Chapultepec is the famous castle-like fortress located atop a rocky piece of ground in the southwest corner of Mexico City. It has been the home of Aztec Indian emperors, Spanish governors, the French puppet emperor Maximilian, and later the Mexican leadership. During the Mexican War the American General Scott had to successfully storm Chapultepec before American troops could capture Mexico City. Since 1937 the castle has become a Mexican National War Museum and Park.

At the end of another series of arduous and brilliant operations, of more than forty-eight hours' continuance, this glorious army hoisted, on the morning of the 14th, the colors of the United States on the walls of this palace.

This city stands upon a slight swell of ground, near the center of an irregular basin, and is girdled with a ditch in its greater extent—a navigable canal of great breadth and depth—very difficult to bridge in the presence of an enemy, and serving at once for drainage, custom-house purposes, and military defense; leaving eight entrances or gates over arches, each of which we found defended by a system of strong works, that seemed to require nothing but some men and guns to be impregnable.

After a close personal survey of the southern gates, covered by Pillow's division and Riley's brigade, and Twigg's, with four times our numbers concentrated in our immediate front, I determined, on the 11th, to avoid that network of obstacles, and to seek, by a sudden inversion to the southwest and west, less unfavorable approaches.

The first step in the new movement was to carry Chapultepec, a natural and isolated mound, of great elevation, strongly fortified at its base, on its acclivities and heights. Besides a numerous garrison, here was the military college of the republic, with a large number of sub-lieutenants and other students. Those works were within direct gunshot of the village of Tacubaya, and, until carried, we could not approach the city on the west without making a circuit too wide and too hazardous.

Both columns now advanced with an alacrity that gave assurance of prompt success. The batteries, seizing opportunities, threw shots and shells upon the enemy over the heads of our men, with good effect, particularly at every attempt to reinforce the works from without to meet our assault.

The broken acclivity was still to be ascended, and a strong redoubt, midway, to be carried, before reaching the castle on the heights. The advance of our brave men, led by brave officers, tho necessarily slow, was unwavering, over rocks, chasms, and mines, and under the hottest fire of cannon and musketry. The redoubt now yielded to resistless valor, and the shouts that followed announced to the castle the fate that impended. The enemy were steadily driven from shelter to shelter. The retreat allowed not time to fire a single mine, without the certainty of blowing up friend and foe. Those who at a distance attempted to apply matches to the long trains were shot down by our men. There was death below, as well as above ground.

At length the ditch and wall of the main work were reached; the scaling-ladders were brought up and planted by the storming parties; some of the daring spirits first in the assault were cast down—killed or wounded; but a lodgment was soon made; streams of heroes followed; all opposition was overcome, and several of the regimental colors flung out from the upper walls, amid long-continued shouts and cheers, which sent dismay into the capital. No scene could have been more animating or glorious.

At a junction of roads, we first passed one of the formidable systems of city defenses, and it had not a gun!—a strong proof: 1. That the enemy had expected us to fall in the attack upon Chapultepec, even if we meant anything more than a feint; 2. That, in either case, we designed, in his belief, to return and double our forces against the southern gates, a delusion kept up by the active demonstrations of Twiggs and the forces posted on that side; and 3. That advancing rapidly from the reduction of Chapultepec, the enemy had not time to shift guns—our previous captures had left him, comparatively, but few—from the southern gates.

Within those disgarnished works I found our troops engaged in a street fight against the enemy posted in gardens, at windows, and on housetops —all flat, with parapets. Worth ordered forward the mountain-howitzers of Cadwalader's brigade, preceded by skirmishers and pioneers, with pickaxes and crowbars, to force windows and doors, or to burrow through walls. The assailants were soon in an equality of position fatal to the enemy. By eight o'clock in the evening, Worth had carried two batteries in this suburb. According to my instructions, he here posted guards and sentinels, and placed his troops under shelter for the night. There was but one more obstacle—the San Cosme gate (custom-house) between him and the great square in front of the cathedral and palace—the heart of the city;

and that barrier, it was known, could not, by daylight, resist our siege guns thirty minutes.

At about 4 o'clock next morning (September 14) a deputation of the *ayuntamiento* (city council) waited upon me to report that the Federal Government and the army of Mexico had fled from the capital some three hours before, and to demand terms of capitulation in favor of the church, the citizens, and the municipal authorities. I promptly replied, that I would sign no capitulation; that the city had been virtually in our possession from the time of the lodgments effected by Worth and Quitman the day before; that I regretted the silent escape of the Mexican army; that I should levy upon the city a moderate contribution, for special purposes; and that the American army should come under no terms, not *self-imposed*—such only as its own honor, the dignity of the United States, and the spirit of the age should, in my opinion, imperiously demand and impose.

At the termination of the interview with the city deputation, I communicated, about daylight, orders to Worth and Quitman to advance slowly and cautiously (to guard against treachery) toward the heart of the city, and to occupy its stronger and more commanding points. Quitman proceeded to the great plaza or square, planted guards, and hoisted the colors of the United States on the national palace—containing the halls of Congress and executive apartments of Federal Mexico.

THE DISCOVERY OF GOLD IN CALIFORNIA
(1847)
by James W. Marshall

James W. Marshall is the hero of the California gold discovery. In a letter dated January 28, 1856, and addressed to Charles E. Pickett, Marshall gives this account.

Toward the end of August, 1847, Captain Sutter and I formed a copartnership to build and run a sawmill upon a site selected by myself (since known as Coloma). We employed P. L. Weimer and family to remove from the Fort (Sutter's Fort) to the mill-site, to cook and labor for us. Nearly the first work done was the building of a double log cabin, about half a mile from the mill-site. We commenced the mill about Christmas. Some of the mill-hands wanted a cabin near the mill. This was built, and I went to the

Fort to superintend the construction of the mill-irons, leaving orders to cut a narrow ditch where the race was to be made. Upon my return, 1848, I found the ditch cut, as directed, and those who were working on the same were doing so at a great disadvantage, expending their labor upon the head of the race instead of the foot.

I immediately changed the course of things, and upon the 19th of the same month of January discovered the gold near the lower end of the race, about two hundred yards below the mill. William Scott was the second man to see the metal. He was at work at a carpenter's bench near the mill. I showed the gold to him. Alexander Stephens, James Brown, Henry Bigler, and William Johnston were likewise working in front of the mill, framing the upper story. They were called up next, and, of course, saw the precious metal. P. L. Weimer and Charles Bennett were at the old double log cabin (where Hastings and Company afterward kept a store).

In the mean time we put in some wheat and peas, nearly five acres, across the river. In February the Captain (Captain Sutter) came to the mountains for the first time. Then we consummated a treaty with the Indians, which had been previously negotiated. The tenor of this was that we were to pay them two hundred dollars yearly in goods, at Yerba Buena prices, for the joint possession and occupation of the land with them; they agreeing not to kill our stock, viz., horses, cattle, hogs, or sheep, nor burn the grass within the limits fixt by the treaty. At the same time Captain Sutter, myself, and Isaac Humphrey, entered into a copartnership to dig gold. A short time afterward, P. L. Weimer moved away from the mill, and was away two or three months, when he returned. With all the events that subsequently occurred, you and the public are well informed.

The preceding article by Marshall is the most precise and is generally considered to be the most correct account of the gold discovery. Other versions of the story have been published, however, and the following, from an article published in the Coloma Argus, in the latter part of the year 1855, is one of them. The statement was evidently derived from Weimer, who lived at Coloma.

"That James W. Marshall picked up the first piece of gold is beyond doubt. Peter L. Weimer, who resides in this place, states positively that Marshall picked up the gold in his presence; they both saw it, and each spoke at the same time, 'What's that yellow stuff?' Marshall, being a step in advance, picked it up. This first piece of gold is now in the possession of Mrs. Weimer, and weighs six pennyweights eleven grains. The piece was given to her by Marshall himself. The dam was finished early in January, the frame for the mill also erected, and the flume and bulkhead completed. It was at this time that Marshall and Weimer adopted the plan of raising the gate during the night to wash out sand from the mill-race, closing it during the day, when work would be continued with shovels, etc.

"Early in February—the exact day is not remembered—in the morning, after shutting off the water, Marshall and Weimer walked down the race together to see what the water had accomplished during the night. Having gone about twenty yards below the mill, they both saw the piece of gold before mentioned, and Marshall picked it up. After an examination, the gold was taken to the cabin of Weimer, and Mrs. Weimer instructed to boil it in saleratus water; but she, being engaged in making soap, pitched the piece into the soapkettle, where it was boiled all day and all night. The following morning the strange stuff was fished out of the soap, all the brighter for the boiling.

"Discussion now commenced, and all exprest the opinion that perhaps the yellow substance might be gold. Little was said on the subject; but every one each morning searched in the race for more, and every day found several small scales. The Indians also picked up many small thin pieces, and carried them always to Mrs. Weimer. About three weeks after the first piece was obtained, Marshall took the fine gold, amounting to between two and three ounces, and went to San Francisco to have the strange metal tested. On his return he informed Weimer that the stuff was gold."

It was not until more than three months after Marshall's discovery that the San Francisco papers stated that gold-mining had became a regular and profitable business in the new placers.

In the latter part of 1848 adventurers began to arrive from Oregon, the Sandwich Islands, and Mexico. The winter found the miners with very little preparation, but most of them were accustomed to a rough manner of life in the Western wilds, and they considered their large profits an abundant compensation for their privations and hardships. The weather was so mild in December and January that they could work almost as well as in the summer, and the rain gave them facilities for washing such as they could not have in the dry season.

In September, 1848, the first rumors of the gold discovery began to reach New York; in October they attracted attention; in November people looked with interest for new reports; in December the news gained general credence, and a great excitement arose. Preparations were made for a migration to California by somebody in nearly every town in the United States. The great body of the emigrants went across the plains with ox or mule teams or around Cape Horn in sailing vessels. A few took passage in the steamer by way of Panama.

Not fewer than one hundred thousand men, representing in their nativity every State in the Union, went to California that year. Of these, twenty thousand crossed the continent by way of the South Pass; and nearly all of them started from the Missouri River between Independence and St. Joseph, in the month of May. They formed an army; in daytime their trains filled up the roads for miles, and at night their campfires glittered in every direction about the places blest with grass and water. The excitement continued from 1850 to 1853; emigrants continued to come by land and sea, from Europe and America, and in the last-named year from China also. In 1854 the migration fell off, and since that time until the completion of the Union Pacific Railroad California received the chief accessions to her white population by the Panama steamers.

THE UNDERGROUND RAILROAD
(1850)
by Levi Coffin

The Underground Railroad designated the methods by which abolitionists in the North aided and protected slaves who ran away from their Southern masters. The routes over which slaves escaped ran mostly through Ohio and Pennsylvania, and thence to Canada. Coffin was actively engaged in the work in Cincinnati.

The fugitives generally arrived in the night, and were secreted among the friendly colored people or hidden in the upper room of our house. They came alone or in companies, and in a few instances had a white guide to direct them.

One company of twenty-eight that crossed the Ohio River at Lawrenceburg, Indiana—twenty miles below Cincinnati—had for conductor a white man whom they had employed to assist them. The company of twenty-eight slaves referred to, all lived in the same neighborhood in Kentucky, and had been planning for some time how they could make their escape from slavery. This white man—John Fairfield—had been in the neighborhood for some weeks buying poultry, etc., for market, and tho among the whites he assumed to be very pro-slavery, the negroes soon found that he was their friend.

He was engaged by the slaves to help them across the Ohio River, and conduct them to Cincinnati. They paid him some money which they had managed to accumulate. The amount was small, considering the risk the conductor assumed, but it was all they had. Several of the men had their wives with them, and one woman a little child with her, a few months old. John Fairfield conducted the party to the Ohio River, opposite the mouth of the Big Miami, where he knew there were several skiffs tied to the bank, near a woodyard. The entire party crowded into three large skiffs or yawls, and made their way slowly across the river. The boats were overloaded and sank so deep that the passage was made in much peril. The boat John

Fairfield was in was leaky, and began to sink when a few rods from the Ohio bank, and he sprang out on the sand-bar, where the water was two or three feet deep, and tried to drag the boat to the shore. He sank to his waist in mud and quick-sands, and had to be pulled out by some of the negroes. The entire party waded out through mud and water and reached the shore safely, tho all were wet, and several lost their shoes. They hastened along the bank toward Cincinnati, but it was now late in the night and daylight appeared before they reached the city.

Their plight was a most pitiable one. They were cold, hungry, and exhausted; those who had lost their shoes in the mud suffered from bruised and lacerated feet, while to add to their discomfort a drizzling rain fell during the latter part of the night. They could not enter the city for their appearance would at once proclaim them to be fugitives. When they reached the outskirts of the city, below Mill Creek, John Fairfield hid them as well as he could, in ravines that had been washed in the sides of the steep hills, and told them not to move until he returned. He then went directly to John Hatfield, a worthy colored man, a deacon in the Zion Baptist church, and told his story. He had applied to Hatfield before, and knew him to be a great friend to the fugitives—one who had often sheltered them under his roof and aided them in every way he could. When he arrived, wet and muddy, at John Hatfield's house, he was scarcely recognized. He soon made himself and his errand known, and Hatfield at once sent a messenger to me, requesting me to come to his house without delay, as there were fugitives in danger. I went at once and met several prominent colored men who had also been summoned. While dry clothes and a warm breakfast were furnished to John Fairfield, we anxiously discust the situation of the twenty-eight fugitives who were lying hungry and shivering, in the hills in sight of the city.

Several plans were suggested, but none seemed practicable. At last I suggested that some one should go immediately to a certain German livery stable in the city and hire two coaches, and that several colored men should go out in buggies and take the women and children from their hiding places, then that the coaches and buggies should form a procession as if going to a funeral, and march solemnly along the road leading to Cumminsville, on the west side of Mill Creek. In the western part of Cumminsville was the Methodist Episcopal burying-ground, where a certain lot of ground had been set apart for the use of the colored people. They should pass this and continue on the Colerain pike till they reached a right-hand road leading to College Hill. At the latter place they would find a few colored families, living in the outskirts of the village, and could take refuge among them. Jonathan Cable, a Presbyterian minister, who lived near Farmer's College, on the west side of the village, was a prominent Abolitionist, and I knew that he would give prompt assistance to the fugitives.

I advised that one of the buggies should leave the procession at Cumminsville, after passing the burying-ground, and hasten to College Hill to apprize friend Cable of the coming of the fugitives, that he might make arrangements for their reception in suitable places. My suggestions and advice were agreed to, and acted upon as quickly as possible.

While the carriages and buggies were being procured, John Hatfield's wife and daughter, and other colored women of the neighborhood, busied themselves in preparing provisions to be sent to the fugitives. A large stone jug was filled with hot coffee, and this, together with a supply of bread and other provisions, was placed in a buggy and sent on ahead of the carriages, that the hungry fugitives might receive some nourishment before starting. The conductor of the party, accompanied by John Hatfield, went in the buggy, in order to apprize the fugitives of the arrangements that had been made, and have them in readiness to approach the road as soon as the carriages arrived. Several blankets were provided to wrap around the women and children, whom we knew must be chilled by their exposure to the rain and cold. The fugitives were very glad to get the supply of food; the hot coffee especially was a great treat to them, and much revived them. About the time they finished their breakfast the carriages and buggies drove up and halted in the road, and the fugitives were quickly conducted to them and placed inside. The women in the tight carriages wrapt themselves in the blankets, and the woman who had a young babe muffled it closely to keep it warm, and to prevent its cries from being heard. The little thing seemed to be suffering much pain, having been exposed so long to the rain and cold.

All the arrangements were carried out, and the party reached College Hill in safety, and were kindly received and cared for.

When it was known by some of the prominent ladies of the village that a large company of fugitives were in the neighborhood, they met together to prepare some clothing for them. Jonathan Cable ascertained the number and size of the shoes needed, and the clothes required to fit the fugitives for traveling, and came down in his carriage to my house, knowing that the Anti-Slavery Sewing Society had their depository there. I went with him to purchase the shoes that were needed, and my wife selected all the clothing we had that was suitable for the occasion; the rest was furnished by the noble women of College Hill.

I requested friend Cable to keep the fugitives as secluded as possible until a way could be provided for safely forwarding them on their way to Canada. Friend Cable was a stockholder in the Underground Railroad, and we consulted together about the best route, finally deciding on the line by way of Hamilton, West Elkton, Eaton, Paris, and Newport, Indiana. I wrote to one of my particular friends at West Elkton, informing him that I had some valuable stock on hand which I wished to forward to Newport, and requested him to send three two-horse wagons—covered—to College Hill, where the stock was resting, in charge of Jonathan Cable.

The three wagons arrived promptly at the time mentioned, and a little after dark took in the party, together with another fugitive, who had arrived the night before, and whom we added to the company. They went through to West Elkton safely that night, and the next night reached Newport, Indiana. With little delay they were forwarded on from station to station through Indiana and Michigan to Detroit, having fresh teams and conductors each night, and resting during the day. I had letters from different stations, as they progressed, giving accounts of the arrival and departure of the train, and I also heard of their safe arrival on the Canada shore.

THE SWEDISH NIGHTINGALE COMES TO NEW YORK

(1850)

from the New York Tribune

Jenny Lind, known as the Swedish nightingale, studied in Europe under one of the great tenors of all time, Manuel Garcia, the inventor of the laryngoscope. She toured the United States under the management of P. T. Barnum (1850–52), and was probably the greatest soprano of her time.

September 2, 1850.—The long expectation is over—Jenny Lind has landed on our shores. It was confidently expected yesterday morning that the *Atlantic* would arrive in the course of the day, and crowds collected on all points where a lookout down the bay could be had, eager to catch the first glimpse of her hull in the distance.

Toward 1 o'clock, two guns were heard in the direction of Sandy Hook, and immediately after the signal-flag of a steamer was run up at the telegraph station above Clifton. In a few minutes the *Atlantic* hove in sight, her giant bulk looming through the light mist which still lay on the outer bay. On the top of a light deckhouse, erected over the forward companionway, sat the subject of the day's excitement—the veritable Jenny Lind—as fresh and rosy as if the sea had spared her its usual discomforts, and enjoying the novel interest of everything she saw, with an apparent unconsciousness of the observation she excited. At her side stood Mr. Jules Benedict, the distinguished composer, and Signor Giovanni Belleti, the celebrated basso, her artistic companion.

Mr. P. T. Barnum, who had by this time climbed on board, with a choice bouquet carefully stuck in the bosom of his white vest, was taken forward and presented by Captain West. But Mr. Collins had for once stolen a march on him, having got on board in advance, and presented to Miss Lind a bouquet about three times the size of Barnum's. The songstress received the latter with great cordiality.

Her manners are very frank and engaging, and there is an expression of habitual good humor in her clear, blue eye, which would win her the heart of a crowd by a single glance. She is about twenty-nine years of age, and rather more robust in face and person that her portraits would indicate. Her forehead is finely formed, shaded by waves of pale brown hair; her eyes, light blue and joyous; her nose and mouth, tho molded on the large Swedish type, convey an impression of benevolence and sound goodness of heart, which is thoroughly in keeping with the many stories we have heard of her charitable doings. Mademoiselle Lind was drest with great taste and simplicity. She wore a visite of rich black cashmere over a dress of silver-gray silk, with a pale blue silk hat and black veil. At her feet lay a silky little lap-dog, with ears almost half the length of its body; it was of that rare breed which are worth their weight in gold, and was a present from Queen Victoria.

September 12.—Jenny Lind's first concert is over, and all doubts are at an end. She is the greatest singer we have ever heard, and her success is all that was anticipated from her genius and her fame. All the preparatory arrangements for the concert were made with great care, and from an admirable system observed none of the usual disagreeable features of such an event were experienced. Outside of the gate there was a double row of policemen extending up the main avenue of the Battery grounds. Carriages only were permitted to drive up to the gate from the Whitehall side, and pass over into Battery Place. At one time the line of carriages extended to Whitehall and up State Street into Broadway. The chief of police with about sixty men came on the ground at five o'clock, and maintained the most complete order to the end. Mr. Barnum, according to promise, had put up a substantial framework, and thrown an immense awning over the bridge, which is some 200 feet in length. This was brilliantly lighted, and had almost the appearance of a triumphal avenue on entering the gate. There was an immense crowd on the Battery clustering around the gates during the whole evening, but no acts of disorder occurred. When Jenny Lind's carriage came, but very few persons knew it, and no great excitement followed. The sight of the grand hall, with its gay decorations, its glittering lamps, and its vast throng of expectant auditors, was in itself almost worth a $5 ticket. We were surprized to notice that not more than one-eighth of the audience were ladies. They must stay at home, it seems, when the tickets are high, but the gentlemen go, nevertheless. For its size, the audience was one of the most quiet, refined and appreciative we ever saw assembled in this city.

Now came a moment of breathless expectation. A moment more, and Jenny Lind, clad in a white dress which well became the frank sincerity of her face, came forward through the orchestra. It is impossible to describe the spontaneous burst of welcome which greeted her. The vast assembly rose as one man, and for some minutes nothing could be seen but the waving of hands and handkerchiefs, nothing heard but a storm of tumultuous cheers. The enthusiasm of the moment, for a time beyond all bounds, was at last subdued, after prolonging itself by its own fruitless efforts to subdue itself, and the divine songstress, with that perfect bearing, that air of a dignity and sweetness, blending a childlike simplicity and half-trembling womanly modesty with the beautiful confidence of genius and serene wisdom of art, addrest herself to song, as the orchestral symphony prepared the way for the voice in "Casta Diva."

If it were possible, we would describe the quality of that voice, so pure, so sweet, so fine, so whole and all-pervading, in its lowest breathings a miniature *fioriture* as well as in its strongest volume. We never heard tones which in their sweetness went so far. They brought the most distant and ill-seated auditor close to her. They were tones, every one of them, and the whole air had to take the law of their vibrations. The voice and the delivery had in them all the good qualities of all the good singers. Song in her has that integral beauty which at once proclaims it as a type for all, and is most naturally worshiped as such by the multitude.

At the close, the audience (who made no movement to leave till the last note had been uttered), broke out in a tempest of cheers, only less vehement than those which welcomed her in "Casta Diva." She came forward again, bowed with a bright, grateful face, and retired. Everybody went home quietly, with a new joy at his heart, and a new thought in his brain.

THE PUBLICATION OF UNCLE TOM'S CABIN
(1852)
by Harriet Beecher Stowe

Uncle Tom's Cabin, *by Harriet Beecher Stowe, was the most influential book of the pre-Civil War period. It transformed slavery from a social problem into a dynamic political issue. Mrs. Stowe writes here in the third person.*

The author had for many years lived in Ohio on the confines of a slave State, and had thus been made familiar with facts and occurrences in relation to the institution of American slavery. Some of the most harrowing incidents related in the story had from time to time come to her knowledge in conversation with former slaves now free in Ohio. The cruel sale and separation of a married woman from her husband, narrated in Chapter XII, "Select Incident of Lawful Trade," had passed under her own eye while a passenger on a steamboat on the Ohio River. Her husband and brother had once been obliged to flee with a fugitive slave woman by night, as described in Chapter IX; and she herself had been called to write the letters for a former slave woman, servant in her own family, to a slave husband in Kentucky, who, trusted with unlimited liberty, free to come and go on business between Kentucky and Ohio, still refused to break his pledge of honor to his master, tho that master from year to year deferred the keeping of his promise of freedom to the slave. It was the simple honor and loyalty of this Christian black man, who remained in slavery rather than violate a trust, that first imprest her with the possibility of such a character as, years after, was delineated in Uncle Tom.

From time to time incidents were brought to her knowledge which deepened her horror of slavery. But it was not for many years that she felt any call to make use of the materials thus accumulating. In fact, it was a sort of general impression upon her mind, as upon that of many humane people in those days, that the subject was so dark and painful a one, so involved in difficulty and obscurity, so utterly beyond human hope or help, that it was of no use to read or think or distress one's self about it. There was a class of profest Abolitionists in Cincinnati and the neighboring regions, but they were unfashionable persons and few in number. Like all asserters of pure abstract right as applied to human affairs, they were regarded as a species of moral monomaniacs, who, in the consideration of one class of interests and wrongs, had lost sight of all proportion and all good judgment. Both in church and in State they were looked upon as "those that troubled Israel."

After many years' residence in Ohio, Mrs. Stowe returned to make her abode in New England, just in the height of the excitement produced by the Fugitive Slave Law. Settled in Brunswick, Me., she was in constant communication with friends in Boston, who wrote to her from day to day of the terror and despair which that law had occasioned to industrious, worthy colored people who had from time to time escaped to Boston, and were living in peace and security. She heard of families broken up and fleeing in the dead of winter to the frozen shores of Canada. But what seemed to her more inexplicable, more dreadful, was the apparent apathy of the Christian world of the free North to these proceedings. The pulpits that denounced them were exceptions, the voices raised to remonstrate few and far between.

In New England, as at the West, profest Abolitionists were a small, despised, unfashionable band, whose constant remonstrances from year to year had been disregarded as the voices from impracticable fanatics. It seemed now as if the system once confined to the Southern States was rousing itself to new efforts to extend itself all over the North, and to overgrow the institutions of free society.

With astonishment and distress Mrs. Stowe heard on all sides, from humane and Christian people, that the slavery of the blacks was a guaranteed constitutional right, and that all opposition to it endangered the national Union. With this conviction she saw that even earnest and tenderhearted Christian people seemed to feel it a duty to close their eyes, ears, and hearts to the harrowing details of slavery, to put down all discussion of the subject, and even to assist slave-owners to recover fugitives in Northern States. She said to herself, These people can not know what slavery is: they do not see what they are defending; and hence arose a purpose to write some sketches which should show to the world slavery as she had herself seen it. Pondering this subject, she was one day turning over a little bound volume of an anti-slavery magazine, edited by Mrs. Dr. Bailey, of Washington, and there she read the account of the escape of a woman with her child on the ice of the Ohio River from Kentucky. The incident was given by an eye-witness, one who had helped the woman to the Ohio shore. This formed the first salient point of the story. She began to meditate. The faithful slave husband in Kentucky occurred to her as a pattern of Uncle Tom, and the scenes of the story began gradually to form themselves in her mind.

The first part of the book ever committed to writing was the death of Uncle Tom. This scene presented itself almost as a tangible vision to her mind while sitting at the communion-table in the little church in Brunswick. She was perfectly overcome by it, and could scarcely restrain the convulsion of tears and sobbings that shook her frame. She hastened home, and wrote it; and, her husband being away, she read it to her two sons of ten and twelve years of age. The little fellows broke out into convulsions of weeping, one of them saying, through his sobs, "O mamma, slavery is the most curst thing in the world!"

From that time the story can less be said to have been composed by her than imposed upon her. Scenes, incidents, conversations, rushed upon her with a vividness and importunity that would not be denied. The book insisted upon getting itself into being, and would take no denial. After the first two or three chapters were written, she wrote to Dr. Bailey of the *National Era* that she was planning a story that might probably run through several numbers of the *Era.* In reply she received an instant application for it, and began immediately to send off weekly instalments.

As the narrative appeared in the *Era,* sympathetic words began to come to her from old workers who had long been struggling in the anti-slavery cause. She visited Boston, went to the Anti-slavery Rooms, and reenforced her repertoire of facts by such documents as Theodore D. Weld's "Slavery

As It Is," the Lives of Josiah Henson and Lewis Clarke, particulars whose lives were inwoven with the story in the characters of Uncle Tom and George Harris.

In shaping her material, the author had but one purpose, to show the institution of slavery truly, just as it existed. She had visited in Kentucky, had formed the acquaintance of people who were just, upright, and generous, and yet slaveholders. She had heard their views, and appreciated their situation. She felt that justice required that their difficulties should be recognized and their virtues acknowledged. It was her object to show that the evils of slavery were the inherent evils of a bad system, and not always the fault of those who had become involved in it and were its actual administrators.

As the story progrest, a young publisher, J. P. Jewett, of Boston, set his eye upon it, and made overtures for the publication of it in book form, to which she consented. After a while she had a letter from him expressing his fears that she was making the story too long for a one-volume publication. He reminded her that it was an unpopular subject, and that people would not willingly hear much about it: that one short volume might possibly sell, but, if it grew to two, it might prove a fatal obstacle to its success. Mrs. Stowe replied that she did not make the story, that the story made itself, and that she could not stop it till it was done. The feeling that pursued her increased in intensity to the last, till, with the death of Uncle Tom, it seemed as if the whole vital force had left her. A feeling of profound discouragement came over her. Would anybody read it? Would anybody listen? Would this appeal, into which she had put heart, soul, mind, and strength, which she had written with her heart's blood—would it, too, go for nothing, as so many prayers and groans and entreaties of these poor suffering souls had gone?

"Uncle Tom's Cabin" was published March 20, 1852. The despondency of the author as to the question whether anybody would read or attend to her appeal was soon dispelled. Ten thousand copies were sold in a few days, and over 300,000 within a year; and eight powerpresses, running day and night, were barely able to keep pace with the demand for it. It was read everywhere, apparently, and by everybody; and she soon began to hear echoes of sympathy all over the land. The indignation, the pity, the distress that had long weighed upon her soul, seemed to pass off from her and into the readers of the book.

A more cheering result was in the testimony of many colored persons and fugitive slaves who said to her: "Since that book has come out, everybody is good to us: we find friends everywhere. It's wonderful how kind everybody is."

In one respect, Mrs. Stowe's expectations were strikingly different from fact. She had painted slaveholders as amiable, generous, and just. She had shown examples among them of the noblest and most beautiful traits of character, had admitted fully their temptations, their perplexities, and their difficulties, so that a friend of hers who had many relatives in the South wrote to her in exultation, "Your book is going to be the great pacificator: it will unite both North and South." Her expectation was that the profest Abolitionists would denounce it as altogether too mild in its dealings with slaveholders. To her astonishment, it was the extreme Abolitionists who received it, and the entire South who rose up against it.

THE CAPTURE OF JOHN BROWN
(1858)
by Colonel Robert E. Lee

John Brown, an ardent abolitionist, had with his followers seized a federal military arsenal at Harper's Ferry, in what is now West Virginia. They hoped thus to spark an insurrection of slaves.

Colonel Lee, afterward General Lee of the Civil War, commanded the forces sent to Harper's Ferry to oppose Brown. He had graduated from West Point in 1829, served in the Mexican War, and been superintendent of West Point.

I have the honor to report, for the information of the Secretary of War, that on arriving here on the night of the 17th instant, in obedience to Special Orders No. 194 of that date from your office, I learn that a party of insurgents, about 11 P.M. on the 16th, had seized the watchmen stationed at the armory, arsenal, rifle factory, and bridge across the Potomac, and taken possession of those points. They then dispatched six men, under one of their party, called Captain Aaron C. Stevens, to arrest the principal citizens in the neighborhood and incite the negroes to join in the insurrection. The party took Colonel L. W. Washington from his bed about 1:30 A.M. on the 17th, and brought him, with four of his servants, to this place. Mr. J. H. Allstadt and six of his servants were in the same manner seized about 3 A.M., and arms placed in the hands of the negroes. Upon their return here, John E. Cook, one of the party sent to Mr. Washington's, was dispatched to Maryland, with Mr. Washington's wagon, two of his servants, and three of Mr. Allstadt's, for arms and ammunition, etc.

As day advanced, and the citizens of Harper's Ferry commenced their usual avocations, they were separately captured, to the number of forty, as well as I could learn, and confined in one room of the fire-engine house of the armory, which seems early to have been selected as a point of defense. About 11 A.M. the volunteer companies from Virginia began to arrive, and the Jefferson Guards and volunteers from Charlestown, under Captain J. W. Rowen, I understood, were first on the ground. The Hamtramck Guards, Captain V. M. Butler; the Shepherdstown troop, Captain Jacob Reinhart; and Captain Alburtis's company from Martinsburg arrived in the afternoon. These companies, under the direction of Colonels R. W. Taylor and John T. Gibson, forced the insurgents to abandon their positions at the bridge and in the village, and to withdraw within the armory inclosure, where they fortified themselves in the fire-engine house, and carried ten of their prisoners for the purpose of insuring their safety and facilitating their escape, whom they termed hostages.

After sunset more troops arrived. Captain B. B. Washington's company from Winchester, and three companies from Fredericktown, Md., under Colonel Shriver. Later in the evening the companies from Baltimore, under General Charles C. Edgerton, second light brigade, and a detachment of marines, commanded by Lieutenant J. Green accompanied by Major Russell, of that corps, reached Sandy Hook, about one and a half miles east of Harper's Ferry. At this point I came up with these last-named troops, and leaving General Edgerton and his command on the Maryland side of the river for the night, caused the marines to proceed to Harper's Ferry, and placed them within the armory grounds to prevent the possibility of the escape of the insurgents. Having taken measures to halt, in Baltimore, the artillery companies ordered from Fort Monroe, I made preparations to attack the insurgents at daylight. But for the fear of sacrificing the lives of some of the gentlemen held by them as prisoners in a midnight assault, I should have ordered the attack at once.

Their safety was the subject of painful consideration, and to prevent, if possible, jeopardizing their lives, I determined to summon the insurgents to surrender. As soon after daylight as the arrangements were made, Lieutenant J. E. B. Stewart, First Calvary, who had accompanied me from Washington as staff officer, was dispatched, under a flag, with a written summons. Knowing the character of the leader of the insurgents, I did not expect it would be accepted. I had therefore directed that the volunteer troops, under their respective commanders, should be paraded on the lines assigned them outside the armory, and had prepared a storming party of twelve marines, under their commander, Lieutenant Green, and had placed them close to the engine-house, and secure from its fire. Three marines were furnished with sledge-hammers to break in the doors, and the men were instructed how to distinguish our citizens from the insurgents; to attack with the bayonet, and not to injure the blacks detained in custody unless they resisted. Lieutenant Stewart was also directed not to receive from the insurgents any counter propositions. If they accepted the terms offered, they must immediately deliver up their arms and release their prisoners. If they did not, he must, on leaving the engine-house, give me the signal. My object was, with a view of saving our citizens, to have as short an interval as possible between the summons and the attack.

The summons, as I had anticipated, was rejected. At the concerted signal the storming party moved quickly to the door and commenced the attack. The fire-engines within the house had been placed by the besieged close to the doors. The doors were fastened by ropes, the spring of which prevented their being broken by the blows of the hammers. The men were therefore ordered to drop the hammers, and, with a portion of the reserve, to use as a battering-ram a heavy ladder, with which they dashed in a part of the door and gave admittance to the storming party. The fire of the insurgents up to this time had been harmless. At the threshold one marine fell mortally wounded. The rest, led by Lieutenant Green and Major Russell, quickly ended the contest. The insurgents that resisted were bayoneted. Their leader, John Brown, was cut down by the sword of Lieutenant Green, and our citizens were protected by both officers and men. The whole was over in a few minutes.

From the information derived from the papers found upon the persons and among the baggage of the insurgents, and the statement of those now in custody, it appears that the party consisted of nineteen men—fourteen white and five black. That they were headed by John Brown, of some notoriety in Kansas, who in June last located himself in Maryland, at the Kennedy farm, where he has been engaged in preparing to capture the United States works at Harper's Ferry. He avows that his object was the liberation of the slaves of Virginia, and of the whole South; and acknowledges that he has been disappointed in his expectations of aid from the black as well as white population, both in the Southern and Northern States. The blacks whom he forced from their homes in this neighborhood, as far as I could learn, gave him no voluntary assistance. The result proves that the plan was the attempt of a fanatic or madman, which could only end in failure; and its temporary success was owing to the panic and confusion he succeeded in creating by magnifying his numbers.

THE RIGHT OF THE SOUTH TO SECEDE

(1861)

by Robert Toombs

From Toombs's speech in the United States Senate, made shortly before the Southern states began to secede, and he resigned. Toombs had served from Georgia in the lower house of Congress from 1845 to 1853, and had entered the Senate in 1853. He belonged to the old-time Whig party, but refused to follow other Whigs into the Republican, or Union party, and became a Disunionist on issues raised by Lincoln's election. During the war he served in the Confederate Army as a brigadier-general, and at one time was secretary of state of the Confederacy. He never took the oath required of Confederates of allegiance to the United States Government, although he lived for twenty years after the war ended.

The South's defense of a state's right to secede from the Union was not the first of its kind. Representatives of the New England states first defended secession in the Hartford Convention of 1814.

These thirteen colonies originally had no bond of union whatever; no more than Jamaica and Australia have to-day. They were wholly separate communities, independent of each other, and dependent on the Crown of Great Britain. All the union between them that was ever made is in writing. They made two written compacts.

Senators, the Constitution is a compact. It contains all our obligations and duties of the Federal Government. All the obligations, all the chains that fetter the limbs of my people, are nominated in the bond, and they wisely excluded any conclusion against them, by declaring that the powers not granted by the Constitution to the United States, or forbidden by it to the States, belonged to the States respectively or the people. Now I will try it by that standard; I will subject it to that test. The law of nature, the law of justice, would say—and it is so expounded by the publicists—that equal rights in the common property shall be enjoyed. This right of equality being, then, according to justice and natural equity, a right belonging to all States, when did we give it up? You say Congress has a right to pass rules and regulations concerning the territory and other property of the United States. Very well. Does that exclude those whose blood and money paid for it? Does "dispose of" mean to rob the rightful owners? You must show a better title than that, or a better sword than we have.

In a compact where there is no common arbiter, where the parties finally decide for themselves, the sword alone at last becomes the real, if not the constitutional, arbiter. Your party says that you will not take the decision of the Supreme Court. You said so at Chicago; you said so in committee; every man of you in both Houses says so. What are you going to do? You say we shall submit to your construction. We shall do it, if you can make us; but not otherwise, or in any other manner. That is settled. You may call it secession, or you may call it revolution; but there is a big fact standing before you, ready to oppose you—that fact is, freemen with arms in their hands. The cry of the Union will not disperse them; we have passed that point; they demand equal rights; you had better heed the demand.

I have, then, established the proposition—it is admitted—that you seek to outlaw $4,000,000,000 of property of our people in the territories of the United States. Is not that a cause of war? Is it a grievance that $4,000,- 000,000 of the property of the people should be outlawed in the territories of the United States by the common government? Then you have declared, Lincoln declares, your platform declares, your people declare, your legislatures declare—there is one voice running through your entire phalanx —that we shall be outlawed in the territories of the United States. I say we will not be; and we are willing to meet the issue; and rather than submit to such an outlawry, we will defend our territorial rights as we would our household goods.

You will not regard confederate obligations; you will not regard constitutional obligations; you will not regard your oaths. What, then, am I to do? Am I a freemen? Is my State a free State, to lie down and submit because political fossils raise the cry of the glorious Union? Too long already have we listened to this delusive song. We are freemen. We have rights; I have stated them. We have wrongs; I have recounted them. I have demonstrated that the party now coming into power has declared us outlaws, and is determined to exclude four thousand million of our property from the common territories; that it has declared us under the ban of the empire; and out of the protection of the laws of the United States everywhere. They have refused to protect us from invasion and insurrection by the Federal power, and the Constitution denies to us in the Union the right either to raise fleets or armies for our own defense. All these charges I have proven by the record; and I put them before the civilized world, and demand the judgment of to-day, of to-morrow, of distant ages, and of Heaven itself, upon the justice of these causes.

I am content, whatever it be, to peril all in so noble, so holy a cause. We have appealed, time and time again, for these constitutional rights. You have refused them. We appeal again. Restore us these rights as we had them, as your court adjudges them to be, just as all our people have said they are; redress these flagrant wrongs, seen of all men, and it will restore fraternity, and peace, and unity, to all of us. Refuse them, and what then?

We shall then ask you, "let us depart in peace." Refuse that, and you present us war. We accept it; and inscribing upon our banners the glorious words, "liberty and equality," we will trust to the blood of the brave and the God of battles for security and tranquillity.

LINCOLN AS PRESIDENT
A. Brief Autobiography
(1859)
by Abraham Lincoln

Writing, in 1859, to one who had asked him for some biographic particulars, Abraham Lincoln said:

"I was born February 12, 1809, in Hardin County, Kentucky. My parents were both born in Virginia, of undistinguished families—second families, perhaps I should say. My mother, who died in my tenth year, was of a family of the name of Hanks. My paternal grandfather, Abraham Lincoln, emigrated from Rockingham County, Virginia, to Kentucky about 1781 or 1782, where, a year or two later, he was killed by the Indians, not in battle, but by stealth when he was laboring to open a farm in the forest.

"My father (Thomas Lincoln) at the death of his father was but six years of age. By the early death of his father, and the very narrow circumstances of his mother, he was, even in childhood, a wandering laboring boy, and grew up literally without education. He never did more in the way of writing than bunglingly to write his own name. He removed from Kentucky to what is now Spencer County, Indiana, in my eighth year. It was a wild region with many bears and other animals still in the woods.

"There were some schools, so-called, but no qualification was ever required of a teacher beyond 'readin', writin', and cipherin' to the rule of three.' If a straggler supposed to understand Latin happened to sojourn in the neighborhood he was looked upon as a wizard. Of course, when I came of age I did not know much. Still, somehow, I could read, write, and cipher to the rule of three. But that was all. The little advance I now have upon this store of education I have picked up from time to time under the pressure of necessity.

"I was raised to farm work till I was twenty-two. At twenty-one I came to Illinois—Macon County. Then I got to New Salem, where I remained a year as a sort of clerk in a store. Then came the Black Hawk war; and I was elected captain of a volunteer company, a success that gave me more pleasure than any I have had since. I went into the campaign—was elated—ran for the legislature the same year (1832), and was beaten—the only time I ever have been beaten by the people. The next, and three succeeding biennial elections, I was elected to the Legislature. I was not a candidate afterward. During the legislative period I had studied law and removed to Springfield to practice it. In 1846 I was elected to the lower house of Congress. Was not a candidate for reëlection. From 1849 to 1854, inclusive, practiced law more assiduously than ever before. Always a Whig in politics, and generally on the Whig electoral tickets, making active canvasses. I was losing interest in politics when the repeal of the Missouri Compromise aroused me again.

"If any personal description of me is thought desirable, it may be said that I am in height six feet four inches, nearly; lean in flesh, weighing on an average one hundred and eighty pounds; dark complexion, with coarse black hair and gray eyes. No other marks or brands recollected."

There is the whole story, told by himself, and brought down to the point where he became a figure of national importance.

LINCOLN AS PRESIDENT
B. Mr. Lincoln
(1861)
by William H. Russell

From Russell's My Diary, North and South. *The author has been commonly known in this country as "Bull Run" Russell, a name bestowed upon him in consequence of his report of the battle of Bull Run, printed in the London* Times, *of which he was the war correspondent in America, the tone of the report being sympathetic toward the South. The first paragraphs in the passage here given are dated March 27, 1861—that is, about three weeks after Lincoln was inaugurated.*

Soon afterward there entered, with a shambling, loose, irregular, almost unsteady gait, a tall, lank, lean man, considerably over six feet in height, with stooping shoulders, long pendulous arms, terminating in hands of extraordinary dimensions, which, however, were far exceeded in proportion by his feet. He was drest in an ill-fitting, wrinkled suit of black, which put one in mind of an undertaker's uniform at a funeral; round his neck a rope of black silk, knotted in a large bulb, with flowing ends projecting beyond the collar of his coat; his turned-down shirtcollar disclosed a sinewy, muscular, yellow neck, and above that, nestling in a great black mass of hair, bristling and compact like a ruff of mourning pins, rose the strange, quaint face and head, covered with its thatch of wild, republican hair, of President Lincoln.

The impression produced by the size of his extremities, and by his flapping and wide-projecting ears, may be removed by the appearance of kindliness, sagacity, and the awkward bonhomie of his face; the mouth is absolutely prodigious; the lips, straggling and extending almost from one line of black beard to the other, are only kept in order by two deep furrows from the nostril to the chin; the nose itself—a prominent organ—stands out from the face, with an inquiring, anxious air, as tho it were sniffing for some good thing in the wind; the eyes, dark, full, and deeply set, are penetrating, but full of an expression which almost amounts to tenderness; and above them projects the shaggy brow, running into the small, hard frontal space, the development of which can scarcely be estimated accurately, owing to the irregular flocks of thick hair carelessly brushed across it.

One would say that, altho the mouth was made to enjoy a joke, it could also utter the severest sentence which the head could dictate, but that Mr. Lincoln would be ever more willing to temper justice with mercy, and to enjoy what he considers the amenities of life, than to take a harsh view of men's nature and of the world, and to estimate things in an ascetic or puritan spirit. A person who met Mr. Lincoln in the street would not take him to be what—according to the usages of European society—is called a "gentleman"; and, indeed, since I came to the United States I have heard more disparaging allusions made by Americans to him on that account than I could have expected among simple republicans, where all should be equals; but, at the same time, it would not be possible for the most indifferent observer to pass him in the street without notice.

In the conversation which occurred before dinner, I was amused to observe the manner in which Mr. Lincoln used the anecdotes for which he is famous. Where men bred in courts, accustomed to the world, or versed in diplomacy, would use some subterfuge, or would make a polite speech, or give a shrug of the shoulders as the means of getting out of an embarrassing position, Mr. Lincoln raised a laugh by some bold west-country anecdote, and moves off in the cloud of merriment produced by his joke.

The first "state dinner," as it is called, of the President was not remarkable for ostentation. The conversation was suited to a state dinner of a cabinet at which women and strangers were present, and except where there was an attentive silence caused by one of the President's stories, there was a Babel of small talk round the table.

LINCOLN AS PRESIDENT
C. The President and His Cabinet
(1861–65)
by Charles A. Dana

*Mr. Dana was assistant secretary of war under Stanton. Before the war he had
long been managing editor of the New York Tribune. After the war he became editor
of the New York Sun, and so remained until his death.*

During the first winter I spent in Washington in the War Department
I had constant opportunities of seeing Mr. Lincoln, and of conversing with
him in the cordial and unofficial manner which he always preferred. Not
that there was ever any lack of dignity in the man. Even in his freest
moments one always felt the presence of a will and of an intellectual power
which maintained the ascendancy of his position. He never posed, or put
on airs, or attempted to make any particular impression; but he was always
conscious of his ideas and purposes, even in his most unreserved moments.

I knew, too, and saw frequently, all the members of his Cabinet. When
Mr. Lincoln was inaugurated as President, his first act was to name his
Cabinet; and it was a common remark at the time that he had put into it
every man who had competed with him for the nomination. The first in
importance was William H. Seward, of New York, Mr. Lincoln's most
prominent competitor. Mr. Seward was made Secretary of State. The second man in importance and ability to be put into the Cabinet was Mr.
Chase, of Ohio. His administration in the Treasury Department was satisfactory to the public. Mr. Chase authored the national banking law. Mr.
Stanton was the energetic Secretary of War, and the Secretary of the Navy
throughout the war was Gideon Welles, of Connecticut.

The relations between Mr. Lincoln and the members of his Cabinet
were always friendly and sincere on his part. He treated every one of them
with unvarying candor, respect, and kindness; but, though several of them
were men of extraordinary force and self-assertion—this was true especially of Mr. Seward, Mr. Chase, and Mr. Stanton— and though there was
nothing of self-hood or domination in his manner toward them, it was
always plain that he was the master and they the subordinates. They constantly had to yield to his will in questions where responsibility fell upon
him. If he ever yielded to theirs, it was because they convinced him that

the course they advised was judicious and appropriate. I fancied during the whole time of my intimate intercourse with him and with them, that he was always prepared to receive the resignation of any one of them. At the same time I do not recollect a single occasion when any member of the Cabinet had got his mind ready to quit his post from any feeling of dissatisfaction with the policy of conduct of the President. Not that they were always satisfied with his actions; the members of the Cabinet, like human beings in general, were not pleased with everything. In their judgment much was imperfect in the administration; much, they felt, would have been done better if their views had been adopted and they individually had had charge of it. Not so with the President.

He was calm, equable, uncomplaining. In the discussion of important questions, whatever he said showed the profoundest thought, even when he was joking. He seemed to see every side of every question. He never was impatient, he never was in a hurry, and he never tried to hurry anybody else. To every one he was pleasant and cordial. Yet they all felt it was his word that went at last; that every case was open until he gave his decision.

This impression of authority, of reserve force, Mr. Lincoln always gave to those about him. Even physically he was impressive. According to the record measurements, he was six feet four inches in height. There was no waste or excess of material about his frame; nevertheless, he was very strong and muscular. I remember that the last time I went to see him at the White House—the afternoon before he was killed—I found him in a side-room with coat off and sleeves rolled up, washing his hands. He had finished his work for the day and was going away. I noticed then the thinness of his arms, and how well-developed, strong, and active his muscles seemed to be. In fact, there was nothing flabby or feeble about Mr. Lincoln physically. He was a very quick man in his movements when he chose to be, and he had immense physical endurance. Night after night he would work late and hard without being wilted by it, and he always seemed as ready for the next day's work as though he had done nothing the day before.

Mr. Lincoln's face was thin, and his features were large. His hair was black, his eyebrows heavy, his forehead square and well-developed. His complexion was dark and quite sallow. His smile was something most lovely. I have never seen a woman's smile that approached it in its engaging quality, nor have I ever seen another face which would light up as Mr. Lincoln's did when something touched his heart or amused him. I have heard it said that he was ungainly, that his step was awkward. He never imprest me as being awkward. In the first place, there was such a charm and beauty about his expression, such good humor and friendly spirit looking from his eyes, that when you were near him you never thought whether he was awkward or graceful; you thought of nothing except, What a kindly character this man has! Then, too, there was such shrewdness in his kindly features that one did not care to criticize him. His manner was always dignified, and even if he had done an awkward thing, the dignity of his character and manner would have made it seem graceful and becoming.

The great quality of his appearance was benevolence and benignity; the wish to do somebody some good if he could; and yet there was no flabby philanthropy about Abraham Lincoln. He was all solid, hard, keen intelligence, combined with goodness. Indeed, the expression of his face and of his bearing which impressed one most, after his benevolence and benignity, was his intelligent understanding. You felt that here was a man who saw through things, who understood, and you respected him accordingly.

Another remarkable peculiarity of Mr. Lincoln's was that he seemed to have no illusions. He had no freakish notions that things were so, or might be so, when they were not so. All his thinking and reasoning, all his mind, in short, was based continually upon actual facts, and upon facts of which, as I said, he saw the essence. I never heard him say anything that was not so. I never heard him foretell things; he told what they were, but I never heard him intimate that such and such consequences were likely to happen without the consequences following. I should say, perhaps, that his greatest quality was wisdom. And this is something superior to talent, superior to education. It is again genius; I do not think it can be acquired. All the advice that he gave was wise, and it was always timely. This wisdom, it is scarcely necessary to add, had its animating philosophy in his own famous words, "With malice toward none, with charity for all."

THE FIRING ON FORT SUMTER
(1861)
by Mary Boykin Chesnut

From Mrs. Chesnut's Diary from Dixie. Mrs. Chesnut was a daughter of Stephen Decatur Miller, governor of South Carolina in the Nullification period, and afterward a United States Senator from the state. Mrs. Chesnut spent a considerable part of the war period in Richmond, where she became a close friend of Mrs. Davis. Her Diary sheds much vivid light on the social life of the city during that time. She and her husband survived the war many years.

Colonel Anderson, the union commander of Fort Sumter, surrendered on April 13, 1861, the day after the Confederate forces under Beauregard opened fire.

April 11th.—To-day at dinner there was no allusion to things as they stand in Charleston Harbor. There was an undercurrent of intense excitement. There could not have been a more brilliant circle. In addition to our usual quartet (Judge Withers, Langdon Cheves, and Trescott), our two ex-Governors dined with us, Means and Manning. These men all talked so delightfully. For once in my life I listened. That over, business began in earnest. Governor Means had rummaged a sword and red sash from somewhere and brought it for Colonel Chesnut, who had gone to demand the surrender of Fort Sumter. And patience—we must wait.

April 12th.—Anderson will not capitulate. Mr. Chesnut returned. His interview with Colonel Anderson had been deeply interesting, but Mr. Chesnut was not inclined to be communicative. He wanted his dinner. He felt for Anderson and had telegraphed to President Davis for instructions—what answer to give Anderson, etc. He has now gone back to Fort Sumter with additional instructions. I do not pretend to go to sleep. How can I? If Anderson does not accept terms at four, the orders are, he shall be fired upon. I count four, St. Michael's bells chime out, and I begin to hope. At half past four the heavy booming of a cannon. I sprang out of bed, and on my knees, prostrate; I prayed as I never prayed before.

There was a sound of stir all over the house, pattering of feet in the corridors. All seemed hurrying one way. I put on my double-gown and a shawl and went, too. It was to the housetop. The shells were bursting. In the dark I heard a man say, "Waste of ammunition." I knew my husband was rowing about in a boat somewhere in that dark bay, and that the shells were roofing it over, bursting toward the fort. If Anderson were obstinate, Colonel Chesnut was to order the fort on our side to open fire. Certainly fire had begun. The regular roar of the cannon, there it was. And who could tell what each volley accomplished of death and destruction? The women were wild there on the housetop. Prayers came from the women and imprecations from the men. And then a shell would light up the scene.

THE FIRST BATTLE OF BULL RUN
(1861)
by General Joseph E. Johnston

The first battle of Bull Run was fought on July 21, 1861, the Confederates being commanded by Beauregard and the Federals by McDowell. A second battle was fought near the same place in August, 1862. The battle takes its name from a small river tributary to the Potomac. The field of conflict lies about twenty-five miles southwest of Washington. In the South both battles then were known as the battles of Manassas. General Johnston here writes in the third person.

General Joseph E. Johnston, who had an army of about 8,000 men in the valley of the Shenandoah, beyond the mountains of the Blue Ridge— was immediately informed by telegraph from the War Department, at Richmond, of the situation; and directed to pursue such course as he might think best under the circumstances.

"The enemy, under cover of a strong demonstration on our right, made a long detour through the woods on his right, crossed Bull Run two miles above our left, and threw himself upon the flank and rear of our position. This movement was fortunately discovered in time for us to check its progress, and ultimately to form a new line of battle nearly at right angles with the defensive line of Bull Run.

"On discovering that the enemy had crossed the stream above him, Colonel Evans moved to his left with eleven companies and two field pieces, to oppose his advance, and disposed his little force under cover of the wood, near the intersection of the Warrenton Turnpike and the Sudley Road. Here he was attacked by the enemy in immensely superior numbers, against which he maintained himself with skill and unshrinking courage. General Bee, moving toward the enemy, guided by the firing, had, with a soldier's eye, selected the position near the Henry House, and formed his troops upon it. They were the 7th and 8th Georgia, 4th Alabama, 2d Mississippi, and two companies of the 11th Mississippi Regiments, with Imboden's battery. Being compelled, however, to sustain Colonel Evans, he crossed the valley and formed on the right and somewhat in advance of his position. Here the joint force, little exceeding five regiments, with six field-pieces, held the ground against about 15,000 United States troops for an hour, until, finding themselves outflanked by the continually arriving troops of the enemy, they fell back to General Bee's first position, upon the line of which Jackson, just arriving, formed his brigade and Stanard's battery. Colonel Hampton, who had by this time advanced with his legion as far as the turnpike, rendered efficient service in maintaining the orderly character of the retreat from that point; and here fell the gallant Lieutenant-Colonel Johnson, his second in command.

"In the meantime I awaited with General Beauregard near the center, the full development of the enemy's designs. About 11 o'clock the violence of the firing on the left indicated a battle, and the march of a large body of troops from the enemy's center toward the conflict was shown by the clouds of dust. I was thus convinced that his great effort was to be made with his right. I stated that conviction to General Beauregard, and the absolute necessity of immediately strengthening our left as much as possible. Orders were, accordingly at once sent to General Holmes and Colonel Early, to move with all speed to the sound of the firing, and to General

Bonham to send up two of his regiments and a battery. General Beauregard and I then hurried at a rapid gallop to the scene of action, about four miles off. On the way I directed my chief of artillery, Colonel Pendleton, to follow with his own and Alburtis's batteries. We came not a moment too soon. The long contest against five-fold odds and heavy losses, especially of field officers, had greatly discouraged the troops of General Bee and Colonel Evans. Our presence with them under fire, and some example, had the happiest effect on the spirit of the troops. Order was soon restored, and the battle reestablished, to which the firmness of Jackson's brigade greatly contributed.

Then, in a brief and rapid conference, General Beauregard was assigned to the command of the left, which, as the younger officer, he claimed, while I returned to that of the whole field. The aspect of affairs was critical, but I had full confidence in the skill and indomitable courage of General Beauregard, the high soldierly qualities of Generals Bee and Jackson, and Colonel Evans, and the devoted patriotism of their troops. Orders were first despatched to hasten the march of General Holmes's, Colonel Early's, and General Bonham's regiments. General Ewell was also directed to follow with all speed. Many of the broken troops, fragments of companies, and individual stragglers, were reformed and brought into action with the aid of my staff and a portion of General Beauregard's. Colonel (Governor) Smith, with his battalion, and Colonel Hunton, with his regiment, were ordered up to reenforce the right. I have since learned that General Beauregard had previously ordered them into the battle. They belonged to his corps. Colonel Smith's cheerful courage had a fine influence, not only upon the spirit of his own men, but upon the stragglers from the troops engaged.

The largest body of these, equal to about four companies, having no competent field-officer, I placed under command of one of my staff, Colonel F. J. Thomas, who fell while gallantly leading it against the enemy. These reenforcements were all sent to the right to reestablish more perfectly that part of our line. Having attended to these pressing duties at the immediate scene of conflict, my eye was next directed to Colonel Cocke's brigade, the nearest at hand. Hastening to his position, I desired him to lead his troops into action. He informed me, however, that a large body of the enemy's troops, beyond the stream and below the bridge, threatened us from that quarter. He was, therefore, left in his position.

"We had now sixteen guns and 260 cavalry, and a little above nine regiments of the Army of the Shenandoah, and six guns, and less than the strength of three regiments of that of the Potomac, engaged with about 35,000 United States troops, among whom were full 3,000 men of the old regular army. Yet this admirable artillery and brave infantry and cavalry lost no foot of ground. For nearly three hours they maintained their position, repelling five successive assaults by the heavy masses of the enemy, whose numbers enabled him continually to bring up fresh troops as their preceding columns were driven back. Colonel Stuart contributed to one of these repulses by a well-timed and vigorous charge on the enemy's right flank, with two companies of his cavalry. The efficiency of our infantry and cavalry might have been expected from a patriotic people, accustomed, like ours, to the management of arms and horses, but that of the artillery was little less than wonderful. They were opposed to batteries far superior in the number, range and equipment of their guns, with educated officers, and thoroughly instructed soldiers. We had but one educated artillerist, Colonel Pendleton—that model of a Christian soldier—yet they exhibited as much superiority to the enemy in skill as in courage. Their fire was superior, both in rapidity and precision.

"The expected reenforcements appeared soon after. Colonel Cocke was then desired to lead his brigade into action, to support the right of the troops engaged, which he did with alacrity and effect. Within a half hour the two regiments of General Bonham's brigade (Cash's and Kershaw's), came up, and were directed against the enemy's right, which he seemed to be strengthening. Fisher's North Carolina regiment was soon after sent in the same direction. About 3 o'clock, while the enemy seemed to be striving to outflank and drive back our left, and thus separate us from Manassas, General E. K. Smith arrived with three regiments of Elzey's brigade. He was instructed to attack the right flank of the enemy now exposed to us. Before the movement was completed he fell, severely wounded. Colonel Elzey at once taking command, executed it with great promptitude and vigor. General Beauregard rapidly seized the opportunity thus afforded him, and threw forward his whole line. The enemy was driven back from the long-contested hill, and victory was no longer doubtful. He made yet another attempt to retrieve the day. He again extended his right, with a still wider sweep, to turn our left. Just as he reformed to renew the battle, Colonel Early's three regiments came upon the field. The enemy's new formation exposed his right flank more even than the previous one. Colonel Early was, therefore, ordered to throw himself directly upon it, supported by Colonel Stuart's cavalry and Beckham's battery. He executed this attack bravely and well, while a simultaneous charge was made by General Beauregard in front. The enemy was broken by this combined attack. He lost all the artillery which he had advanced to the scene of the conflict. He had no more fresh troops to rally on, and a general rout ensued.

"Our victory was as complete as one gained by infantry and artillery can be. An adequate force of cavalry would have made it decisive.

STONEWALL JACKSON'S RUSE
(1862)
by Brigadier-General John D. Imboden

A veteran cavalry officer who fought with Jackson during the early part of the Civil War and later with Breckinridge (the former United States Vice-President and electoral runner-up to Lincoln in the presidential race of 1860), Brigadier-General Imboden here recalls an amusing incident of the war.

From the very beginning of the war the Confederacy was greatly in need of rolling-stock for the railroads. We were particularly short of locomotives, and were without the shops to build them. Jackson, appreciating this, hit upon a plan to obtain a good supply from the Baltimore and Ohio road. Its line was double-tracked, at least from Point of Rocks to Martinsburg, a distance of 25 or 30 miles. We had not interfered with the running of trains, except on the occasion of the arrest of General Harney. The coal traffic from Cumberland was immense, as the Washington government was accumulating supplies of coal on the seaboard. These coal trains passed Harper's Ferry at all hours of the day and night, and thus furnished Jackson with a pretext for arranging a brilliant "scoop." When he sent me to Point of Rocks, he ordered Colonel Harper with the 5th Virginia Infantry to Martinsburg. He then complained to President Garrett, of the Baltimore and Ohio, that the night trains, eastward bound, disturbed the repose of his camp, and requested a change of schedule that would pass all east-bound trains by Harper's Ferry between 11 and 1 o'clock in the day-time. Mr. Garrett complied, and thereafter for several days we heard the constant roar of passing trains for an hour before and an hour after noon. But since the "empties" were sent up the road at night, Jackson again complained that the nuisance was as great as ever, and, as the road had two tracks, said he must insist that the west-bound trains should pass during the same two hours as those going east. Mr. Garrett promptly complied, and we then had, for two hours every day, the liveliest railroad in America. One night, as soon as the schedule was working at its best, Jackson sent me an order to take a force of men across to the Maryland side of the river the next day at 11 o'clock, and, letting all west-bound trains pass till 12 o'clock, to permit none to go east, and at 12 o'clock to obstruct the road so that it would require several days to repair it. He ordered the reverse to be done at Martinsburg. Thus he caught all the trains that were going east or west between those points, and these he ran up to Winchester, thirty-two miles on the branch road, where they were safe, and whence they were removed by horse-power to the railway at Strasburg. I do not remember the number of trains captured, but the loss crippled the Baltimore and Ohio road seriously for some time, and the gain to our scantily stocked Virginia roads of the same gage was invaluable.

THE EMANCIPATION PROCLAMATION
(1862)
by Francis C. Carpenter

From Carpenter's Six Months in the White House with Abraham Lincoln. *The author was a portrait painter of considerable reputation in his time. His picture of the "Signing of the Emancipation Proclamation" is one of the most familiar American historical paintings. While making sketches for this picture Carpenter developed personal relations with the President and with members of his cabinet, whom he saw with frequency.*

The President received me pleasantly, giving me a seat near his own armchair; took off his spectacles, and said, "Well, Mr. Carpenter, we will turn you in loose here, and try to give you a good chance to work out your idea." Then, he proceeded to give me a detailed account of the history and issue of the great proclamation.

"It had got to be," said he, "midsummer, 1862. Things had gone on from bad to worse, until I felt that we had reached the end of our rope on the plan of operations we had been pursuing; that we had about played our last card, and must change our tactics, or lose the game! I now determined upon the adoption of the emancipation policy; and, without consultation with, or the knowledge of the Cabinet, I prepared the original draft of the proclamation, and, after much anxious thought, called a Cabinet meeting upon the subject. This was the last of July, or the first part of the month of August, 1862."(The exact date he did not remember.) "This Cabinet meeting took place, I think, upon a Saturday. All were present, excepting Mr. Blair, the Postmaster-General, who was absent at the opening of the discussion, but came in subsequently. I said to the Cabinet that I had resolved upon this step, and had not called them together to ask their advice, but to lay the subject-matter of a proclamation before them; suggestions as to which would be in order, after they had heard it read. Secretary Seward said in substance: 'Mr. President, I approve of the proclamation, but I question the expediency of its issue at this juncture. The depression of public mind, consequent upon our repeated reverses, is so great that I fear the effect of so important a step. It may be viewed as the last measure of an exhausted government, a cry for help; the government stretching forth its hands to Ethiopia, instead of Ethiopia stretching forth her hands to the government.' His idea," said the President, "was that it would be considered our last shriek, on the retreat." (This was his precise expression.) " 'Now,' continued Mr. Seward, 'while I approve the measure, I suggest, sir, that you postpone its issue, until you can give it to the country supported by military success, instead of issuing it, as would be the case now, upon the greatest disasters of the war!' "

Mr. Lincoln continued: "The wisdom of the view of the Secretary of State struck me with very great force. It was an aspect of the case that, in all my thought upon the subject, I had entirely overlooked. The result was that I put the draft of the proclamation aside, as you do your sketch for a picture, waiting for a victory. From time to time I added or changed a line, touching it up here and there, anxiously watching the progress of events. Well, the next news we had was of Pope's disaster, at Bull Run. Things looked darker than ever. Finally, came the week of the Battle of Antietam.[3] I determined to wait no longer. The news came, I think, on Wednesday, that the advantage was on our side. I was then staying at the Soldiers' Home (three miles out of Washington). Here I finished writing the second draft of the preliminary proclamation; came up on Saturday; called the Cabinet together to hear it, and it was published the following Monday."

At the meeting of September 20th, another interesting incident occurred in connection with Secretary Seward. The President had written the important part of the proclamation in these words:

"That, on the first day of January, in the year of our Lord one thousand eight hundred and sixty-three, all persons held as slaves within any State or designated part of a State, the people whereof shall then be in rebellion against the United States, shall be then, thenceforward, and forever free; and the Executive Government of the United States, including the military and naval authority thereof, will recognize the freedom of such persons, or any of them, in any efforts they may make for their actual freedom."

"When I finished reading this paragraph," resumed Mr. Lincoln, "Mr. Seward stopt me, and said, 'I think, Mr. President, that you should insert after the word "recognize," in that sentence, the words "and maintain." ' I replied that I had already fully considered the import of that expression

---

[3] The second battle of Bull Run was fought on August 29, 1862. Lee commanded the Confederates. Antietam was fought on September 17 of the same year.

in this connection, but I had not introduced it, because it was not my way to promise what I was not entirely sure that I could perform, and I was not prepared to say that I thought we were exactly able to 'maintain' this.

"But," said he, "Seward insisted that we ought to take this ground; and the words finally went in!" The President then proceeded to show me the various positions occupied by himself and the different members of the Cabinet, on the occasion of the first meeting. "As nearly as I remember," said he, "I sat near the head of the table; the Secretary of the Treasury and the Secretary of War were here, at my right hand; the others were grouped at the left."

SHERMAN'S MARCH TO THE SEA
(1864)
by Major General William Tecumseh Sherman

From Sherman's Memoirs. The march through Georgia of Sherman's Northern Army crippled the railway system and farms supporting the Confederate armies, thus hastening the South's defeat.

On the 12th of November the railroad and telegraph communications with the rear were broken, and the army stood detached from all friends, dependent on its own resources and supplies. The strength of the army, as officially reported shows an aggregate of fifty-five thousand three hundred and twenty-nine infantry, five thousand and sixty-three cavalry, and eighteen hundred and twelve artillery—in all, sixty-two thousand two hundred and four officers and men.

The most extraordinary efforts had been made to purge this army of non-combatants and of sick men so that all on this exhibit may be assumed to have been able-bodied, experienced soldiers, well armed, well equipped, and provided, as far as human foresight permitted, with all the essentials of life, strength, and vigorous action.

The two general orders made for this march appear to me, even at this late day, so clear, emphatic, and well digested, that no account of that historic event is perfect without them and, tho they called for great sacrifice and labor on the part of the officers and men, I insist that these orders were obeyed as well as any similar orders ever were, by an army operating wholly in an enemy's country, and dispersed, as we necessarily were, during the subsequent period of nearly six months. The wagon-trains were divided equally between the four corps, so that each had about eight hundred wagons, and these usually on the march occupied five miles or more of road.

The march from Atlanta began on the morning of November 15th, the right wing and cavalry following the railroad southeast toward Jonesboro, and General Slocum with the Twentieth Corps leading off to the east by Decatur and Stone Mountain, toward Madison. These were divergent lines, designed to threaten both Macon and Augusta at the same time, so as to prevent a concentration at our intended destination, or "objective," Milledgeville, the capital of Georgia, distant southeast about one hundred miles.

About 7 A.M. of November 16th we rode out of Atlanta by the Decatur road. Some band, by accident struck up the anthem of "John Brown's soul goes marching on"; the men caught up the strain, and never before or since have I heard the chorus of "Glory, glory, hallelujah!" done with more spirit, or in better harmony of time and place.

The first night out we camped by the roadside near Lithonia. The whole horizon was lurid with the bonfires of rail-ties, and groups of men all night were carrying the heated rails to the nearest trees, and bending them around the trunks. Colonel Poe had provided tools for ripping up the rails and twisting them when hot; but the best and easiest way is the one of heating the middle of the iron rails on bonfires made of the cross-ties, and then winding them around a telegraph-pole or the trunk of some convenient sapling. I attached some importance to this destruction of the railraod, gave it my own personal attention, and made reiterated orders to others on the subject.

We found abundance of corn, molasses, meal, bacon, and sweet potatoes. We also took a good many cows and oxen, and a large number of mules. In all these the country was quite rich, never before having been visited by a hostile army; the recent crop had been excellent, had been just gathered and laid by for the winter. As a rule, we destroyed none, but kept our wagons full, and fed our teams bountifully.

The skill and success of the men in collecting forage was one of the features of this march. Each brigade commander had authority to detail a company of foragers, usually about fifty men, with one or two commissioned officers selected for their boldness and enterprise. This party would be dispatched before daylight with a knowledge of the intended day's march and camp; would proceed on foot five or six miles from the route traveled by their brigade, and then visit every plantation and farm within range. They would usually procure a wagon or family carriage, load it with bacon, corn-meal, turkeys, chickens, ducks, and everything that could be used as food or forage, and would then regain the main road, usually in advance of their train. When this came up, they would deliver to the brigade commissary the supplies thus gathered by the way.

Often would I pass these foraging-parties at the roadside, waiting for their wagons to come up, and was amused at their strange collections—mules, horses, even cattle, packed with old saddles and loaded with hams, bacon, bags of corn-meal, and poultry of every character and description. Altho this foraging was attended with great danger and hard work, there seemed to be a charm about it that attracted the soldiers, and it was a privilege to be detailed on such a party. Daily they returned mounted on all sorts of beasts, which were at once taken from them and appropriated to the general use; but the next day they would start out again on foot, only to repeat the experience of the day before.

No doubt, many acts of pillage, robbery, and violence were committed by these parties of foragers, usually called "bummers"; for I have since heard of jewelry taken from women, and the plunder of articles that never reached the commissary; but these acts were exceptional and incidental.

November 23d, we rode into Milledgeville, the capital of the State, whither the Twentieth Corps had preceded us; and during that day the left wing was all united, in and around Milledgeville. The first stage of the journey was, therefore, complete, and absolutely successful.

Meantime orders were made for the total destruction of the arsenal and its contents, and of such public buildings as could be easily converted to hostile uses. Meantime the right wing continued its movement along the railroad toward Savannah, tearing up the track and destroying its iron. Kilpatrick's cavalry was brought into Milledgeville, and crossed the Oconee by the bridge near the town; and on the 23d I made the general orders for the next stage of the march as far as Millen.

THE DESTRUCTION OF THE ALABAMA
(1864)
by Captain Raphael Semmes

From Semmes' official report, dated Southhampton, England, June 21, 1864. The Alabama was a wooden ship of about a thousand tons, built for the Confederacy at Birkenhead, England. Her crew and equipments were English. When she met the Kearsarge off Cherbourg, she had destroyed, as a cruiser, much American shipping. Because she was built and manned in England, claims for damages were preferred against England by the United States. These were finally adjusted at the Geneva Arbitration Tribunal in June, 1872. The gross award for damages caused by the

Alabama *and other ships for whose acts England was held to be responsible amounted to $15,000,000.*

I steamed out of the harbor of Cherbourg between 9 and 10 o'clock on the morning of June 19 for the purpose of engaging the enemy's steamer *Kearsarge,* which had been lying off and on the port for several days previously. After clearing the harbor we descried the enemy, with his head offshore, at a distance of about nine miles. We were three-quarters of an hour in coming up with him.

Let me say I had previously pivoted my guns to starboard, and made all my preparations for engaging the enemy on that side. When within about a mile and a quarter of the enemy he suddenly wheeled, and bringing his head inshore presented his starboard battery to me.

By this time we were distant about one mile from each other, when I opened on him with solid shot, to which he replied in a few minutes, and the engagement became active on both sides. When we got within good shell range, we opened upon him with shell.

The firing became very hot, and the enemy's shot and shell soon began to tell upon our hull, knocking down, killing, and disabling a number of men in different parts of the ship. Perceiving that our shell, tho apparently exploding against the enemy's sides, were doing but little damage, I returned to solid shot firing, and from this time onward alternated with shot and shell.

After the lapse of about one hour and ten minutes our ship was ascertained to be in a sinking condition, the enemy's shell having exploded in our sides and between decks, opening large apertures, through which the water rushed with great rapidity. For some few minutes I had hopes of being able to reach the French coast, for which purpose I gave the ship all steam and set such of the fore-and-aft sails as were available. The ship filled so rapidly, however, that before we had made much progress the fires were extinguished in the furnaces, and we were evidently on the point of sinking.

I now hauled down my colors to prevent the further destruction of life, and dispatched a boat to inform the enemy of our condition. Altho we were now but 400 yards from each other, the enemy fired upon me five times after my colors had been struck, dangerously wounding several of my men. It is charitable to suppose that a ship of war of a Christian nation could not have done this intentionally. We now turned all our exertions toward the wounded, and such of the boys as were unable to swim. These were dispatched in my quarterboats, the only boats remaining to me, the waitboats having been torn to pieces.

Some twenty minutes after my furnace fires had been extinguished, and the ship being on the point of settling, every man, in obedience to a previous order which had been given to the crew, jumped overboard and endeavored to save himself. There was no appearance of any boat coming to me from the enemy until after the ship went down. Fortunately, however, the steam-yacht *Deerhound,* owned by a gentleman of Lancashire, England (Mr. John Lancaster), who was himself on board, steamed up in the midst of my drowning men and rescued a number of both officers and men from the water. I was fortunate enough myself thus to escape to the shelter of the neutral flag, together with about forty others, all told. About this time the *Kearsarge* sent one and then, tardily, another boat. It was discovered by those of our officers who went alongside the enemy's ship with the wounded that her midship section on both sides was thoroughly iron-coated, this having been done with chains constructed for the purpose, placed perpendicularly from the rail to the water's edge, the whole covered over by a thin outer planking, which gave no indication of the armor beneath. This planking had been ripped off in every direction by our shot and shell, the chain broken and indented in many places, and forced partly into the ship's side.

My officers and men behaved steadily and gallantly, and tho they have lost their ship they have not lost honor. Where all behaved so well it would be invidious to particularize; but I can not deny myself the pleasure of saying that Mr. Kell, my first lieutenant, deserves great credit for the fine condition in which the ship went into action, with regard to her battery, magazine, and shellrooms; also that he rendered me great assistance by his coolness and judgment.

The enemy was heavier than myself, both in ship, battery, and crew; but I did not know until the action was over that she was also ironclad. Our total loss in killed and wounded is 30, to wit, 9 killed and 21 wounded.

GETTYSBURG

(1864)
by General John B. Gordon

The following extract is taken from General John B. Gordon's lecture, "The Last Days of the Confederacy." It is an example of the maintenance of a humane spirit in the midst of a brutal war.

As my command came back from the Susquehanna River to Gettysburg, it was thrown squarely on the right flank of the Union army. The fact that that portion of the Union army melted was no disparagement either of its courage or its lofty American manhood, for any troops that had ever been marshaled, the Old Guard itself, would have been as surely and swiftly shattered. It was that movement that gave to the Confederate army the first day's victory at Gettysburg; and as I rode forward over that field of green clover, made red with the blood of both armies, I found a major-general among the dead and the dying. But a few moments before, I had seen the proud form of that magnificent Union officer reel in the saddle and then fall in the white smoke of the battle; and as I rode by, intensely looking into his pale face, which was turned to the broiling rays of that scorching July sun, I discovered that he was not dead. Dismounting from my horse, I lifted his head with one hand, gave him water from my canteen, inquired his name and if he was badly hurt. He was General Francis C. Barlow, of New York. He had been shot from his horse while grandly leading a charge. The ball had struck him in front, passed through the body and out near the spinal cord, completely paralyzing him in every limb; neither he nor I supposed he could live for one hour. I desired to remove him before death from that terrific sun. I had him lifted on a litter and borne to the shade in the rear. As he bade me good-bye, and upon my inquiry what I could do for him, he asked me to take from his pocket a bunch of letters. Those letters were from his wife, and as I opened one at his request, and as his eye caught, as he supposed for the last time, that wife's signature, the great tears came like a fountain and rolled down his pale face; and he said to me, "General Gordon, you are a Confederate; I am a Union soldier; but we are both Americans; if you should live through this dreadful war and ever see my wife, will you not do me the kindness to tell my wife for me that you saw me on this field? Tell her for me, that my last thought on earth was of her; tell her for me that you saw me fall in this battle, and that her husband fell, not in the rear, but at the head of his column; tell her for me, general, that I freely give my life to my country, but that my unutterable grief is that I must now go without the privilege of seeing her once more, and bidding her a long and loving fare-well." I at once said: "Where is Mrs. Barlow, general? Where could I find her?" for I was determined that wife should receive that gallant husband's message. He replied: "She is very close to me; she is just back of the Union line of battle with the commander-in-chief at his headquarters." That announcement of Mrs. Barlow's presence with the Union army struck in this heart of mine another chord of deepest and tenderest sympathy; for my wife had followed me, sharing with me the privations of the camp, the fatigues of the march; again and again was she under fire, and always on the very verge of the battle was that devoted wife of mine, like an angel of protection and an inspiration to duty. I replied: "Of course, General Barlow, if I am alive, sir, when this day's battle, now in progress is ended —if I am not shot dead before the night comes—you may die satisfied that I will see to it that Mrs. Barlow has your message before to-morrow's dawn."

And I did. The moment the guns had ceased their roar on the hills, I sent a flag of truce with a note to Mrs. Barlow. I did not tell her—I did not have the heart to tell her that her husband was dead, as I believed him to be; but I did tell her that he was desperately wounded, a prisoner in my hands; but that she should have safe escort through my lines to her husband's side. Late that night, as I lay in the open field upon my saddle, a picket from my front announced a lady on the line. She was Mrs. Barlow. She had received my note and was struggling, under the guidance of officers of the Union army, to penetrate my lines and reach her husband's side. She was guided to his side by my staff during the night. Early next morning the battle was renewed, and the following day, and then came the retreat of Lee's immortal army. I thought no more of that gallant son of the North, General Barlow, except to count him among the thousands of Americans who had gone down on both sides in the dreadful battle. Strangely enough, as the war progressed, Barlow concluded not to die; Providence decreed that he should live. He recovered and rejoined his command; and just one year after that, Barlow saw that I was killed in another battle. The explanation is perfectly simple. A cousin of mine, with the same initials, General J. B. Gordon, of North Carolina, was killed in a battle near Richmond. Barlow, who, as I say, had recovered and rejoined his command—although I knew he was dead, or thought I did—picked up a newspaper and read this item in it: "General J. B. Gordon of the Confederate army was killed to-day in battle." Calling his staff around him, Barlow read that item and said to them, "I am very sorry to see this; you will remember that General J. B. Gordon was the officer who picked me up on the battlefield at Gettysburg, and sent my wife through his lines to me at night. I am very sorry."

Fifteen years passed. Now, I wish the audience to remember that during all those fifteen years which intervened, Barlow was dead to me, and for fourteen of them I was dead to Barlow. In the meantime, the partiality of the people of Georgia had placed me in the United States senate. Clarkson Potter was a member of Congress from New York. He invited me to dine with him to meet his friend, General Barlow. Now came my time to think. "Barlow," I said, "Barlow? That is the same name, but it can't be my Barlow, for I left him dead at Gettysburg." And I endeavored to understand what it meant, and thought I had made the discovery. I was told, as I made the inquiry, that there were two Barlows in the United States army. That satisfied me at once. I concluded, as a matter of course, that it was the other fellow I was going to meet; that Clarkson Potter had invited me to dine with the living Barlow and not with the dead one. Barlow had a similar reflection about the Gordon he was to dine with. He supposed that I was the other Gordon. We met at Clarkson Potter's table. I sat just opposite to Barlow; and in the lull of the conversation I asked him, "General, are you related to the Barlow who was killed at Gettysburg?" He replied: "I am the man, sir." "Are you related," he asked, "to the Gordon who killed me?" "Well," I said, "I am the man sir." No language could describe that scene at Clarkson Potter's table in Washington, fifteen years after the war was over. Truth is indeed stranger than fiction. There we met, both dead, each of us presenting to the other the most absolute proof of the resurrection of the dead.

But stranger still, perhaps, is the friendship true and lasting begun under such auspices. What could be further removed from the realms of probabilities than a confiding friendship between combatants, which is born on the field of blood, amidst the thunders of battle, and while the hostile legions rush upon each other with deadly fury and pour into each other's breasts their volleys of fire and of leaden hail. Such were the circumstances under which was born the friendship between Barlow and myself, and which I believe is more sincere because of its remarkable birth, and which has strengthened and deepened with the passing years. For the sake of our reunited and glorious Republic may we not hope that similar ties will bind together all the soldiers of the two armies—indeed all Americans in perpetual unity until the last bugle call shall have summoned us to the eternal camping grounds beyond the stars?

SOCIAL LIFE IN THE SOUTH IN THE LAST YEARS OF THE WAR
(1863–65)
by Mary Boykin Chesnut

This excerpt from Mrs. Chesnut's Diary from Dixie *shows the hardships produced in the South by the Northern blockade and inflation—caused by the widespread use of paper money unbacked by a precious metal.*

RICHMOND, Va., Nov. 28, 1863.—I gave a party; Mrs. Davis very witty; Preston girls very handsome; Isabella's fun fast and furious. No party could have gone off more successfully, but my husband decides we are to have no more festivities. This is not the time, or the place, for such gaieties. Maria Freeland is perfectly delightful on the subject of her wedding. Lucy Haxall is positively engaged to Captain Coffey, an Englishman. She is convinced that she will marry him. He is her first fancy. Mr. Venable, of Lee's staff, was at our party, so out of spirits. He knows everything that is going on. His depression bodes us no good. To-day, General Hampton sent James Chesnut a fine saddle that he had captured from the Yankees in battle array. Charleston is bombarded night and day. It fairly makes me dizzy to think of that everlasting racket they are beating about people's ears down there. Bragg defeated, and separated from Longstreet. It is a long street that knows no turning, and Rosecrans is not taken after all.

Nov. 30.—Anxiety pervades. Lee is fighting Meade. Misery is everywhere. Bragg is falling back before Grant. Longstreet, the soldiers call him Peter the Slow, is settling down before Knoxville. And now I am in a fine condition for Hetty Cary's starvation party, where they will give thirty dollars for the music and not a cent for a morsel to eat. My husband bought yesterday at the commissary's one barrel of flour, one bushel of potatoes, one peck of rice, five pounds of salt beef, and one peck of salt—all for sixty dollars. In the street a barrel of flour sells for one hundred and fifteen dollars. Spent seventy-five dollars to-day for a little tea and sugar, and have five hundred left. My husband's pay never has paid for the rent of our lodgings. My husband laid the law down last night. I felt it to be the last drop in my full cup. "No more feasting in this house," said he. "This is no time for junketing and merrymaking." "And you said you brought me here to enjoy the winter before you took me home and turned my face to a dead wall." He is the master of the house; to hear is to obey.

Sunday, Christopher Hampton walked to church with me. Coming out, General Lee was seen slowly making his way down the aisle, bowing royally to right and left. I pointed him out to Christopher Hampton when General Lee happened to look our way. He bowed low, giving me a charming smile of recognition. I was ashamed of being so pleased. I blushed like a schoolgirl.

We went to the White House. They gave us tea. The President said he had been on the way to our house, coming with all the Davis family, to see me, but the children became so troublesome they turned back. Just then, little Joe rushed in and insisted on saying his prayers at his father's knee, then and there. He was in his nightclothes.

December 19th.—A box has come from home for me. Taking advantage of this good fortune and a full larder, have asked Mrs. Davis to dine with me. Wade Hampton sent me a basket of game. We had Mrs. Davis and Mr. and Mrs. Preston. After dinner we walked to the church to see the Freeland-Lewis wedding. Mr. Preston had Mrs. Davis on his arm. My husband and Mrs. Preston, and Burton Harrison and myself brought up the rear. Willie Allan joined us, and we had the pleasure of waiting one good hour. Then the beautiful Maria, loveliest of brides, sailed in on her father's arm, and Major John Coxe Lewis followed with Mrs. Freeland. After the ceremony such a kissing was there up and down the aisle.

Christmas Day.—Yesterday dined with the Prestons. Wore one of my handsomest Paris dresses (from Paris before the war). Three magnificent

Kentucky generals were present, with Senator Orr from South Carolina, and Mr. Miles. Others dropt in after dinner; some without arms, some without legs; von Borcke, who can not speak because of a wound in his throat. Isabella said: "We have all kinds now, but a blind one," Poor fellows, they laugh at wounds. "And they yet can show many a scar." We had for dinner oyster soup, besides roast mutton, ham, boned turkey, wild duck, partridge, plum pudding, sauterne, burgundy, sherry, and Madeira. There is life in the old land yet!

My husband says I am extravagant. "No, my friend, not that," said I. "I had fifteen hundred dollars and I have spent every cent of it in my housekeeping. Not one cent for myself, not one cent for dress, nor any personal want whatever." He calls me "hospitality run mad."

To-day, for a pair of forlorn shoes I have paid $85. Colonel Ives drew my husband's pay for me. I sent Lawrence for it (Mr. Chesnut ordered him back to us; we needed a man servant here). Colonel Ives wrote that he was amazed I should be willing to trust a darky with that great bundle of money, but it came safely. Mr. Petigru says you take your money to market in the market-basket, and bring home what you buy in your pocketbook.

January 18.—Lamar was asked to dinner here yesterday; so he came to-day. We had our wild turkey cooked for him yesterday, and I drest myself within an inch of my life with the best of my four-year-old finery. Two of us, my husband and I, did not damage the wild turkey seriously. So Lamar enjoyed the *réchauffé*, and commended the art with which Molly had hid the slight loss we had inflicted upon its mighty breast. She had piled fried oysters over the turkey so skilfully, that unless we had told about it, no one would ever have known that the huge bird was making his second appearance on the board. Lamar was more absent-minded and distrait than ever. My husband behaved like a trump—a well-bred man, with all his wits about him; so things went off smoothly enough.

January 25.—The President walked home with me from church (I was to dine with Mrs. Davis). He walked so fast I had no breath to talk; so I was a good listener for once. The truth is I am too much afraid of him to say very much in his presence. We had such a nice dinner. After dinner Hood came for a ride with the President.

February 9.—This party for Johnny was the very nicest I have ever had, and I mean it to be my last. I sent word to the Carys to bring their own men. They came alone, saying, "they did not care for men." "That means a raid on ours," growled Isabella. Mr. Lamar was devoted to Constance Cary. He is a free lance; so that created no heart-burning. Afterward, when the whole thing was over, and a success, the lights put out, etc., here trooped in the four girls, who stayed all night with me. In dressing-gowns they stirred up a hot fire, relit the gas, and went in for their supper; *réchauffé* was the word, oysters, hot coffee, etc. They kept it up till daylight. Isabella says that war leads to love-making. She says these soldiers do more courting here in a day than they would do at home, without a war, in ten years. In the pauses of conversation, we hear, "She is the noblest woman God ever made!" "Goodness!" exclaims Isabella. "Which one?" The amount of courting we hear in these small rooms. Men have to go to the front, and they say their say desperately. I am beginning to know all about it. The girls tell me.

February 23d.—At the President's, where General Lee breakfasted, a man named Phelan told General Lee all he ought to do; planned a campaign for him. General Lee smiled blandly the while, tho he did permit himself a mild sneer at the wise civilians in Congress who refrained from trying the battle-field in person, but from afar dictated the movements of armies.

February 26th.—We went to see Mrs. Breckenridge, who is here with her husband. Then we paid our respects to Mrs. Lee.[4] Her room was like an industrial school; everybody so busy. Her daughters were all three plying their needles, with several other ladies. Mrs. Lee showed us a beautiful sword, recently sent to the General by some Marylanders, now in Paris. On the blade was engraved, *"Aide toi et Dieu t'aidera."*[5] When we came out some one said, "Did you see how the Lees spend their time? What a rebuke to the taffy parties!"

March 11th.—Letters from home, including one from my husband's father, now over ninety, written with his own hand, and certainly in his own mind still. I quote: "Bad times; worse coming. Starvation stares me in the face. Neither John's nor James's overseer will sell me any corn." Now, what has the Government to do with the fact that, on all his plantations, he made corn enough to last for the whole year, and by the end of January his negroes had stolen it all? Poor old man, he has fallen on evil days, after a long life of ease and prosperity.

March 12th.—Somebody counted fourteen generals in church to-day, and suggested that less piety and more drilling of commands would suit the times better. There were Lee, Longstreet, Morgan, Hoke, Clingman, Whiting, Pegram, Elzey, Gordon, and Bragg.

March 15th.—Old Mrs. Chesnut is dead. A saint is gone and James Chesnut is broken-hearted. He adored his mother. I gave $375 for my mourning, which consists of a black alpaca dress and a crape veil. With bonnet, gloves, and all it came to $500. Before the blockade such things as I have would not have been thought fit for a chambermaid. Everybody is in trouble. Mrs. Davis says paper money has depreciated so much in value that they can not live within their income; so they are going to dispense with their carriage and horses.

Yesterday, we went to the Capitol grounds to see our returned prison-

---

[4] Mrs. Robert E. Lee, wife of the General.
[5] This is the sword that Lee wore at the time of the surrender at Appomattox.

ers. We walked slowly up and down until Jeff Davis was called upon to speak. There I stood, almost touching the bayonets when he left me. I looked straight into the prisoners' faces, poor fellows. They cheered with all their might, and I wept for sympathy, and enthusiasm. I was deeply moved. These men were so forlorn, so dried up, and shrunken, with such a strange look in some of their eyes; others so restless and wild-looking; others again placidly vacant, as if they had been dead to the world for years.

April 1st.—Mrs. Davis is utterly deprest. She said the fall of Richmond must come; she would send her children to me and Mrs. Preston. We begged her to come to us also. My husband is as deprest as I ever knew him to be. He has felt the death of that angel mother of his keenly, and now he takes his country's woe to heart.

CAMDEN, S.C., May 8, 1864.—My friends crowded around me so in those last days in Richmond, I forgot the affairs of this nation utterly; tho I did show faith in my Confederate country by buying poor Bones's (my English maid's) Confederate bonds. I gave her gold thimbles, bracelets; whatever was gold and would sell in New York or London, I gave. My friends grieved that I had to leave them—not half so much, however, as I did that I must come away. Those last weeks were so pleasant. No battle, no murder, no sudden death, all went merry as a marriage bell. Clever, cordial, kind, brave friends rallied around me.

It is sad enough at Mulberry without old Mrs. Chesnut, who was the good genius of the place. It is so lovely here in spring. The giants of the forest—the primeval oaks, water-oaks, willow-oaks, such as I have not seen since I left here—with opopanax, violets, roses, and yellow jessamine. The air is laden with perfume. Araby the Blest was never sweeter. Inside, creature comforts of all kinds—green peas, strawberries, asparagus, spring lamb, spring chicken, fresh eggs, rich, yellow butter, clean white linen for one's beds, dazzling white damask for one's table. It is such a contrast to Richmond, where I wish I were.

September 19th.—My pink silk dress I have sold for $600, to be paid in instalments, two hundred a month for three months. And I sell my eggs and butter from home for two hundred dollars a month. Does it not sound well—four hundred dollars a month regularly. But in what? In Confederate money. Hélas!

A thousand dollars have slipped through my fingers already this week. At the commissary's I spent five hundred to-day for candles, sugar, and a lamp, etc. Tallow candles are bad enough, but of them there seems to be an end, too. Now we are restricted to smoky, terrabine lamps—terrabine is a preparation of turpentine. When the chimney of the lamp cracks, as crack it will, we plaster up the place with paper, thick old letterpaper, preferring the highly glazed kind. In the hunt for paper queer old letters come to light.

Sherman is thundering at Augusta's very doors. My General was on the wing, somber, and full of care. The girls are merry enough; the staff, who fairly live here, no better. Cassandra, with a black shawl over her head, is chased by the gay crew from sofa to sofa, for she avoids them, being full of miserable anxiety. There is nothing but distraction and confusion.

We have lost nearly all of our men, and we have no money, and it looks as if we had taught the Yankees how to fight since Manassas. Our best and bravest are under the sod; we should have to wait till another generation grows up. Here we stand, despair in our hearts ("Oh, Cassandra, don't!" shouts Isabella), with our houses burning, or about to be, over our heads. The North have just got things ship-shape; a splendid army, perfectly disciplined, with new levies coming in day and night. Their gentry do not go into the ranks. They hardly know there is war up there.

Serena's account of money spent: Paper and envelopes, $12.00; tickets to concert, $10.00; toothbrush, $10.00; total, $32.00. To-day Mrs. McCord exchanged $16,000 in Confederate bills for $300 in gold—sixteen thousand for three hundred.

LINCOLNTON, N.C., February 16, 1865.—A change has come o'er the spirit of my dreams. Dear old quire of yellow, coarse, Confederate home-made paper, here you are again. An age of anxiety and suffering has passed over my head since last I wrote and wept over your forlorn pages. My husband urged me to go home. He said Camden would be safe enough. They had no spite against that old town, as they had against Charleston and Columbia. My husband does not care a fig for the property question, and never did. Perhaps, if he had ever known poverty, it would be different. He talked beautifully about it, as he always does about everything. I have told him often that, if at Heaven's gate St. Peter would listen to him a while, and let him tell his own story, he would get in, and the angels might give him a crown extra. Now he says he has only one care—that I should be safe, and not so harassed with dread; and then there is his blind old father. "A man," said he, "can always die like a patriot and a gentleman, with no fuss, and take it coolly. It is hard not to envy those who are out of all this, their difficulties ended—those who have met death gloriously on the battle-field, their doubts all solved. One can but do his best and leave the result to a higher power."

CHESTER, S.C., March 21, 1865.—Another flitting has occurred. As the train rattled and banged along, and I waved my handkerchief in farewell to Miss Middleton, Isabella, and other devoted friends, I could only wonder if fate would ever throw me again, with such kind, clever, agreeable, congenial companions? The McLeans refused to be paid for their rooms. No plummet can sound the depths of the hospitality and kindness of the North Carolina people.

April 7th.—Richmond has fallen, and I have no heart to write about it. Grant broke through our lines and Sherman cut through them. Stoneman is this side of Danville. They are too many for us. Everything is lost in Richmond, even our archives. Blue-black is our horizon. Hood says we shall all be obliged to go West—to Texas, I mean, for our own part of the country will be overrun. Yes, a solitude and a wild waste it may become, but, as to that, we can rough it in the bush at home.

April 22.—It has been a wild three days, with aides galloping around with messages, Yankees hanging over us like a sword of Damocles. We have been in queer straits. We sat up at Mrs. Bedon's drest, without once going to bed for forty-eight hours.

CAMDEN, S.C., May 2, 1865.—Since we left Chester nothing but solitude, nothing but tall, blackened chimneys, to show that any man has ever trod this road before. This is Sherman's track. It is hard not to curse him. I wept incessantly at first. The roses of the gardens are already hiding the ruins. My husband said Nature is a wonderful renovator. He tried to say something else and then I shut my eyes and made a vow that if we were a crusht people, crusht by weight, I would never be a whimpering, pining slave. When we crossed the river coming home, the ferryman at Chesnut's Ferry asked for his fee. Among us all we could not muster the small silver coin he demanded. There was poverty for you.

May 18th.—A feeling of sadness hovers over me now, day and night, which no words of mine can express. There is a chance for plenty of character study in this Mulberry house, if one only had the heart for it. Colonel Chesnut, now ninety-three, blind and deaf, is apparently as strong as ever, and certainly as resolute of will. Partly patriarch, partly grand seigneur, this old man is of a species that we shall see no more—the last of a race of lordly planters who ruled this Southern world, but now a splendid wreck. His manners are unequaled still, but underneath this smooth exterior lies the grip of a tyrant whose will has never been crossed. I will not attempt what Lord Byron says he could not do, but must quote again: "Everybody knows a gentleman when he sees him. I have never met a man who could describe one." We have had three very distinct specimens of the genus in his house—three generations of gentlemen, each utterly different from the other—father, son, and grandson.

African Scipio walks at Colonel Chesnut's side. He is six feet two, a black Hercules, and as gentle as a dove in all his dealings with the blind old master, who boldly strides forward, striking with his stick to feel where he is going. Sometimes this old man will stop himself, just as he is going off in a fury, because they try to prevent his attempting some feat impossible in his condition of lost faculties. He will ask gently, "I hope that I never say or do anything unseemly! Sometimes I think I am subject to mental aberrations." At every footfall he calls out, "Who goes there?" If a lady's name is given, he uncovers and stands, with hat off, until she passes. He still has the old-world art of bowing low and gracefully.

Colonel Chesnut came of a race that would brook no interference with their own sweet will by man, woman, or devil. But then such manners has he, they would clear any man's character, if it needed it. Mrs. Chesnut, his wife, used to tell us that when she met him at Princeton, in the nineties of the eighteenth century, they called him "the Young Prince."

SECOND INAUGURAL ADDRESS
(1865)
by Abraham Lincoln

Fellow-Countrymen: At this second appearing to take the oath of the Presidential office there is less occasion for an extended address than there was at the first. Then a statement somewhat in detail of a course to be pursued seemed fitting and proper. Now, at the expiration of four years, during which public declarations have been constantly called forth on every point and phase of the great contest which still absorbs the attention and engrosses the energies of the nation, little that is new could be presented. The progress of our arms, upon which all else chiefly depends, is as well known to the public as to myself, and it is, I trust, reasonably satisfactory and encouraging to all. With high hope for the future, no prediction in regard to it is ventured.

On the occasion corresponding to this four years ago all thoughts were anxiously directed to an impending civil war. All dreaded it, all sought to avert it. While the inaugural address was being delivered from this place, devoted altogether to *saving* the Union without war, insurgent agents were in the city seeking to *destroy* it without war—seeking to dissolve the Union and divide effects by negotiation. Both parties deprecated war, but one of them would *make* war rather than let the nation survive, and the other would *accept* war rather than let it perish, and the war came.

One-eighth of the whole population were colored slaves, not distributed generally over the Union, but localized in the southern part of it. These slaves constituted a peculiar and powerful interest. All knew that this interest was somehow the cause of the war. To strengthen, perpetuate, and extend this interest was the object for which the insurgents would rend the union even by war, while the Government claimed no right to do more than to restrict the territorial enlargement of it. Neither party expected for the war the magnitude or the duration which it has already attained. Neither anticipated that the *cause* of the conflict might cease with or even before the conflict itself should cease. Each looked for an easier triumph, and a result less fundamental and astounding. Both read the same Bible and pray to the same God, and each invokes His aid against the other. It may seem strange that any men should dare to ask a just God's assistance in wringing their bread from the sweat of other men's faces, but let us judge not, that we be not judged. The prayers of both could not be answered. That of neither has been answered fully. The Almighty has His own purposes. "Woe unto the world because of offenses; for it must needs be that offenses come, but woe to that man by whom the offense cometh." If we shall suppose that American slavery is one of those offenses which, in the providence of God, must needs come, but which, having continued through His appointed time, He now wills to remove, and that He gives to both North and South this terrible war as the woe due to those by whom the offense came, shall we discern therein any departure from those divine attributes which the believers in a living God always ascribe to Him? Fondly do we hope, fervently do we pray, that this mighty scourge of war may speedily pass away. Yet, if God wills that it continue until all the wealth piled by the bondsman's two hundred and fifty years of unrequited toil shall be sunk, and until every drop of blood drawn with the lash shall be paid by another drawn with the sword, as was said three thousand years ago, so still it must be said "the judgments of the Lord are true and righteous altogether."

With malice toward none, with charity for all, with firmness in the right as God gives us to see the right, let us strive on to finish the work we are in, to bind up the nation's wounds, to care for him who shall have borne the battle and for his widow and his orphan, to do all which may achieve and cherish a just and lasting peace among ourselves and with all nations.

THE SURRENDER OF LEE
(1865)
by General Fitzhugh Lee

From Lee's Life of Robert E. Lee. *Fitzhugh Lee was a nephew of Robert E. Lee, a graduate of West Point, and a cavalry commander during all the campaigns of the Army of Northern Virginia. After the war he became governor of Virginia and later United States consul at Havana, Cuba. He filled the latter office at the time of the blowing up of the* Maine *in Havana Harbor.*

A white flag went out from the Southern ranks, the firing ceased; the war in Virginia was over. Colonel Babcock, the bearer of General Grant's last note, found General Lee near Appomattox Court House, lying under an apple tree upon a blanket spread on some rails, from which circumstance the widespread report originated that the surrender took place under an apple tree.

General Lee, Colonel Marshall of his staff, Colonel Babcock of General Grant's, and a mounted orderly rode to the village, and found Mr. Wilmer McLean, a resident, who, upon being told that General Lee wanted the use of a room in some house, conducted the party to his dwelling, a comfortable two-story brick, with a porch in front running the length of the house. General Lee was ushered into the room on the left of the hall as you enter, and about one o'clock was joined by General Grant, his staff, and Generals Sheridan and Ord. Grant sat at a marble-topped table in the center of the room, Lee at a small oval table near the front window. "The contrast between the commanders," said one who was present, "was striking."

Grant, not yet forty-three years old, five feet eight inches tall, shoulders slightly stooped, hair and beard nut-brown, wearing a dark-blue flannel blouse unbuttoned, showing vest beneath; ordinary top boots, trousers inside; dark-yellow thread gloves; without spurs or sword, and no marks of rank except a general's shoulder-straps. Lee, fifty-eight years old, six feet tall, hair and beard silver gray; a handsome uniform of Confederate gray buttoned to the throat, with three stars on each side of the turned-down collar, fine top-boots with handsome spurs, elegant gauntlets, and at his side a splendid sword. With a magnificent physique, not a pound of superfluous flesh, ruddy cheeks bronzed by exposure, grave and dignified, he was the focus for all eyes. "His demeanor was that of a thoroughly possest gentleman who had a disagreeable duty to perform, but was determined to get through it as well and as soon as he could" without the exhibition of temper or mortification.

Generals Lee and Grant had met once, eighteen years before, when both were fighting for the same cause in Mexico—one an engineer-officer and on the staff of Scott, the commanding general, the other a subaltern of infantry in Garland's brigade. After a pleasant reference to that event, Lee promptly drew attention to the business before them, the terms of surrender were arranged, and at General Lee's request reduced to writing, as follows:

APPOMATTOX COURT HOUSE, VA.,

April 9, 1865.

GENERAL: In accordance with the substance of my letter to you of the 8th inst., I propose to receive the surrender of the Army of Northern Virginia on the following terms, to wit: Rolls of all the officers and men to be made in duplicate, one copy to be given to an officer to be designated by me, the other to be retained by such officer or officers as you may designate. The officers to give their individual paroles not to take up arms against the Government of the United States until properly exchanged; and each company and regimental commander sign a like parole for the men of their commands. The arms, artillery, and public property to be parked and stacked, and turned over to the officers appointed by me to receive them. This will not embrace the side-arms of the officers nor the private horses or baggage. This done, each officer and man will be allowed to return to his home, not to be disturbed by United States authority so long as he observes his parole, and the laws in force where he may reside.

U. S. GRANT, *Lieutenant-General.*

General R. E. LEE.

"Unless you have some suggestion to make, I will have a copy of the letter made in ink and sign it," said Grant; and it gave Lee the opportunity to tell him that the cavalrymen and many of the artillerymen owned their own horses, and he wished to know whether these men would be permitted to retain their horses. The terms gave to the officers only that privilege, and so Grant stated; but seeing that Lee's face showed plainly that he would like that concession made, the former said feelingly that he supposed that most of the men in ranks were small farmers, that their horses would be useful in putting in a crop to carry themselves and families through the next winter, and that he would give instructions "to let all men who claim to own a horse or mule take the animals home with them to work their little farms." The Union commander was in touch with his President.

General Weitzel, who had entered Richmond with his Twenty-fifth Corps and received its formal capitulation, asked Mr. Lincoln what he "should do in regard to the conquered people?" The latter is reported to have replied that he did not wish to give any orders on that subject, but added, "If I were in your place I'd let 'em up easy, I'd let 'em up easy." It was the fear of his men losing their horses in case of surrender that made the Confederate cavalry commander ask permission at the council the night before to extricate his cavalry in case of surrender, provided it was done before the flag of truce changed the status. To Grant's written proposition for the surrender of the Army of Northern Virginia, General Lee replied:

HEADQUARTERS ARMY OF NORTHERN VIRGINIA,

April 9, 1865.

GENERAL: I received your letter of this date, containing the terms of the surrender of the Army of Northern Virginia as proposed by you. As they are substantially the same as those exprest in your letter of the 8th instant, they are accepted. I will proceed to designate the proper officers to carry the stipulation into effect.

R. E. LEE, *General.*

Lieutenant-General U. S. GRANT.

The formalities were concluded without dramatic accessories, and then Lee's thoughts turned to his hungry veterans and to his prisoners. "I have a thousand or more of your men and officers, whom we have required to march along with us for several days," said Lee to Grant. "I shall be glad to send them to your lines as soon as it can be arranged, for I have no provisions for them. My own men have been living for the last few days principally upon parched corn, and we are badly in need of both rations and forage." The rations sent from Lynchburg to the Southerners were captured. When Grant suggested that he should send Lee twenty-five thousand rations, the latter told him it would be ample, and assured him it would be a great relief. The Confederate commander then left, and rode away to break the sad news to the brave troops he had so long commanded.

General Grant's behavior at Appomattox was marked by a desire to spare the feelings of his great opponent. There was no theatrical display; his troops were not paraded with bands playing and banners flying, before whose lines the Confederates must march and stack arms. He did not demand Lee's sword, as is customary, but actually apologized to him for not having his own, saying it had been left behind in the wagon; promptly stopt salutes from being fired to mark the event, and the terms granted were liberal and generous. "No man could have behaved better than General Grant did under the circumstances," said Lee to a friend in Richmond. "He did not touch my sword; the usual custom is for the sword to be received when tendered, and then handed back, but he did not touch mine." Neither did the Union chief enter the Southern lines to show himself or to parade his victory, or go to Richmond or Petersburg to exult over a fallen people, but mounted his horse and with his staff started for Washington. Washington, at Yorktown, was not as considerate and thoughtful of the feelings of Cornwallis or his men. Charges were now withdrawn from the guns, flags furled, and the Army of the Potomac and the Army of Northern Virginia turned their backs upon each other for the first time in four long, bloody years.

THE ASSASSINATION OF LINCOLN
(1865)
I
by Secretary of War Stanton

As printed in the newspapers of April 15, 1865. Lincoln was shot shortly after 10 o'clock P.M., and died at 7:22 the following morning.

This evening at about 9:30 P.M., at Ford's Theater, the President, while sitting in his private box with Mrs. Lincoln, Miss Harris, and Major Rathbone, was shot by an assassin who suddenly entered the box and approached the President. The assassin then leapt upon the stage, brandished a large dagger or knife, and made his escape in the rear of the theater. The pistol-ball entered the back of the President's head and penetrated nearly through the head. The wound is mortal. The President has been insensible ever since it was inflicted and is now dying.

About the same hour an assassin, whether the same or not, entered Mr. Seward's apartments, and under the pretense of having a prescription, was shown to the Secretary's sick chamber. The assassin immediately rushed to the bed, and inflicted two or three stabs on the throat and two on the face. It is hoped the wounds may not be mortal. My apprehension is that they will prove fatal. The nurse alarmed Mr. Frederick Seward, who was in an adjoining room, and hastened to the door of his father's room, when he met the assassin, who inflicted upon him one or more dangerous wounds. The recovery of Frederick Seward is doubtful.

It is not probable that the President will live throughout the night. General Grant and wife were advertised to be at the theater this evening, but he started for Burlington at six o'clock this evening. At a cabinet meeting at which General Grant was present, the subject of the state of the country, and the prospect of a speedy peace was discust. The President was very cheerful and hopeful, and spoke very kindly of General Lee and others of the Confederacy, and of the establishment of government in Virginia. All the members of the cabinet, except Mr. Seward, are now in attendance upon the President.

I have seen Mr. Seward, but he and Frederick are both unconscious.

EDWIN M. STANTON,
Secretary of War.

April 14, 1865.

II

As Reported in the New York Tribune

From the Tribune *of April 15, 1865. So late was the hour, and so great the excitement and confusion in Washington, that none of the regular editions of the papers of the following morning had more than disconnected reports. The* Tribune's *fifteen short dispatches, here given as then printed, illustrate alike the confusion and the difficulties reporters had in learning details.*

We give the dispatches in the order in which they reached us, the first having been received a little before midnight, for we know that every line, every letter will be read with the intensest interest. In the sudden shock of a calamity so appalling, we can do little else than give such details of the murder of the President as have reached us. Sudden death is always overwhelming; assassination of the humblest of men is always frightfully startling; when the head of thirty millions of people is hurried into eternity by the hand of a murderer—that head a man so good, so wise, so noble as Abraham Lincoln, the chief magistrate of a nation in the condition of ours at this moment—the sorrow and the shock are too great for many words. There are none in all this broad land to-day, who love their country, who wish well to their race, that will not bow down in profound grief at the event it has brought upon us. For once all party rancor will be forgotten, and no right-thinking man can hear of Mr. Lincoln's death without accepting it as a national calamity. We can give in these its first moments, no thought of the future. God, in His inscrutable Providence, has thus visited the nation; the future we must leave to Him.

First Dispatch.
Washington, Friday, April 14, 1865.
To the Associated Press:
The President was shot in a theater tonight, and perhaps mortally wounded.

Second Dispatch.
To the Editors: Our Washington agent orders the dispatch about the President "stopt." Nothing is said about the truth or falsity of the dispatch.

Third Dispatch.
Special Dispatch to the New York Tribune:
The President was shot at Ford's Theater. The ball entered his neck. It is not known whether the wound is mortal. Intense excitement.

Fourth Dispatch.
Special to the New York Tribune:
The President expired at a quarter to 12.

Fifth Dispatch.
Washington, April 15—12:30 A.M.

To the Associated Press:

The President was shot in a theater tonight, and is perhaps mortally wounded. The President is not expected to live through the night. He was shot at the theater. Secretary Seward was also assassinated. No arteries were cut. Particulars soon.

Sixth Dispatch.
Washington, Friday, April 14, 1865.

Special Dispatch to the New York Tribune:

Like a clap of thunder out of a clear sky spread the announcement that President Lincoln was shot while sitting in his box at Ford's Theater. The city is wild with excitement. A gentleman who was present thus describes the event: At about 10:30 o'clock in the midst of one of the acts, a pistol-shot was heard, and at the same instant a man leapt upon the stage from the same box occupied by the President, brandished a long knife, and shouted, "*Sic semper tyrannis!*" then rushed to rear of the scenes and out of the back door of the theater. So sudden was the whole thing that most persons in the theater supposed it a part of the play, and it was some minutes before the fearful tragedy was comprehended. The man was pursued, however, by some one connected with the theater to the outer door and seen to mount a horse and ride rapidly away. A regiment of cavalry have started in all directions, with orders to arrest every man found on horseback. Scarce had the news of this horror been detailed, when couriers came from Secretary Seward's, announcing that he also had been assassinated.

Seventh Dispatch.
Washington, Friday, April 14, 1865.

Special Dispatch to the New York Tribune:

The President attended Ford's Theater, and about 10 o'clock an assassin entered his private box and shot him in the back of the head. The ball lodged in his head, and he is now lying insensible in a house opposite the theater. No hopes are entertained of his recovery. Laura Keene[6] claims to have recognized the assassin as the actor, J. Wilkes Booth. A feeling of gloom like a pall has settled on the city.

About the same hour a horseman rode up to Secretary Seward's, and, dismounting, announced that he had a prescription to deliver to the Secretary in person. Major Seward and Miss Seward were with their father at the time. Being admitted the assassin delivered the pretended prescription to the Secretary in bed, and immediately cut his throat from ear to ear. Fortunately the jugular vein was not severed, and it is possible that Mr.

---

[6] Laura Keene was playing in *The American Cousin.*

Seward may survive. Secretary Stanton was undisturbed at his residence. Thus far, no other murderous demonstrations are reported. It is deemed Providential that General Grant left tonight for New Jersey. He was publicly announced to be present at the theater with the President. Ten thousand rumors are afloat, and the most intense and painful excitement pervades the city.

Eighth Dispatch
Washington, Friday, April 14, 1865.
Special Dispatch to the New York Tribune:
The assassin is said to have gained entrance to the President's box by sending in his card requesting an interview. The box was occupied by Mrs. Lincoln and Colonel Parker of General Grant's staff. The villain drew his pistol across Mrs. Lincoln's shoulder and fired. Colonel Parker sprang up and seized the assassin, but he wrested himself from his grip and sprang down upon the stage as described. His spur caught in the American flag as he descended, and threw him at length. He unloosed the spur and dashed to the rear, brandishing his knife and revolver.

Ninth Dispatch.
Washington, Friday, April 14, 1865.
To the Associated Press:
The screams of Mrs. Lincoln first disclosed the fact to the audience that the President had been shot, when all present rose to their feet, rushed toward the stage, many exclaiming, "Hang him, hang him!" The excitement was of the wildest possible description, and of course there was an abrupt termination to the theatrical performance.

There was a rush toward the President's box, when cries were heard: "Stand back and give him air." "Has any one stimulants?" On a hasty examination, it was found that the President had been shot through the head, above and back of the temporal bone, and that some of the brains were oozing out. He was removed to a private house opposite to the theater, and the Surgeon General of the army and other surgeons sent for to attend to his condition.

On an examination of the private box, blood was discovered on the back of the cushioned rocking-chair on which the President had been sitting, also on the partition and on the floor. A common single-barreled pocket-pistol was found on the carpet. A military dispatch was placed in front of the private residence to which the President had been conveyed. An immense crowd was in front of it, all deeply anxious to learn the condition of the President. It had been previously announced that the wound was mortal, but all hoped otherwise. The shock to the community was terrible. At midnight the Cabinet, together with Messrs. Sumner, Colfax, and Farnsworth, Judge Curtis, Governor Oglesby, General Meigs, Colonel Hay and a few personal friends, with Surgeon General Barnes and his immediate assistants, were around his bedside. The President was in a state of syncope, totally insensible, and breathing slowly. The blood oozed from the wound at the back of his head. The surgeons exhausted every possible effort of medicinal skill, but all hope was gone.

The President and Mrs. Lincoln did not start for the theater until 8:15 o'clock. Speaker Colfax was at the White House at the time, and the President stated to him that he was to go. Mrs. Lincoln had not been well, but because the papers had announced that General Grant and they were to be present, and, as General Grant had gone North, he did not wish the audience to be dispirited. He went with apparent reluctance, and urged Mr. Colfax to go with him, but that gentleman had made other engagements, and with Mr. Ashman, of Massachusetts, bade him good night.

Tenth Dispatch.

Washington, April 15—1 A.M.

Special Dispatch to the New York Tribune:

One of our reporters is just in from the Presidential mansion, who says an orderly reports the President still breathing, but beyond all probable recovery. The circumstances of Secretary Seward's assassination were thus narrated by a member of his household: A man on horseback rode to the Secretary's house, rang the bell and told the servant attending upon the door that he had a prescription from Dr. Verdi, Mr. Seward's attending physician, for the suffering Secretary, which he must deliver in person. The servant took him upstairs, and ushered him into Mr. Frederick Seward's room, where he delivered the same message, but was assured by young Mr. Seward that he could not see his father. He then started to retire, but he turned with an inaudible mutter and leveled a blow at Frederick with a slung-shot. A scuffle then ensued, in which the assassin used his knife, and very seriously wounded the Assistant Secretary; then rushing by him he passed through the door into the father's room. He found the Secretary in charge of his male nurse, and with an instantaneous rush he drew his knife and cut the Secretary's throat from ear to ear, then, lunging his knife into the nurse, he darted out, when he encountered young Major Seward, who seized him and endeavored to detain him, without knowing the horrible tragedy he had enacted. He again used his knife and billy, but was most eager to escape, and as soon as he had cut himself loose fled to the outer door, mounting his horse and was off before the inmates could give to any one an alarm. In fact the wonderful suddenness with which both acts of brutality were enacted, is perhaps the most surprizing feature of this dire national calamity.

Eleventh Dispatch.

Washington, Friday, April 14—1:15 A.M.

Special Dispatch to the New York Tribune:

The President is slowly dying. The brain is slowly oozing through the bullet-hole in his forehead. He is of course insensible. There is an occasional lifting of his hand, and heavy stentorous breathing; that is all. Mrs. Lincoln and her two sons are in a room opposite to Ford's Theater, where the President was taken, and adjoining that where he is lying. Mr. Sumner is seated at the head of the bed. Secretary Stanton, Welles, Dennison, Usher, and McCulloch, and Mr. Speed are in the room. A large number of surgeons, generals, and personal family friends of Mr. Lincoln fill the house. All are in tears. "Andy" Johnson is here. He was in bed in his room at the Kirkwood when the assassination was committed. He was immediately apprized of the event, and got up. The precaution was taken to provide a guard of soldiers for him, and these were at his door before the news was well through the evening. Captain [Major] Rathbone of Albany was in the box with the President. He was slightly wounded.

Later—The accounts are confused and contradictory. One dispatch announces that the President died at 12:30 P.M. Another, an hour later, states that he is still living, but dying slowly. We go to press without knowing the exact truth, but presume there is not the slightest ground for hope. Mr. Seward and his son are both seriously wounded, but are not killed. But there can be little hope that the Secretary can rally with this additional and frightful wound.

Twelfth Dispatch.
Washington, Friday, April 14, 1865.

Special Dispatch to the New York Tribune:

Secretaries Stanton, Welles, and other prominent officers of the Government called at Secretary Seward's house to inquire into his condition, and there heard of the assassination of the President. They then proceeded to the house where he was lying, exhibiting, of course, intense anxiety and solicitude. An immense crowd was gathered in front of the President's house, and a strong guard was also stationed there, many persons evidently supposing he would be brought to his home. The entire city to-night presents a scene of the wildest excitement, accompanied by violent expressions of indignation, and the profoundest sorrow; many shed tears. The military authorities have dispatched mounted patrols in every direction, in order, if possible, to arrest the assassins. The whole metropolitan police are likewise vigilant for the same purpose. The attacks, both at the theater and at Secretary Seward's house, took place at about the same hour—ten o'clock—thus showing a preconcerted plan to assassinate those gentlemen. Some evidences of the guilt of the party who attacked the President are in the possession of the police. Vice-President Johnson is in the city, and his headquarters are guarded by troops.

Thirteenth Dispatch.
Washington, Friday, April 14, 1865.

Special Dispatch to the New York Tribune:

It was Major Rathbone, late of General Burnside's staff, and stepson of Senator Harris, with Miss Harris, who were in the box with Mr. and

Mrs. Lincoln. The captain received a wound in the arm in his effort to detain the assassin. The President is rapidly sinking, and the attending surgeons say he will expire in a very short time. Secretary Seward has just dropt into a comfortable sleep. His pulse remains full, and his physicians pronounce him in a hopeful state.

A burden of anxiety has been lifted by a dispatch just received from General Grant. The train reached Philadelphia all right. The six rebel generals accompanied him on this train, while the remainder of the three or four hundred other officers below that rank, who arrived today, were sent to the Old Capitol. There is one universal acclaim of accusation rising against J. Wilkes Booth as the assassin. If he be indeed innocent, popular feeling against him must be to him unbearable.

Fourteenth Dispatch.
Washington, Saturday, April 15—1:30 A.M.

Special Dispatch to the New York Tribune:

I have just visited the dying couch of Abraham Lincoln. He is now in the agonies of death, and his physicians say he cannot live more than an hour. He is surrounded by the members of his Cabinet, all of whom are bathed in tears. Senator Sumner is seated on the right of the couch on which he is lying, the tears streaming down his cheeks and sobbing like a child. All around him are his physicians, Surgeon-General Barnes directing affairs. The President is unconscious, and the only sign of life he exhibits is by the movement of his right hand, which he raises feebly. Mrs. Lincoln and her two sons are in an adjoining room, into which Secretary Stanton has just gone to inform them that the President's physicians have pronounced his case hopeless. As I passed through the passage to the front door I hear shrieks and cries proceeding from the room in which the grief-stricken wife and children are seated.

Fifteenth Dispatch.
Washington, Saturday, April 15—2:12 A.M.

Special Dispatch to the New York Tribune:

The President is still living, but he is growing weaker. The ball is lodged in the brain three inches from where it entered the skull. He remains insensible, and his condition is utterly hopeless. The Vice-President has been to see him; but all company, except the members of the Cabinet and of the family, is rigidly excluded. Large crowds still continue in the street, as near to the house as the line of guards allows.

ROBERT E. LEE'S ATTITUDE AFTER THE WAR

(1865)

by General Robert E. Lee

From a letter addressed by General Lee to a personal friend in September, 1865. This letter has been accepted as an important document pertaining to the attitude Lee himself assumed after the war, the spirit of which he sought to inculcate in others.

I have received your letter of the 23d ult. [August, 1865], and in reply will state the course I have pursued under circumstances similar to your own, and will leave you to judge of its propriety. Like yourself, I have, since the cessation of hostilities, advised all with whom I have conversed on the subject, who come within the terms of the President's proclamations, to take the oath of allegiance, and accept in good faith the amnesty offered.

But I have gone further, and have recommended to those who were excluded from their benefits, to make application under the proviso of the proclamation of the 29th of May, to be embraced in its provisions. Both classes, in order to be restored to their former rights and privileges, were required to perform a certain act, and I do not see that an acknowledgment of fault is exprest in one more than the other. The war being at an end, the Southern States have laid down their arms, and the question at issue between them and the Northern States having been decided, I believe it to be the duty of every one to unite in the restoration of the country, and the reestablishment of peace and harmony.

These considerations governed me in the counsels I gave to others, and induced me on the 13th of June to make application to be included in the terms of the amnesty proclamation.[7] I have not received an answer, and can not inform you what has been the decision of the President. But, whatever that may be, I do not see how the course I have recommended and practised can prove detrimental to the former President of the Confederate States.

It appears to me that the allayment of passion, the dissipation of preju-

---

[7] General Lee's application dissappeared for nearly one hundred years after its filing. It reappeared in 1970, and in 1975 the United States Congress passed a bill granting the great Southern leader posthumous citizenship.

dice, and the restoration of reason, will alone enable the people of the country to acquire a true knowledge and form a correct judgment of the events of the past four years. It will, I think, be admitted that Mr. Davis has done nothing more than all the citizens of the Southern States, and should not be held accountable for acts performed by them in the exercise of what had been considered by them unquestionable right. I have too exalted an opinion of the American people to believe that they will consent to injustice; and it is only necessary, in my opinion, that truth should be known, for the rights of every one to be secured. I know of no surer way of eliciting the truth than by burying contention with the war.

RECONSTRUCTION
A. THE SOUTH AFTER THE WAR
(1866)
by General Carl Schurz

General Schurz, as well as General Grant, made a tour of the South at the request of President Andrew Johnson. In the accompanying passages from his report will be found the main conclusions at which he arrived.

There is, at present, no danger of another insurrection against the authority of the United States on a large scale, and the people are willing to reconstruct their State governments, and to send their Senators and Representatives to Congress.

But as to the moral value of these results, we must not indulge in any delusions. There are two principal points to which I beg to call your attention. In the first place, the rapid return to power and influence of so many of those who but recently were engaged in a bitter war against the Union, has had one effect which was certainly not originally contemplated by the Government. Treason does, under existing circumstances, not appear odious in the South. The people are not imprest with any sense of its criminality. And, secondly, there is, as yet, among the Southern people an *utter absence* of national feeling.

The principal cause of that want of national spirit which has existed in the South so long, and at last gave birth to the rebellion, was, that the Southern people cherished, cultivated, idolized their peculiar interests and institutions in preference to those which they had in common with the rest of the American people. Hence the importance of the negro question as an integral part of the question of union in general, and the question of reconstruction in particular.

Aside from the assumption that the negro will not work without physical compulsion, there appears to be another popular notion prevalent in the South, which stands as no less serious an obstacle in the way of a successful solution of the problem. It is that the negro exists for the special object of raising cotton, rice and sugar for the whites, and that it is illegitimate for him to indulge, like other people, in the pursuit of his own happiness in his own way. Altho it is admitted that he has ceased to be the property of a master, it is not admitted that he has a right to become his own master. An ingrained feeling like this is apt to bring forth that sort of class legislation which produces laws to govern one class with no other view than to benefit another. This tendency can be distinctly traced in the various schemes for regulating labor which here and there see the light.

As to what is commonly termed "reconstruction," it is not only the political machinery of the States and their constitutional relations to the general government, but the whole organism of Southern society that must be reconstructed, or rather constructed anew, so as to bring it in harmony with the rest of American society. The difficulties of this task are not to be considered overcome when the people of the South take the oath of allegiance and elect governors and legislatures and members of Congress, and militia captains.

The true nature of the difficulties of the situation is this: The general government of the republic has, by proclaiming the emancipation of the slaves, commenced a great social revolution in the South, but has, as yet, not completed it. Only the negative part of it is accomplished. The slaves are emancipated in point of form, but free labor has not yet been put in the place of slavery in point of fact.

The planters, who represented the wealth of the Southern country, are partly laboring under the severest embarrassments, partly reduced to absolute poverty. Many who are stript of all available means, and have nothing but their land, cross their arms in gloomy despondency, incapable of rising to a manly resolution. Others, who still possess means, are at a loss how to use them, as their old way of doing things is, by the abolition of slavery, rendered impracticable, at least where the military arm of the Government has enforced emancipation. Others are still trying to go on in the old way, and that old way is in fact the only one they understand, and in which they have any confidence. Only a minority is trying to adopt the new order of things. A large number of the plantations, probably a considerable majority of the more valuable estates, is under heavy mortgages, and the owners know that, unless they retrieve their fortunes in a comparatively short space of time, their property will pass out of their hands. Almost all are, to some extent, embarrassed. The nervous anxiety which such a state of things produces extends also to those classes of society which, altho not composed of planters, were always in close business connection with the planting interest, and there was hardly a branch of commerce or industry in the South which was not directly or indirectly so connected. Besides, the Southern soldiers, when returning from the war, did not, like the Northern soldiers, find a prosperous community which merely waited for their arrival to give them remunerative employment. They found, many of them, their homesteads destroyed, their farms devastated, their families in distress; and those that were less unfortunate found, at all events, an impoverished and exhausted community which had but little to offer them. Thus a great many have been thrown upon the world to shift as best they can.

RECONSTRUCTION
B. Phases of Reconstruction in South Carolina
(1868–1872)
by Daniel H. Chamberlain

From a letter written by Mr. Chamberlain in 1871. He was a Northern man, born and reared in Massachusetts, and had served in the Union Army during the Civil War. In 1866 he settled in South Carolina, where he became a cotton planter. From 1868 to 1872 he was attorney-general of the state. The letter here given was written while he was attorney-general.

Let us look at our State when the reconstruction acts first took effect in 1868. A social revolution had been accomplished—an entire reversal of the political relations of most of our people had ensued. The class which formerly held all the political power of our State were stript of all.

The class which had formerly been less than citizens, with no political power or social position, were made the sole depositaries of the political power of the State. I refer now to practical results, not to theories. The numerical relations of the two races here were such that one race, under the new laws, held absolute political control of the State.

The attitude and action of both races under these new conditions, while not unnatural, was, as I must think, unwise and unfortunate. One race stood aloof and haughtily refused to seek the confidence of the race which was just entering on its new powers; while the other race quickly grasped all the political power which the new order of things had placed within their reach.

From the nature of the case, the one race were devoid of political experience, of all or nearly all education, and depended mainly for all these qualities upon those who, for the most part, chanced to have drifted here from other States, or who, in very rare instances, being former residents of the State, now allied themselves with the other race. No man of common prudence, or who was even slightly familiar with the working of social forces, could have then failed to see that the elements which went to compose the now dominant party were not of the kind which produce public virtue and honor, or which could long secure even public order and peace.

I make all just allowance for exceptional cases of individual character, but I say that the result to be expected, from the very nature of the situation in 1868, was that a scramble for office would ensue among the members of the party in power, which, again, from the nature of the case, must result in filling the offices of the State, local and general, with men of no capacity and little honesty or desire to really serve the public.

The nation had approved the reconstruction measures, not because they seemed to be free of danger, nor because they were blind to the very grave possibilities of future evils, but in the hope that the one race, wearing its new laurels and using its new powers with modesty and forbearance, would gradually remove the prejudices and enlist the sympathies and cooperation of the other race, until a fair degree of political homogeneity should be reached, and race lines should cease to mark the limits of political parties.

Three years have passed and the result is—what? Incompetency, dishonesty, corruption in all its forms, have "advanced their miscreated fronts," have put to flight the small remnant that opposed them, and now rules the party which rules the State.

You may imagine the chagrin with which I make this statement. Truth alone compels it. My eyes see it—all my senses testify to the startling and sad fact. I can never be indifferent to anything which touches the fair fame of that great national party to which all my deepest convictions attach me, and I repel the libel which the party bearing that name in this State is daily pouring upon us. I am a Republican by habit, by conviction, by association, but my republicanism is not, I trust, composed solely of equal parts of ignorance and rapacity.

Such is the plain statement of the present condition of the dominant party of our State. What is the remedy? That a change will come, and come speedily, let no man doubt. Corruption breeds its own kind. Ignorance rushes to its downfall. Close behind any political party which tolerates such qualities in its public representatives stalks the headsman. If the result is merely political disruption let us be profoundly thankful. Let us make haste to prevent it from being social disruption—the sundering of all the bonds which make society and government possible.

HOW THE ATLANTIC CABLE
WAS LAID

(1866)
by Cyrus W. Field

From an account which Mr. Field wrote in 1866. Mr. Field had been the chief promoter of the cable from the beginning. He was born in Stockbridge, Massachusetts, in 1819, and died in New York in 1892. His activity in promoting the cable had begun in 1854, when, after two years of work, he was able to connect Newfoundland with the mainland. Then followed his work in laying a cable across the Atlantic in 1858. Mr. Field was a brother of Stephen J. Field, a justice of the Supreme Court of the United States, of David Dudley Field, an eminent lawyer of New York, and of Henry M. Field, the author of many books of travel.

At first the Atlantic cable project was wholly an American enterprise. It was begun, and for two years and a half was carried on, solely by American capital. Our brethren across the sea did not even know what we were doing away in the forests of Newfoundland. Our little company raised and expended over a million and a quarter of dollars before an Englishman paid a single pound sterling.

It was not till 1856 that the enterprise had any existence in England. In that summer I went to London, and there, with Mr. John W. Brett, Mr. (now Sir) Charles Bright, and Doctor Whitehouse, organized the Atlantic Telegraph Company. Science had begun to contemplate the necessity of such an enterprise; and the great Faraday cheered us with his lofty enthusiasm. Then, for the first time, was enlisted the support of English capitalists; and then the British Government began that generous course which it has continued ever since—offering us ships to complete soundings across the Atlantic and to assist in laying the cable, and an annual subsidy for the transmission of messages. The expedition of 1857 and the two expeditions of 1858 were joint enterprises, in which the *Niagara* and the *Susquehanna* took part with the *Agamemnon,* the *Leopard,* the *Gordon,* and the *Valorous;* and the officers of both navies worked with generous rivalry for the same great object. The capital—except one-quarter which was taken by myself—was subscribed wholly in Great Britain. The directors were almost all English bankers and merchants, tho among them was one gentleman whom we are proud to call an American—Mr. George Peabody, a name honored in two countries, since he has showered his princely benefactions upon both.

After two unsuccessful attempts, on the third trial we gained a brief success. The cable was laid, and for four weeks it worked—tho never very brilliantly. It spoke, tho only in broken sentences. But while it lasted no less than four hundred messages were sent across the Atlantic. Great was the enthusiasm it excited. It was a new thing under the sun, and for a few weeks the public went wild over it. Of course, when it stopt, the reaction was very great. People grew dumb and suspicious. Some thought it was all a hoax; and many were quite sure that it never had worked at all. That kind of odium we have had to endure for eight years, till now. I trust, we have at last silenced the unbelievers.

After the failure of 1858 came our darkest days. When a thing is dead, it is hard to galvanize it into life. It is more difficult to revive an old enterprise than to start a new one. The freshness and novelty are gone, and the feeling of disappointment discourages further effort.

Other causes delayed a new attempt. The United States had become involved in a tremendous war; and while the nation was struggling for life, it had no time to spend in foreign enterprises. But in England the project was still kept alive. The Atlantic Telegraph Company kept up its organization. It had a noble body of directors, who had faith in the enterprise and looked beyond its present low estate to ultimate success. It was plain that our main hope must be in England, and I went to London. There, too, it dragged heavily. There was a profound discouragement. Many had lost before, and were not willing to throw more money into the sea. We needed six hundred thousand pounds, and with our utmost efforts we had raised less than half, and there the enterprise stood in a deadlock. It was plain that we must have help from some new quarter. I looked around to find a man who had broad shoulders and could carry a heavy load, and who would be a giant in the cause.

At this time I was introduced to a gentleman, whom I would hold up to the American public as a specimen of a great-hearted Englishman, Mr. Thomas Brassey. In London he is known as one of the men who have made British enterprise and British capital felt in all parts of the earth. I went to see him, tho with fear and trembling. He received me kindly, but put me through such an examination as I never had before. I thought I was in the witness-box. He asked me every possible question, but my answers satisfied him, and he ended by saying it was an enterprise that should be carried out, and that he would be one of ten men to furnish the money to do it. This was a pledge of sixty thousand pounds sterling! Encouraged by this noble offer, I looked around to find another such man, tho it was almost like trying to find two Wellingtons. But he *was* found in Mr. John Pender, of Manchester. I went to his office in London one day, and we walked together to the House of Commons, and before we got there he said he would take an equal share with Mr. Brassey.

The action of these two gentlemen was a turning-point in the history of our enterprise; for it led shortly after to a union of the well-known firm of Glass, Eliott & Company, with the Guttapercha Company, making of the two one concern known as the Telegraph Construction and Maintenance Company. We needed, I have said, six hundred thousand pounds, and with all our efforts in England and America we raised only two hundred eighty-five thousand pounds. This new company now came forward, and offered to take the whole remaining three hundred fifteen thousand pounds, besides one hundred thousand pounds of the bonds, and to make its own profits contingent on success.

A few days after, half a dozen gentlemen joined together and bought the *Great Eastern* to lay the cable; and at the head of this company was placed Mr. Daniel Gooch, a member of Parliament, and chairman of the Great Western Railway, who was with us in both the expeditions which followed. His son, Mr. Charles Gooch, a volunteer in the service, worked faithfully on board the *Great Eastern.*

The good-fortune which favored us in our ship favored us also in our commander, Captain Anderson, who was for years in the Cunard Line. How well he did his part in two expeditions the result has proved, and it was just that a mark of royal favor should fall on that manly head. Thus organized, the work of making a new Atlantic cable was begun. The core was prepared with infinite care, under the able superintendence of Mr. Chatterton and Mr. Willoughby Smith, and the whole was completed in about eight months. As fast as ready, it was taken on board the *Great Eastern* and coiled in three enormous tanks, and on July 15, 1865, the ship sailed.

I will not stop to tell the story of that expedition. For a week all went well; we had paid out one thousand two hundred miles of cable, and had only six hundred miles farther to go, when, hauling in the cable to remedy a fault, it parted and went to the bottom. That day I never can forget—how men paced the deck in despair, looking out on the broad sea that had swallowed up their hopes; and then how the brave Canning for nine days and nights dragged the bottom of the ocean for our lost treasure, and, tho he grappled it three times, failed to bring it to the surface. We returned to England defeated, yet full of resolution to begin the battle anew. It was finally concluded that the best course was to organize a new company, which should assume the work; and so originated the Anglo-American Telegraph Company. It was formed by ten gentlemen who met around a table in London and put down ten thousand pounds apiece. The great Telegraph Construction and Maintenance Company, undaunted by the failure of last year, answered us with a subscription of one hundred thousand pounds. Soon after the books were opened to the public, through the eminent banking-house of J. S. Morgan and Company, and in fourteen days we had raised the six hundred thousand pounds. Then the work began again, and went on with speed. Never was greater energy infused into any enterprise. It was only the last day of March that the new company was formed, and it was registered as a company the next day; and yet such was the vigor and dispatch that in five months from that day the cable had been manufactured, shipt on the *Great Eastern,* stretched across the Atlantic, and was sending messages, literally swift as lightning, from continent to continent.

But our work was not over. After landing the cable safely at Newfoundland, we had another task—to return to mid-ocean and recover that lost in the expedition of last year. This achievement has perhaps excited more surprize than the other. Many even now "don't understand it," and every day I am asked "How it was done?" Well, it does seem rather difficult to fish for a jewel at the bottom of the ocean two and a half miles deep. But it is not so very difficult when you know how. You may be sure we did not go fishing at random, nor was our success mere "luck." It was the triumph of the highest nautical and engineering skill. We had four ships, and on board of them some of the best seamen in England—men who knew the ocean as a hunter knows every trail in the forest. There was Captain Moriarty, who was in the *Agamemnon* in 1857-1858. He was in the *Great Eastern* in 1865, and saw the cable when it broke; and he and Captain Anderson at once took observations so exact that they could go right to the spot. After finding it, they marked the line of the cable by buoys; for fogs would come, and shut out sun and stars, so that no man could take an observation.

These buoys were anchored a few miles apart, they were numbered, and each had a flagstaff on it so that it could be seen by day, and a lantern by night. Having thus taken our bearings, we stood off three or four miles, so as to come broadside on, and then, casting over the grapnel, drifted slowly down upon it, dragging the bottom of the ocean as we went. At first it was a little awkward to fish in such deep water, but our men got used to it, and soon could cast a grapnel almost as straight as an old whaler throws a harpoon. Our fishing line was of formidable size. It was made of rope, twisted with wires of steel, so as to bear a strain of thirty tons. It took about two hours for the grapnel to reach bottom, but we could tell when it struck. I often went to the bow, and sat on the rope, and could feel by the quiver that the grapnel was dragging on the bottom two miles under us. But it was a very slow business. We had storms and calms and fogs and squalls.

Still we worked on day after day. Once, on August 17th, we got the cable up, and had it in full sight for five minutes, a long, slimy monster, fresh from the ooze of the ocean's bed, but our men began to cheer so wildly that it seemed to be frightened and suddenly broke away and went down into the sea. This accident kept us at work two weeks longer, but, finally, on the last night of August we caught it. We had cast the grapnel thirty times. It was a little before midnight on Friday night that we hooked the cable, and it was a little after midnight Sunday morning when we got it on board. What was the anxiety of those twenty-six hours! The strain on every man was like the strain on the cable itself. When finally it appeared, it was midnight; the lights of the ship, and those in the boats around our bows, as they flashed in the faces of the men, showed them eagerly watching for the cable to appear on the water.

At length it was brought to the surface. All who were allowed to approach crowded forward to see it. Yet not a word was spoken save by the officers in command who were heard giving orders. All felt as if life and death hung on the issue. It was only when the cable was brought over the bow and on to the deck that men dared to breathe. Even then they hardly believed their eyes. Some crept toward it to feel of it, to be sure it was there. Then we carried it along to the electricians' room, to see if our long-sought-for treasure was alive or dead. A few minutes of suspense, and a flash told of the lightning current again set free. Then did the feeling long pent up burst forth. Some turned away their heads and wept. Others broke into cheers, and the cry ran from man to man, and was heard down in the engine-rooms, deck below deck, and from the boats on the water, and the other ships, while rockets lighted the darkness of the sea. Then with thankful hearts we turned our faces again to the west.

But soon the wind rose, and for thirty-six hours we were exposed to all the dangers of a storm on the Atlantic. Yet in the very height and fury of the gale, as I sat in the electricians' room, a flash of light came up from the deep, which having crossed to Ireland, came back to me in mid-ocean, telling that those so dear to me, whom I had left on the banks of the Hudson, were well and following us with their wishes and their prayers. This was like a whisper of God from the sea, bidding me keep heart and hope. The *Great Eastern* bore herself proudly through the storm, as if she knew that the vital cord, which was to join two hemispheres, hung at her stern; and so, on Saturday, September 7th, we brought our second cable safely to the shore.

JOHNSON'S IMPEACHMENT
(1868)
by Senator S. M. Cullom

Shelby Moore Cullom, United States senator from Illinois, nominated General Ulysses Simpson Grant at the Republican national convention in 1872. He was chairman of the Senate committee that investigated malpractice in railroads and instigated the proceedings that later brought into existence the Interstate Commerce

Bill. In addition to practicing law in Illinois, as well as being elected speaker in the Illinois House of Representatives, he was noted for his thorough grasp of American problems at the turn of the century.

As I look back now over the vista of the years that have come and gone, it seems to me that I entered the Lower House of Congress just at the beginning of the most important period in all our history. The great President had been assassinated; the war was over; Andrew Johnson, a Union Democrat, was President of the United States. Reconstruction was the problem which confronted us, how to heal up the nation's wounds and remake a Union which would endure for all time to come. These were the difficult conditions that had to be dealt with by the Thirty-ninth Congress.

Andrew Johnson was the queerest character that ever occupied the White House, and, with the exception of Lincoln only, he entered it under the most trying and difficult circumstances in all our history; but Lincoln had, what Johnson lacked, the support and confidence of the great Republican party. Johnson was never a Republican, and never pretended to be one. He was a lifelong Democrat, and a slaveholder as well; but he was loyal to the Union, no man living more so. As a Senator from Tennessee, alone of all the Southern Senators he faced his colleagues from the South in denouncing secession as treason. His subsequent phenomenal course in armed opposition to the Rebellion brought about his nomination for the Vice-Presidency as a shrewd stroke to secure the support of the War Democrats of the North and the Union men· of his State and section.

There were two striking points in Johnson's character, and I knew him well: first, his loyalty to the Union; and, second, his utter fearlessness of character. He could not be cowed; old Ben Wade, Sumner, Stevens, all the great leaders of that day could not, through fear, influence him one particle.

In 1861, when he was being made the target of all sorts of threats on account of his solitary stand against secession in the Senate, he let fall this characteristic utterance: "I want to say, not boastingly, with no anger in my bosom, that these two eyes of mine have never looked upon anything in the shape of mortal man that this heart has feared." This utterance probably illustrates Johnson's character more clearly than anything that I could say. He sought rather than avoided a fight. Headstrong, domineering, having fought his way in a State filled with aristocratic Southerners, from the class of so-called "low whites" to the highest position in the United States, he did not readily yield to the dictates of the dominating forces in Congress.

Lincoln had a well-defined policy of reconstruction. Indeed, so liberal was he disposed to be in his treatment of the Southern States, that immediately after the surrender of Richmond he would have recognized the old State Government of Virginia had it not been for the peremptory veto of

Stanton. Congress was not in session when Johnson came to the Presidency in April, 1865. To do him no more than simple justice, I firmly believe that he wanted to follow out, in reconstruction, what he thought was the policy of Mr. Lincoln, and in this he was guided largely by the advice of Mr. Seward.

But there was this difference. Johnson was, probably in good faith, pursuing the Lincoln policy of reconstruction; but when the legislatures and executives of the Southern States began openly passing laws and executing them so that the negro was substantially placed back into slavery, practically nullifying the results of the awful struggle, the untold loss of life and treasure, Mr. Lincoln certainly would have receded and would have dealt with the South with an iron hand, as Congress had determined to do, and as General Grant was compelled to do when he assumed the Presidency.

From April to the reassembling of Congress in December, Johnson had a free hand in dealing with the seceding States, and he was not slow to take advantage of it. He seemed disposed to recognize the old State governments; to restrict the suffrage to the whites; to exercise freely the pardoning power in the way of extending executive clemency not only to almost all classes, but to every individual who would apply for it. The result was, it seemed to be certain that if the Johnson policy were carried out to the fullest extent, the supremacy of the Republican party in the councils of the nation would be at stake.

To express it in a word, the motive of the opposition to the Johnson plan of reconstruction was the firm conviction that its success would wreck the Republican party, and by restoring the Democrats to power bring back Southern supremacy and Northern vassalage. The impeachment, in a word, was a culmination of the struggle between the legislative and the executive departments of the Government over the problem of reconstruction. The legislative department claimed exclusive jurisdiction over reconstruction; the executive claimed that it alone was competent to deal with the subject.

This is a very brief summary of the conditions which confronted us when I entered the Thirty-ninth Congress. Representatives of the eleven seceding States were there to claim their seats in Congress. The Republican members met in caucus the Saturday evening preceding the meeting of Congress on Monday. I, as a member-elect, was present, and I remember how old Thaddeus Stevens at once assumed the dominating control in opposition to the President's plan. Stevens was a most remarkable character—one of the most remarkable in the legislative history of the United States. He believed firmly in negro equality and negro suffrage. As one writer eloquently expresses it:

"According to his creed, the insurgent States were conquered provinces to be shaped into a paradise for the freedman and a hell for the rebel. His eye shot over the blackened southern land; he saw the carnage, the desolation, the starvation, and the shame; and like a battered old warhorse, he flung up his frontlet, sniffed the tainted breeze, and snorted 'Ha, Ha!' "

It was at once determined by the Republican majority in Congress that the representatives of the eleven seceding States should not be admitted. The Constitution expressly gives to the House and Senate the exclusive power to judge of the admission and qualification of its own members.

We were surprised at the moderation of the President's message, which came in on Tuesday after Congress assembled.

Aside from the worst radicals, the message pleased every one, the country at large and the majority in Congress; and there was a general disposition to give the President a reasonably free hand in working out his plan of reconstruction. But as I stated, the legislatures of the Southern States and their executives assumed so domineering an attitude, practically wiping out the results of the war, that the Republican majority in Congress assumed it to be its duty to take control from the Executive.

What determined Johnson in his course, I do not know. It was thought that he would be a radical of radicals. Being of the "poor white" class, he may have been flattered by the attentions showered on him by the old Southern aristocrats. Writers of this period have frequently given that as a reason. My own belief has been that he was far too strong a man to be governed in so vital a matter by so trivial a cause. My conviction is that the radical Republican leaders in the House were right; that he believed in the old Democratic party, aside from his loyalty to the Union; and was a Democrat determined to turn the Government over to the Democratic party, reconstructed on a Union basis. An extension to the Freedman's Bureau bill was passed, was promptly vetoed by the executive, the veto was as promptly overruled by the House, where there was no substantial opposition, but the Senate failed to pass the bill, the veto of the President to the contrary notwithstanding.

I had not the remotest idea that Johnson would dare to veto the Freedman's Bureau bill, and I made a speech on the subject, declaring a firm conviction to that effect. A veto at that time was almost unheard of. Except during the administration of Tyler, no important bill had ever been vetoed by an executive. It came as a shock to Congress and the country. Excitement reigned supreme. The question was: "Should the bill pass the veto of the President regardless thereof?"

Not the slightest difficulty existed in the House; Thaddeus Stevens had too complete control of that body to allow any question concerning it there. The bill, therefore, was promptly passed over the veto of the President. But the situation in the Senate was different. At that time the Sumner-Wade radical element did not have the necessary two-thirds majority, and the bill failed to pass over the veto of the President. The war between the executive and legislative departments of the Government had fairly commenced, and the first victory had been won by the President. The Civil Rights bill, drawn and introduced by Judge Trumbull, than whom there was no greater lawyer in the United States Senate, in January, 1866, on the reassembling of Congress, was passed. Then began the real struggle on the part of the radicals in the Senate, headed by Sumner and Wade, to muster the necessary two-thirds majority to pass a bill over the veto of the President.

Let me digress here to say a word in reference to Charles Sumner. For ten years he was chairman of the Foreign Relations Committee of the United States Senate, and no man, by education, experience, knowledge of world politics, and travel, was ever more fitted to occupy that high position. He was one of the most cultivated men of his day, a radical, and filled one of the most important places in the history of his time. When he entered the Senate, the South dominated this Government; the great triumvirate, Webster, Clay, and Calhoun, had just passed. Compromise was the word, and the Southerners so dominated that it was considered treason to mention the slavery question. Charles Sumner was an Abolitionist; he was not afraid, and at the very first opportunity he took the floor and denounced the institution in no unmeasured terms. Chase and Seward were present that day, and quickly followed Sumner's lead. Seward, however, was far more conservative than either Sumner or Chase.

It was the mission of Charles Sumner to awake the public conscience to the horrors of slavery. He performed his duty unfalteringly, and it almost cost him his life. Mr. Lincoln was the only man living who ever managed Charles Sumner, or could use his for his purpose. Sumner's end has always seemed to me most pitiful. Removed from his high position as chairman of the Foreign Relations Committee of the Senate, followed relentlessly by the enmity of President Grant, then at the very acme of his fame; drifting from the Republican party, his own State repudiating him, Charles Sumner died of a broken heart.

But to return to the struggle between the President and Congress. Trumbull, Sumner, Wade, and the leaders were bound in one way or another to get the necessary two-thirds. The vote was taken in the Senate: "Shall the Civil Rights bill pass the veto of the President to the contrary notwithstanding?" It was understood the vote would be very close, and the result uncertain.

The excitement was intense. The galleries were crowded; members of the House were on the Senate floor. The result seemed to depend entirely on the vote of Senator Morgan, of New York, and he seemed to be irresolute, uncertain in his own mind which way he would vote. The call of the roll proceeded. When his name was reached there was profound silence. He first voted nay, and then immediately changed to yea. A wonderful demonstration burst forth, as it was then known that the bill would pass over the veto of the President, and that the Republican party in Congress at last had complete control. Senator Trumbull made a remarkable speech on that occasion, and I was never prouder of any living man.

So the struggle went on from day to day and year to year, growing all the time more intense. I have always been disposed to be conservative; I was then; and it was with profound regret that I saw the feeling between the President and Congress becoming more and more strained.

I disliked to follow the extreme radical element, and when the row was at its height, Judge Orth, a colleague in the House from Indiana, and I concluded to go and see the President and advise with him, in an attempt to smooth over the differences. I will never forget that interview. It was at night. He received us politely enough, and without mincing any words he gave us to understand that we were on a fool's errand and that he would not yield. We went away, and naturally joined the extreme radicals in the House, always voting with them afterward.

The row continued in the Fortieth Congress. Bills were passed, promptly vetoed, and the bills immediately passed over the President's veto. Many of the bills were not only unwise legislation, but were unconstitutional as well. We passed the Tenure of Office bill; we attempted to restrict the President's pardoning power; and as I look back over the history of the period, it seems to me that we did not have the slightest regard for the Constitution. Some of President Johnson's veto messages were admirable. He had the advice and assistance of one of the ablest lawyers of his day, Jeremiah Black.

To make the feeling more intense, just about this time Johnson made his famous "swing around the circle," as it was termed. His speeches published in the opposition press were intemperate and extreme. He denounced Congress. He threatened to "kick people out of office," in violation of the Tenure of Office act. He was undignified in his actions and language, and many people thought he was intoxicated most of the time, altho I do not believe this.

The radicals in both the House and Senate determined that he should be impeached and removed from office. They had the votes in the House easily, and they thought they could muster the necessary number in the Senate, as we had been passing all sorts of legislation over the President's veto.

It seems to me difficult to realize that it was as far back as March 2, 1868, that I address the House in favor of the impeachment articles. I think I made a pretty good speech on that occasion and supported my position very well. I took rather an extreme view in favor of the predominance of the legislative department of the Government, contending that the executive and judiciary departments of the Government, while they are finally responsible to the people, are directly accountable to the legislative department.

The first and principal article in the impeachment proposed by the

House was the President's issuance of an order removing Edwin M. Stanton as Secretary of War, he having been duly appointed and commissioned by and with the advice and consent of the Senate, and the Senate having been in session at the time of his removal. I contended then, on the floor of the House, that such a removal was a violation of the Constitution, and could not be excused on any pretext whatever, in addition to being a direct violation of the Tenure of Office act.

I do not intend to go into the details of the various articles proposed by the House; suffice it to say that they were mainly based on the attempted removal of Mr. Stanton, and the appointment of Mr. Thomas as Secretary of War.

Needless for me to say, that as the subject continued, feeling remained at a high pitch in the House. It was debated from day to day. Stevens was urging the impeachment with all the force at his command; some were doubtful and holding back, as I was; some changed—for instance, James G. Blaine, who was taunted by Stevens and sneered at for his change of front.

Under the law then existing the President of the Senate succeeded a Vice-President who became, by the death or removal of the President, President of the United States. The radicals in complete control—and I have no doubt that Stevens had a hand in it—elected the most radical of their number as President of the Senate—Ben Wade, of Ohio. Johnson removed, Wade would have been President, and the extreme radicals would have been in supreme control of the legislative and executive departments of the Government.

This condition is what made Mr. Blaine hesitate. He told me on one occasion: "Johnson in the White House is bad enough, but we know what we have; Lord knows what we would get with old Ben Wade there. I do not know but I would rather trust Johnson than Wade." But in the end Blaine supported the impeachment articles, just as I did, and as Senator Allison and other somewhat conservative members did, all feeling at the same time not a little doubtful of our course.

Stevens, Logan, Boutwell, Williams, and Wilson were appointed managers on the part of the House, and solemnly and officially notified the Senate of the action of the House in impeaching the President of the United States. The Senate proceeded without long delay to resolve itself as a High Court of Impeachment, for the purpose of trying the President of the United States for high crimes and misdemeanors. The most eminent counsel of the nation were engaged. Mr. Evarts was President Johnson's principal counsel. He was ably assisted by lawyers of scarcely less renown.

The trial dragged along from day to day. Part of the time the Senate considered the matter in executive session. The corridors were crowded. All sorts of coercing methods were used to influence wavering Senators. Old Bob Schenck was the chairman of this movement, and he sent telegrams broadcast all over the United States to the effect that there was great danger to the peace of the country and the Republican cause if impeachment failed, and asking the recipients to send to their Senators public opinion by resolutions and delegations. And responses came from all over the North, urging and demanding the impeachment of the President.

It is difficult now to realize the intense excitement of that period. General Grant was there, tacitly acknowledged as the next nominee of the Republican party for the Presidency. He took no active part, but it was pretty well understood, from the position of his friends such as Logan and Washburne, that the impeachment had his sympathy; and in the Senate Conkling was especially vindictive. Grimes, Fessenden, and Trumbull led the fight for acquittal. Many were non-committal; but in the end the struggle turned on the one doubtful Senator, Edmund G. Ross of Kansas.

It was determined to vote on the tenth article first, as that article was the strongest one and more votes could be mustered for it than any other. It was well understood that the vote on that article would settle the matter.

More than forty-three years have passed into history since that memorable day when the Senate of the United States was sitting as a Court of Impeachment for the purpose of trying the President of the United States for high crimes and misdemeanors. The occasion is unforgettable. As I look back now, I see arising before me the forms and features of the great men who were sitting in that high court: I see presiding Chief Justice Chase; I see Sumner, cold and dignified; Wade, Trumbull, Hendricks, Conkling, Yates; I see Logan as one of the managers on the part of the House; I see old Thad Stevens, weak and wasted from illness, being carried in—all long since have passed to the beyond, the accused President, the members of the high court, the counsel. Of all the eminent men who was present on that day, aside from the Hon. J. B. Henderson, I do not know of a single one now living.

As the roll was called, there was such a solemn hush as only comes when man stands in the presence of Deity. Finally, when the name of Ross was reached and he voted "No"; when it was understood that his vote meant acquittal, the friends of the President in the galleries thundered forth in applause. And thus ended for the first, and I hope the last, time the trial of a President of the United States before the Senate, sitting as a Court of Impeachment for high crimes and misdemeanors.

THE GREAT CHICAGO FIRE
(1871)
by Horace White

Mr. White, who afterward became one of the editors of the New York Evening Post, *was then one of the editors of the Chicago* Tribune. *He was an eyewitness of the great Chicago conflagration, and wrote this account as a letter to Murat Halstead, then editor of the Cincinnati* Commercial. *It was written in the office of the Chicago* Tribune, *and bears the date October 14, 1871.*

As a slight acknowledgment of your thoughtful kindness in forwarding to us, without orders, a complete outfit of type and cases, when you heard that we had been burned out, I send you a hastily written sketch of what I saw at the great fire.

The history of the great fire in Chicago, which rises to the dignity of a national event, can not be written until each witness, who makes any record whatever, shall have told what he saw. Nobody could see it all—no more than one man could see the whole of the battle of Gettysburg. It was too vast, too swift, too full of smoke, too full of danger, for anybody to see it all. My experience derives its only public importance from the fact that what I did, substantially, a hundred thousand others did or attempted—that is, saved or sought to save their lives and enough of their wearing apparel to face the sky in.

I had retired to rest, tho not to sleep (Sunday, October 8), when the great bell struck the alarm, but fires had been so frequent of late, and had been so speedily extinguished, that I did not deem it worth while to get up and look at it, or even to count the strokes on the bell to learn where it was. The bell paused for fifteen minutes before giving the general alarm, which distinguishes a great fire from a small one. When it sounded the general alarm I rose and looked out. There was a great light to the southwest of my residence, but no greater than I had frequently seen in that quarter, where vast piles of pine lumber have been stored all the time I have lived in Chicago, some eighteen years. But it was not pine lumber that was burning this time. It was a row of wooden tenements in the South Division of the city, in which a few days ago were standing whole rows of the most costly buildings which it hath entered into the hearts of architects to conceive. I watched the increasing light for a few moments. Red tongues of light began to shoot upward; my family were all aroused by this time, and

I drest myself for the purpose of going to the *Tribune* office to write something about the catastrophe. Once out upon the street, the magnitude of the fire was suddenly disclosed to me.

I went to the *Tribune* office, ascended to the editorial rooms, took the only inflammable thing there, a kerosene lamp, and carried it to the basement, where I emptied the oil into the sewer. This was scarcely done when I perceived the flames breaking out of the roof of the court house, the old nucleus of which, in the center of the edifice, was not constructed of fireproof material, as the new wings had been. As the flames had leapt a vacant space of nearly two hundred feet to get at this roof, it was evident that most of the business portion of the city must go down, but I did not reflect that the city water works, with their four great pumping engines, were in a straight line with the fire and wind. Nor did I know then that this priceless machinery was covered by a wooden roof. The flames were driving thither with demon precision.

Billows of fire were rolling over the business palaces of the city and swallowing up their contents. Walls were falling so fast that the quaking of the ground under our feet was scarcely noticed, so continuous was the reverberation. Sober men and women were hurrying through the streets from the burning quarter, some with bundles of clothes on their shoulders, others dragging trunks along the sidewalks by means of strings and ropes fastened to the handles, children trudging by their sides or borne in their arms. Now and then a sick man or woman would be observed, half concealed in a mattress doubled up and borne by two men. Droves of horses were in the streets, moving by some sort of guidance to a place of safety. Vehicles of all descriptions were hurrying to and fro, some laden with trunks and bundles, others seeking similar loads and immediately finding them, the drivers making more money in one hour than they were used to see in a week or a month. Everybody in this quarter was hurrying toward the lake shore. All the streets crossing that part of Michigan Avenue which fronts on the lake (on which my own residence stood) were crowded with fugitives, hastening toward the blessed water.

We saw the tall buildings on the opposite sides of the two streets melt down in a few moments without scorching ours. The heat broke the plate-glass windows in the lower stories, but not in the upper ones. After the fire in our neighborhood had spent its force, the editorial and composing rooms did not even smell of smoke. Several of our brave fellows who had been up all night had gone to sleep on the lounges, while others were at the sink washing their faces, supposing that all danger to us had passed. So I supposed, and in this belief went home to breakfast. The smoke to the northward was so dense that we could not see the North Division, where sixty thousand people were flying in mortal terror before the flames. The immense store of Field, Leiter & Co. I observed to be under a shower of water from their own fire-apparatus, and since the First National Bank, a fire-proof building, protected it on one corner, I concluded that the progress of the flames in that direction was stopt, as the *Tribune* building had stopt it where we were. Here, at least, I thought was a saving of twenty millions of property, including the great Central depot and the two grain-elevators adjoining, effected by two or three buildings which had been erected with a view to such an emergency. The post-office and custom-house building (also fire-proof, according to public rumor) had stopt the flames a little farther to the southwest, altho the interior of that structure was burning. A straight line drawn northeast from the post-office would nearly touch the *Tribune,* First National Bank, Field, Leiter & Co.'s store, and the Illinois Central Railroad land department, another fire-proof. Everything east of that line seemed perfectly safe. And with this feeling I went home to breakfast.

There was still a mass of fire to the southwest, in the direction whence it originally came, but as the engines were all down there, and the buildings small and low, I felt sure that the firemen would manage it. As soon as I had swallowed a cup of coffee and communicated to my family the facts that I had gathered, I started out to see the end of the battle. Reaching State Street, I glanced down to Field, Leiter & Co.'s store, and to my surprize noticed that the streams of water which had before been showering it, as tho it had been a great artificial fountain, had ceased to run. But I did not conjecture the awful reality, viz., that the great pumping engines had been disabled by a burning roof falling upon them. I thought perhaps the firemen on the store had discontinued their efforts because the danger was over. But why were men carrying out goods from the lower story?

This query was soon answered by a gentleman who asked me if I had heard that the water had stopt! The awful truth was here! The pumping engines were disabled, and tho we had at our feet a basin sixty miles wide by three hundred and sixty long, and seven hundred feet deep, all full of clear green water, we could not lift enough to quench a cooking-stove. Still the direction of the wind was such that I thought the remaining fire would not cross State Street, or reach the residences on Wabash and Michigan avenues and the terrified people on the lake shore. I determined to go down to the black cloud of smoke which was rising away to the southwest, the course of which could not be discovered on account of the height of the intervening buildings, but thought it most prudent to go home again, and tell my wife to get the family wearing apparel in readiness for moving. I found that she had already done so. I then hurried toward the black cloud, some ten squares distant, and there found the rows of wooden houses on Third and Fourth avenues falling like ripe wheat before the reaper. At a glance I perceived that all was lost in our part of the city, and I conjectured that the *Tribune* building was doomed too, for I had noticed with consternation that the fireproof postoffice had been completely gutted, notwithstanding it was detached from other buildings. The *Tribune* was fitted into a niche, one side of which consisted of a wholesale stationery store, and the other of McVicker's Theater. But there was now no time to think of property. Life was in danger. The lives of those most dear to me depended upon their getting out of our house, out of our street, through an infernal gorge of horses, wagons, men, women, children, trunks, and plunder.

My brother was with me, and we seized the first empty wagon we could find, pinning the horse by the head. A hasty talk with the driver disclosed that we could have his establishment for one load for twenty dollars. I had not expected to get him for less than a hundred, unless we should take him by force, and this was a bad time for a fight. He proved himself a muscular as well as a faithful fellow, and I shall always be glad that I avoided a personal difficulty with him. One peculiarity of the situation was that nobody could get a team without ready money. I had not thought of this when I was revolving in my mind the offer of one hundred dollars, which was more greenbacks than our whole family could have put up if our lives had depended upon the issue. This driver had divined that, as all the banks were burned, a check on the Commercial National would not carry him very far, altho it might carry me to a place of safety. All the drivers had divined the same. Every man who had anything to sell perceived the same. "Pay as you go" had become the watchword of the hour. Never was there a community so hastily and so completely emancipated from the evils of the credit system.

With some little difficulty we reached our house, and in less time than we ever set out on a journey before, we dragged seven trunks, four bundles, four valises, two baskets, and one hamper of provisions into the street and piled them on the wagon. For one square southward from the corner of Monroe Street we made pretty fair progress. The dust was so thick that we could not see the distance of a whole square ahead. It came, not in clouds, but in a steady storm of sand, the particles impinging against our faces like needle points. Pretty soon we came to a dead halt. We could move neither forward, nor backward, nor sidewise. The gorge had caught fast somewhere. Yet everybody was good-natured and polite.

Presently the jam began to move; the contributions from the cross-streets grew less; and soon we began to move on a walk without interruption.

At Eldridge Court, I turned into Wabash Avenue, where the crowd was thinner. Arriving at the house of a friend, who was on the windward side of the fire, I tumbled off my load and started back to get another. Half-way down Michigan Avenue, which was now perceptibly easier to move in, I perceived my family on the sidewalk with their arms full of light household effects. My wife told me that the house was already burned, that the flames burst out ready-made in the rear hall before she knew that the roof had been scorched, and that one of the servants, who had disobeyed orders in her eagerness to save some article, had got singed, tho not burned, in coming out. My wife and my mother and all the rest were begrimed with dirt and smoke, like blackamoors; everybody was. The "bloated aristocrats" all along the streets, who supposed they had lost both home and fortune at one swoop, were a sorry but not despairing congregation. They had saved their lives at all events, and they knew that many of their fellow creatures must have lost theirs. I saw a great many kindly acts done as we moved along. The poor helped the rich, and the rich helped the poor (if anybody could be called rich at such a time), to get on with their loads. I heard of cartmen demanding one hundred and fifty dollars (in hand, of course) for carrying a single load. Very likely it was so, but those cases did not come under my own notice. It did come under my notice that some cartmen worked for whatever the sufferers felt able to pay, and one I knew worked with alacrity for nothing. It takes all sorts of people to make a great fire.

Presently we heard loud detonations, and a rumor went around that buildings were being blown up with gunpowder. The depot of the Hazard Powder Company was situated at Brighton, seven or eight miles from the nearest point of the fire. At what time the effort was first made to reach this magazine, and bring powder into the service, I have not learned, but I know that Col. M. C. Stearns made heroic efforts with his great lime-wagons to haul the explosive material to the proper point.

This is no time to blame anybody, but in truth there was no directing head on the ground. Everybody was asking everybody else to pull down buildings. There were no hooks, no ropes, no axes. I had met General Sheridan[8] on the street in front of the post-office two hours before. He had been trying to save the army records, including his own invaluable papers relating to the war of the rebellion. He told me they were all lost, and then added that "the post-office didn't seem to make a good fire." This was when we supposed the row of fire-proof buildings, already spoken of, had stopt the flames in our quarter. Where was General Sheridan now? everybody asked. Why didn't he do something when everybody else had failed? Presently a rumor went around that Sheridan was handling the gunpowder; then everybody felt relieved. The reverberations of the powder, who ever was handling it, gave us all heart again. Think of a people feeling encouraged because somebody was blowing up houses in the midst of the city, and that a shower of bricks was very likely to come down on their heads!

I had paid and discharged my driver after extorting his solemn promise to come back and move me again if the wind should shift to the north—in which event everybody knew that the whole South Division, for a distance of four miles, must perish. We soon arrived at the house of the kind friend on Wabash Avenue, where our trunks and bundles had been deposited.

---

[8] General Sheridan was then living in Chicago, and commanded the Western military division.

This was south of the line of fire, but this did not satisfy anybody, since we had all seen how resolutely the flames had gone transversely across the direction of the wind.

The wind continued to blow fiercely from the southwest, and has not ceased to this hour (Saturday, October 14). But it was liable to change. If it chopped around to the north, the burning embers would be blown back upon the South Division. If it veered to the east, they would be blown into the West Division, tho the river afforded rather better protection there. Then we should have nothing to do but to keep ahead of the flames and get down as fast as possible to the open prairie, and there spend the night houseless and supperless—and what of the morrow? A full hundred thousand of us. And if we were spared, and the West Division were driven out upon their prairie (a hundred and fifty thousand according to the Federal census), how would the multitude be fed? If there could be anything more awful than what we had already gone through, it would be what we would certainly go through if the wind should change; for with the embers of this great fire flying about, and no water to fight them, we knew that there was not gunpowder enough in Illinois to stop the inevitable conflagration. But this was not all.

A well-authenticated rumor came up to the city that the prairie was on fire south of Hyde Park, the largest of the southern suburbs. The grass was as dry as tinder, and so were the leaves in Cottage Grove, a piece of timber several miles square, containing hundreds of residences of the better class, some of them of palatial dimensions. A fire on the prairie, communicating itself to the grove, might cut off the retreat of the one hundred thousand people in the South Division; might invade the South Division itself, and come up under the impulsion of that fierce wind, and where should we all be then? There were three or four bridges leading to the West Division, the only possible avenues of escape; but what were these among so many? And what if the "Commune" should go to work and start incendiary fires while all was yet in confusion? These fiends were improving the daylight by plundering along the street. Before dark the whole male population of the city was organized by spontaneous impulse into a night patrol, with pallid determination to put every incendiary to instant death.

About five o'clock P.M. I applied to a friend on Wabash Avenue for the use of a team to convey my family and chattels to the southern suburbs, about four miles distant, where my brother happened to own a small cottage, which, up to the present time, nobody could be induced to occupy and pay rent for. My friend replied that his work-teams were engaged hauling water for people to drink. Here was another thing that I had not thought of—a great city with no water to drink. Plenty in the lake, to be sure, but none in the city mains or the connecting pipes. Fortunately the extreme western limits were provided with a number of artesian wells, bored for manufacturing establishments. Then there was the river—the horrible, black, stinking river of a few weeks ago, which has since become clear enough for fish to live in, by reason of the deepening of the canal, which draws to the Mississippi a perpetual flow of pure water from Lake Michigan. With the city pumping-works stopt, the sewers could no longer discharge themselves into the river. So this might be used; and it was. Twenty-four hours had not passed before tens of thousands of people were drinking the water of Chicago River, with no unpleasant taste or effects.

The work-teams of my friend being engaged in hauling water for people who could not get any from the wells or the river or lake, he placed at my disposel his carriage, horses and coachman, whom he directed to take me and the ladies to any place we desired to reach. While we were talking he hailed another gentleman on the street, who owned a large stevedore wagon, and asked him to convey my trunks, etc., to Cottage Grove Avenue, near Forty-third Street, to which request an immediate and most gracious assent was given. And thus we started again, our hostess pressing a mattress upon us from her store. All the streets leading southward were yet filled with fugitives. Where they all found shelter that night I know not, but every house seemed to be opened to anybody who desired to enter. Arrived at our new home, about dusk, we found in it, as we expected, a cold reception, there being neither stove, nor grate, nor fireplace, nor fuel, nor light therein. But I will not dwell upon these things. We really did not mind them, for when we thought of the thousands of men, women, and tender babes huddled together in Lincoln Park, seven miles to the north of us, with no prospect of food, exposed to rain, if it should come, with no canopy but the driving smoke of their homes, we thought how little we had suffered.

MANILA BAY
(1898)
by Admiral Dewey

From Dewey's official report. The Battle of Manila Bay occurred on May 1, 1898. Since the blowing up of the Maine in Havana Harbor on February 15, matters leading to war with Spain had moved rapidly. An ultimatum was finally sent to Spain on April 20, in which April 23 was made the last date on which a satisfactory reply would be received. This was virtually a declaration of war, although the formal declarations were not made until April 24 and April 25.

Admiral Dewey, then a commodore in Chinese waters, commanding the Asiatic squadron, was at once ordered "to proceed to the Philippine Islands; commence operations at once against the Spanish fleet; capture vessels or destroy."

The *Boston* and *Concord* were sent to reconnoiter Port Subio, I having been informed that the enemy intended to take position there. A thorough search of the port was made by the *Boston* and *Concord*, but the Spanish fleet was not found, altho from a letter afterward found in the arsenal, it appears that it had been their intention to go there.

Entered the Boca Grande, or south channel, at 11:30 P.M., steaming in column at distance at 8 knots. After half the squadron had passed, a battery on the south side of the channel opened fire, none of the shots taking effect. The *Boston* and *McCulloch* returned the fire. The squadron proceeded across the bay at slow speed, and arrived off Manila at daybreak, and was fired upon at 5:15 A.M. by three batteries at Manila, and two at Cavite, and by the Spanish fleet anchored in an approximately east and west line across the mouth of Bakor Bay, with their left in shoal water in Canacao Bay.

The squadron then proceeded to the attack, the flagship *Olympia*, under my personal direction, leading, followed at distance by the *Baltimore, Raleigh, Petrel, Concord,* and *Boston,* in the order named, which formation was maintained throughout the action. The squadron opened fire at 5:41 A.M. While advancing to the attack, two mines were exploded ahead of the flagship, too far to be effective. The squadron maintained a continuance and precise fire at ranges varying from 5,000 to 2,000 yards, countermarching in a line approximately parallel to that of the Spanish fleet. The enemy's fire was vigorous, but generally ineffective.

Early in the engagement two launches put out toward the *Olympia* with the apparent intention of using torpedoes. One was sunk and the other disabled by our fire and beached before an opportunity occurred to fire torpedoes. At 7 A.M. the Spanish flagship *Reina Christina* made a desperate attempt to leave the line and come out to engage at short range, but was received with such galling fire, the entire battery of the *Olympia* being concentrated upon her, that she was barely able to return to the shelter of the point. The fires started in her by our shell at this time were not extinguished until she sank.

At 7:35 A.M., it having been erroneously reported to me that only 15 rounds per gun remained for the 5-inch rapid-fire battery, I ceased firing and withdrew the squadron for consultation and a redistribution of ammunition, if necessary. The three batteries at Manila had kept up a continuous fire from the beginning of the engagement, which fire was not returned by this squadron. The first of these batteries was situated on the south mole head at the entrance to the Pasig River, the second on the south bastion of the walled city of Manila, and the third at Malate, about one-half mile farther south. At this point I sent a message to the Governor-General to the effect that if the batteries did not cease firing the city would be shelled. This had the effect of silencing them.

At 11:16 A.M., finding that the report of scarcity of ammunition was incorrect, I returned with the squadron to the attack. By this time the flagship and almost the entire Spanish fleet were in flames, and at 12:30 P.M., the squadron ceased firing, the batteries being silenced and the ships sunk, burned, and deserted.

I am happy to report that the damage done to the squadron under my command was inconsiderable. There were none killed, and only 7 men in the squadron very slightly wounded. Several of the vessels were struck and even penetrated, but the damage was of the slightest, and the squadron is in as good condition now as before the battle.

A GLOBAL POWER

A GLOBAL POWER

As the twentieth century opened, the United States was emerging as one of the most powerful and populous nations in the world. The tidal wave of newcomers had increased to such proportions that by the turn of the century almost fifteen million European immigrants had arrived. While thousands of Chinese and other Orientals were brought in to assist the building of railroads in the West, thousands more from Germany and the Scandinavian countries landed and moved on to the western states of Indiana, Illinois, Wisconsin, Minnesota, and the Dakotas. Lithuanians, Slovaks, Bohemians, Poles, Hungarians, and Russians by the hundreds worked the steel mills of Chicago and Gary, Indiana. New York City became the home of thousands of Jews who had fled from imperial Russia, while the coal fields of Pennsylvania provided refuge for a hundred thousand Slovaks. Yet the new century saw not only the penniless, homeless, and persecuted come to a new nation, but likewise the brilliant and educated. Steinmetz, Einstein, and Carnegie were such immigrants.

The twentieth century brought with it new sights, new sounds, and new names. Lee De Forest invented the radio vacuum tube (1907); Vladimir Zworykin, television (1934). Mechanically-minded Americans such as Henry Ford, the Wright Brothers, and Samuel Langley pioneered research in solar radiation and flying machines. Europe's economic might was already taking second seat to that of the United States. The free enterprise system had made this country, and with it came new hopes and dreams. Marshall Field of Chicago and John Wanamaker of Philadelphia made their fortunes as merchants; John D. Rockefeller made it big in oil. The Vanderbilts, Morgans, Goulds, Hills, and the Harrimans controlled the railroads and great banking houses, while Philip Armour and the Swifts were making Chicago the "hog butcher of the world." The McCormicks and Deerings made millions in the manufacture of farm machinery.

Yet while hundreds thrived and lolled in riches, thousands of poor worked for pennies. Reform movements soon sprang up, and the opening decade of the twentieth century became known as the progressive era. It was during this period that unions organized by socialists and radical leaders like Eugene V. Debs achieved some small success. Theirs was a short-lived victory, however, as employers formed associations, blacklisted workers, and were generally successful in breaking strikes.

Theodore Roosevelt's dedication to public service and the American way of life brought progress and change with his "square deal." He was a man of action; and having succeeded McKinley after the assassination and then being reelected on his own in 1904, he proceeded to make the Federal Government a titanic referee. If free enterprise was to succeed, monopolies and trusts had to be controlled by a government idealistic enough to punish even the rich when they broke the law.

President Woodrow Wilson was another notable idealist. Wilson entered office in 1913 concerned with domestic interests and ended his days in the White House pressed by foreign relations. In June of 1914, a Serbian student, Gavrilo Princep, assassinated Archduke Franz Ferdinand of Austria-Hungary, touching off a chain of events resulting in World War I. America remained neutral. However, in 1915 the Germans announced that all ships found in British waters would be subject to "unrestricted submarine warfare"; soon after American citizens were killed on English ships. On May 7 of the same year the English luxury liner *Lusitania* was torpedoed off the coast of Ireland; 1,198 passengers and crewmen perished; 128 of them were American citizens. Americans did not know that England was guilty of carrying armaments in the holds of supposedly neutral ships. Public opinion in the United States slowly but surely moved against the Germans. Although reelected in 1916 as the President who "kept us out of war," Wilson signed the Declaration of War on April 6, 1917.

General John J. "Blackjack" Pershing was appointed commander of the American Expeditionary Force, which launched its first attack at Cantigny on May 28, 1917, and proved to the world that the Yanks could fight. Thousands of American troops started arriving to buttress the exhausted allies. A year and a half later, on the eleventh day of November at eleven o'clock, 1918, an armistice was agreed upon. Almost three-hundred fifty thousand Americans had been killed or wounded.

World War I gave Americans new heroes, such as air aces General Billy Mitchell, Eddy Rickenbacker, and Raoul Lufberry. A red-haired mountain man from Tennessee, Alvin York, single-handedly killed twenty-five Germans and captured more than one hundred more; he was subsequently awarded the Congressional Medal of Honor.

The Treaty of Versailles, which brought an end to the war, required ratification by the United States Senate as outlined in the Constitution. Many senators, however, had genuine convictions against certain sections of the treaty. Moreover, the treaty was not popular among American minorities such as the German Americans. In September of 1919 President Wilson suffered a paralitic stroke. This unfortunate turn of events allowed Senator Henry Cabot Lodge, leader of the Republican wing of the Senate, to defeat the treaty in a close vote. It was only after Wilson's death that the next President's secretary of state secured senate ratification of a separate American peace treaty with Germany.

The decade of the twenties was heralded as a "return to normalcy." The Republicans had promised it; and their candidate, Warren G. Harding, was swept into office accordingly. A pleasant incompetent from Ohio, he died soon after taking office, amidst a flurry of scandals. Affairs such as The Teapot Dome scandal, brought on by Federal bureaucrats, permitting oil companies to drill on government land without competition, angered the electorate. In 1924 American voters sent a man of unimpeachable integrity to the Presidency. Calvin Coolidge's Puritan background revived people's confidence in the White House and the Federal Government. Coolidge took the oath of office at the beginning of a spectacular growth spurt in American industry. Known as a pro-business President, he once made the remark that "the chief business of the American people is business."

The era after World War I is described by many names. Not only the era of normalcy, but also the red scare; the revolution of morals; the scandalous years; the ballyhoo years; "the time of the highbrows"; the prohibition era; and "the time of the big bull market." This last ended with the spectacular crash of the stock market in 1929, which kicked off a violent economic reaction. So vast and far-reaching was the economic crisis that it is known as the Great Depression. Unemployment rose in 1929 to a million and a half, and by 1932 as high as sixteen million.

Herbert Hoover had been elected President in 1928, but because of the Great Depression, he was defeated in the elections of 1932 by Franklin D. Roosevelt. A Harvard graduate from an old New York family, Roosevelt had served as state senator and New York governor. In March of 1933, after taking the oath of office, Roosevelt turned to meet the terrible depression by asserting that "the only thing we have to fear is fear itself. . . ." After proclaiming a bank holiday across the country, he asked Congress for unusual powers. During Roosevelt's first months in office, called The Hundred Days, dozens of new bills passed Congress, all designed to bolster the nation's sagging economy. Roosevelt's method of solving problems was to hire brillant men from academic circles and industry who became known as "the brain trust." In 1936, after swamping Governor Alf Landon of Kansas, the GOP flag bearer, Roosevelt moved blithely on his way. He was at the zenith of his popularity. Yet his ill-advised attempt to "pack" the Supreme Court, the severe recession of 1937–38, and a new wave of economic woes and strikes brought fresh apprehensions to the White House and the country. In 1939 Roosevelt defeated Wendell Willkie by over five million votes for an unprecedented third term.

Meanwhile, our relations with Japan had deteriorated. Mutual distrust over economics finally caused the Japanese to strike first on December 7, 1941, with a stunning sneak attack at the headquarters of our Pacific fleet—Pearl Harbor in the Hawaiian Islands. In a matter of minutes the Japanese took apart the military might of the United States in the Pacific, destroying almost two hundred planes, sinking or damaging eighteen ships, and killing more than twenty-four hundred Americans. The next day President Roosevelt asked for, and got, a Declaration of War against Japan from Congress.

The war brought about an economic boom. Weekly earnings rose phenomenally, and war plant overtime gave many who had done without for so long during the Great Depression a chance at prosperity. The Federal bureaucrats imposed all kinds of restrictions including the rationing of meat, rubber, gasoline, nylon stockings, and tobacco products. In addition, price controls were maintained while federal spendings soared to astronomical heights, eventually doubling the total of all federal expenditures in all the previous history of the country.

The strategy of the war consisted of a holding action until men could be trained and supplies brought to use, followed by a gradual shift to the attack. In the Pacific, General Douglas MacArthur used an "island-hopping" strategy, leap-frogging Japanese strongholds to capture islands with airfields from which to attack the Japanese homeland. Meanwhile, another war was raging on the other side of the globe. Although we had helped drive the Nazis and Fascist Italians from Africa, it was not until the mighty invasion of Hitler's Fortress Europe that a real breakthrough came. The famous Normandy invasion of June 6, 1944, better known as D-Day, sparked a race across France toward Germany, while General Mark Clark and his forces combined to slog their way up the Italian Peninsula, the "soft underbelly" of Europe.

Slowly the military might of America grew. American bombers became a common sight as they took off from fields in England to fly devastating raids on German factories and communications. American air power had a major role in the defeat of Germany, a feat accomplished on V. E. Day, May 7, 1945. MacArthur and his naval counterparts, Admiral William F. "Bull" Halsey and Admiral Chester Nimitz continued island hopping across the Pacific islands. An attack on the Japanese homeland seemed inevitable. With it would come the loss of thousands of American lives; therefore, in a final desperate gesture to end the war and to prevent more American deaths, President Truman ordered an atomic bomb dropped on the Japanese city of Hiroshima. In spite of eighty thousand deaths and countless injuries, the Japanese refused to give up. Three days later a second A-bomb was detonated over the city of Nagasaki, and forty thousand more Japanese died. Japan's military rulers finally accepted terms.

Franklin Roosevelt did not live to see the final surrender on the deck of the world's largest battleship, the U.S.S. *Missouri* on September 2, 1945. He had died of a cerebral hemorrhage in Warm Springs, Georgia, on April 12, 1945. Vice-President Harry Truman succeeded him.

The war ended in 1945 for many, but the Russians violated one agreement after another, taking over eastern European countries by force or trickery. A new era known as Cold War brought increasing friction between the USSR and the West. As President Truman and American leaders became increasingly weary of Soviet lies and duplicity, a new policy of containing Communist imperialism was slowly evolving. In March of 1947 the famous Truman Doctrine extended economic and military aid to foreign countries to assist in fighting aggression. Later the Marshall Plan sent massive economic aid to Europe.

The years after the war brought myriads of new scientific concepts and ideas. Polio was conquered by the discovery of a new vaccine pioneered by Dr. Jonas Salk, while breakthroughs in technology brought harder plastics, the use of laser lights, communications electronic satellites, and scores of new antibiotics.

America gradually settled down into peace. But on June 25, 1950, Communist forces from North Korea attacked South Korea, and within days American (and later United Nations) forces entered combat. Because of surprise and overwhelming military superiority, the South Korean and American forces were soon pushed into a small perimeter in the southeastern corner of the country. It was only after a bold amphibious landing by General MacArthur's troops at Inchon that American troops were able to take the offensive. Soon U. N. troops were chasing the Communists north across their own territory, and victory seemed imminent. Suddenly thousands of "volunteers" from Communist China swept down across the Yalu River and forced MacArthur's troops back to a stabilized position where an armistice was finally agreed upon. Today the United States continues to aid South Korea with supplies and the presence of American troops.

For twenty years the Democrats had controlled the White House. In 1952 and again in 1956 the World War II general, Dwight David Eisenhower, ran as a Republican and was elected President. During his tenure he ordered troops into Little Rock, Arkansas to enforce school desegregation; he continued a strong defense program; he saw the world's first atomic submarine the *Nautilus* launched. His cabinet was big-business oriented and somewhat conservative.

As the election of 1960 drew near, the Republican party nominated Eisenhower's vice-president, Richard Nixon, for President, while the Democrats selected John F. Kennedy of Massachusetts as their nominee, with Senator Lyndon B. Johnson of Texas as his running mate. Kennedy won by less than one percent of the total popular vote. His assassination in November of 1963 permitted him to live long enough to see an American-backed invasion of Castro's Cuba fail and the beginning of American military involvement in South Vietnam. The space program started by Kennedy allowed the United States to put the first man on the moon in 1969.

Lyndon Johnson finished Kennedy's term and was reelected over Senator Barry Goldwater of Arizona in 1964 for his own term. His administration was notable for its civil rights legislation. Johnson inherited the Vietnam problem, he augmented it further, and it finally drove him from office in 1968. The Republicans were returned to the White House with Richard Nixon, who helped to end the war. Nixon was reelected in 1972 only to be forced to withdraw from the Presidency because of his part in the Watergate scandal. Vice-President Gerald Ford ascended to the Presidency in 1974.

DECLARATION OF WAR
(1917)
by President Woodrow Wilson

*When the conflict opened during the summer of 1914, the United States at-
tempted to stay out of it. American neutrality, however, was soon violated by the
sinking of the* Lusitania *(1915), the announcement and implementation of unrestricted submarine warfare (1916), and interference in Western Hemispheric problems (e.g., the Zimmerman plot). On April 6, 1917, President Wilson went before
Congress and asked for a declaration of war in the following message.*

Gentlemen of the Congress:

I have called the Congress into extraordinary session because there are
serious, very serious, choices of policy to be made, and made immediately,
which it was neither right nor constitutionally permissible that I should
assume the responsibility of making.

On the third of February last I officially laid before you the extraordinary announcement of the Imperial German Government that on and after
the first day of February it was its purpose to put aside all restraints of law
or of humanity and use its submarines to sink every vessel that sought to
approach either the ports of Great Britian and Ireland or the western
coasts of Europe or any of the ports controlled by the enemies of Germany
within the Mediterranean. That had seemed to be the object of the German
submarine warfare earlier in the war, but since April of last year the Imperial Government had somewhat restrained the commanders of its under-
sea craft, in conformity with its promise, then given to us, that passenger
boats should not be sunk and that due warning would be given to all other
vessels which its submarines might seek to destroy, when no resistance was
offered or escape attempted, and care taken that their crews were given at
least a fair chance to save their lives in their open boats. The precautions
taken were meagre and haphazard enough, as was proved in distressing
instance after instance in the progress of the cruel and unmanly business,
but a certain degree of restraint was observed.

The new policy has swept every restriction aside. Vessels of every kind, whatever their flag, their character, their cargo, their destination, their errand, have been ruthlessly sent to the bottom without warning and without thought of help or mercy for those on board, the vessels of friendly neutrals along with those of belligerents. Even hospital ships and ships carrying relief to the sorely bereaved and stricken people of Belgium, though the latter were provided with safe conduct through the proscribed areas by the German Government itself and were distinguished by unmistakable marks of identity, have been sunk with the same reckless lack of compassion or of principle.

I was for a little while unable to believe that such things would in fact be done by any Government that had hitherto subscribed to humane practices of civilized nations. International law had its origin in the attempt to set up some law which would be respected and observed upon the seas, where no nation has right of dominion and where lay the free highways of the world. By painful stage after stage has that law been built up, with meagre enough results, indeed, after all was accomplished that could be accomplished, but always with a clear view, at least, of what the heart and conscience of mankind demanded.

This minimum of right the German Government has swept aside, under the plea of retaliation and necessity and because it had no weapons which it could use at sea except these, which it is impossible to employ, as it is employing them, without throwing to the wind all scruples of humanity or of respect for the understanding that were supposed to underlie the intercourse of the world.

I am not now thinking of the loss of property involved, immense and serious as that is, but only of the wanton and wholesale destruction of the lives of noncombatants, men, women, and children, engaged in pursuits which have always, even in the darkest periods of modern history, been deemed innocent and legitimate. Property can be paid for; the lives of peaceful and innocent people cannot be. The present German submarine warfare against commerce is a warfare against mankind.

The German Government denies the right of neutrals to use arms at all within the areas of the sea which it has proscribed, even in the defense of rights which no modern publicist has ever before questioned their right to defend. The intimation is conveyed that the armed guards which we have placed on our merchant ships will be treated as beyond the pale of law and subject to be dealt with as pirates would be. Armed neutrality is ineffectual enough at best; in such circumstances and in the face of such pretensions it is worse than ineffectual; it is likely only to produce what it was meant to prevent; it is practically certain to draw us into the war without either the rights or the effectiveness of belligerents. There is one choice we cannot make, we are incapable of making; we will not choose the path of submission and suffer the most sacred rights of our nation and our people to be ignored or violated. The wrongs against which we now array ourselves are no common wrongs; they cut to the very roots of human life.

With a profound sense of the solemn and even tragical character of the step I am taking and of the grave responsibilities which it involves, but in unhesitating obedience to what I deem my constitutional duty, I advise that the Congress declare the recent course of the Imperial German Government to be in fact nothing less than war against the Government and people of the United States; that it formally accept the status of belligerent which has thus been thrust upon it; and that it take immediate steps not only to put the country in a more thorough state of defense, but also to exert all its power and employ all its resources to bring the Government of the German Empire to terms and end the war.

What this will involve is clear. It will involve the utmost practicable cooperation in counsel and action with the Governments now at war with Germany, and, as incident to that, the extension to those Governments of the most liberal financial credits, in order that our resources may so far as possible be added to theirs.

It will involve the organization and mobilization of all the material resources of the country to supply the materials of war and serve the incidental needs of the nation in the most abundant and yet the most economical and efficient way possible.

It will involve the immediate full equipment of the navy in all respects, but particularly in supplying it with the best means of dealing with the enemy's submarines.

It will involve the immediate addition to the armed forces of the United States, already provided for by law in case of war, of at least 500,000 men, who should, in my opinion, be chosen upon the principle of universal liability to service, and also the authorization of subsequent additional increments of equal force so soon as they may be needed and can be handled in training.

It will involve also, of course, the granting of adequate credits to the Government, sustained, I hope, so far as they can equitably be sustained by the present generation, by well conceived taxation.

We have no quarrel with the German people. We have no feeling toward them but one of sympathy and friendship. It was not upon their impulse that their Government acted in entering this war. It was not with their previous knowledge or approval. It was a war determined upon as wars used to be determined upon in the old, unhappy days, when peoples were nowhere consulted by their rulers and wars were provoked and waged in the interest of dynasties or of little groups of ambitious men who were accustomed to use their fellow men as pawns and tools.

Self-governed nations do not fill their neighbor States with spies or set the course of intrigue to bring about some critical posture of affairs which will give them an opportunity to strike and make conquest. Such designs can be successfully worked out only under cover and where no one has the right to ask questions. Cunningly contrived plans of deception or aggression, carried, it may be, from generation to generation, can be worked out and kept from the light only within the privacy of courts or behind the carefully guarded confidences of a narrow and privileged class. They are happily impossible where public opinion commands and insists upon full information concerning all the nation's affairs.

A steadfast concert for peace can never by maintained except by a partnership of democratic nations. No autocratic Government could be trusted to keep faith within it or observe its covenants. It must be a league of honor, a partnership of opinion. Intrigue would eat its vitals away; the plottings of inner circles who could plan what they would and render account to no one would be a corruption seated at its very heart. Only free peoples can hold their purpose and their honor steady to a common end and prefer the interests of mankind to any narrow interest of their own.

One of the things that has served to convince us that the Prussian autocracy was not and could never be our friend is that from the very outset of the present war it has filled our unsuspecting communities, and even our offices of government with spies and set criminal intrigues every where afoot against our national unity of counsel, our peace within and without, our industries and our commerce. Indeed, it is now evident that its spies were here even before the war began; and it is unhappily not a matter of conjecture, but a fact proved in our courts of justice, that the intrigues which have more than once come perilously near to disturbing the peace and dislocating the industries of the country, have been carried on at the instigation, with the support, and even under the personal direction of official agents of the Imperial Government, accredited to the Government of the United States.

Even in checking these things and trying to extripate them we have sought to put the most generous interpretation possible upon them because we knew that their source lay, not in any hostile feeling or purpose of the German people toward us (who were, no doubt, as ignorant of them as we ourselves were), but only in the selfish designs of a Government that did what it pleased and told its people nothing. But they have played their part in serving to convince us at last that that Government entertains no real friendship for us, and means to act against our peace and security at its convenience. That it means to stir up enemies against us at our very doors the intercepted note to the German Minister at Mexico City is eloquent evidence.

We are accepting this challenge of hostile purpose because we know that in such a Government, following such methods, we can never have a friend; and that in the presence of its organized power, always lying in wait to accomplish we know not what purpose, can be no assured security for the democratic Governments of the world. We are now about to accept the gauge of battle with this natural foe to liberty and shall, if necessary spend the whole force of the nation to check and nullify its pretensions and its power. We are glad, now that we see the facts with no veil of false pretense about them, to fight thus for the ultimate peace of the world and for the liberation of its peoples, the German peoples included; for the rights of nations, great and small, and the privilege of men everywhere to choose their way of life and of obedience.

The world must be made safe for democracy. Its peace must be planted upon the tested foundations of political liberty. We have no selfish ends to serve. We desire no conquest, no dominion. We seek no indemnities for ourselves, no material compensation for the sacrifices we shall freely make. We are but one of the champions of the rights of mankind. We shall be satisfied when those rights have been made as secure as the faith and the freedom of nations can make them.

The right is more precious than peace, and we shall fight for the things which we have always carried nearest our hearts—for democracy, for the right of those who submit to authority to have a voice in their own Governments, for the rights and liberties of small nations, for a universal dominion of right by such a concert of free peoples as shall bring peace and safety to all nations and make the world itself at last free.

To such a task we dedicate our lives and our fortunes, everything that we are and everything that we have, with the pride of those who know that the day has come when America is privileged to spend her blood and her might for the principles that gave her birth and happiness and the peace which she has treasured.

God helping her, she can do no other.

CHATEAU-THIERRY
(1918)
by Major Robert L. Denig

Since its founding as the Continental Marines in 1775, the United States Marine Corps has always been in the vanguard defending its country. Among the many laurels that this proud organization bears was the operation at Chateau-Thierry, a tiny town in northern France on the Marne River. It was here that the last great German offensive in 1918 was stopped. In this, the high point of the second battle of the Marne, counterattacking United States Marine units spearheaded the drive that broke the German offensive at tremendous cost. This description of the battle was written by Major Robert L. Denig of Philadelphia in a letter to his wife.

The day before we left for this big push we had a most interesting fight between a fleet of German planes and a French observation balloon, right over our heads. We saw five planes circle over our town, then put on, what we thought afterwards, a sham fight. One of them, after many fancy stunts, headed right for the balloon. They were all painted with our colors except one. This one went near the balloon. One kept right on. The other four shot the balloon up with incendiary bullets. The observers jumped into their parachutes just as the outfit went up in a mass of flame.

The next day we took our positions at various places to wait for camions that were to take us somewhere in France, when or for what purpose we did not know. Wass passed me at the head of his company—we made a date for a party on our next leave. He was looking fine and was as happy as could be. Then Hunt, Keyser and a heap of others went by. I have the battalion and Holcomb the regiment. Our turn to en-buss did not come until near midnight.

We at last got under way after a few big "sea bags" had hit nearby. Wilmer and I led in a touring car. We went at a good clip and nearly got ditched in a couple of new shell holes. Shells were falling fast by now, and as the tenth truck went under the bridge a big one landed near with a crash, and wounded the two drivers, killed two marines and wounded five more. We did not know it at the time, and did not notice anything wrong till we came to a crossroad when we found we had only eleven cars all told. We found the rest of the convoy after a hunt, but even then were not told of the loss, and did not find it out until the next day.

We were finally, after twelve hours' ride, dumped in a big field and after a few hours' rest started our march. It was terribly hot—and we had had nothing to eat since the day before. We at last entered a forest; troops seemed to converge on it from all points. We marched some six miles in the forest, a finer one I have never seen—deer would scamper ahead and we could have eaten one raw. At 10 that night without food, we lay down in a pouring rain to sleep. Troops of all kinds passed us in the night—a shadowy stream, over a half-million men. Some French officers told us that they had never seen such concentration since Verdun, if then.

The next day, the 18th of July, we marched ahead through a jam of troops, trucks, etc., and came at last to a ration dump where we fell to and ate our heads off for the first time in nearly two days. When we left there, the men had bread stuck on their bayonets. I lugged a ham. All were loaded down.

Here I passed one of Wass' lieutenants with his hand wounded. He was pleased as Punch and told us the drive was on, the first we knew of it. I then passed a few men of Hunt's company, bringing prisoners to the rear.

They had a colonel and his staff. They were well dressed, cleaned and polished, but mighty glum looking.

We finally stopped at the far end of the forest near a dressing station, where Holcomb again took command. This station had been a big fine stone farm but was now a complete ruin—wounded and dead lay all about. Joe Murray came by with his head all done up—his helmet had saved him. The lines had gone on ahead so we were quite safe. Had a fine aero battle right over us. The stunts that those planes did cannot be described by me.

Late in the afternoon we advanced again. Our route lay over an open field covered with dead.

We lay down on a hillside for the night near some captured German guns, and until dark I watched the cavalry—some four thousand, come up and take positions.

At 3.30 the next morning Sitz woke me up and said we were to attack. The regiment was soon under way and we picked our way under cover of a gas infested valley to a town where we got our final instructions and left our packs. I wished Sumner good luck and parted.

We formed up in a sunken road on two sides of a valley that was perpendicular to the enemy's front; Hughes right, Holcomb left, Sibley support. We now began to get a few wounded; one man with ashen face came charging to the rear with shell shock. He shook all over, foamed at the mouth, could not speak. I put him under a tent, and he acted as if he had a fit.

I heard Overton call to one of his friends to send a certain pin to his mother if he should get hit.

At 8.30 we jumped off with a line of tanks in the lead. For two "kilos" the four lines of Marines were as straight as a die, and their advance over the open plain in the bright sunlight was a picture I shall never forget. The fire got hotter and hotter, men fell, bullets sung, shells whizzed-banged and the dust of battle got thick. Overton was hit by a big piece of shell and fell. Afterwards I heard he was hit in the heart, so his death was without pain. He was buried that night and the pin found.

A man near me was cut in two. Others when hit would stand, it seemed, an hour, then fall in a heap. I yelled to Wilmer that each gun in the barrage worked from right to left, then a rabbit ran ahead and I watched him wondering if he would get hit. Good rabbit—it took my mind off the carnage. Looked for Hughes way over to the right; told Wilmer that I had a hundred dollars and be sure to get it. You think all kinds of things.

About sixty Germans jumped out of a trench and tried to surrender, but their machine guns opened up, we fired back, they ran and our left company after them. That made a gap that had to be filled, so Sibley advanced one of his to do the job, then a shell lit in a machine-gun crew of ours and cleaned it out completely.

At 10.30 we dug in—the attack just died out. I found a hole or old trench and when I was flat on my back I got some protection. Holcomb was next me; Wilmer some way off. We then tried to get reports. Two companies we never could get in touch with. Lloyd came in and reported he was holding some trenches near a mill with six men. Cates, with his trousers blown off, said he had sixteen men of various companies; another officer on the right reported he had and could see forty men, all told. That, with the headquarters, was all we could find out about the battalion of nearly 800. Of the twenty company officers who went in, three came out, and one, Cates, was slightly wounded.

From then on to about 8 P.M. life was a chance and mighty uncomfortable. It was hot as a furnace, no water, and they had our range to a "T." Three men lying in a shallow trench near me were blown to bits.

I went to the left of the line and found eight wounded men in a shell hole. I went back to Cates' hole and three shells landed near them. We thought they were killed, but they were not hit. You could hear men calling for help in the wheat fields. Their cries would get weaker and weaker and die out. The German planes were thick in the air; they were in groups of from three to twenty. They would look us over and then we would get a pounding. One of our planes got shot down; he fell about a thousand feet, like an arrow, and hit in the field back of us. The tank exploded and nothing was left.

We had a machine gun officer with us and at six a runner came up and reported that Sumner was killed. He commanded the machine-gun company with us. He was hit early in the fight by a bullet, I hear; I can get no details. At the start he remarked: "This looks easy—they do not seem to have much art." Hughes' headquarters were all shot up. Turner lost a leg.

Well, we just lay there all through the hot afternoon.

It was great—a shell would land near by and you would bounce in your hole.

As twilight came, we sent out water parties for the relief of the wounded. Then we wondered if we would get relieved. At 9 o'clock we got a message congratulating us and saying the Algerians would take over at midnight. We then began to collect our wounded. Some had been evacuated during the day, but at that, we soon had about twenty on the field near us. A man who had been blinded wanted me to hold his hand. Another, wounded in the back, wanted his head patted, and so it went; one man got up on his hands and knees. I asked him what he wanted. He said, "Look at the full moon," then fell dead. I had him buried, and all the rest I could find. All the time bullets sung and we prayed that shelling would not start until we had our wounded on top.

The Algerians came up at midnight and we pushed out. They went over at daybreak and got all shot up. We made the relief under German flares and the light from a burning town.

We went out as we came, through the gulley and town, the latter by now all in ruins. The place was full of gas, so we had to wear our masks. We pushed on to the forest and fell down in our tracks and slept all day. That afternoon a German plane got a balloon and the observer jumped and landed in a high tree. It was some job getting him down. The wind came up and we had to dodge falling trees and branches. As it was, we lost—two killed and one wounded from that cause.

That night the Germans shelled us and got three killed and seventeen wounded. We moved a bit further back to the crossroad and after burying a few Germans, some of whom showed signs of having been wounded before, we settled down to a short stay.

It looked like rain, and so Wilmer and I went to an old dressing station to salvage some cover. We collected a lot of bloody shelter halves and ponchos that had been tied to poles to make stretchers, and were about to go, when we stopped to look at a new grave. A rude cross made of two slats from a box had written on it:

"Lester S. Wass, Captain U.S. Marines, July 18, 1918"

The old crowd at St. Nazaire and Bordeaux, Wass and Sumner killed, Baston and Hunt wounded, the latter on the 18th, a clean wound, I hear, through the left shoulder. We then moved further to the rear and camped for the night. Dunlap came to look us over. His car was driven by a sailor who got out to talk to a few of the marines, when one of the latter yelled out, "Hey, fellows! Anyone want to see a real live gob, right this way." The gob held a regular reception. A carrier pigeon perched on a tree with a message. We decided to shoot him. It was then quite dark, so the shot missed. I then heard the following as I tried to sleep: "Send up a flare;" "Call for a barrage," etc. The next day further to the rear still, a Ford was towed by with its front wheels on a truck.

We are now back in a town for some rest and to lick our wounds.

As I rode down the battalion, where once companies 250 strong used to march, now you see fifty men, with a kid second lieutenant in command; one company commander is not yet twenty-one.

After the last attack I cashed in the gold you gave me and sent it home along with my back pay. I have no idea of being "bumped off" with money on my person, as if you fall into the enemy's hands you are first robbed, then buried perhaps, but the first is sure.

Baston, the lieutenant that went to Quantico with father and myself, and of whom father took some pictures, was wounded in both legs in the Bois de Belleau. He nearly lost his legs, I am told, but is coming out O.K. Hunt was wounded in the last attack, got his wounds fixed up and went back again till he had to be sent out. Coffenburg was hit in the hand,—all near him were killed. Talbot was hit twice, but is about again. That accounts for all the officers in the company that I brought over. In the first fight 103 of the men in that outfit were killed or wounded. The second fight must have about cleaned out the old crowd.

The tanks, as they crushed their way through the wet, gray forest looked to me like beasts of the pre-stone age.

In the afternoon as I lay on my back in a hole that I dug deeper, the dark gray German planes with their sinister black crosses, looked like Death hovering above. They were for many. Sumner, for one. He was always saying, "Denig, let's go ashore!" Then here was Wass, whom I usually took dinner with—dead, too. Sumner, Wass, Baston and Hunt— the old crowd that stuck together; two dead, one may never be any good any more; Hunt, I hope, will be as good as ever.

UNKNOWN SOLDIER EULOGY
(1921)
by President Warren G. Harding

The bloodshed of World War I ended on November 11, 1918, at 11:00 A.M. In memory of those who had sacrificed their lives, a grateful America set aside November 11 each year as Armistice Day, now celebrated as Veterans Day. For years after that on Armistice Day it was customary for the nation to pause for a moment of silence at 11:00 A.M. on November 11 to honor and reflect upon the sacrifice of our fallen heroes. On November 11, 1921, a solemn burial ceremony of America's unknown soldier took place at Arlington National Cemetery, led by President Harding. The man buried there was just one of many nameless casualties from the great war; he represented, however, all those who had given their "last full measure of devotion." Also now at Arlington are shrines to the unknown dead of World War II and the Korean War.

Mr. Secretary of War, Ladies and Gentlemen—We are met today to pay the impersonal tribute. The name of him whose body lies before us took flight with his imperishable soul. We know not whence he came, but only that his death marks him with the everlasting glory of an American dying for his country.

We do not know his station in life, because from every station came the patriotic response of the five million. The service flag marked mansion and cottage alike, and riches were common to all homes in the consciousness of service to country.

We do not know the eminence of his birth, but we do know the glory of his death. He died for his country, and greater devotion hath no man than this. He died unquestioning, uncomplaining, with faith in his heart and hope on his lips, that his country should triumph and its civilization survive. As a typical soldier of the representative democracy, he fought and died, believing in the indisputable justice of his country's cause. Conscious of the world's upheaval, appraising the magnitude of a war the like of which had never horrified humanity before, perhaps he believed his to be a service destined to change the tide of human affairs.

With the din of battle, the glow of conflict, and the supreme trial of courage come involuntarily the hurried appraisal of life and the contemplation of death's great mystery. On the threshold of eternity many a soldier, I can well believe, wondered how his ebbing blood would color the stream of human life flowing on after his sacrifice. His patriotism was none less if he craved more than triumph of country: rather it was greater if he hoped for a victory of all humankind.

Indeed, I revere that citizen whose confidence in the righteousness of his country inspired belief that its triumph is the victory of humanity.

This American soldier went forth to battle with no hatred for any people in the world, but hating war and hating the purpose of every war for conquest. He cherished our national rights and abhorred the threat of armed domination; and in the maelstrom of destruction and suffering and death he fired his shot for liberation of the captive conscience of the world.

On such an occasion as this, amid such a scene, our thoughts alternate between defenders living and defenders dead. A grateful republic will be worthy of them both. Our part is to atone for the losses of heroic dead by making a better republic for the living.

Ours are lofty resolutions today, as with tribute to the dead we consecrate ourselves to a better order for the living. With all my heart I wish we might say to the defenders who survive, to mothers who sorrow, to widows and children who mourn, that no such sacrifice shall be asked again.

It was my fortune recently to see a demonstration of modern warfare. It is no longer a conflict in chivalry, no more a test of militant manhood. It is only cruel, deliberate, scientific destruction. There was no contending enemy, only the theoretic defense of a hypothetic objective. But the attack was made with all the relentless methods of modern destruction.

There was the rain of ruins from the aircraft, the thunder of artillery followed by the unspeakable devastation wrought by bursting shells. There were mortars belching their bombs of desolation, machine guns concentrating their leaden storms. There was the infantry advancing, firing, and falling—like men with souls sacrificing for the decision. The flying missiles were revealed by illumination tracers so that we could note their flight and appraise their deadliness. The air was streaked with tiny flames marking the flight of massed destruction, while the effectiveness of the theoretical defense was impressed by the simulation of dead and wounded among those going forward, undaunted and unheeding.

As this panorama of unutterable destruction visualized the horrors of modern conflict, there grew on me the sense of the failure of a civilization which can leave its problems to such cruel arbitrament. Surely no one in authority, with human attributes and full appraisal of the patriotic loyalty of his countrymen, could ask the manhood of kingdom, empire, or republic to make such a sacrifice until all reason had failed, until appeal to justice through understanding had been denied, until every effort of love and consideration for fellowmen had been exhausted, until freedom itself and inviolate honor had been brutally threatened.

I speak not as a pacifist fearing war, but as one who loves justice and hates war. I speak as one who believes the highest function of government is to give its citizens the security of peace, the opportunity to achieve, and the pursuit of happiness.

The loftiest tribute we can bestow today is the commitment of this republic to an advancement never made before. If American achievement is a cherished pride at home, if our unselfishness among nations is all we wish it to be and ours is a helpful example in the world, then let us give of our influence and strength, yea, of our aspirations and convictions, to put mankind on a little higher plane, exulting and exalting with war's distressing and depressing tragedies barred from the stage of righteous civilization.

Standing today on hallowed ground, conscious that all America has halted to share in the tribute of heart and mind and soul to this fellow American and knowing that the world is noting this expression of the republic's mindfulness, it is fitting to say that his sacrifice, and that of the millions dead, shall not be in vain. There must be, there shall be, the commanding voice of a conscious civilization against armed warfare.

As we return this poor clay to its mother soil, garlanded by love and covered with the decorations that only nations can bestow, I can sense the prayers of our poeple, of all peoples, that this Armistice day shall mark the beginning of a new and lasting era of peace on earth, good will among men. Let us join in that prayer.

Our Father who art in heaven, hallowed be Thy name, Thy kingdom come, Thy will be done on earth as it is in heaven. Give us this day our daily bread and forgive us our trespasses as we forgive those who trespass against us, and lead us not into temptation, but deliver us from evil, for Thine is the kingdom, and the power and the glory forever. Amen.

JOHN BARLEYCORN'S FUNERAL
(1920)
by a Journalist of the Period

Barleycorn is literally "the grain of the barley," but the term also was used to describe any strong alcoholic liquor such as whisky. During that "noble experiment" know as Prohibition the term John Barleycorn was a personification used to poke fun at strong drink.

"Bone-dry" prohibition went into effect at one minute past midnight this morning and the fast-gathering snowflakes wove a winding sheet for the inanimate form of J. Barleycorn. The evening, at the hotels and restaurants, witnessed almost sedate contrasts, but for rare exceptions, to the bibulous scenes of the preceding evening. Gone was the zest and sparkle, the brilliant gayety which had attended the great outpouring of Bohemia for the final oblations to Bacchus, more or less mistakenly set for January 15.

"Why have so few brought liquor tonight?" I asked at hostelry after hostelry, and the answer came almost invariable: "They drank it all last night." The striking variation to this response was: "It costs too much."

More than one waiter confided to me that consumption the preceding evening was on a larger scale than he had ever before witnessed, and its effects, naturally, would be more lasting. "It was more convenient to carry small packages, and as a result they had to bring hard stuff as a rule."

Sharp were the contrasts to the spectacles of the previous evening. Instead of crowds struggling to present precious pasteboards as the "Open Sesame" to reserved tables from seven to eight per cover, while imperious waiters waved meek though richly attired guest hither and thither, there were great empty spaces in dining rooms, and some were closed altogether.

With the effervescence of the night of the sixteenth vanished, a considerable proportion of the troop of cabaret entertainers and orchestras generally were cut down.

At the American House, the coffin of J. Barleycorn was still on exhibition, with its contents of empty bottles and its artistic epitaph on the wall above.

THE ST. VALENTINE'S DAY MASSACRE

(1929)

A Newspaper Account

The Prohibition amendment (18) brought with it organized crime such as this country had never known. Gangsters took over the illegal liquor industry and fought for control of large urban areas. It has been estimated that over five hundred murders were committed by these hoodlums in the city of Chicago alone during the 1920s. Probably the most spectacular was perpetrated on the North Side of Chicago on February 14, 1929, when six members of the Bugs Moran Gang were massacred by men masquerading in police uniforms. Although the crime has never been solved, it was widely held that Al Capone (Moran's biggest competitor) was responsible.

It's too much to tell. You go into the door marked "S-M-C Cartage company." You see a bunch of big men talking with restrained excitement in the cigarette smoke. You go through another door back of the front office. You go between two close-parked trucks in the garage.

Then you almost stumble over the head of the first man, with a clean gray felt hat still placed at the precise angle of gangster toughness.

The dull yellow light of a lamp in daytime shows dark rivulets of blood heading down to the drain that was meant for the water from washed cars. There are six of the red streams from six heads. The bodies—four of them well dressed in civilian clothes—two of them with their legs crossed as they whirled to fall.

It's too much, so you crowd on past the roadster with bullet holes in it to the big truck behind.

You look at the truck. It is something to look at because the men were fixing it. It's jacked up, with one wheel off. You look and the big man called "commissioner" looks and a crowd gathers, and then it gets too much for the police dog you had failed to notice lying under the truck, tied to it by a cheap yellow rope.

It gets too much for the big brown and gray police dog and he goes crazy. He barks, he howls, he snarls, showing wicked white teeth in bright red gums.

The crowd backs away. The dog yowls once more and subsides.

Your thoughts snap with a crack back to the circle of yellow lamplight, where six things that were men are sprawled.

It's still too much. You push out into the fresh air.

You find that traffic was quiet in front of 3122 North Clark street at 10:30 this morning. A streetcar rattled down the narrow way left by parked cars. Across from the high garage, two windows of one of those old-fashioned gray-stone apartment houses were open. Two women exchanged their curiosities about it and then went back to gossip.

They jumped as a muffled roar reached them. The blue and black car sped away and turned the corner.

Out of nowhere the crowd came, pouring in from the rooming houses, the little stores, the automobiles, the street cars. They set up a hum. A policeman arrived—another. A police siren sounded—the clang of a patrol wagon.

The two women ran down and joined the buzzing in the street.

By this time people from the big apartment hotels on Lincoln Park West, half a block away, had heard and had come. The crowd was a cross section. Gold coast and Clark street merged in the gathering.

"What is it? Who were they? What did they do? Were they in the know? Double-crossers. Them guys had the pull and pulled it too strong——"

Inside six pairs of lips failed to answer.

"NOTHING TO FEAR" SPEECH

(1933)

by President Franklin D. Roosevelt

Franklin Delano Roosevelt assumed office while the country was in the throes of the Great Depression. At his inauguration he gave the following speech, sometimes known as his "fear" speech because of its famous phrase, "We have nothing to fear but fear itself." To those who did not experience the depression, this topic may seem peculiar. Yet to a newly industrialized nation whose people had been reared on hard work, the closed factories, foreclosures, bank failures, and soup lines were fearsome indeed. In this speech Roosevelt urges self-reliance and fortitude. As the decade wore on, however, his administration emphasized solutions through new Federal programs. It is difficult to try to reconcile the apparent disparity in the policies of this President before and after the depression.

I am certain that my fellow Americans expect that on my induction into the Presidency I will address them with a candor and a decision which the present situation of our nation impels. This is preeminently the time to speak the truth, the whole truth, frankly and boldly. Nor need we shrink from honestly facing conditions in our country today. This great nation will endure as it has endured, will revive, and will prosper. So, first of all, let me assert my firm belief that the only thing we have to fear is fear itself—nameless, unreasoning, unjustified terror which paralyzes needed efforts to convert retreat into advance. In every dark hour of our national life a leadership of frankness and vigor has met with that understanding and support of the people themselves which is essential to victory. I am convinced that you will again give that support to leadership in these critical days.

In such a spirit on my part and on yours we face our common difficulties. They concern, thank God, only material things. Values have shrunken to fantastic levels; taxes have risen; our ability to pay has fallen; government of all kinds is faced by serious curtailment of income; the means of exchange are frozen in the currents of trade; the withered leaves of industrial enterprise lie on every side; farmers find no markets for their produce, the savings of many years in thousands of families are gone.

More important, a host of unemployed citizens face the grim problem of existence, and an equally great number toil with little return. Only a foolish optimist can deny the dark realities of the moment.

Yet our distress comes from no failure of substance. We are stricken by no plague of locusts. Compared with the perils which our forefathers conquered because they believed and were not afraid, we have still much to be thankful for. Nature still offers her bounty and human efforts have multiplied it. Plenty is at our doorstep, but a generous use of it languishes in the very sight of the supply. Primarily this is because rulers of the exchange of mankind's goods have failed through their own stubbornness and their own incompetence, have admitted their failure, and have abdicated. Practices of the unscrupulous money changers stand indicted in the court of public opinion, rejected by the hearts and minds of men.

True they have tried, but their efforts have been cast in the pattern of an outworn tradition. Faced by failure of credit, they have proposed only the lending of more money. Stripped of the lure of profit by which to induce our people to follow their false leadership, they have resorted to exhortations, pleading tearfully for restored confidence. They know only the rules of a generation of self-seekers. They have no vision, and when there is no vision the people perish.

The money changers have fled from their high seats in the temple of our civilization. We may now restore that temple to the ancient truths. The measure of the restoration lies in the extent to which we apply social values more noble than mere monetary profit.

Happiness lies not in the mere possession of money; it lies in the joy of achievement, in the thrill of creative effort. The joy and moral stimulation of work no longer must be forgotten in the mad chase of evanescent profits. These dark days will be worth all they cost us if they teach us that our true destiny is not to be ministered unto but to minister to ourselves and to our fellow men.

Recognition of the falsity of material wealth as the standard of success goes hand in hand with the abandonment of the false belief that public office and high political position are to be valued only by the standards of pride of place and personal profit; and there must be an end to a conduct in banking and in business which too often has given to a sacred trust the likeness of callous and selfish wrongdoing. Small wonder that confidence languishes, for it thrives only on honesty, on honor, on the sacredness of obligations, on faithful protection, on unselfish performance; without them it cannot live.

Restoration calls, however, not for changes in ethics alone. This nation asks for action, and action now.

Our greatest primary task is to put people to work. This is no unsolvable problem if we face it wisely and courageously. It can be accomplished in part by direct recruiting by the government itself, treating the task as we would treat the emergency of a war, but at the same time, through this employment, accomplishing greatly needed projects to stimulate and reorganize the use of our natural resources.

Hand in hand with this we must frankly recognize the overbalance of population in our industrial centers and, by engaging on a national scale in a redistribution, endeavor to provide a better use of the land for those best fitted for the land. The task can be helped by definite efforts to raise the values of agricultural products and with this the power to purchase the output of our cities. It can be helped by preventing realistically the tragedy of the growing loss through foreclosure of our small homes and our farms. It can be helped by insistence that the federal, state, and local governments act forthwith on the demand that their cost be drastically reduced. It can be helped by the unifying of relief activities which today are often scattered, uneconomical, and unequal. It can be helped by national planning for and supervision of all forms of transportation and of communications and other utilities which have a definitely public character. There are many ways in which it can be helped, but it can never be helped merely by talking about it. We must act and act quickly.

Finally, in our progress toward a resumption of work we require two safeguards against a return of the evils of the old order: there must be a strict supervision of all banking and credits and investments, so that there will be an end to speculation with other people's money; and there must be provision for an adequate but sound currency.

These are the lines of attack. I shall presently urge upon a new Congress, in special session, detailed measures for their fulfillment, and I shall seek the immediate assistance of the several states.

Through this program of action we address ourselves to putting our own national house in order and making income balance outgo. Our international trade relations, though vastly important, are in point of time and necessity secondary to the establishment of a sound national economy. I favor as a practical policy the putting of first things first. I shall spare no effort to restore world trade by international economic readjustment, but the emergency at home cannot wait on that accomplishment.

The basic thought that guides these specific means of national recovery is not narrowly nationalistic. It is the insistence, as a first consideration, upon the interdependence of the various elements in and parts of the United States—a recognition of the old and permanently important manifestation of the American spirit of the pioneer. It is the way to recovery. It is the immediate way. It is the strongest assurance that the recovery will endure.

In the field of world policy I would dedicate this nation to the policy of the good neighbor—the neighbor who resolutely respects himself and, because he does so, respects the rights of others—the neighbor who respects his obligations and respects the sanctity of his agreements in and with a world of neighbors.

If I read the temper of our people correctly, we now realize as we have never realized before our interdependence on each other; that we cannot merely take but we must give as well; that if we are to go forward, we must move as a trained and loyal army willing to sacrifice for the good of a common discipline, because without such discipline no progress is made, no leadership becomes effective. We are, I know, ready and willing to submit our lives and property to such discipline, because it makes possible a leadership which aims at a larger good. This I propose to offer, pledging that the larger purposes will bind upon us all as a sacred obligation with a unity of duty hitherto evoked only in time of armed strife.

With this pledge taken, I assume unhesitatingly the leadership of this great army of our people dedicated to a disciplined attack upon our common problems.

Action in this image and to this end is feasible under the form of government which we have inherited from our ancestors. Our Constitution is so simple and practical that it is possible always to meet extraordinary needs by changes in emphasis and arrangement without loss of essential form. That is why our constitutional system has proved itself the most superbly enduring political mechanism the modern world has produced. It has met every stress of vast expansion of territory, of foreign wars, of bitter internal strife, of world relations.

It is to be hoped that the normal balance of executive and legislative authority may be wholly adequate to meet the unprecedented task before us. But it may be that an unprecedented demand and need for undelayed action may call for temporary departure from that normal balance of public procedure.

I am prepared under my constitutional duty to recommend the measures that a stricken nation in the midst of a stricken world may require. These measures, or such other measures as the Congress may build out of its experience and wisdom, I shall seek, within my constitutional authority, to bring to speedy adoption.

But in the event that the Congress shall fail to take one of these two courses, and in the event that the national emergency is still critical, I shall not evade the clear course of duty that will then confront me. I shall ask the Congress for the one remaining instrument to meet the crisis—broad executive power to wage a war against the emergency, as great as the power that would be given to me if we were in fact invaded by a foreign foe.

For the trust reposed in me I will return the courage and the devotion that befit the time. I can do no less.

We face the arduous days that lie before us in the warm courage of national unity; with the clear consciousness of seeking old and precious moral values; with the clean satisfaction that comes from the stern performance of duty by old and young alike. We aim at the assurance of a rounded and permanent national life. . . .

"DAY OF INFAMY" SPEECH
(1941)
by President Franklin D. Roosevelt

Though Europe was already at war and our relations with Japan were deteriorating precipitously, the United States was not prepared for war. Certainly the President and his administration were partly responsible for these things.

Soldiers and sailors, however, reacted valiantly to the Japanese strike at our Pearl Harbor naval base on the quiet Sunday morning of December 7, 1941. The two-hour attack cost the United States dearly in lives, aircraft, and ships. Ultimately, though, it would cost Japan the war, for it mobilized the American public and made "Remember Pearl Harbor!" a battle cry throughout the Pacific.

In the scope of the attack and the casualties suffered, Pearl Harbor was not the great battle of the Pacific war. The American attack on the Japanese fleet at Truk in 1944 has been estimated as fifteen times more powerful than the attack on Pearl Harbor. Later at Okinawa—an American victory!—we suffered fifty thousand casu-

alties and lost many ships. So it was not really the size of the battle that made Pearl Harbor significant, but the treachery behind it. This was the theme of Roosevelt's speech to Congress.

Yesterday, December 7, 1941—a date which will live in infamy—the United States of America was suddenly and deliberately attacked by naval and air forces of the Empire of Japan.

The United States was at peace with that Nation and, at the solicitation of Japan, was still in conversation with its Government and its Emperor looking toward the maintenance of peace in the Pacific. Indeed, one hour after Japanese air squadrons had commenced bombing in Oahu, the Japanese Ambassador to the United States and his colleague delivered to the Secretary of State a formal reply to a recent American message. While this reply stated that it seemed useless to continue the existing diplomatic negotiations, it contained no threat or hint of war or armed attack.

It will be recorded that the distance of Hawaii from Japan makes it obvious that the attack was deliberately planned many days or even weeks ago. During the intervening time the Japanese Government has deliberately sought to deceive the United States by false statements and expressions of hope for continued peace.

The attack yesterday on the Hawaiian Islands has caused severe damage to American naval and military forces. Very many American lives have been lost. In addition American ships have been reported torpedoed on the high seas between San Francisco and Honolulu.

Yesterday the Japanese Government also launched an attack against Malaya.

Last night Japanese forces attacked Hong Kong.

Last night Japanese forces attacked Guam.

Last night Japanese forces attacked Wake Island.

This morning the Japanese attacked Midway Island.

Japan has, therefore, undertaken a surprise offensive extending throughout the Pacific area. The facts of yesterday speak for themselves. The people of the United States have already formed their opinions and well understand the implications to the very life and safety of our Nation.

As Commander in Chief of the Army and Navy I have directed that all measures be taken for our defense.

Always we will remember the character of the onslaught against us.

No matter how long it may take us to overcome this premeditated invasion, the American people in their righteous might will win through to absolute victory.

I believe I interpret the will of the Congress and of the people when I assert that we will not only defend ourselves to the uttermost but will make very certain that this form of treachery shall never endanger us again.

Hostilities exist. There is no blinking at the fact that our people, our territory, and our interests are in grave danger.

With confidence in our armed forces—with the unbounded determination of our people—we will gain the inevitable triumph—so help us God.

I ask that the Congress declare that since the unprovoked and dastardly attack by Japan on Sunday, December 7, a state of war has existed between the United States and the Japanese Empire.

THE SURRENDER OF CORREGIDOR
(1942)
Military Radio Logs

After their attack on Pearl Harbor, which severely crippled America's Pacific fleet, Japan overran resource–rich southeast Asia. Japanese troops soon assaulted the Philippines, which were defended by American forces under General Douglas MacArthur. It became evident that, because of a lack of supplies and reinforcements, America could not retain control of the Philippines; President Roosevelt ordered General MacArthur to Australia, to command from there America's war effort in the Pacific. He left the Philippines, vowing, "I shall return." Lieutenant General Jonathan Wainwright, headquartered on the island fortress of Corregidor, then assumed command of the beleaguered American and Filipino forces.

After an heroic and desperate resistance, General Wainwright surrendered to the Japanese on May 6, 1942. Here is the story of that surrender, as told in the radio messages sent to and from Corregidor in its last twelve hours under the American flag.

Wainwright spent the next three years in a Japanese prison camp; finally liberated by victorious American troops, he was chosen to accompany General MacArthur in receiving Japan's final capitulation aboard the U.S.S. Missouri in Tokyo Bay on September 2, 1945.

3:00 A.M., *President Roosevelt to General Wainwright:*

DURING RECENT WEEKS WE HAVE BEEN FOLLOWING WITH GROWING ADMIRATION THE DAY-BY-DAY ACCOUNTS OF YOUR HEROIC STAND AGAINST THE MOUNTING INTENSITY OF BOMBARDMENT BY ENEMY PLANES AND HEAVY SIEGE GUNS.

IN SPITE OF ALL THE HANDICAPS OF COMPLETE ISOLATION, LACK OF FOOD AND AMMUNITION YOU HAVE GIVEN THE WORLD A SHINING EXAMPLE OF PATRIOTIC FORTITUDE AND SELF-SACRIFICE.

THE AMERICAN PEOPLE ASK NO FINER EXAMPLE OF TENACITY, RE-

SOURCEFULNESS, AND STEADFAST COURAGE. THE CALM DETERMINA-
TION OF YOUR PERSONAL LEADERSHIP IN A DESPERATE SITUATION SETS
A STANDARD OF DUTY FOR OUR SOLDIERS THROUGHOUT THE WORLD.

IN EVERY CAMP AND ON EVERY NAVAL VESSEL SOLDIERS, SAILORS,
AND MARINES ARE INSPIRED BY THE GALLANT STRUGGLE OF THEIR COM-
RADES IN THE PHILIPPINES. THE WORKMEN IN OUR SHIPYARDS AND MU-
NITIONS PLANTS REDOUBLE THEIR EFFORTS BECAUSE OF YOUR EXAMPLE.

YOU AND YOUR DEVOTED FOLLOWERS HAVE BECOME THE LIVING
SYMBOLS OF OUR WAR AIMS AND THE GUARANTEE OF VICTORY.

FRANKLIN D. ROOSEVELT

General Wainwright's response:

YOUR GRACIOUS AND GENEROUS MESSAGE OF MAY 4 HAS JUST NOW
REACHED ME. I AM WITHOUT WORDS TO EXPRESS TO YOU, MR. PRESI-
DENT, MY GRATITUDE FOR THE DEEP APPRECIATION OF YOUR GREAT
KINDNESS. AS I WRITE THIS AT 3:30 A.M. OUR PATROLS ARE ATTEMPTING
TO LOCATE THE ENEMY POSITIONS AND I WILL COUNTERATTACK AT
DAWN TO DRIVE HIM INTO THE SEA OR DESTROY HIM. THANK YOU
AGAIN, MR. PRESIDENT, FOR YOUR WONDERFUL MESSAGE WHICH I WILL
PUBLISH TO MY ENTIRE COMMAND.

10:30 A.M., *Wainwright to Roosevelt:*

WITH BROKEN HEART AND HEAD BOWED IN SADNESS BUT NOT IN
SHAME I REPORT TO YOUR EXCELLENCY THAT TODAY I MUST ARRANGE
TERMS FOR THE SURRENDER OF THE FORTIFIED ISLANDS OF MANILA BAY.

THERE IS A LIMIT OF HUMAN ENDURANCE AND THAT LIMIT HAS
LONG SINCE BEEN PAST. WITHOUT PROSPECT OF RELIEF I FEEL IT IS MY
DUTY TO MY COUNTRY AND TO MY GALLANT TROOPS TO END THIS USE-
LESS EFFUSION OF BLOOD AND HUMAN SACRIFICE.

IF YOU AGREE, MR. PRESIDENT, PLEASE SAY TO THE NATION THAT MY
TROOPS AND I HAVE ACCOMPLISHED ALL THAT IS HUMANLY POSSIBLE
AND THAT WE HAVE UPHELD THE BEST TRADITIONS OF THE UNITED
STATES AND ITS ARMY.

MAY GOD BLESS AND PRESERVE YOU AND GUIDE YOU AND THE NA-
TION IN THE EFFORT TO ULTIMATE VICTORY.

WITH PROFOUND REGRET AND WITH CONTINUED PRIDE IN MY GAL-
LANT TROOPS I GO TO MEET THE JAPANESE COMMANDER. GOOD BYE, MR.
PRESIDENT.

Then Navy Captain K. M. Hoeffel sent out this message:

ONE HUNDRED AND SEVENTY-THREE OFFICERS AND TWENTY-THREE
HUNDRED AND SEVENTEEN MEN OF THE NAVY REAFFIRM THEIR LOY-
ALTY AND DEVOTION TO COUNTRY, FAMILIES AND FRIENDS. . . .

11:00 A.M.

GOING OFF AIR NOW. GOOD-BYE AND GOOD LUCK, CALLAHAN AND MCCOY (communications officers). NOTIFY ANY AND ALL VESSELS HEADED TOWARD THIS AREA TO RETURN TO THEIR HOME PORTS.

This was the last official radiogram from Corregidor. But the radio operator, Army Corporal Irving Strobing, kept tapping out signals:

THEY ARE NOT NEAR YET. WE ARE WAITING FOR GOD ONLY KNOWS WHAT. HOW ABOUT A CHOCOLATE SODA? . . . LOTS OF HEAVY FIGHTING GOING ON. WE MAY HAVE TO GIVE UP BY NOON, WE DON'T KNOW YET. THEY ARE THROWING MEN AND SHELLS AT US AND WE MAY NOT BE ABLE TO STAND IT. THEY HAVE BEEN SHELLING US FASTER THAN YOU CAN COUNT. . . .

WE'VE GOT ABOUT FIFTY-FIVE MINUTES AND I FEEL SICK AT MY STOMACH. I AM REALLY LOW DOWN. THEY ARE AROUND NOW SMASHING RIFLES. THEY BRING IN THE WOUNDED EVERY MINUTE. WE WILL BE WAITING FOR YOU GUYS TO HELP. THIS IS THE ONLY THING I GUESS THAT CAN BE DONE. GENERAL WAINWRIGHT IS A RIGHT GUY AND WE'RE WILLING TO GO ON FOR HIM, BUT SHELLS WERE DROPPING ALL NIGHT. . . . DAMAGE TERRIFIC. TOO MUCH FOR GUYS TO TAKE. CORREGIDOR USED TO BE A NICE PLACE BUT IT'S HAUNTED NOW.

THE JIG IS UP. EVERY ONE IS BAWLING LIKE A BABY. THEY ARE PILING DEAD AND WOUNDED IN OUR TUNNEL. . . . I KNOW NOW HOW A MOUSE FEELS, CAUGHT IN A TRAP WAITING FOR GUYS TO COME ALONG AND FINISH IT UP.

12:30 P.M.

MY NAME IS IRVING STROBING. GET THIS TO MY MOTHER, MRS. MIN-NIE STROBING, 605 BARBEY STREET, BROOKLYN, NEW YORK. THEY ARE TO GET ALONG O.K. GET IN TOUCH WITH THEM SOON AS POSSIBLE. MES-SAGE: MY LOVE TO PA, JOE, SUE, MAC, GARRY, JOY AND PAUL. ALSO TO ALL FAMILY AND FRIENDS. GOD BLESS 'EM ALL. HOPE THEY WILL BE THERE WHEN I COME HOME. MY LOVE TO YOU ALL. GOD BLESS YOU AND KEEP YOU. LOVE. SIGN MY NAME AND TELL MOTHER HOW YOU HEARD FROM ME.

With this last message, Corregidor's radio went silent.

Irving Strobing was captured and spent most of the next three and a half years doing forced labor in a Japanese prisoner-of-war camp. In October, 1945, he was safely reunited with his family on Barbey Street in Brooklyn.

BASTOGNE
(1944)
by General Anthony McAuliffe and three American soldiers

Six months after the Allies had invaded Hitler's "Fortress Europe" at Normandy, the German forces counterattacked through southern Belgium and Luxembourg. It was a desperate attempt to turn the tide of the war that was inexorably approaching the German Fatherland. On December 16, 1944, a quarter-million Axis soldiers attacked. Their numbers, the inclement weather, and the element of surprise produced German successes and created an ominous bulge in the Allied lines. The turning point in the "Battle of the Bulge" came when the Germans surrounded the Americans at the crucial crossroads town of Bastogne. The Germans demanded surrender. General McAuliffe's reply: "Nuts!"

Brigadier General Anthony McAuliffe (101st Airborne Division; commander of U.S. forces at Bastogne): We lost our only hospital the night of December 19. A German column shot it up before they found out it was a hospital. Then a German officer came up and gave them thirty minutes to get ready to leave—took the whole bunch as prisoners of war. But some of our soldiers managed to get away.

Our casualties were comparatively light because the Germans were attacking. Still there were seven or eight hundred wounded. They were wonderful. I tried to visit them every day.

One paratrooper suffering from trench foot said to me, "General, I can't get my shoes over these swollen feet, but I 'traded' a pair of galoshes off a truck driver and they fit okay. Can't I go back?"

It cleared on the fourth day and we began to get some air support. Our boys took some casualties from our own fighters, but not much. We didn't warn off the fighter-bombers because they were doing such a good job.

We had a captain, a man named Parker, with us who acted as liason officer with the air force. He'd sit there and call down the air all around the perimeter whenever things were getting tough. He was a card, called himself the 'maestro.' Got so we had to put up ropes to keep the crowd back when he was talking to the fliers.

(later)

We always had tanks, tank destroyers and a battalion of infantry in reserve, and we never were really in tough shape. I resent any implication we were desperate or needed rescue. The whole thing was just our dish.

* * *

Sergeant George L. Williams (mortar observer in the woods northeast of Mande St. Etienne):

Throughout the siege the general's orders were "Let the tanks go through but clean up the infantry; we'il take care of the tanks inside the perimeter." But it's not very nice lying there and looking up while a Tiger tank goes past.

The tank destroyers let the Germans come right through. I guess the Krauts thought the TD's were their own because one of their tank commanders cussed them out for being in the way. Then when the tanks went further, they knocked them out.

Technical Sergeant Warren Lee: Everybody became a doughboy or fought a tank. They chopped us up a good bit—there were lots of mortars —and when we got back to Magerotte we really caught it from the 88's [88mm artillery]. I remember one tank was on fire and we could hear the guys inside who couldn't get out screaming.

One night we stayed in a barn. We had given our coats and jackets to the wounded; so to stay warm we sort of got in the stalls with the cows.

Their bombers hit a first aid station Christmas Eve. There were a hundred and eleven men there. We got most of them out—I remember one of the guy's bandages were on fire—but some we couldn't get to. There was a Belgian woman, a nurse, who helped us. She was pinned by a falling beam, and we had to leave her. The Krauts were coming in on the southwest and we had to go down to Villadour and try and stop them.

Corporal William Fowler: The Nazis came through after the moon had set, some of them in regular uniforms, some of them in white uniforms to blend with the snow. We let them come, and then I started to fire my machine gun. You could hear them holler, begging for mercy, when they were hit, but that wasn't any good. We just kept firing, although they were hollering 'Kamerad' and all that stuff. They got pretty well in. One sergeant stood in the door of a house we were using as a platoon command post and killed six of them with a Thompson gun.

Ten tanks had overrun our forward positions. There was a fella in a foxhole. These tanks had gone past and he saw a German clinging to the side of one. He picked up his rifle, shot the German, put the rifle down, picked up a bazooka and knocked the tank out. He was a cool fella.

CHRONOLOGY OF THE A-BOMB
(1939 - 1945)

In the latter part of the 1930's, physicists in several countries came to believe that Uranium-235 would split when hit with a neutron, and then fission of this atom would free other neutrons which would set off a chain reaction. On August 2, 1939, Albert Einstein sent this letter to President Roosevelt:

In the course of the last four months it has been made probable through the work of Joliot in France, as well as [Enrico] Fermi and [Leo] Szilard in America, that it may become possible to set up a nuclear chain reaction in a large mass of uranium, by which vast amounts of power and large quantities of new radium-like elements would be generated. Now it appears this could be achieved in the immediate future.

This new phenomenon would also lead to the construction of bombs, and it is conceivable, though much less certain—that extremely powerful bombs of a new type may thus be constructed. A single bomb of this type, carried by boat and exploded in a port, might very well destroy the whole port, together with some of the surrounding territory. . . .

Roosevelt embarked on the project. It would ultimately cost $2.5 billion and directly involve 125,000 workers. Yet, only a handful of people, not even the Congress or the subsequent Vice-President, Truman, knew of the project. At Roosevelt's death Truman was told of the bomb and approved of its use. It was estimated the A-Bomb saved half a million Americans lives that would have been lost in invading mainland Japan. After the war, Truman explained his reasons for giving the go-ahead:

Let there be no mistake about it, I regarded the bomb as a military weapon and never had any doubt that it should be used. The top military advisers to the President recommended its use, and when I talked to Churchill he unhesitatingly told me that he favored the use of the atomic bomb if it might aid to end the war.

The atomic bomb was so secret that only three men on the B-29 which bombed Hiroshima knew the real nature of the mission. Colonel Paul W. Tibbits, Jr., was the pilot of that plane, the Enola Gay. *This is his report:*

After we dropped the bomb we did a roundhouse turn to get out of the shock wave.

When the shock wave hit us the plane was in a bank. The plane snapped like a tin roof, but there was more noise than shock. . . .

Twice we made our S-shaped maneuvers taking pictures with our two cameras, one in the nose and one in the tail. We were never closer than a mile from the cloud, but we were close enough to watch it boil. It turned many different colors—orange and blue and gray. It was like looking over a tar barrel boiling. There was lots of black smoke and dust and rubble that gave the appearance of boiling. We couldn't see the city at all through the thick layer of dust nor could we see the fires beneath. A circle of dust outlined the area of destruction.

Navy Captain William S. Parsons was also on board the aircraft, specifically to observe the blast.

It was 0915 when we dropped our bomb and we turned the plane broadside to get the best view. Then we made as much distance from the ball of fire as we could.

We were at least ten miles away and there was a visual impact even though every man wore colored glasses for protection. We had braced ourselves when the bomb was gone for the shock and Tibbets said "close flak" and it was just like that—a close burst of antiaircraft fire.

The crew said "My God" and couldn't believe what had happened.

A mountain of smoke was going up in a mushroom with the stem coming down. At the top was white smoke but up to 1,000 feet from the ground there was swirling, boiling dust. Soon afterward small fires sprang up on the edge of town, but the town was entirely obscured. We stayed around two or three minutes and by that time the smoke had risen to 40,000 feet. As we watched the top of the white cloud broke off and another soon formed.

Truman at that time was in the Atlantic on the cruiser Augusta, *returning from the Potsdam conference. This message was flashed to him:*

TO THE PRESIDENT
FROM THE SECRETARY OF WAR
BIG BOMB DROPPED ON HIROSHIMA AUGUST 5 AT 7:15 P.M. WASHINGTON TIME. FIRST REPORTS INDICATE COMPLETE SUCCESS WHICH WAS EVEN MORE CONSPICUOUS THAN EARLIER TEST.

In a few minutes additional information followed:

FOLLOWING INFO REGARDING MANHATTAN [code name for bomb project] RECEIVED. HIROSHIMA BOMBED VISUALLY WITH ONLY ONE TENTH [cloud] COVER AT 052315A [date/time/month]. THERE WAS

NO FIGHTER OPPOSITION AND NO FLAK. PARSONS REPORTS 15 MINUTES AFTER DROP AS FOLLOWS: "RESULTS CLEAR CUT SUCCESSFUL IN ALL RESPECTS. VISIBLE EFFECTS GREATER THAN IN ANY TEST. CONDITIONS NORMAL IN AIRPLANE FOLLOWING DELIVERY."

The President then released statement to the newsmen which included the following:

Sixteen hours ago an American airplane dropped one bomb on Hiroshima, an important Japanese Army base. That bomb had more power than 20,000 tons of TNT. It had more than two thousand times the blast power of the British "Grand Slam," which is the largest bomb ever yet used in the history of warfare.

The Japanese began the war from the air at Pearl Harbor. They have been repaid manyfold. And the end is not yet. With this bomb we have now added a new and revolutionary increase in destruction to supplement the growing power of our armed forces. In their present form these bombs are now in production and even more powerful forms are in development.

It is an atomic bomb. It is a harnessing of the basic power of the universe. The force from which the sun draws its powers has been loosened against those who brought war to the Far East.

Before 1939, it was the accepted belief of scientists that it was theoretically possible to release atomic energy. But no one knew any practical method of doing it. By 1942, however, we knew that the Germans were working feverishly to find a way to add atomic energy to the other engines of war with which they hoped to enslave the world. But they failed. We may be grateful to Providence that the Germans got the V-1's and the V-2's late in limited quantities and even more grateful that they did not get the atomic bomb at all.

The battle of the laboratories held fateful risks for us as well as the battles of the air, land and sea, and we have now won the battle of the laboratories as we have won the other battles.

Beginning in 1940, before Pearl Harbor, scientific knowledge useful in war was pooled between the United States and Great Britian, and many priceless helps to victories have come from the arrangement. Under that general policy the research on the atomic bomb was begun. With American and British scientists working together, we entered the race of discovery against the Germans.

Both science and industry worked under the direction of the United States Army, which achieved a unique success in managing so diverse a problem in the advancement of knowledge in an amazingly short time. It is doubtful if such another combination could be got together in the world. What has been done is the greatest achievement of organized science in history. It was done under high pressure and without failure.

We are now prepared to obliterate more rapidly and completely every productive enterprise the Japanese have above ground in any city. We shall destroy their docks, their factories and their communications. Let there be no mistake; we shall completely destroy Japan's power to make war.

It was to spare the Japanese people from utter destruction that the ultimatum of July 26 was issued at Potsdam. Their leaders promptly rejected that ultimatum. If they do not now accept our terms they may expect a rain of ruin from the air, the like of which has never been seen on this earth. Behind this air attack will follow sea and land forces in such numbers and power as they have not yet seen and with the fighting skill of which they are already well aware.

The fact that we can release atomic energy ushers in a new era in man's understanding of nature's forces. Atomic energy may, in the future, supplement the power that now comes from coal, oil and falling water, but at present it cannot be produced on a basis to compete with them commercially. Before that comes there must be a long period of intensive research.

I shall recommend that the Congress of the United States consider promptly the establishment of an appropriate commission to control the production and use of atomic power within the United States. I shall give further consideration and make further recommendations to the Congress as to how atomic power can become a powerful and forceful influence toward the maintenance of world peace.

OLD SOLDIERS NEVER DIE
(1951)
by General Douglas MacArthur

General MacArthur entered World War II with the respect of the American people and by its conclusion had won their open adulation. When the Communists attacked South Korea, MacArthur was charged with stopping them. In this "police action" (said one infantryman, "They told us it was a sort of police action. Some police action! Some cops! Some robbers! What is this police action?") MacArthur was faced with a limited war, a fight he could not take to the enemies' homeland. He openly chafed under these restrictions, so much so that, on April 11, 1951, President Truman abruptly relieved the General of his command. He had executed a brilliant military campaign in Korea and the American public was aghast: it gave MacArthur a hero's welcome home and vilified Truman. The General was invited to address Congress soon after his return to the United States. In his speech on April 19, he reviewed the military situation in Asia and the Pacific, then gave this moving conclusion.

Once war is forced upon us, there is no other alternative than to apply every available means to bring it to a swift end. War's very object is victory—not prolonged indecision. In war, indeed, there can be no substitute for victory.

There are some who for varying reasons would appease Red China. They are blind to history's clear lesson. For history teaches with unmistakable emphasis that appeasement but begets new and bloodier war. It points to no single instance where the end has justified that means—where appeasement has led to more than a sham peace. Like blackmail, it lays the basis for new and successively greater demands, until, as in blackmail, violence becomes the only other alternative. Why, my soldiers asked of me, surrender military advantages to an enemy in the field? I could not answer. Some may say to avoid spread of the conflict into an all-out war with China; others, to avoid Soviet intervention. Neither explanation seems valid. For China is already engaging with the maximum power it can commit and the Soviet will not necessarily mesh its actions with our moves. Like a cobra, any new enemy will more likely strike whenever it feels that the relativity in military or other potential is in its favor on a world-wide basis.

The tragedy of Korea is further heightened by the fact that as military action is confined to its territorial limits, it condemns that nation, which it is our purpose to save, to suffer the devastating impact of full naval and air bombardment, while the enemy's sanctuaries are fully protected from such attack and devastation. Of the nations of the world, Korea alone, up to now, is the sole one which has risked its all against communism. The magnificence of the courage and fortitude of the Korean people defies description. They have chosen to risk death rather than slavery. Their last words to me were "Don't scuttle the Pacific."

I have just left your fighting sons in Korea. They have met all tests there and I can report to you without reservation they are splendid in every way. It was my constant effort to preserve them and end this savage conflict honorably and with the least loss of time and a minimum sacrifice of life. Its growing bloodshed has caused me the deepest anguish and anxiety. Those gallant men will remain often in my thoughts and in my prayers always.

I am closing my 52 years of military service. When I joined the Army even before the turn of the century, it was the fulfillment of all my boyish hopes and dreams. The world has turned over many times since I took the oath on the plain at West Point, and the hopes and dreams have long since vanished. But I still remember the refrain of one of the most popular barracks ballads of that day which proclaimed most proudly that—

"Old soldiers never die; they just fade away." And like the old soldier of that ballad, I now close my military career and just fade away—an old soldier who tried to do his duty as God gave him the light to see that duty. Good-by.

KOREAN TREATMENT OF AMERICAN POW'S
(1952)
Two American Soldiers
(testimony to U.S. Senate investigators)

The horror of the crimes against mankind by international Communism is beyond dispute. Since the Russian revolution and the subsequent murder and starvation of thousands of Kulaks, the insatiable blood appetite of the Communists has grown stronger. Outside of Russia, hundreds of thousands more have been murdered in the Baltic nations and in East Germany, Poland, Hungary, and Czechoslovakia, to name only a few. The same was true in Korea, and more recently thousands were slaughtered in Vietnam and Cambodia.

Such atrocities continue on a daily basis. Generally Americans are aware of them only when their fellow Americans are confronted with Communist torture and murder. Such was the case when American prisoners of war came home from Korea. The story was repeated when our men were freed from Vietnamese prisons, some after nine years of captivity and abuse. Our men in Korean prisons resisted their captors far better than is often conceded: the first account gives an idea of how American humor helped the men resist their captors, the second is a mild anecdote of torture and subsequent death. There are many accounts which more graphically describe sadistic tortures (wounded soldiers thrown live into a fire; scantily clad prisoners taken outdoors in sub-zero weather, doused with water until frozen to the ground; grisly, day-long beatings; and worse) but this book is for the general interest reader and inclusion of these nauseating accounts in full here does not seem proper.

For documented studies of Red atrocities by Russians, the reader is commended to Roy A. Medvedev's Let History Judge *and Alexander Solshenitsyn's* Gulag Archipeligo.

An Army sergeant: All I told them is I was in the Army, and this actually started on what they called autobiography. It had a big bunch of things on there. To us it was a joke. I mean, questions they asked. One of the questions was "Who is your best friend?" At that time we was fed up with it. We didn't care what they did with us. So I put "The only friend

I have wants to borrow money." Then they went along and asked other information such as "Who was your commander," and I put on there, like most of us put, "Military secret, can't be given."

. . . This is one thing I would like to bring up. What makes me feel proud to be part of America is no matter how bad they had us down, no matter how bad we were, as long as they were around, we never showed them we was down. That is one thing and they could never understand, how we could still laugh and joke in the conditions we were in. So that is why, as I say this, we were not in a good mood when we did it, but it is just the way an American GI reacts.

This one kid put on his paper, "I filled out something like this before and I ended up in the Army."

Another one put "This is too much for me. I request transportation to go back and have my lawyer fill it out."

It was all humorous things like that, and it kind of made the Chinese mad but we didn't care.

Lt. Col. Robert Abbott, formerly with the United States 8th Infantry Division and a prisoner of war for 33 months, related the following incident concerning treatment afforded prisoners who objected to Communist indoctrination:

COLONEL ABBOTT. They died of malnutrition and lack of medical attention; yes, sir.

It was in this camp that we also experienced our first real sadistic treatment of individuals, and I cite one case, the story of a prisoner who when exposed to one of these political indoctrination speeches came back to his quarters and sat down and talking to another prisoner made the statement that the speech that he had just listened to wasn't worth the paper that it was written on. It so happened that there was a Chinese interpreter standing outside who came in, had heard the statement, took the prisoner out of the room, took him to headquarters where he was taken out and tied up in front of the headquarters where we could all see him. He was required to stand there for a prolonged period of time—until such time as he completely collapsed from exhaustion, couldn't stand any longer.

At this time, the Chinese guard came and dragged him away and kicked him as they took him away, hitting him with the butts of their rifles and so on, and actually visibly mistreated him before the bulk of the prisoners in the compound.

He was taken to an air-raid shelter where he was confined for a period of probably 3 to 4 days.

During this time he received very little food or water and was kept tied up during the entire period.

He returned to the compound sometime later and in a very weak and sick condition and he never fully recovered from that and I would say he died within a period of 3 weeks after he was brought back to us.

VIETNAM
(1969)
by Colonel Robert R. Scott

After decades of French colonial rule, French Indochina was partitioned and divided leaving the countries of North Vietnam, South Vietnam, Laos, and Cambodia. After years of bloodshed, subterfuge, and betrayal, Communism in its various forms now controls the entire area.

I break lock with the refueling boom, back away from the tanker and slide slowly left so my number two pilot can refuel. In the process I look down and to the rear to check the others. There are 25 F-105s around the tanker—a strike force of 20, plus a spare 105 for each flight of four.

I'm looking for flaws, but mostly my attitude is that of a leader proudly watching professional jet jockeys. I know my pilots are all professionals or they wouldn't be here. They all have considerable background and experience. The number two man in my flight moves in and locks onto the tanker, rock-steady—like he is part of it. Yes, they are truly professionals.

Right now everything is as peaceful as a training mission. Even the weather is good. But when you see those bombs hanging on pylons beneath each bird, you know you can rule out the training mission. The green and brown camouflage paint job on each aircraft also smacks of combat. This peaceful lull won't last long, for soon we will be within twenty miles of Hanoi.

Although it is April, the monsoon season has not yet reached us at our base in Takhli, Thailand. But it's in full swing in the target area. In addition to the weather, we will have to be ever alert for surface to air missiles (SAMs). And we can never discount the swift, wraith-like *MiGs* and the scores of ack-ack positions, waiting to light up like the Fourth of July. The unfavorable odds bring us to parody a popular television program. We call our task "Mission Improbable."

The last pilot has refueled and we move quickly into formation. Throttles forward, we rapidly leave our tankers and spares behind. Now the spares move in for their refueling, still alert for any abort. After refueling, the spares will join up as one flight and return home, their mission finished for today.

As we speed north, more and more clouds appear. We press on and soon the lush, green terrain below is replaced by the moving, white fluff.

Our target is an Army barracks at Son Toy, twenty miles west-north-west of Hanoi. We have deliberately flown north beyond our turn-in point to deceive and confuse the enemy—we hope.

Now I waggle my wings and all our aircraft move swiftly into close formation. We are descending through the first layer of clouds so we fly close in order to see one another. Our navigation lights are on bright as an additional aid. Another group of F-105s is ahead of us to suppress flak just prior to our scheduled time on target. But now our radios tell us the flak suppression flight is unable to locate the target because of the weather. This message brings all the short hair on my neck to rigid attention. The odds against us go up another notch.

Some of the mountains in this area rise to ten thousand feet; so I start to level off at eleven thousand feet when, suddenly, we burst through the clouds. Continuing our descent down a ridge to the southeast, we fly close to the terrain in hopes that the enemy radar will have trouble locking onto us—this is SAM country!

As we drop toward the level floor of the valley, broken clouds are in abundance about four thousand feet above the ground. Beneath the clouds it is hazy, reducing visibility to three miles or less. When you're zapping along at six hundred knots, this kind of visibility is like looking through a peephole into a fog bank. My eyes are straining in their sockets, trying to make out key landmarks. But right now speed is our only protection and we're determined to maintain it, even in the low visibility.

We're close now and I give directions in short bursts. This allows my pilots to anticipate changes in direction and elevation as I try to zero in on the IP (initial point). Now I'm *really* straining my eyeballs to see the IP so we can pop up, spread the flights and roll in on the dive bomb run. I can sense without looking that the wingmen are tucked in tight on my wings. The visibility is really poor—missed the IP! I bark into the radio.

"Scotch Lead: Tight left to pick up IP!" I'm tensed up, fighting G's and looking desperately for the IP. There it is! It was only a small S-curve in a stream but a most welcome sight.

"Rolling in, left. Flights, take your spacing."

Now I see the target through the broken clouds.

"Line up," I tell myself, "get six hundred on the airspeed—thumb on bomb button—Now!"

I pull back hard on the stick and light the after-burner. I can sense when the bombs release. From now on we are operating as individual flights.

We know there are at least a hundred guns in the immediate vicinity and right now I think they are all firing at me—37 and 57mm plus radar-controlled 85mm.

My number three yells, *"MiGs!"* At almost the same instant I see two missiles go overhead. Then I see two *MiG*-21s flash up and away. They missed us—too eager.

We had been briefed about a new *MiG* field (Hoa Lac) just south of our target. Almost automatically after the near fatal encounter I lower a wing and pull hard, bending my bird in the direction of the field. Zing! I meet a *MiG* head-on, right after takeoff. He whistles under me to make like an air-show thriller. I latch onto a *MiG*-17 in the traffic pattern but he turns too tight. With my excess speed I am unable to line up for a missile shot. I yo-yo up and down, reducing my speed to 475 knots. The *MiG* reverses—I pull up. As I go down, he reverses again and we both go across the runway at five hundred feet. He pulls up to the clouds, five hundred then down to the treetops. I'm pulling 7 Gs in after-burner, determined to nail him! Now the *MiG* relaxes his turn and heads west—his mistake. I open up with my 20mm Gatling gun and a steady stream of metal closes the gap. For a fraction of a second, his left wing lights up, then—pow! Half the wing snaps off and he crashes inverted in a split second.

Two heartbeats later, a scream in my earphones, "SAM at three o'clock!"

Instinctively, I whip the controls right and forward. My bird responds violently to the right and down. The SAM arches over me at about two hundred feet. I'm impressed but there isn't time for fear—everything's at high speed. The SAM left a telltale smoke trail right back to the site. Too bad! My wingmen bore down the smoke trail preceded by their deadly 20mm emissaries. Scratch one SAM mobile unit!

Knocking out this missile site may have saved our necks because my number two had already called bingo (low fuel) so we must head for home. But here lies a dilemma: jets use tremendous quantities of fuel at low level and high speed, yet to get altitude now would make us extremely vulnerable to the other SAMs in the area. Fortunately, we meet the hills to the west. Now we are able to stay low over the ground and still climb, following the terrain upward. This should give their radar a few problems. Finally, I feel we are far enough away for safety so we reach for altitude in a hurry.

Once in level flight, I set about checking our position relative to the tankers. We need fuel—and quick! After a short period, my number four man moves in close indicating with hand signals that his radio is out and that he is very low on fuel. I quickly call our tanker to ascertain exactly how far away it is. Luck is with us; we are closer than I had hoped for. I give him a readiness call.

"Big Blue, this is Scotch Lead. Extend your boom and fly heading two four zero."

Now I see our tanker. My number four needs fuel desperately, and I cross my fingers that we will be there in time. We reach the tanker and number four loses no time getting plugged in and starting the flow of that precious fluid. After the four of us take on our seven thousand pounds each, I give the tanker an A-okay and we depart for Takhli. We know them all because they are assigned to the wing and are based with us at Takhli.

As our long runway comes into view, I flick my wings, putting the flight into echelon. The flight tucks in very tight and we come in for the break.

There are several thousand officers and airmen on the ground watching. Some are just enjoying the sight and sound but many will search anxiously for damage and identification.

We touch down in two's with the drag chutes billowing behind.

It's a good feeling. We complete another "Mission Improbable!"

THE FIRST MEN ON THE MOON
(1969)
Taped Transcript

The Russian word for satellite is "sputnik." In 1957 the Soviet Union launched the first Sputnik into space and touched off the race to the moon. American technological know-how and industrial might placed the first man on the moon in July of 1969.

Three astronauts made the voyage: Michael Collins orbited the moon in the command and service module Columbia, while Neil Armstrong and "Buzz" Aldrin put down on the moon's surface in the lunar module Eagle. Their landing spot was entitled Tranquility Base. The flight was controlled from America's Manned Spacecraft Center at Houston, Texas.

EAGLE (the lunar module): Houston, Tranquility Base here. The *Eagle* has landed.

HOUSTON: Roger, Tranquility, we copy you on the ground. You've got a bunch of guys about to turn blue. We're breathing again. Thanks a lot.

TRANQUILITY BASE: Thank you.

HOUSTON: You're looking good here.

TRANQUILITY BASE: A very smooth touchdown.

COLUMBIA (the command and service module): How do you read me?

HOUSTON: *Columbia,* he has landed Tranquility Base. *Eagle* is at Tranquility. I read you five by. Over.

COLUMBIA: Yes, I heard the whole thing.

HOUSTON: Well, it's a good show.

COLUMBIA: Fantastic.

TRANQUILITY BASE: I'll second that.

APOLLO CONTROL: We have an unofficial time for that touchdown of 102 hours, 45 minutes, 42 seconds after blastoff, and we will update that.

APOLLO CONTROL: We're now less than four minutes from our next stay-no stay. It will be for one complete revolution of the command module.

One of the first things that Armstrong and Aldrin will do after getting their next stay-no stay will be to remove their helmets and gloves.

That's stay for another two minutes plus. The next stay-no stay will be for one revolution.

TRANQUILITY BASE: Houston, that may have seemed like a very long final phase but the auto targeting was taking us right into a football field-sized crater with a large number of big boulders and rocks for about one or two crater diameters around it. And it required us to fly manually over the rock field to find a reasonably good area.

HOUSTON: Roger. We copy. It was beautiful from here, Tranquility. Over.

TRANQUILITY BASE: We'll get to the details of what's around here, but it looks like a collection of just about every variety of shape, angularity, granularity; about every variety of rock you could find. The colors vary pretty much depending on how you are looking relative to the zero phase length [direction of sunlight]. There doesn't appear to be too much of a general color at all. However, it looks as though some of the rocks and boulders—of which there are quite a few in the near area—it looks as though they're going to have some interesting colors to them. Over.

HOUSTON: Roger. Copy. Sounds good to us, Tranquility. We'll let you press on through the simulated countdown, and we'll talk to you later. Over.

TRANQUILITY BASE: Okay. This one-sixth G [pull of gravity] is just like an airplane.

HOUSTON: Roger, Tranquility. Be advised there are lots of smiling faces in this room and all over the world. Over.

TRANQUILITY BASE: There are two of them up here.

HOUSTON: Roger. It was a beautiful job, you guys.

COLUMBIA: And don't forget one in the command module.

TRANQUILITY BASE: Roger.

APOLLO CONTROL [television hook-up]: That last remark from Mike Collins at an altitude of sixty miles. The comments on the landing, on the manual take-over, came from Neil Armstrong. Buzz Aldrin followed that with a description of the lunar surface and the rocks and boulders that they are able to see out the window of the LM.

COLUMBIA: Thanks for putting me on relay, Houston. I was missing all the action.

HOUSTON: Roger. We'll enable relay.

COLUMBIA (later): I just got it, I think.

HOUSTON: Roger, *Columbia.* This is Houston. Say something; they ought to be able to hear you. Over.

COLUMBIA: Roger. Tranquility Base. It sure sounded great from up here. You guys did a fantastic job.

TRANQUILITY BASE: Thank you. Just keep that orbiting base ready for us up there, now.

COLUMBIA: Will do.

APOLLO CONTROL: That request from Neil Armstrong.

APOLLO CONTROL: We've just gotten a report from the telcom here in mission control that LM [Lunar Module] systems look good after that landing. We're about twenty-six minutes now from loss of signal from the command module.

TRANQUILITY BASE: Houston, the guys that bet that we wouldn't be able to tell precisely where we are are the winners today. We were a little busy worrying about program alarms and things like that in the part of the descent where we would normally be picking out our landing spot; and aside from a good look at several of the craters we came over in the final descent, I haven't been able to pick out the things on the horizon as a reference as yet.

HOUSTON: Rog, Tranquility. No sweat. We'll figure out—we'll figure it out. Over.

TRANQUILITY BASE: You might be interested to know that I don't think we noticed any difficulty at all in adapting to one-sixth G. It seems immediately natural to live in this environment.

HOUSTON: Roger, Tranquility. We copy. Over.

TRANQUILITY BASE: [Unintelligible] . . . window, with relatively level plain cratered with a fairly large number of craters of the five- to fifty-foot variety. And some ridges twenty to thirty feet high, I would guess. And literally thousands of little one- and two-foot craters around the area. We see some angular blocks out several hundred feet in front of us that are probably two feet in size and have angular edges. There is a hill in view just about on the ground track ahead of us. Difficult to estimate, but might be a half a mile or a mile.

HOUSTON: Roger, Tranquility. We copy. Over.

COLUMBIA: Sounds like it looks a lot better than it did yesterday. At that very low sun angle, it looked rough as a cob then.

TRANQUILITY BASE: It really was rough, Mike, over the targeted landing area. It was extremely rough, cratered with large numbers of rocks that were probably many larger than five or ten feet in size.

COLUMBIA: When in doubt, land long.

TRANQUILITY BASE: Well, we did.

COLUMBIA: Do you have any idea whether they landed left or right of center line—just a little bit long? Is that all we know?

HOUSTON: Apparently that's about all we can tell. Over.

COLUMBIA: Okay, thank you.

TRANQUILITY BASE: Okay. I'd say the color of the local surface is very comparable to that we observed from orbit at this sun angle. It's pretty much without color. Some of the surface rocks in close here that have been fractured or disturbed by the rocket engine plume are coated with this light gray on the outside. But where they've been broken, they display a dark—very dark—gray interior and it looks like it could be country basalt.

From the surface we could not see any stars out the window, but on my overhead patch I'm looking at the earth. It's big and bright—beautiful. Buzz is going to give a try at seeing some stars through the optics.

HOUSTON: Roger, Tranquility. We understand; must be a beautiful sight.

Two minutes to LOS [loss of signal]. You're looking great. Going over the hill. Over.

COLUMBIA: Okay. Thank you. Glad to hear it's looking good. Do you have a suggested attitude for me? This one here seems all right.

HOUSTON: Stand by.

COLUMBIA: Let me know when it's lunch time, will ya?

HOUSTON: Say again?

HOUSTON: *Columbia,* Houston. You got a good attitude right there.

APOLLO CONTROL: This is Apollo Control. We've had loss of signal now from the command module. Of course, we'll maintain constant communication with the lunar module on the lunar surface. We have some heart rates for Neil Armstrong during that powered descent to lunar surface. At the time the burn was initiated, Armstrong's heart rate was 110. At touchdown on the lunar surface, he had a heart rate of 156 beats per minute, and the flight surgeon reports that his heart rate is now in the 90s. We do not have biomedical data on Buzz Aldrin.

[later]

We also have updated information on the landing point. It appears that the spacecraft *Eagle* touched down at .799 degrees north or just about on the lunar equator and 23.46 degrees east longitude, which would have put it about four miles from the targeted landing point downrange. We're now 54 minutes—or rather 27 minutes from reacquisition of the command module, and of course we're in constant contact with the lunar module on the surface.

At this point all LM systems continue to look very good.

HOUSTON: Hello Tranquility Base, Houston. You can start your power down now. Over.

TRANQUILITY BASE: Roger.

HOUSTON: Tranquility Base, the white team is going off now and the maroon team takes over. We appreciate the great show; it was a beautiful job, you guys.

TRANQUILITY BASE: Roger. Couldn't ask for better treatment from all the way back there.

TRANQUILITY BASE: Houston, our recommendation at this point is planning an EVA [Extra Vehicular Activity], with your concurrence, starting at about eight o'clock this evening, Houston time. That is about three hours from now.

HOUSTON: Stand by.

TRANQUILITY BASE: We will give you some time to think about that.

HOUSTON: Tranquility Base, Houston. We thought about it. We will support it. We'll go at that time.

TRANQUILITY BASE: Roger.

HOUSTON: You guys are getting prime time on TV there.

TRANQUILITY BASE: I hope that little TV set works. We'll see.

About six and a half hours after landing, Neil Armstrong opened the landing craft's hatch, stepped slowly down the ladder, and declared as he planted the first human footprint on the lunar crust:

"That's one small step for [a] man, one giant leap for mankind."

His first step on the moon came at 10:56:20 P.M., as a television camera outside the craft transmitted his every move to an awed and excited audience of hundreds of millions of people on earth.

WATERGATE SPEECH
(1974)
by President Richard M. Nixon

The administrations of other American Presidents had been under fire for wrong-doing, but none of these scandals were as devastating as was Richard Nixon's "Watergate affair." Stemming from an otherwise minor burglary, the subsequent cover-up and related scandals were pursued by a hostile Congress and a vindictive press until the President stood on the brink of impeachment. His original vice-president, Spiro Agnew, had resigned a year earlier to avoid prosecution for income tax evasion and Nixon had appointed Gerald Ford to replace Agnew. As Nixon opted to exit Washington, Ford became the first unelected American President. Nixon's resignation speech came on August 8, 1974. He was the first American President to resign his office.

Good evening.

This is the thirty-seventh time I have spoken to you from this office in which so many decisions have been made that shape the history of this nation.

Each time I have done so to discuss with you some matters that I believe affected the national interest. And all the decisions I have made in my public life I have always tried to do what was best for the nation.

Throughout the long and difficult period of Watergate, I have felt it was my duty to persevere; to make every possible effort to complete the term of office to which you elected me.

In the past few days, however, it has become evident to me that I no longer have a strong enough political base in the Congress to justify continuing that effort.

As long as there was such a base, I felt strongly that it was necessary to see the constitutional process through to its conclusion; that to do otherwise would be unfaithful to the spirit of that deliberately difficult process, and a dangerously destabilizing precedent for the future.

But with the disappearance of that base, I now believe that the constitutional purpose has been served. And there is no longer a need for the process to be prolonged.

I would have preferred to carry through to the finish whatever the personal agony it would have involved, and my family unanimously urged me to do so.

But the interests of the nation must always come before any personal considerations. From the discussions I have had with Congressional and other leaders I have concluded that because of the Watergate matter I might not have the support of the Congress that I would consider necessary to back the very difficult decisions and carry out the duties of this office in the way the interests of the nation will require.

I have never been a quitter.

To leave office before my term is completed is opposed to every instinct in my body. But as President I must put the interests of America first.

America needs a full-time President and a full-time Congress, particularly at this time with problems we face at home and abroad.

To continue to fight through the months ahead for my personal vindication would almost totally absorb the time and attention of both the President and the Congress in a period when our entire focus should be on the great issues of peace abroad and prosperity without inflation at home.

Therefore, I shall resign the Presidency effective at noon tomorrow.

Vice-President Ford will be sworn in as President at that hour in this office.

As I recall the high hopes for America with which we began this second term, I feel a great sadness that I will not be here in this office working on your behalf to achieve those hopes in the next two and a half years.

But in turning over direction of the government to Vice President Ford I know, as I told the nation when I nominated him for that office ten months ago, that the leadership of America will be in good hands.

In passing this office to the Vice President I also do so with the profound sense of the weight of responsibility that will fall on his shoulders tomorrow, and therefore of the understanding, the patience, the cooperation he will need from all Americans.

As he assumes that responsibility, he will deserve the help and the support of all of us. As we look to the future, the first essential is to begin healing the wounds of this nation. To put the bitterness and divisions of the recent past behind us and to rediscover those shared ideals that lie at the heart of our strength and unity as a great and as a free people.

By taking this action, I hope that I will have hastened the start of that process of healing which is so desperately needed in America.

I regret deeply any injuries that may have been done in the course of the events that led to this decision. I would say only that if some of my judgments were wrong—and some were wrong—they were made in what I believed at the time to be the best interests of the nation.

To those who have stood with me during these past difficult months—to my family, my friends, the many others who've joined in supporting my cause because they believed it was right—I will be eternally grateful for your support.

And to those who have not felt able to give me your support, let me say I leave with no bitterness toward those who have opposed me, because all of us in the final analysis have been concerned with the good of the country, however our judgments might differ.

So let us all now join together in affirming that common commitment and in helping our new President succeed for the benefit of all Americans.

I shall leave this office with regret at not completing my term but with gratitude for the privilege of serving as your President for the past five and a half years.

These years have been a momentous time in the history of our nation and the world. They have been a time of achievement in which we can all be proud—achievements that represent the shared efforts of the administration, the Congress and the people. But the challenges ahead are equally great.

And they, too, will require the support and the efforts of a Congress and the people, working in cooperation with the new administration.

We have ended America's longest war. But in the work of securing a lasting peace in the world, the goals ahead are even more far-reaching and more difficult. We must complete a structure of peace, so that it will be said of this generation—our generation of Americans—by the people of all nations, not only that we ended one war but that we prevented future wars.

We have unlocked the doors that for a quarter of a century stood between the United States and the People's Republic of China. We must now insure that the one-quarter of the world's people who live in the People's Republic of China will be and remain not our enemies, but our friends.

In the Middle East, one hundred million people in the Arab countries, many of whom have considered us their enemies for nearly twenty years, now look on us as their friends. We must continue to build on that friendship so that peace can settle at last over the Middle East and so that the cradle of civilization will not become its grave.

Together with the Soviet Union we have made the crucial breakthroughs that have begun the process of limiting nuclear arms. But we must set as our goal not just limiting but reducing and finally destroying these terrible weapons so that they cannot destroy civilization.

And so that the threat of nuclear war will no longer hang over the world and the people, we have opened a new relation with the Soviet Union. We must continue to develop and expand that new relationship so that the two strongest nations of the world will live together in cooperation rather than confrontation.

Around the world—in Asia, in Africa, in Latin America, in the Middle East—there are millions of people who live in terrible poverty, even starvation. We must keep as our goal turning away from production for war and expanding production for peace so that people everywhere on this earth can at least look forward, in their children's time if not in our time, to having the necessities for a decent life.

Here in America we are fortunate that most of our people have not only the blessings of liberty but also the means to live full and good, and by the world's standards, even abundant lives.

We must press on, however, toward a goal not only of more and better jobs but of full opportunity for every man, and of what we are striving so hard right now to achieve—prosperity without inflation.

For more than a quarter of a century in public life, I have shared in the turbulent history of this evening.

I have fought for what I believe in. I have tried, to the best of my ability, to discharge those duties and meet those responsibilities that were entrusted to me.

Sometimes I have succeeded. And sometimes I have failed. But always I have taken heart from what Theodore Roosevelt said about the man in the arena whose face is marred by dust and sweat and blood, who strives valiantly, who errs and comes short again and again because there is not effort without error and shortcoming, but who does actually strive to do the deed, who knows the great enthusiasm, the great devotion, who spends himself in a worthy cause, who at the best knows in the end the triumphs of high achievements and with the worst if he fails, at least fails while daring greatly.

I pledge to you tonight that as long as I have a breath of life in my body I shall continue in that spirit. I shall continue to work for the great causes to which I have been dedicated throughout my years as a Congressman, a Senator, Vice President and President, the cause of peace—not just for America but among all nations—prosperity, justice and opportunity for all of our people.

There is one cause above all to which I have been devoted and to which I shall always be devoted for as long as I live.

When I first took the oath of office as President five and a half years ago, I made this sacred commitment: to consecrate my office, my energies and all the wisdom I can summon to the cause of peace among nations.

I've done my very best in all the days since to be true to that pledge.

As a result of these efforts, I am confident that the world is a safer place today, not only for the people of America but for the people of all nations, and that all of our children have a better chance than before of living in peace rather than dying in war.

This, more than anything, is what I hoped to achieve when I sought the Presidency. This, more than anything, is what I hope will be my legacy to you, to our country, as I leave the Presidency.

To have served in this office is to have felt a very personal sense of kinship with each and every American. In leaving it, I do so with this prayer: May God's grace be with you in all the days ahead.

EPILOGUE

Together we have traced our nation's course from a handful of settlements struggling for existence on the shores of the Atlantic to the liberator and savior of Old Europe in two World Wars. The independent, indomitable spirit of our forefathers achieved independence and freedom for them and their posterity. Is there a lesson in this history for us?

To observe men such as Washington, Houston, Lee, and Lincoln grappling with yesterday's challenges increases our insight into their lives, their times, and the history they shaped. It should also increase our courage to face a difficult present and an uncertain future.

America is not free of faults. Man's nature is corrupt: "There is none righteous, no not one," the Bible tells us. What has been true of other nations has in some measure been repeated with us. Some Americans have exhibited excessive greed, thus giving observers the unsavory stereotype of the fat capitalist. Other Americans have callously exploited their land's superb natural resources. Still others have succumbed to the arrogance of power.

There is, however, a more positive side. America is still the land of opportunity. In many countries there is little upward or downward social mobility; in America it is still possible for a young man of poor parentage and humble surroundings to become, through hard work and a tenacious spirit, a great surgeon, lawyer, or national leader. Today there are more black American millionaires than ever before. Men whose parents came over from the "old country" find themselves college graduates, successful in their fields, filled with self-esteem.

But economic and social opportunity are only part of the story. America's Constitution grants her citizens the opportunity to worship more freely and to express themselves more openly than can the people of almost any other nation. Along with these opportunities Americans possess a host of other freedoms. There, indeed, lies the real meaning of American freedom—opportunity.

This American ideal we must pledge ourselves to uphold. Tobias Smollett said most aptly that "true patriotism is a matter of deeds, not words; of unselfish acts, not hero dreams; of devoted service, not mere sentiment. True patriotism is of no party."

Sincere patriotism is not only good and ennobling but also very necessary. Nevertheless, patriotism is not enough. For a nation that does not put God on the throne of its heart cannot long prosper. The Bible says that "righteousness exalteth a nation: but sin is a reproach to any people." Let us purpose not only to serve our country devotedly, but also to accept the leadership of our God and Saviour.

"Blessed is the nation whose God is the LORD."